# The Third Reich and Yugoslavia

# The Third Reich and Yugoslavia

*An Economy of Fear, 1933–1941*

Perica Hadži-Jovančić

BLOOMSBURY ACADEMIC
LONDON • NEW YORK • OXFORD • NEW DELHI • SYDNEY

BLOOMSBURY ACADEMIC
Bloomsbury Publishing Plc
50 Bedford Square, London, WC1B 3DP, UK
1385 Broadway, New York, NY 10018, USA
29 Earlsfort Terrace, Dublin 2, Ireland

BLOOMSBURY, BLOOMSBURY ACADEMIC and the Diana logo
are trademarks of Bloomsbury Publishing Plc

First published in Great Britain 2020
This paperback edition published in 2022

Copyright © Perica Hadži-Jovančić, 2020

Perica Hadži-Jovančić has asserted his right under the Copyright,
Designs and Patents Act, 1988, to be identified as Author of this work.

For legal purposes the Acknowledgements on p. ix constitute
an extension of this copyright page.

Cover design by: Tjaša Krivec
Cover image: Berlin, Berlin/City State, Germany, Hermann Göring (2nd from left) and the
Yugoslav Prime Minister Milan Stojadinović (3rd from left) take the salute of the guard of
honour of the Air Force. (© SZ Photo/Scherl/Bridgeman Images)

All rights reserved. No part of this publication may be reproduced or transmitted
in any form or by any means, electronic or mechanical, including photocopying,
recording, or any information storage or retrieval system, without prior
permission in writing from the publishers.

Bloomsbury Publishing Plc does not have any control over, or responsibility for,
any third-party websites referred to or in this book. All internet addresses given
in this book were correct at the time of going to press. The author and publisher
regret any inconvenience caused if addresses have changed or sites have
ceased to exist, but can accept no responsibility for any such changes.

Every effort has been made to trace copyright holders and to obtain their
permissions for the use of copyright material. The publisher apologizes for any errors
or omissions and would be grateful if notified of any corrections that should be
incorporated in future reprints or editions of this book.

A catalogue record for this book is available from the British Library.

A catalog record for this book is available from the Library of Congress.

Library of Congress Control Number: 2020940858

ISBN: HB: 978-1-3501-3805-6
PB: 978-1-3502-0175-0
ePDF: 978-1-3501-3806-3
eBook: 978-1-3501-3807-0

Typeset by Integra Software Services Pvt. Ltd.

To find out more about our authors and books visit www.bloomsbury.com
and sign up for our newsletters.

*To my parents*

# Contents

| | | |
|---|---|---|
| Acknowledgements | | ix |
| Abbreviations | | xi |
| | | |
| Introduction | | 1 |
| Sources and literature overview | | 3 |
| Notes on terminology and disclaimers | | 5 |
| | | |
| 1 | Yugoslavia, South-Eastern Europe and economic decision-making in Hitler's Germany | 9 |
| | *Mitteleuropa*, *Grosswirtschaftsraum* and German economic theories | 9 |
| | Polycracy in the Third Reich | 12 |
| | | |
| 2 | The Austrian partnership | 19 |
| | The political context before 1933 | 20 |
| | Germany, Yugoslavia and the Austrian question | 22 |
| | The road to neutrality | 27 |
| | From player to played | 32 |
| | | |
| 3 | Economic relations under the auspices of Schacht's New Plan | 35 |
| | The transition years 1930–3 in the Danube region | 36 |
| | End of German reparations | 37 |
| | German-Yugoslav economic relations in the wake of Hitler's rise to power | 40 |
| | The May 1934 Trade Agreement | 42 |
| | Little Entente's economic cooperation | 46 |
| | The war economy, Hjalmar Schacht and the New Plan | 47 |
| | German-Yugoslav economic relations after May 1934 | 50 |
| | Towards import controls | 53 |
| | Political prey or economic outlet? | 57 |
| | | |
| 4 | In the web of the Axis | 59 |
| | Germany and Italy in the Danube region | 59 |
| | Germany comes to the fore | 65 |
| | A mouse between the cats | 74 |

## Contents

| | | |
|---|---|---|
| 5 | Yugoslavia and the Four-Year Plan | 77 |
| | The beginnings of the Four-Year Plan | 78 |
| | Dresden and Berlin meetings | 79 |
| | Between Berlin and Dubrovnik | 83 |
| | Economic relations after the Anschluss | 86 |
| | Armament deliveries | 90 |
| | Elusive freedom | 95 |
| 6 | The Third Reich and the industrialization of Yugoslavia | 97 |
| | The consequences of the Abyssinian Crisis | 97 |
| | German investments in Yugoslavia | 101 |
| | Yugoslavia's state purchases in Germany | 105 |
| | Germany and modernization of Yugoslavia's agriculture | 110 |
| | Mutual importance | 112 |
| | The deployment of Germany's soft power | 114 |
| | Yugoslav reaction to German economic theories | 121 |
| | Conflicting directions | 125 |
| 7 | Ideological traps in the Nazi decade | 127 |
| | Antisemitism in pre-1941 Yugoslavia | 128 |
| | Native fascism in the 1930s | 134 |
| | The Third Reich and Yugoslavia on ideological crossroads | 138 |
| | Yugoslav *Volksdeutsche* between homeland and fatherland | 142 |
| | Limited fear | 147 |
| 8 | Bringing Yugoslavia in line | 149 |
| | German armament deliveries after September 1939 | 150 |
| | Before the fall of France | 152 |
| | Pre-1914 credits | 158 |
| | Economy and politics become one | 160 |
| | Economy of fear | 165 |
| 9 | Yugoslavia commits suicide | 167 |
| | Uncomfortable neutrality | 168 |
| | War comes to the Balkans | 171 |
| | The end | 180 |
| Conclusion | | 191 |
| Notes | | 194 |
| Bibliography | | 245 |
| Index | | 261 |

# Acknowledgements

Researching, analysing, writing and preparing this manuscript for publication were a challenging and windy path which would not have been possible without selfless assistance and help from many individuals and institutions. As is usually customary in situations such as this one, I should mention those who helped the most and to anyone I might have omitted to mention, I humbly apologize.

As this book is based on the research I conducted for my PhD studies at Cambridge University between 2013 and 2017, I owe a special praise to my mentor Professor Brendan Simms (Peterhouse, Cambridge), with whom this topic had been discussed and agreed long before I even came to Cambridge and without whose assistance and guidance it would have not come to its conclusion. I am also very grateful to both Professor Chris Clark (St Catharine's College, Cambridge) and Professor Milan Ristović (Belgrade University) for their suggestions for improvements of the text and critics where the critic was needed. I owe a special praise to everyone at the History Faculty of Cambridge University and to my alma mater Wolfson College, Cambridge. Wolfson has been a wonderful place to be part of, a huge support in any mater academic or non-academic related for a number of years and remains a special place for me for the rest of my life. I would especially like to thank my college tutor Professor Lesley MacVinish, Gillian Sanders and Kim Allen of the Wolfson's postgraduate department, Dr Evelyn Lord, Emeritus Fellow of Wolfson who frequently helped in correcting the flaws of my written English and to Wolfson's former president at the time of my studies, Professor Richard J. Evans. Very useful for my deeper and broader understanding of modern German history was Richard's workshop at the college premises which after many years of running and helping young scholars with the interest in German history ended in 2014.

I am very grateful to a number of academics, colleagues and friends, either experts in this topic or simply wonderful people willing to help. I would here like to mention Professor Hannes Grandits (Humboldt University, Berlin), Srdjan Mićić and Zoran Janjetović (both from the Institute for Recent History of Serbia in Belgrade), Saša Ilić (Archive of the National Bank of Serbia), Ljiljana Macura (National Library of Serbia), Annegret Wilke (Political Archive of the German Foreign Office), Ivan Marinković who frequently helped explaining the finer details of economic theory, and my dear friends and fellow historians Anne-Christin Saß and Jan Mittenzwei. Of course, the scope of this research would have never been possible without the professionalism and dedication of the personnel of all the archives and libraries where I conducted my research. I am especially grateful to members of staff of the Cambridge University Library and Staatsbibliothek in Berlin, where I was spending most of my time during this project.

Finally, I would like to mention those who especially supported me throughout these years. Thanks to my father-in-law David, who has proof-read through every piece of text I have written since beginning the journey at Cambridge. Thank you to Ana, my sister and the closest friend. To Laura, the woman who became my partner and wife, for being there with her love and support when I needed it the most. To our beautiful children Todor and Olivia, for all the joy, smiles and hugs. I could not have done it without all of you. For the end, I would love to dedicate this book to my beloved parents, mother Snežana and father Todor, as a thank you for all their love and everything they have ever done for me. If in my lifetime I manage to offer my own children only half of all the support I had from my mother and father, I will consider myself a successful parent.

# Abbreviations

| | |
|---|---|
| AJ | Arhiv Jugoslavije |
| ADAP | Akten zur deutschen auswärtigen Politik |
| ANB | Arhiv Narodne banke Srbije |
| BArch | Bundesarchiv |
| DBFP | Documents on British Foreign Policy |
| FRUS | Foreign Relations of the United States |
| IfZG | Institut für Zeitgeschichte |
| MWT | Mitteleuropäischer Wirtschaftstag |
| PA | Politisches Archiv des Auswärtigen Amts |
| TNA | The National Archives |
| VA | Vojni Arhiv |
| YNB | Narodna Banka Kraljevine Jugoslavije |

# Introduction

This book analyses economic and political relations between the Third Reich and Yugoslavia during the National Socialist regime in Germany, before the German attack on Yugoslavia on 6 April 1941. The analysis is done through an in-depth study of economic policies in both countries, of mutual trade, expectations, ideology and underlying motives behind the decision-making in both Germany and Yugoslavia. It is set within the wider regional, continental and worldwide economic background of the era, without which it is impossible to understand the reasons why events took a particular course. The book also addresses the period before the Nazis seized power in Berlin, in order to show a continuity in mutual economic relations, existing with the period of tenure of successive German governments prior to 1933. It will point to the role Germany played in the industrialization of Yugoslavia, both directly through capital investments in infrastructure and the modernization of Yugoslavia's industrial capacities and indirectly through German export of machinery which helped the development of some branches of Yugoslav industry.

There is no comprehensive study on economic relations between these two countries to date. There have been studies of a narrower scope which addressed certain facets of this complex relationship, or addressed economic relations in general, only as part of a wider, regional framework. However, there is always the danger that a study of mutual relations between two countries will remain narrow in focus, and yet such studies are the bread and butter of historical research. To avoid such a narrow focus, this analysis offers the broader regional context and one which brings other great powers into consideration wherever necessary.

German-Yugoslav relations in the Nazi era can be divided into three phases: 1933–6, 1936–9 and 1939–41. While the beginning of the Second World War represented one of the divisions, the case for determining the summer of 1936 as a boundary in phases of German-Yugoslav relations is less self-evident. However, the period between March and September 1936 brought important changes in Yugoslavia's foreign policy and changed the dynamics of economic relations with Germany. In April 1936, Yugoslavia introduced import controls which increased the volume of trade with Germany to a level which steered the country towards economic dependence on the German market, but more importantly represented a break with the system of free trade. Politically, this period witnessed the German reoccupation of the Rhineland, the end of the Abyssinian Crisis and sanctions on Italy (which ruined the reputation of the League of Nations as protector of the weak and compromised collective security as a system for preserving peace) and the signing of the German-Austrian agreement on 11 July 1936, which put Austria under German influence. As a consequence of these events and an absence of any response from the Western democracies whose interests were equally endangered, Yugoslavia retreated to a stance of neutrality.

The book challenges some commonplaces of the current historiography. Older Yugoslav historiography suggested that Germany used the economy as a tool for the political subordination of Yugoslavia, taking the example of the 1 May 1934 Trade Agreement between the two countries and some of its provisions as proof of this claim. Economy was indeed one of the interstate activities where a complex interplay of hidden political goals of the Third Reich and normal everyday business probably reached its climax. Yugoslavia, just like other agricultural countries of the region, needed economic assistance from larger industrial nations, especially after the start of the Great Depression. As Britain, France and Italy were not to be counted on, Germany was the only remaining economic outlet in the 1930s. However, as this book demonstrates, economic policies in both countries were mostly driven by economic needs. Furthermore, Yugoslavia's leading officials rarely brought economic considerations into account when making foreign policy decisions. Yugoslavia's foreign policy in the interwar period was always determined by diplomatic implications and the reality of its geo-political surroundings, the most important being its complex relationship with Italy, the fear of a Habsburg restoration in Hungary and Austria and opposition to border revisions in the region. This book observes economic relations between Germany and Yugoslavia primarily from an economic perspective, with political relations forming a backdrop within which the economy operated.

The suggestion that Yugoslavia was part of the French security system in Eastern Europe, which sometime in the 1930s shifted towards Berlin for various reasons, some of which imply alleged fascist leanings of the government in Belgrade during the tenure of the Prime Minister Milan Stojadinović, is also widespread in historiography. However, this book demonstrates that Yugoslavia, instead of belonging to any ideological blocs or alliances with other great powers, simply belonged to the camp of anti-revisionist states, like France and unlike Germany, which does not automatically indicate its alliance with France. To be sure, Serbian elites and military were predominantly Francophile and Anglophile and there was a sense of brotherhood in arms with their former war allies. However, through the greater part of this period Yugoslavia's relationship with France was strained due to the French courting of Italy, Yugoslavia's archenemy. At the same time, there were no significant points of disagreement with Germany which was geographically distant and whose attitude towards some important foreign policy issues in the region, such as the Habsburg restoration, was identical to Yugoslavia's standpoint. Furthermore, German economic presence was always considered welcome in Yugoslavia and the repayment of German reparations in the 1920s, partly in goods, played an important role in the modernization of Yugoslavia's economy. After the economic crisis, both countries lacked foreign currencies and willingly continued mutual trade through the clearing system. However, as this book will demonstrate, this system was considered to be only a transitional phase for Yugoslavia, until the recovery of the world economy and a return to free trade. Germany under the Nazis however favoured a centralized economy and foreign trade which operated through the exchange of goods wherever possible. These two economic models were incompatible and eventually would have clashed.

This book argues that both German economic and foreign policy plans for Yugoslavia largely failed to achieve its ultimate goals. The expression of that failure in economy was Yugoslavia's independent economic policy until the fall of France in June 1940 and Yugoslavia's resistance to supplying the Third Reich with raw materials necessary for German war production beyond quotas agreed shortly after the outbreak of war. Yugoslavia's plans for the further industrialization and development of heavy industry, just like the leaning of its economic and financial elites towards liberal capitalism, diverged from German economic policy and its imperialistic plans for South-Eastern Europe. Simultaneously, the book demonstrates the failure of Germany's political approach to Yugoslavia, which adamantly withstood German pressure to abandon its position of neutrality in regard to the two opposed ideological blocs in Europe until March 1941, when Yugoslavia's government adherence to the Axis merely paralysed with fear of German might. The deployment of German soft power in an attempt to win over the Yugoslav society and intellectual elite demonstrated the same failure. The expression of all these failures was the military coup of 27 March 1941, against the government which had signed the Tripartite Pact two days earlier and the subsequent people's demonstrations in support of putschists.

This topic importantly relates to a contemporary question of European order and the place of smaller nations in it. Understanding why one great power failed to win over a smaller country, despite the seemingly clear economic and political benefits it bore for the latter, is important. Yugoslavia aimed to find its place in a turbulent geo-political space defined by economic crisis, protectionism, aggressive political and economic approaches by autocratic states, a lack of political and economic support by liberal states, the rise of nationalism in the region and the continent, blackmailing and various demands of subordination. This topic equally relates to another important relationship in modern European history, that of a smaller nation and its dominant neighbour. The deployment of both soft and hard power by larger political entities, in the form of cultural penetration, the use of economy and of minorities' problems as a means of pressure are mechanisms frequently used both before and after the Second World War in international relations.

## Sources and literature overview

Original and unpublished material in three languages was used for this research, in Serbo-Croatian, German and English. The majority of German sources used are kept in the Political Archive of the Federal Foreign Office (*Politisches Archiv des Auswärtigen Amts*), the Berlin section of Federal Archive (*Bundesarchiv, Abteilung Berlin*) and to a lesser extent the Institute of Contemporary History (*Institut für Zeitgeschichte*) in Munich. Research of German theoretical approaches to the problem of Yugoslavia's industrialization would not be possible without the material kept in the Institute for World Economy (*Institut für Weltwirtschaft*) in Kiel. Documents available on the Yugoslav side mainly come from the Archive of the Serbian National Bank (*Arhiv Narodne banke Srbije*) and the Archive of Yugoslavia (*Arhiv Jugoslavije*), both in Belgrade. The folders kept in the Archive of Yugoslavia are rarely complete, with many documents missing; those kept in the Archive of the Serbian National Bank are better preserved and organized and are of particular importance as they either naturally complement or are often saved copies of the National Bank's correspondence with other official institutions, otherwise lost or only partially preserved in the Archive of Yugoslavia's collections. The use of contemporary British sources from the National Archives in London was a welcome addition, as they offered a broader perspective from an outside viewpoint.

I did not cite archival sources in situations when a satisfying printed version was available. Published primary sources include volumes of selected documents from ministries for foreign affairs of both countries, *Akten zur deutschen auwärtigen Politik* (Documents on German Foreign Policy), series C and D and *Izveštaji Ministarstva inostranih poslova Kraljevine Jugoslavije* (Reports of the Kingdom of Yugoslavia's Foreign Ministry) and other publications containing various excerpts of German and Yugoslav documents. Also used are the diaries and memoirs of some prominent contemporaries on both sides: among others Hjalmar Schacht, the president of the Reichsbank and German Economics Minister; Franz Halder, the Chief of the Army High Command; Milan Stojadinović, the Yugoslav Prime Minister between 1935 and 1939; Vladko Maček, the Croatian leader and Yugoslavia's Deputy Prime Minister between 1939 and 1941; Mihailo Konstantinović, the Justice Minister in the Yugoslav government; Konstantin Fotić, Yugoslavia's Minister in Washington and others. Also widely used are diaries of the Italian Foreign Minister Galeazzo Ciano, both Yugoslav and British editions, as they do not contain the same selection of diary entries. Daily newspapers are occasionally referenced; more important were economic periodicals in both countries and these are widely quoted, such as *Mitteilungen des Mitteleuropäischer Wirtschaftstag, Narodno blagostanje, Industrijski pregled, Jugoslovenski Ekonomist*, etc.

The list of books dealing specifically with the German-Yugoslav political and economic relations is not long. In 1982, Dušan Lukač published *Treći Rajh i zemlje jugoistočne Evrope* (The Third Reich and the countries of South-Eastern Europe), a voluminous study of German foreign policy in the Balkans; Lukač's contribution to understanding of the topic is undeniable, but his ideological prejudices more than once bring into question some conclusions he reaches. Very useful is a selection of articles on the Yugoslav-German relations from 1918 to 1945, published in Belgrade in 1977 by a number of prominent Yugoslav and German historians and others, in both English and German. Most of these articles are frequently quoted throughout this book. A solitary attempt to examine mutual relations between the Third Reich and Kingdom of Yugoslavia before April 1941 in the form of a monograph publication in English is Frank Littlefield's *Germany and Yugoslavia, 1933–1941*, published in 1988. Unfortunately, the author's knowledge and understanding of the two countries he discusses are poor. Obviously not a speaker of either German or Serbo-Croatian, Littlefield, whose motivation for the enterprise is unclear, was neither able to research original, unpublished archival material, nor able to use literature in languages other than English. As a result, he produced a publication of little value, with the repeatedly emphasized central argument that Germany had no other motive in dealings with Yugoslavia except maintaining good economic relations. Equally problematic is Jochan Wüscht's *Jugoslawien und das Dritte Reich*, published in 1969. Being a Yugoslav ethnic German who was forced to flee the country at the end of the Second World War, Wüscht ended up as the archivist of the Federal Archive in Koblenz, where in the 1950s and 1960s he had access to the original archival material stored there. The result of his research was a book burdened with selective use of documents, misinterpretations and overblown statements, obviously written with the aim of justifying Nazi policy towards Yugoslavia. On German economic relations with Yugoslavia, William Grenzebach Jr.'s *Germany's Informal Empire in East-Central Europe*, published in 1988, is a very useful analysis of German trade policies with Yugoslavia and Romania between 1933 and 1939. The author focuses on Germany's decision to pay higher than the world market prices for imports of agricultural goods from these two countries, thus making them increasingly dependent on trade with Nazi Germany. Grenzebach criticized Alan Millward for relying too much on statistical analysis with seemingly sarcastic reference: 'Milward's contribution to this field demonstrates that statistics are not substitute for solid archival work.' However, Grenzebach's own meticulous approach to work in German archives is sadly undermined by an absence of material from Romanian and Yugoslav archives. Important for this research was also *Export Empire: German Soft Power in Southeastern Europe, 1890–1945*, by Stephen G. Gross, published in 2015, which studies the deployment of German soft power in South-Eastern Europe mostly by using German material on Romania and Yugoslavia. Gross establishes a connection between the network made up of unofficial personal contacts by German traders and corporations in the south-east, with the official economic policies of the Weimar Germany and the Third Reich. This study represents an important contribution to our understanding of the methods Germany used for economic penetration in the region. However, there is a feeling that the author overstates the success of German soft power, at least in Yugoslavia, while the reader is denied the reactions of Yugoslav and Romanian elites. *The Third Reich and Yugoslavia: An Economy of Fear* therefore revises current literature on the subject of German-Yugoslav relations before the Second World War and fills in some gaps in current knowledge on the subject of German economic penetration in South-Eastern Europe, in order to create a fuller picture of the events.

## Notes on terminology and disclaimers

One of the central terms the reader will face with while reading this book is *clearing*, with all its variations: clearing agreement, clearing accounts, clearing office, etc. This is a specific economic feature of the era we discuss in this book, rarely applied in modern times; many modern economists are not even familiar with the term. It is a reciprocal trade agreement between the two governments for settling mutual commerce, aimed at avoiding the payment in foreign currency – usually, because both governments lack foreign currency. According to Ivan Berend and György Ranki, as explained in their 1985 book *The Hungarian Economy in the Twentieth Century*, the idea of clearing system arose at the Conference of National Banks held in Prague in 1931. 'The importer paid the National Bank for the value of imported goods in his own currency; similarly, the exporter received from National Bank the value of the exported goods in his own currency. The National Banks of the trading countries however, did not make direct payments to each other.' The system was instead based on the relative balance of trade. In theory: the two countries had no foreign currency to pay for their imports, therefore regulated their mutual trade through clearing, trading goods, while paying their exporters in local currencies. In practice: as we will see, the things were more complicated.

This book does not promise to revise what we know about Yugoslavia's overall economic history of the 1930s; such a task would require much more time for research and space for presenting the research findings. Therefore, the book does not deal with the features and aspects of Yugoslavia's own economic development. Instead, it offers a valuable revision of economic and political relations between the Third Reich and Yugoslavia. In studying the facets of this tense relationship, Yugoslavia's economy, its economic policies and foreign trade were therefore always treated from a distinctly Yugoslav standpoint. Yugoslavia was a new country, founded on 1 December 1918 as one of successors to Austro-Hungary and of both pre-1918 Serbian and Montenegrin Kingdoms. Naturally, the process of integration of such diverse regions, with different social, cultural, economic and political traditions, was not an easy one. During that process, there were many misunderstandings and politically that integration was never successfully completed. This gave birth early on to the so-called national question, which was never resolved before the war and led to even more problems among the Yugoslav nations throughout the rest of the twentieth century. The features of internal economic development in the interwar period were at times equally frustrating; there were measures and policies directed from Belgrade that were sometimes beneficial to some and detrimental to other nations, ethnic groups or historical regions which clustered together to form a new country.

However, the problem of Yugoslavia's uneven economic development and further problems arising from it were not relevant for German-Yugoslav economic relations in the 1930s. Both German and Yugoslav economic officials worked within the frameworks of national policies; any impact which this mutual economic relationship could have had on internal Yugoslav economic development, unless such effects influenced the reasoning and attitude of Yugoslav experts and officials in dealing with their German counterparts, is beyond the scope of this book. Politically, the line of supporting Yugoslavia's unity as opposed to Croatian separatism and other countries' aspirations towards Yugoslavia's territory was adopted early in the German Foreign Ministry, with Hitler's blessing, and did not change until 1941. For these reasons and to avoid any unnecessary pitfalls of the national question and problems of uneven internal economic development in pre-1941 Yugoslavia, this book stays out of it, unless it was deemed necessary to bring it to the fore; this is for example the case in the final chapter. This book deals with German-Yugoslav relations in the 1930s and as such it consistently throughout refers to the Yugoslav economy, Yugoslav industry, Yugoslav banking, Yugoslav institutions, etc.

The name National Bank consistently throughout the book refers to the Yugoslav National Bank; its German counterpart is always referred to as the Reichsbank. Although *Auswärtiges Amt* translates as the Foreign Office, to avoid confusion with the British Foreign Office, the name consistently used for the Ministry of Foreign Affairs in Berlin throughout the book is German Foreign Ministry and sometimes the Wilhelmstrasse. Finally, although initially founded as the Kingdom of Serbs, Croats and Slovenes in 1918, the name which was changed to the Kingdom of Yugoslavia (Land of the South Slavs) only in 1929, for the reader's easier navigation the name Yugoslavia will be used consistently throughout the book.

This book should not be viewed or read as an attempt to rehabilitate Yugoslavia's political leadership. As it will be seen, it carries a great share of blame for Yugoslavia's destiny in March and April 1941. Yugoslavia was not a democratic country with responsible institutions, internal dialogue and transparent politics, but a minor European dictatorship where a small clique in power segregated itself from the wider population, limited public freedoms and prevented non-conformist parties from participating in decision-making. Still, Yugoslavia's foreign policy in the second half of the 1930s was trying to be pragmatic rather than cynical, and this does not necessarily imply a willing subordination to or cooperation with the Nazis. Therefore, the reader is reminded to separate Yugoslavia's shrewd foreign policy and economic decision-making made out of commercial interests and needs of the country, from its autocratic and undemocratic internal practices.

Parts of the first and seventh chapters were published as a journal article in the *Godišnjak za društvenu istoriju* (Annual for Social History), under the title 'Ergänzungswirtschaft, Grosswirtschaftsraum and Yugoslavia's Responses to German Economic Theories and Plans for the Balkans in the 1930s' in 2017.

1

# Yugoslavia, South-Eastern Europe and economic decision-making in Hitler's Germany

This small opening chapter offers contextualization. It sets out the theoretical framework in order to help the reader less versed in this topic to better understand the theory within which the events described in this book operate: which theories currently exist on the subject, where they clash and what the author's perspective is. To this end, it was first imperative to define the key political and ideological concepts which formed the worldview of the German elites and set the background within which German plans and policies towards the Balkans functioned in the interwar period – because Germany was the dominant partner in this relationship and it set the dynamics of events. Secondly, it was equally important to summarize the debates within current historiography about the importance of the economy in Nazi political theory and practice and to establish the relationship between big business and party politics in Hitler's state. This should help readers to navigate more easily through the book and properly assess the importance of German-Yugoslav relations in the history of the Third Reich and their place in the interwar history of Europe.

## *Mitteleuropa, Grosswirtschaftsraum* and German economic theories

Historically, *Mitteleuropa* was both a way of overcoming Germans' perceived isolation in Europe and the means of their hegemonic aspirations.[1] Since the late eighteenth century, German history has been interpreted as a drive for political and economic control of Central Europe. In the early nineteenth century, economist Friedrich List favoured the idea of *Mitteleuropäische Wirtschaftszone*, the Central-European Economic Area, where he combined Adam Smith's ideas of free trade and liberal economy within a politically unified German nation-state, with the idea of a custom union between Germany and the rest of Central Europe.[2] In List's time, this idea basically implied an Austro-German-Hungarian economic union and German expansion in the Balkans, strengthened through the resettlement of German farmers across the lower Danube area.[3] Bismarck was not interested in such theories, but after his dismissal Germany became embroiled in more aggressive and expansionist policies, a precondition for which was seen to be the setting up of a closed zone in Central Europe under German political and economic control. For Friedrich Naumann, who wrote his very influential book *Mitteleuropa* in 1915, Central-European Union was a tool for German survival in a future world dominated by Anglo-American and Russo-Asiatic blocks.[4] According to the author, *Mitteleuropa* comprised a wide swathe of Central Europe, from the Baltic Sea down to the Danube; however, it did not include the territory of the then Kingdom of Serbia. Instead, Naumann claimed that Germany should aspire towards economic leadership over the Balkan states.[5] In the time of Naumann's writing, the Balkans were seen more as a link between the *Mitteleuropa* and Asia Minor and the Mediterranean, and there was much discussion as to whether countries such as Serbia or Bulgaria could be integrated into *Mitteleuropa* in a political sense.[6] The concept gained even greater importance after the First World War and served as a platform for undermining the new system of small nation-states in Central Europe.[7]

The theory of complementary economy, *Ergänzungswirtschaft*, as the name suggests, testifies to the intention of transforming the peripheral regions of Europe into a complementary economic area of Germany.[8] As such, the theory is linked to the envisaged economic bloc known as the *Grosswirtschaftsraum*, Greater Economic Area, a concept popular in Germany at the end of the 1920s and in the Third Reich, which occupied somewhat undefined position towards *Mitteleuropa*. Henry Cord Meyer defines it as 'a larger integrated economy, transcending national boundaries and motivated by considerations of economic exclusiveness and political advantage'.[9] We might say that, while the latter referred to a geo-political concept, the former was a purely economic model covering a geographic space comprising Germany as the core and a dependent economic periphery, of which South-Eastern Europe was part. Still, much of the theory of complementary economies originated from the geo-political, rather than from pure economic considerations, and much of the reasoning was based on common logic.

To contemporaries, South-Eastern Europe was geographic, political and economic space consisting of Yugoslavia, Romania, Bulgaria, Albania and Greece, of which Yugoslavia, Romania and Bulgaria represented the core, while Hungary and Turkey were additional peripheral countries.[10] At first, it was not seen as part of German *Mitteleuropa*.[11] Still, by the end of 1930s South-Eastern Europe began to bear, apart from geographical, an ideological meaning, namely in replacing the derogatory term 'the Balkans'. As such, it deserved to be part of the new, reborn Europe. Left on its own, outside new cultural, economic and political developments on the continent dominated by Germany, it would remain to be simply the backward Balkans.[12] The main characteristic of this region was a high fertility rate, with roughly 80 per cent of the population living and working in rural settlements. Coupled with outdated methods of land cultivation, the most important consequence of these circumstances was that only a small portion of agricultural products were surplus for export.[13] This was the perception, despite certain variations, of most German experts during the Third Reich.

Walter Hoffmann was one of them, a specialist in Balkan affairs. In his book entitled *South-Eastern Europe: Political, Cultural and Economic Profile*, published in 1932, Hoffmann spoke at length and in great detail about the economies of Yugoslavia, Bulgaria and Romania. He recognized the historical striving of the Balkan countries to industrialize, but emphasized that the future development of their industries should be in the context of the agricultural character of the country. When writing about the foreign investments of Germany's western rivals, the author did not miss the opportunity to condemn the possibly harmful political implications.[14]

Seven years later, Hoffmann wrote a short booklet entitled *Greater Germany in the Danube Region*. After providing impressive statistics about German trade with South-Eastern European countries, Hoffmann triumphantly revealed that Germany was now buying and selling more goods from and to the region than all of the rest of the world together. Furthermore, 'it will remain so even if the industrial development of the south-eastern area makes further progress. [Because] In that case, the needs of these countries which they cover from abroad, would have a different character to today.' They would always remain dependant on Germany; even if they progressed into the production of goods for mass consumption, they would still have to import machines and weaponry, as they themselves would never reach the technological level necessary to make products of the highest quality. This did not mean that Hoffmann denied Yugoslavia and its neighbours a right to develop industrially, but such development would be subject to 'circumstances'.[15]

Being the head of the Economic Department of the Institute for South-Eastern Europe in Leipzig, Hermann Gross was another high-profile expert. In his 1937 habilitation thesis called simply *The South Eastern Europe*, Gross concluded that it would be hard for the countries of the south-east to reach the level of the highly industrialized countries. However, this opened up the possibility to become suppliers to Germany of agricultural products and raw materials.[16] The following year, in his book on the economic importance of the south-east for the German Reich, Gross contemplated the prospects of modernization on the Balkan economies. He argued that successful industrialization of the region was simply not possible; in order to industrialize, a country required either large internal market able to absorb the products of a fully employed population of a certain purchasing power, or a strong exports capacity oriented towards the world market. He recognized that region had achieved some success in industrialization, but only in those spheres where industrial activity was complementary to the agricultural character of these countries, that is, light industries. For this reason, Gross praised historical, political and cultural ties with Germany, whose role was that of a supplier of finished goods to the region. Gross tried to prove that the complementary character of the German economy and the economies of South-Eastern Europe was a fact and that this relationship would not change significantly even if their industrial production increased over time. This relationship was only going to get stronger and more dependent on Germany as the living standards of the South-Eastern Europeans grew.[17]

Kurt Erbsland reduced the world market to six large economic areas: North American, Russian, British Empire, French with its colonies, Japanese with the Far East and Italian with its North African possessions. For Germany, he reserved 'the space left on the map between the Soviet Union and France, filled with numerous little countries whose heart is Germany'. This represented 70 million consumers, apparently happy to receive German products in exchange for their raw materials. Such an area should not resemble an empire, but rather a partnership of free national economies. Erbsland raised the issue of the possible danger further industrialization of some of these agricultural countries could pose to the concept of goods exchange on which such an economic area rested, but he dismissed it by claiming that these countries were still far from being able to make products which could match German quality.[18]

Hermann Neubacher, a leading Austrian economic expert on the Balkans, a successful businessman and the first mayor of Vienna after the Anschluss, toyed with the idea of the economic integration of Central and South-Eastern Europe as early as 1930. It would be based on the exchange of agricultural products from the lower Danube region, for industrial products of the upper Danube countries. Neubacher therefore opposed any industrial development of Yugoslavia, Romania and the likes, as in the long run it would jeopardize the trading capacities of Austria and Germany. He was particularly opposed to the development of heavy industry, but was in favour of technical improvements in agriculture, provided that support came from Germany.[19]

Finally, we should mention Hans Zeck, a researcher in the South-Eastern European Society in Vienna. According to him, all the South-Eastern European states should get rid of the foreign capital invested in their industries and strive towards self-sustainability. Particular attention should be paid to modernization of agricultural production. However, they should all turn towards Germany and use its experience and help in this process.[20] Zeck urged Yugoslavia not to tolerate the foreign exploitation anymore and praised the Prime Minister Milan Stojadinović for, in his words, aiming to replace the foreign capital with the domestic Yugoslav.[21] A few pages later, Zeck questioned the wisdom of Yugoslavia's economic agreements with Britain, France or the United States which, within their economic empires, were already producing all that their economies needed. The only solution for Yugoslavia was a continuous economic cooperation with Germany, which (to borrow a phrase from Ian Innerhofer) acted more in a role of a development aid worker and, according to Zeck, unlike others did not intend any economic or political subjection of the country.[22]

This overview of some notable examples of economic writing in Nazi Germany highlights the dominant views about Yugoslavia and the region as a whole among the cohorts of German experts of the Weimar era, who retained their positions in governmental ministries and official institutions after January 1933. For most of them, continuous economic cooperation with Germany was normal and the only logical economic development for the region. Still, it is important to stress that, despite being German nationalists, most of these people did not belong to the party, or had joined the NSDAP only after the *Machtergreifung,* the Nazi seizure of power on 30 January 1933, for practical reasons. The question therefore is: to what extent were their ideas influential in decisions on official German economic policies? Before any assessment of German economic or political relations with Yugoslavia, it is essential to properly understand the structure of the decision-making process and the hierarchy within the political system created by Hitler, as well as the relationship between the economy and politics, that is, between big business and the party.

## Polycracy in the Third Reich

At a government meeting on 7 April 1933, German Foreign Minister Konstantin von Neurath submitted a report with recommended lines of foreign policy. Speaking of the south-east, he emphasized that Germany should pay special attention to Yugoslavia and Romania, which both needed economic assistance, in order for Germany to gain political influence.[23] Živko Avramovski argues that Hitler's plans from the outset were aimed at the breaking up the Little Entente and disrupting all the regional alliances in the region.[24] Avramovski describes the 1934 Trade Agreement between Germany and Yugoslavia as 'the first tangible success of Germany's policy'. The main purpose of the agreement was to assure 'the maximum expansion of economic ties and thus pave the way for the creation of ever closer and stronger political ties'.[25] Leposava Cvijetić also sees the 1934 agreement as an instrument of Germany's foreign policy for economic penetration to the region.[26]

In reaching these conclusions, both Cvijetić and Avramovski analysed two subsequent German political assessments of the 1934 agreement. A Foreign Ministry circular dated 18 June 1934 described the commercial treaties with Hungary, signed in February 1934, and with Yugoslavia signed three months later, as designed to create points of support for German policy in the Danube region, in order to counteract French and Italian policies. It stated that 'the Reich's government made certain financial sacrifices in the interest of German foreign policy in South-Eastern Europe'.[27] A letter from the Foreign Ministry in Berlin to the German Ambassador in Rome Ulrich von Hassell three days later contained further explanations: to increase the base of mutual trade and to open the Yugoslav market to German exports, 'besides providing us with an economic foothold in Yugoslavia and thus also in the Little Entente'.[28] The Foreign Ministry in Berlin tended to see economic relations with Yugoslavia either as a step towards closer political ties or as a means for political pressure. This view was strongly supported by Hans-Jürgen Schröder in the 1970s.[29] The same applies to Johann Wüscht's claim that the German-Yugoslav trade agreement could be understood as an answer to the Rome Protocols, a political and economic agreement between Italy, Hungary and Austria, signed in March 1934.[30] In common to all is that they did not observe the commercial agreement from an economic perspective and instead they immediately established a political connection. Also, they omitted to test the power and influence of Neurath's Ministry in the Reich's polycratic political structure.

There is an ongoing debate about the nature of Hitler's rule in the Third Reich. For 'intentionalists', Hitler was a sole ruler, who purposely allowed the chaos in order to control the party and the state; for 'structuralists', he was a weak, uninterested and indecisive dictator, who could not control various competing institutions within and outside the party.[31] But there is a consensus among historians that the power structure of the Third Reich was not centralized or coherent, but according to Martin Broszat 'it juxtaposed a polycracy of state departments with the heterogeneity of the party auxiliary organizations, and from this there developed all forms of amalgamation, coexistence and conflict between party and state offices and responsibilities'.[32] Soon after the Reichstag fire and the Enabling Act of March 1933, the Nazis began with the *Gleichschaltung* – Nazification of all the state institutions.[33] However, there were fears that purging the Foreign Ministry too hastily would cause problems; their experience was much needed in calming down the fears abroad regarding the true nature of Hitler's regime. To some extent, there were similar concerns about the rush to Nazify services such as the Economic and Finance Ministries.[34]

The Nazis did not have structures in place to deal with foreign affairs and the first attempt to rival the Foreign Ministry was Alfred Rosenberg's Foreign Policy Office of the NSDAP, *Aussenpolitisches Amt der NSDAP*, founded on 1 April 1933. But Rosenberg quickly lost influence with Hitler, who instead started to favour Joachim von Ribbentrop. He served as Hitler's unofficial diplomatic representative and his office, *Dienststelle Ribbentrop*, soon became the Foreign Ministry's most influential rival.[35] Other competitors included the Foreign Organization of the NSDAP, *Auslands-Organisation*, whose aim was to assist German nationals living abroad; the Central Office for Ethnic Germans, *Volksdeutsche Mittelstelle* (henceforth VoMi), with the task of managing the interests of German minorities in other countries; and the most important Nazi authorities, such as Hermann Göring who controlled Prussia and after 1936 the German economy, Joseph Goebbels in charge of propaganda, and Heinrich Himmler in charge of the police and secret service apparatus. They all pursued diplomacies of their own, mostly independent from the Foreign Ministry and German legations abroad. This resulted in numerous disagreements, not only between the state and party institutions whose scopes of authority overlapped, but also between the various competing departments within the party itself. Andor Hencke, a career diplomat and Under-Secretary of State in the Foreign Ministry during the Second World War, in his testimony in front of the State Department Interrogation Mission in Wiesbaden in October 1945, provided an insight into the way in which various institutions competed in the field of foreign affairs. According to him, Hitler never allowed the Foreign Ministry to influence his decisions.[36] The State Secretary at the Foreign Ministry Ernst von Weizsäcker wrote in his memoirs about the enormous energy Ribbentrop invested in defending his department against others interested in foreign affairs, after he took over the post from Neurath in 1938.[37]

Both the Nazis and the Foreign Ministry considered the post-Versailles order as provisional; the League of Nations' system of collective security was seen as only an obstacle to German expansion. But the ultimate aims and methods differed. The Foreign Ministry wanted Germany rearmed, the rectification of its borders, the return of its colonies and the creation of its own sphere of political and economic influence; but *Lebensraum*, a living space for the Germans to be forged by force in the east – the crux of Nazi ideology – was not on its agenda. On the other hand, the concept of economic imperialism was foreign to Hitler and rest of the party.[38] The Foreign Ministry's conservative approach to the great power policy was based on financial and economic dominance; Hitler's was through war. Still, despite this discrepancy and the contempt which the Führer showed for his diplomats, Neurath and key Foreign Ministry's officials and diplomats abroad initially maintained their positions. Hitler needed first to focus on internal consolidation of his power, which temporarily provided a period of relative autonomy to the Foreign Ministry.[39]

The stronger role given to foreign trade as a tool of foreign policy coincided with the succession of right-wing governments in Berlin at the end of the 1920s. Foreign Ministry officials gradually undermined the Reichstag and coordinated policy with various business organizations.[40] For them, the economy was a way to counter French influence in the south-east, even after January 1933. The Economic Ministry usually shared these views. In December 1933, State Secretary of the Economic Ministry

Hans Posse spoke about the need for a closer cooperation with the countries of the Danube region, the north of Europe and the Benelux. Posse's statements were very moderate; he even praised the most-favoured-nation principle as the easiest for everyday business.[41] But by the spring of 1934, the promoters of the *Mitteleuropa* within the ministry, led by Posse himself, gave way and for a while the policy only coexisted parallel to other economic models before it was discarded by 1936. Neurath and the Foreign Ministry officials also struggled to coordinate their attempts towards *Mitteleuropa* with the policy of agrarian overprotection favoured by the Nazis, as the two concepts were mutually exclusive.[42] Appeals to Hitler were usually a gamble; priority to political or economic considerations depended solely on his interests at any one time.[43] Before 1933, Hitler considered the concept of rebuilding Germany's status as a great power through commercial means as the 'greatest nonsense ever raised to be a guiding principle in the policy of a state'.[44] In *Mein Kampf*, Hitler discusses two alternative ways for securing work and bread for Germany's rising population: through conquest, or through trade and colonial policy. The Wilhelmine Germany opted for the latter, but in Hitler's words, 'the healthier way of the two would ... have been the first'.[45] And his preference for territorial expansion as an answer to German economic woes did not change after he became Chancellor. Every dilemma over this question was waived in November 1934, when Hitler explicitly 'forbade once and for all, commodities transfers (*Warengeschäfte*) with the secondary aim of [the exertion of] political influence in other countries'.[46]

The question of the character of the 1934 Trade Agreement between Germany and Yugoslavia thus cuts through the debate of whether there was a major shift in German policy towards South-Eastern Europe after January 1933, or was there a continuity. For Schröder, there is no dilemma: Hitler's policy in the region was a continuation of the conservative Prime Minister Heinrich Brüning's concept of economic penetration in the south-east as a means of foreign policy.[47] Andrej Mitrović sees the year of 1933 as a turning point: 'Previously just a concept – that Germany needed the south-east – was then [in 1933] finally turned into the policy of the Reich, as it was accepted by the state leadership.'[48] Marie-Luise Recker argues that economic conceptions of tying the South-Eastern European and Latin American countries more firmly to Germany, which found its expression and implementation in Schacht's economic policy, did represent a continuity with the policies designed at the turn of the century, but could hardly be a stepping stone for the Nazi concepts of the living space in the east.[49] The crucial question is whether the traditional *Mitteleuropa* of the Wilhelmine and Weimar eras corresponded to Hitler's views. It is hard to argue the case. Central to Hitler's ideology were the terms of *Lebensraum* and *Volk,* not foreign trade, exports or power politics.[50] For Hitler, the economic counterpart to the living space for Germans, *Lebensraum,* was Germany's autarchy enabled through the *Grosswirtschaftsraum*, not some export-oriented economic powerhouse.[51] Schacht, a political conservative and outsider to the party, president of the Reichsbank since March 1933 and the Economics Minister since July 1934, who had a free hand from Hitler in gearing the German economy towards war production, based his policy towards South-Eastern Europe on purely economic grounds. Most likely not intentionally, he created the basis for later Nazi policies of exploitation of neighbouring areas. Still, there were more similarities between his policy and what followed after he fell from Hitler's grace in 1936, than with what preceded it before 1933.

A foreign-trade orientation of Economics and Foreign Ministries in Berlin by the mid-1930s indeed created an economic space which gravitated towards Germany, which was also the crux of the Nazi *Grosswirtschaftsraum*.[52] But a difference in views between the conservative officials of the two ministries and the Nazis was over the war economy, a specific policy of the Nazi era. A continuity in aspirations towards a certain geographical region therefore did exist and the Nazis continued to build on the foundations laid down by their Weimar predecessors, but differences in foreign political and economic agendas before 1933 and afterwards were as big as was the difference between the older, conservative politicians and the Nazis. Furthermore, the long-term Nazi political objectives towards the south-east were never clearly defined and outlined by Hitler. The economy thus at first served as a medium of either creating or confirming cordial relations with the countries of the region, whose raw materials were vitally needed for the initial stages of German rearmament.[53] According to Alfred Kube, Hitler was uninterested in this region before 1940; instead, he relinquished it to Schacht and Göring. As a result, various policies stood side by side pursued by different competing institutions, but in reality South-Eastern Europe was on the periphery of Hitler's political thinking.[54]

The historical debate about the levels of influence within the Nazi state also focused on the relationship between the economy and politics. Tim Mason was among the first who challenged two confronting theories: one which claimed that the economy was subjected to politics, and the second which saw Nazi politics merely as a continuation of the old regime's bourgeois attempts to dominate others. He instead marked 1936 as the year when the Nazi policy freed itself from economic considerations, which had not hitherto been the case.[55] Critics of Mason's paper among the former East Germany's historians replied that such views reduced Nazism to the role of an accidental episode in German history.[56] For Hans-Erich Volkmann, two facts are undoubtedly criteria by which one may assess that the economy and politics went hand in hand in the Third Reich; firstly, the means of production remained in private hands, and secondly Hitler's promise to solve the economic problems of the Weimar era through territorial expansion and therefore a widening of the export market.[57]

Alan Milward criticized the historians who viewed German foreign policy as developing in carefully pre-planned steps using the economy only as a reinforcement to political objectives. Instead, he offered a detailed statistical proof which in his opinion demonstrated that South-Eastern European countries were economic partners with the Third Reich, not merely exploited by the larger and dominant side.[58] The reply came from Bernd-Jürgen Wendt, stating that German economic policies towards South-Eastern Europe could not be studied in isolation from Germany's war economy. He agreed that to use the term 'exploitation' was an overstatement, but saw the German-dominated area in the south-east as a link between the traditional *Grosswirtschaftsraum* and the racial *Lebensraum* of the Nazi era.[59] According to Mitrović, Germany wanted to create a greater economic area mainly in order to solve its own economic problems by establishing economic hegemony over smaller, geographically closer states. However, this excluded use of military power in the south-east, as it was assessed that other means would suffice.[60]

Richard Overy argues that in the period 1933–9, political authorities gradually took full control of the economic sphere and the traditional industrial barons lost the right to determine the conditions of their own development.[61] Ian Kershaw describes an alliance of the ruling elites in the Third Reich as a 'power-cartel', a triad made of Nazis, the army and a group consisting of big businessmen and large landowners. Their relationship altered during the course of Hitler's dictatorship, first at the expense of the businessmen and landowners and later of the army. By the summer of 1936, tensions in the Nazi economy between the needs of rearmament and the needs of consumption decided the destiny of Schacht and those echelons of the business elite which asked for a stronger German role in international trade.[62]

It is obviously not possible to strictly separate the realms of politics and economics in the Nazi Germany. Despite their differences, the political and business elites depended on each other. It is beyond a doubt that the leading industrialists were not just ordinary and innocent bystanders. German industrial and economic elites aimed to create an authoritarian state with an agenda for protecting businesses long before 1933. The new state would rest on economic ideas from Bismarck's time and would in economic and social sense be an antithesis to the Weimar Republic, which they mocked as the 'Trade Union State'. Various organizations, often founded and financed by the likes of the Reich Association of German Industry, *Reichsverband der Deutschen Industrie* (henceforth RDI), or *Langnam-Verein*,[63] contributed significantly to the demise of the Weimar Republic with their propaganda at the turn of the decade.[64] Similarly to conservative officials of the Foreign Ministry, RDI hoped to create a dependent area which would then absorb German exports, by becoming a market for Germany's finished goods.[65] After 1933, corporations such as IG Farben greatly profited from an unprecedented rise in investment. Georg von Schnitzler, second in command of IG Farben, admitted after the war that most of their turnover was guaranteed by the army.[66] Furthermore, in August 1938, IG Farben's director Carl Krauch was appointed plenipotentiary of the Four-Year Plan for production of mineral oil, synthetic rubber, gunpowder and explosives.[67] According to Holm Sundhaussen, the relationship between politics and the economy was irrelevant, because they suitably complemented each other.[68]

Still, it is hard to agree with the suggestion that it was IG Farben and other German heavy industry companies that had the decisive influence on the direction of German south-eastern policy.[69] Any profit made by businessmen was possible only on the party's terms.[70] According to Dietrich Orlow, in the later stages of the Nazi era only the party's policy was allowed to exist and it was 'unthinkable that a policy proposal that lay outside the boundaries of Hitler's ideological principles would have become Reich policy'.[71] By distancing from Schacht after 1936, Hitler emphasized a change in relationship between the state and big business.[72] By 1937, the regime managed to increase government control over the means of production and make the leading industrialists dependent on the state authority.[73] In September 1937, Hitler publicly announced: 'If private enterprise does not carry through the Four-Year Plan, the state will assume full control of business.'[74] The foundation of the Reichswerke 'Hermann Göring' in July 1937, a giant state-run steel production complex by which Hitler bypassed the Ruhr industrialists and monopolized the iron and steel production for the state, was a turning point. In the future, politics would always have primacy over economy, just as the party officials would always dominate conservative politicians from some ministries. Still, the businessmen were not against the foreign expansion, as long as it could provide new markets for exports and profit.

Hitler did not need complementary economies to consume German exports, but to supply his war machine with raw materials and foodstuff. If it was not always clear that the economy was the weaker partner in this relationship, it was thanks to the system imposed by Hitler, which effectively reduced the potential for confrontation, meaning that the state intervention was imposed, but only to the limits where such a controlled economy created a suitable environment for German industrial enterprises, which again had to respect the limits of their own field of action.[75] We can identify two phases in this relationship: one which lasted until the summer of 1936, during which traditional economic and financial elites enjoyed relative autonomy, and another phase after September 1936, marked by the Four-Year Plan, during which complete control of all economic activity passed to Göring and the party officials.

The question therefore is: were economic relations with Yugoslavia motivated by political, or economic reasons, or both? It is obviously not possible to exclude political motives, that is, their significance for the closer relations between the two countries. The Foreign Ministry was overwhelmed with various blueprints of how to best use economic relations with South-Eastern Europe for German political benefits. In general, the traditional argument of the earlier Yugoslav historiography is correct. However, a distinction should be made between German economic and political approaches, as in 1934 they might have, but not necessarily, gone hand in hand and economic motives worked relatively independently from politics.[76] We tend to agree with Rainer Schmidt that Germany's commercial agreements based on compensation deals with the countries of Eastern and South-Eastern Europe and Latin America were motivated by economic needs of the moment, which however had a welcoming side effect in bringing the Balkan states into economic dependence on Germany, thus also politically tying them to Berlin.[77]

# 2

# The Austrian partnership

The crux of the political situation in South-Eastern Europe in the interwar period was a division between revisionist and anti-revisionist countries. The core issue was Hungarian and Bulgarian revisionism; both countries sought rectification of their borders and the return of territories lost after 1918. To isolate Hungary and Bulgaria, by 1934 anti-revisionist countries had formed two alliances, Little Entente (Yugoslavia, Romania and Czechoslovakia) and Balkan Entente (Yugoslavia, Romania, Greece and Turkey). This complex situation left space for great powers to meddle into the affairs of South-Eastern Europe in pursuing their own interests, namely Italy which endorsed Hungary and had its own pretentions on Yugoslavia's territory and France which had close political and military relationship with the Little Entente. Things got more complicated after Hitler's ascent to power in January 1933, which sparked fears around Europe about the destiny of Austria. For Yugoslavia, the Austrian problem had a special dimension, a possible restoration of the Habsburgs in Vienna, which would present *casus belli* for Belgrade. Yugoslavia was therefore wary of any great power intent on challenging the status quo in the region. This implies that Yugoslavia's foreign policy was defined mainly in regard to certain situations, not by feelings of friendship or animosity towards other countries. There is a common perception in historiography that in this period Yugoslavia was part of the French security system in Eastern Europe, which then shifted towards Germany sometime during Stojadinović's term as Prime Minister.[1] As it shall be seen, this was not true. Yugoslavia had its own steady foreign-political course, and its relationship with other countries was constantly reconsidered from the perspective of their value as political and possibly military counterweights against Italy, the Habsburgs and the problem of border revisions.

Politically, Germany's aim after 1933 was clear – Yugoslavia's neutrality in any future European conflict.[2] The upcoming war, once Germany was strong enough, was to be fought eastwards and westwards. The role of the European south-east was to remain peacefully inclined towards the Reich and supply the Nazi war machine with foodstuff and resources until the mineral reaches in Eastern Europe became German. To achieve this, regional anti-revisionist alliances needed to be dismantled, other great powers with interests in the region pushed back and German political positions reinforced until the moment arrived when Berlin became the sole political arbiter in South-Eastern Europe. Therefore, foreign politics was to serve mainly for enabling two aims: beneficial circumstances for a fruitful economic cooperation with the region on Germany's terms and assuring the region's benevolent neutrality towards Germany in the upcoming war.

Political events analysed in this chapter form a backdrop against which the economic relations between Yugoslavia and Germany, described in the following chapter, worked. It takes into consideration the wider regional and European situation which eased Germany's penetration in South-Eastern Europe, such as the Abyssinian crisis and its political aftermaths. Throughout this period, Italy was the bone of contention for Yugoslavia's relations with France, while Austria played a key role in bringing Yugoslavia politically closer to Germany. However, uncertainty over Berlin's ulterior motives, awareness of its revisionism and the true nature of Hitler's regime made Yugoslavs careful in their approach to the Third Reich.

## The political context before 1933

In the heart of Yugoslavia's foreign-political situation throughout the interwar period were its relations with Italy. There were several key areas which were the source of constant grievance between the two countries: Italy's territorial ambitions in Dalmatia, its support for irredentist claims against Yugoslavia, treatment of the Yugoslav minority in Italy, Italian interference in Albanian and Austrian affairs, and after 1929, the support for Croatian terrorists.[3] The question of a possible Habsburg restoration in Austria especially worried Belgrade. With its historical appeal and in the context of internal frictions between Serbs and Croats, the government considered this issue to be dangerous for political stability of the country. Therefore, Belgrade regarded the *Anschluss*, incorporation of Austria into Germany, as a preferable solution for some of its problems long before Hitler's rise to power.[4] French policy, on the contrary, would rather have accepted the Habsburg restoration as a tool against strengthening Germany's position in Central Europe. Obviously, the two countries had different perceptions of the threat in South-Eastern Europe.[5] But as long as there was a danger of border revisions in the Balkans, Yugoslavia had to remain allied to France.

Yugoslavia's attitude towards Austria and the question of Anschluss was not set in stone. In 1926, Belgrade attempted an agreement with Rome on the basis of a mutual opposition to Anschluss.[6] This was repeated at the meeting between King Alexander and Carlo Galli, the Italian Minister in Yugoslavia, in Bled (Slovenia) in July 1930. The King offered a political agreement and a customs union with Italy, provided Rome renounced its territorial ambitions in Yugoslavia and support for revisionism in the Balkans. Alexander even offered a joint Yugoslav-Italian defence along the Austrian border against any future German attack.[7] However, any conciliatory approach from Belgrade was rejected by Rome.[8] At the same time, the British foreign policy in this region, although dedicated to preserving peace with as little British involvement as possible, was more in favour of Italy and Hungary, being aristocratic, traditional and conservative political structures, than Yugoslavia or other anti-revisionist countries.[9] Yugoslavia's membership of the Little Entente was neither an answer to Belgrade's problems in the Danube basin, as there were many misunderstandings between the member states themselves. Bearing all this in mind, Germany eventually stood out as the only powerful ally against Italy's domination over the Danube region at the beginning of the 1930s.

Political rapprochement between Yugoslavia and Germany started in the mid-1920s. In 1926, the former Yugoslav Foreign Minister Momčilo Ninčić, in his capacity of President of the League of Nations, held a series of meetings in Geneva with Gustav Stresemann, German Foreign Minister. During the crisis with Italy in March 1927, when Rome alarmed Europe with a threat of war with Yugoslavia,[10] the government in Berlin supported Belgrade. Another influential believer in the German-Yugoslav friendship was Yugoslavia's Minister in Berlin, Živojin Balugdžić. In October 1927, the two countries signed a trading agreement. The same year, after the approval of the Yugoslav Foreign Ministry, one of the largest German news agencies Telegraphen-Union opened its office in Belgrade; both countries were hoping in this way to increase their presence in the other's public sphere. Yugoslav move was primarily motivated by irritations with the way in which the French news agency Havas hitherto reported about the nature of the Yugoslav conflict with Italy, but also by the wish to create a fertile soil in both German and Yugoslav public for a gradual improvement of mutual relations.[11] However, the introduction of the dictatorship in Yugoslavia at the beginning of 1929 cooled German-Yugoslav relations; one of the consequences of King Alexander's decision was a new Education Bill which drastically reduced cultural freedoms of ethnic minorities, including the German one.[12] Alexander attempted to renew German friendship through acts of his own diplomacy; in December 1929, he sent Father Anton Korošec, political leader of the Yugoslav Slovenes, on a private diplomatic mission without consulting his government. The Slovenian met with the German Foreign Minister Julius Curtius in Berlin and clarified that Yugoslavia would not object to the Anschluss.[13] Overall, German-Yugoslav relations were those of mutual respect between the former enemies; on 6 November 1932, a joint mass for the Serbian and German soldiers who had died during the First World War was held in the military graveyard in Topčider, outside Belgrade, by Orthodox, Catholic and Lutheran priests.[14]

The geo-political situation of the Weimar Republic was not as bad as it initially seemed in 1919. The demise of two neighbouring empires in Central and South-Eastern Europe created a system of small and mutually opposed states with weak economies.[15] A restoration of Germany's great power status seemed especially realistic after the Locarno Treaty in 1925, which, albeit defining Germany's western borders beneficially for France and Belgium, left the question of its eastern borders open. Prospects for revision there seemed promising as Britain was not interested, France was geographically detached from the area and Russia withheld within its own borders due to internal problems.[16] The demand for revision of eastern borders was an ever-present topic in the 1920s Germany and influenced foreign policy decision-making in Berlin.

Another topic was German economic hegemony in Central Europe. The idea of pursuing a distinctively German *Mitteleuropa*, instead of cooperation with France to secure wider European political agreement and economic cooperation, prevailed among the German politicians, diplomats and businessmen after Stresemann's death in November 1929, thus ending the policy of compromising with Western powers.[17] The reins of foreign policy were taken by Curtius and Brüning, who turned their attention towards the south-east. Austria's strong economic ties with agricultural Balkan countries were seen as an opportunity for Germany to rebuild its status as a great power, with Austria as a bridge to these markets.[18] However, the failure of the attempted customs union between the two countries in March 1931 was a proof of Germany's weaknesses and a sign that Berlin was politically still not strong enough to pursue *Mitteleuropa*.

Jürgen Elvert suggests that Berlin tended to see the Balkans only as a reservoir of political power; its main focus was normally on Central and Eastern Europe, while Germany's foreign policy would have focused on the Balkans only in times of political and economic crisis.[19] And this was the case at the beginning of the 1930s, when the world economic crisis hit the region particularly hard. This gave the economy a prominent place in Berlin's mutual relations with the poor states of South-Eastern Europe, as a tool for rebuilding the German status of great power. Berlin's strongest weapon in the Danube region and the Balkans was preferential tariffs, which the struggling agricultural countries there desperately needed. Although this stood in opposition to the most-favoured-nation principle, Brüning's government had already decided to diverge from free trade and opted for protectionism and agricultural subventions in Germany.[20]

## Germany, Yugoslavia and the Austrian question

Whatever Hitler thought of Yugoslavia before 1933, once in power he allowed neither his pan-German prejudices and sentiments towards the *Volksdeutsche*, ethnic Germans scattered around the Danube region, of which half a million lived in Yugoslavia, nor revisionist solidarity with Italy or Hungary, to influence his reasoning. From his constant references of 'the Serbs' whenever he spoke of the Yugoslavs, it is safe to assume that he regarded Yugoslavia as nothing more than the enlarged Serbia, a well-deserved prize for heroic achievements of Serbian soldiers during the First World War; this would fit into the Social Darwinist pattern of his thinking. But in general, the Danube region and the Balkans were beyond his immediate interest; the exception was Austria, which Hitler considered as his own domain in the foreign policy, and it was Yugoslavia to temporarily serve as a fulcrum in Hitler's push towards Anschluss.

As always, Yugoslavia's first priority remained its safety from Italian ambitions. The change of regime in Berlin was a non-event in the German-Yugoslav relationship; Germany seemed distant and the new regime shared the anti-communist sentiment of Yugoslavia's elites. Events in Yugoslavia's neighbourhood in the period before Hitler's rise occupied more attention in Belgrade. In January 1933, the Austrian social-democratic newspaper *Arbeiter Zeitung* revealed the so-called Hirtenberg affair, attempted arms smuggling from Italy to Hungary in December 1932. Forty wagons loaded with old Austro-Hungarian arms and ammunition captured by the Italians in 1918 left the Hirtenberg weapons factory, where they were shipped allegedly for modernization works, towards Hungary. The Austrian government at first tried to deny the report and the Hungarians ignored it. But the scandal quickly spread across Europe and left both governments embarrassed.[21] In such circumstances, any political initiative coming from Rome caused alarm in Belgrade.

The Four-Power Pact was one of those, designed by the Italian leader Benito Mussolini in March 1933 and unwillingly supported by the French.[22] The very idea of a concert of great powers which would replace the League and sponsor revision of peace treaties disturbed the Yugoslavs. On 1 June, King Alexander spoke about the political situation in Europe and inside Germany with Albert Dufour von Feronce, the German Minister in Belgrade. According to the latter's report, the King asked for assurances that the question of border revisions in Europe would only be discussed in Geneva. The King confessed that he 'prefers a customs union between Germany and Austria. Germany as a neighbour would not be a problem for him, as an understanding between Germany and Austria would settle the Austrian question once and for all'.[23] The course of Yugoslavia's foreign policy was determined by Italian ambitions in South-Eastern Europe, which served as a tool for the peace treaties' revision against the Yugoslav interests; who dominated Austria was of essential importance for Yugoslavia.[24]

Berlin understood the importance of maintaining good relations with countries 'from the other side of the Austrian border, namely with Yugoslavia'.[25] Good relations with Belgrade were seen as a valuable lever against Italy and Hungary.[26] Anschluss with Austria was the focal point of German foreign policy during Hitler's first year in power; therefore, relations with Yugoslavia were important to Berlin's plans.[27] At the same time and for the same reason, Germany's relations with Italy were full of tensions.[28] Italy's standing in the region was reinforced when in October 1932 Gyula Gömbös became the Hungarian Prime Minister. At a meeting in Rome in November, Mussolini and Gömbös announced their commitment to Austrian independence and worked out a plan for creating a bloc of three countries opposed to both the Little Entente and the Anschluss. Mussolini then moved to persuade the Austrian Prime Minister Engelbert Dollfuss into joining a customs union with Italy and Hungary and cutting ties with Germany and France.[29] For the time being, Germany and Italy were rivals and their interests in the Danube region were fundamentally opposed.

Berlin learned more about Yugoslavia's diplomatic orientation from the Under-Secretary of the Foreign Ministry in Belgrade, Božidar Purić, in June 1933. The latter explained that Yugoslavia understood the German wish for an understanding with Italy because of ideological similarities between the two countries but admitted that such a rapprochement worried him and expressed the hope that it would not be at the expense of Yugoslavia. Regarding the Anschluss, Purić repeated that Yugoslavia would not object to it, as 'Germany would be a better neighbour than an independent Austria'. However, he warned that Yugoslavia would oppose the unification of Germany and Austria if it meant the awakening of the old *Drang nach Osten* ideology. 'For the sake of [Yugoslavian] survival, any great power setting up in the Balkans would not be tolerated.'[30] At the same time, Gömbös visited Berlin, becoming the first foreign head of state to visit Hitler. The Führer emphasized that his aim was to eliminate French influence in Central Europe and break the Little Entente but rejected any political support for Hungarian revisionism, except towards Czechoslovakia.[31]

The Austrian question was also a factor which determined the German attitude towards Yugoslavia's internal situation. Berlin had a good understanding of Yugoslavia's domestic affairs, and despite an awareness of the problem with Croatia, it was confident of no immediate danger of the country's disintegration.[32] Playing the card of Yugoslavia's unity, as opposed to Italy and Hungary, and gaining in return a strong opponent to Italian domination over the Danube region as a friend, was a logical conclusion. In a letter to Hassell, Gerhard Köpke, one of the departmental directors in the German Foreign Ministry, explained their motivation: 'Nothing could give a stronger impetus to legitimism [the Habsburg restoration] in Austria than the political rapprochement between the independent Croats and Slovenes and Austria and Hungary.'[33] This would inevitably lead to a consolidation of Italian influence in the region.[34] The Foreign Ministry's reasoning soon gained practical implementation. At the end of 1933, problems emerged about the treatment of Croatian émigrés in Germany and their printed propaganda, which gained the support from Rosenberg's Foreign Policy Office.[35] German Foreign Ministry however took a firm stand against anti-Yugoslavian propaganda. Hitler himself stepped in and ruled in favour of the Foreign Ministry; the Gestapo closed down two newspapers on 25 January 1934.[36]

The main German problem in the first years of Hitler's rule was the inherited political weakness of the Weimar era. Foreign Ministry officials maintained older political views of the Wilhelmine era, particularly towards the Central and South-Eastern Europe. But in the early 1930s, the wishes of Wilhelmstrasse were not compatible with the reality of German economic and political strength. They were painfully reminded of this by the events after the signing of the German-Hungarian Trade agreement of February 1934; the Foreign Ministry hoped to circumvent Italian influence in Budapest with it. However, already by 15 March, Hungary, Austria and Italy had signed a political treaty in Rome, the so-called Rome Protocols. Although at the time it looked to contemporaries as a counterbalance to the Little Entente and a reaction to the recently formed Balkan Pact, the agreement had a clear anti-German edge in its provision for safeguarding of Austrian independence.[37]

The Rome Protocols increased the political importance of South-Eastern Europe for Berlin and disturbed Belgrade.[38] It looked like a continuation of the endless stream of Italian designs for encircling Yugoslavia.[39] But reports about the beginning of German-Yugoslav trade negotiations in March equally disturbed governments in Italy and Hungary.[40] In April, Hassell was invited to the Foreign Ministry in Rome to clarify the press attacks against Italy by *Völkischer Beobachter* and various Bavarian newspapers.[41] There were even rumours in Austria that in the event of Anschluss, Germany would cede south Carinthia to Yugoslavia.[42] European diplomatic circles rumoured about the existence of a secret agreement between Belgrade and Berlin, directed against Vienna and Rome.[43] Everybody kept a watchful eye on everyone else in this part of Europe.

In April and May 1934, two of the most important Nazi officials visited Yugoslavia, Ernst Röhm and Hermann Göring. Röhm visited Dubrovnik and the Yugoslav coast privately during his holiday.[44] Göring on the other hand made a stop in Belgrade on his way from Budapest to Athens.[45] Despite the interest which this visit caused in Belgrade, King Alexander, who at the time happened to be in Montenegro, did not find it necessary to cut his trip short and meet the guest. At the same time, a minor French delegation arrived in Belgrade for an official visit, and the most important Yugoslav officials had already been scheduled to meet them. Last but not least, Göring was driven from the airport to the German legation along the streets decorated with French flags. Although Foreign Minister Bogoljub Jevtić made the effort to meet him the following morning, Göring was not pleased.[46] Still, this visit caused more worries in Rome, where it was seen as proof of a political rapprochement between Berlin and Belgrade, particularly as it occurred three weeks after the conclusion of the new German-Yugoslav trade agreement, signed on 1 May.

Clearly, Hitler's meeting with Mussolini in Venice on 14 June 1934 happened during a sensitive period of mutual mistrust between Rome and Berlin. Hitler stressed that Anschluss was not on the table and instead suggested the forming of a new government in Vienna, led by a non-party person, which would include the Austrian National Socialists; to avoid rivalry, Italy and Germany would settle any outstanding political or economic issues regarding Austria between themselves.[47] Essentially, Hitler wanted Mussolini to give up Italian support for Austria, which was unacceptable to Il Duce. However, the Führer misinterpreted the latter's evasive answers, and the chain of well-known events was set, leading to the failed Nazi coup in Vienna and Dollfuss's murder on 25 July. Italy immediately moved its divisions onto the Austrian border but did not cross it, partly out of fear of Yugoslavia's army entering southern Austria.[48] More importantly, as some of the heaviest fighting between the governmental forces and the Austrian Nazis took place in eastern Carinthia, many rebels escaped to Yugoslavia after the Yugoslavs opened border crossings.[49] Yugoslav authorities treated them well but insisted that Germany had to provide for their expenses, both financially and in supplies.[50] In September, Purić expressed his opinion to the new German Minister in Belgrade Viktor von Heeren that as long as Germany remained patient and clever, both Italy and France would soon lose their influence in Austria.[51]

Barely two weeks after the meeting in Venice, the French Foreign Minister Louis Barthou visited Belgrade as part of his Eastern-European tour, with the purpose of promoting the idea of Eastern Locarno for containing Germany.[52] Unlike the wholehearted reception and the cheering crowds which greeted Barthou on every stop along the Danube,[53] his conversation with the Yugoslav king was less cordial. Alexander would not accept any agreement which included the Soviet Union and restricted Germany for Italy's benefit.[54] But Heeren reported after the visit that Yugoslavia was still following the French policy of safeguarding the status quo.[55] This commitment was not as strong as it had been, but feelings of gratitude to France and of brotherhood of arms between the two nations were still strong among the Serbian portion of the Yugoslav nation. The Yugoslavs actually hoped for a German-French rapprochement, which would make it easier for Belgrade to cooperate more closely with Berlin. Heeren recommended more understanding and patience for Yugoslavia's position vis-à-vis France at present, for the sake of future relations.[56]

However, despite its disappointment with the French policy, the Yugoslavs were fearful that once the Austrian question had been settled, Berlin might turn its political support towards Italy and Hungary.[57] Although for the time being Germany was their closest ally in preventing the Italian penetration in the Danube region, the Yugoslavs were aware that the Reich was a revisionist country and not certain about Hitler's long-term goals. In the first years of their rule, the Nazis were careful not to reveal their aims and thus provoke a preventive response from the rival European powers. This was achieved by skilfully using negotiations whenever it was possible to gain time and create a smokescreen of willingness to cooperate.[58] A typical example was the January

1934 Non-Aggression Pact with Poland, which the British Ambassador in Berlin Eric Phips described as 'the act of reconciliation between Germany and Poland'.[59]

The Yugoslavs were aware of the true nature of Hitler's regime. Diplomatic reports from Berlin emphasized that the new government stigmatized as Marxists all those who had in the past fifteen years supported democracy and that the underlying motive behind Hitler's actions was the reorganization of Germany as a one-party state.[60] The Yugoslav press, in full knowledge about the anti-pacifist nature of the Nazis, questioned how could they possibly contribute to peace in Europe.

> Did we not see how easily they used the confusion in their own country to dissolve the Parliament, imprison their political opponents and rule with an iron fist? ... One who does not refrain from the use of force in his own country will show no restrain against the others and would easily go to war once he thinks it is necessary, or assess that he would be successful.[61]

From January 1933, a renowned Serbian poet and writer, Stanislav Vinaver, acting as a Berlin correspondent of the Yugoslav Central Press Bureau, sent frequent reports about the persecutions of political opponents to the new German regime, including communists and Jews.[62] In an article for *Politika* in April 1933, Balugdžić[63] suggested that Hitler's initial approach to foreign affairs was probably moderated by Neurath, but at the price of Hitler's great personal effort to defeat his own instincts and foreign-political ambitions, as they had been trumpeted over the years of work in opposition to successive Weimar governments.[64] *Slovenec*, the newspaper of the Slovenian nationalists, published warnings on the danger of Greater-German nationalism and called upon Austrian Slovenes to support Dollfuss in opposing Hitler.[65] In February 1934, the police in Zagreb searched the apartment of and questioned a German national who attempted to set up a local branch of the NSDAP.[66] In December 1935, police discovered that some younger members of Kulturbund, a cultural association of Yugoslav ethnic Germans, swore oaths by placing right hand on the Reich's flag with Swastika.[67]

At a meeting with Heeren in June 1934, Alexander enquired about the nature of the German-Polish agreement and wondered if this meant that a French-German understanding was now possible.[68] Yet, contrary to some claims in older Yugoslav historiography,[69] he never mentioned the possibility of a Yugoslav-German agreement – an indication that the Yugoslav foreign policy still preferred to operate through existing ties with France. Alexander probably preferred to see some form of German-French rapprochement, not German-Yugoslav.[70] Yugoslavia wanted to use Germany for its political benefit, but not at the price of becoming a German salient in the Balkans, thus replacing French tutelage with the German. It is also possible that, saturated with reports of German internal problems, economic grievances and international isolation, Alexander underestimated Hitler and failed to assess the dangerous long-term implications of a closer Yugoslav relationship with Germany, once Austria stopped being a mutual interest.[71] Anyway, before his last trip, the King himself announced publicly that any hope of an agreement between Rome and Belgrade to protect Austria was an illusion, as Yugoslavia had no intention of defending Central

Europe against Hitler.⁷² At the same time, he let Berlin know that Yugoslavia would not be drawn into any anti-German alliance.⁷³

These events fell in the period which witnessed a change of personnel in the German legation in Belgrade. In 1933, Dufour von Feronce reached retirement age and in October that year the new German Minister arrived. Viktor von Heeren, aged fifty-two at the time, was a professional diplomat who had already served in Madrid and Prague in the 1920s, followed by his promotion to the rank of the Foreign Ministry's senior counsellor of the first rank in 1929. Prior to his arrival in Belgrade, Heeren was head of the Foreign Ministry's Department for South-Eastern Europe in Berlin.⁷⁴ He did not become a party member until 1937. Being an experienced diplomat, Heeren quickly developed a wide circle of acquaintances in Yugoslavia's public life. During his eight years of service in Belgrade, he transformed the legation building into one of the centres of Belgrade's social life, organizing lectures, concerts and other public events, which all helped him gather valuable information and gauge the public opinion.⁷⁵ Heeren supported the political line of closer ties with Yugoslavia and after the military coup of 27 March 1941 tried to prevent the German attack, which brought him in conflict with Ribbentrop and effectively ended his career.⁷⁶

## The road to neutrality

King Alexander was assassinated in Marseilles on 9 October 1934, at the beginning of his state visit to France. It was supposed to be a follow-up to the Belgrade meeting with Barthou in June. Had he arrived safely in Paris, the King would have attempted once again to obtain French support for limiting Italian influence in Central Europe.⁷⁷ The assassin was a Bulgarian and the assassination was organized by the Croatian terrorist émigré organization Ustaše, mostly harboured and supplied by Italy. As Berlin had expected, Yugoslavia did not fall apart. The manifestations of the national unity were strong, equally in the Croatian parts of the country, which left the Italians visibly impressed.⁷⁸ Heeren was pleased to report after the funeral that 'the interest of the whole country was focused on Göring', the head of the German delegation. The Yugoslav press overemphasized feelings of gratitude to Germany for its sincere condolences, while the government in Belgrade struggled to keep under control the public outrage towards France.⁷⁹ Especially cordial was Heeren's first meeting with the Regent Prince Paul, Alexander's first cousin, on 8 November.⁸⁰ This caused the former to recommend patience in dealing with Yugoslavia, now that Germany was gaining momentum. 'Since no one is more interested than us in Yugoslavia's independent foreign policy [from France], it would be useful if our press showed consideration for Yugoslavia's need for peace in foreign affairs.'⁸¹

Determined not to leave the deed unpunished, the government in Belgrade, supported by its Little Entente and Balkan Entente partners, pressed charges against the countries which it considered responsible. Eventually, no accusations were made against Italy, which was omitted from the Yugoslav appeal to the League of Nations on 22 November, largely due to the persistent pressure from Pierre Laval, the new French

Foreign Minister.[82] Yugoslavia's anger was instead directed at Hungary, as there were indications that some of its officials had been involved.[83] Yugoslavia asked that the question of Hungarian responsibility for King Alexander's assassination be placed on the agenda of the forthcoming League's session in December. But despite its desire to strengthen its influence in Belgrade, Berlin was not supportive. For Germany, the assassination was a criminal affair and the League had no business in investigating it. Berlin even condemned the Little Entente for trying to make a political capital out of a tragic event.[84] According to German Foreign Ministry, the Little Entente was trying to use the League for political propaganda, by turning the debate into a trial of Hungarian revisionism.[85] Despite the sound bites about worries for European peace which could be threatened by Yugoslavia's action, its motivation was far more prosaic; being a revisionist country itself, Germany could not have supported the Yugoslav demand, which in reality represented everything that Berlin stood against – namely, the legitimacy of the international order set up after 1918. This was the essence of the German foreign policy, old and new alike, and it had a clear priority over economic or geopolitical considerations.

After the French-Italian rapprochement on 7 January 1935, the so-called Rome Accords, Yugoslavia felt insecure and more than ever threatened by Italy. There was a fear that at some stage, if its interests were at stake in other issues, France could sacrifice Yugoslavia to get Italian support.[86] In light of these doubts, Yugoslavia remained opposed to the idea of the Danube security pact, pursued by both France and Italy in January.[87] Italian motives were linked to the expected military campaign in Africa, which would have left Italy unable to defend Austrian independence against any renewed Nazi's takeover attempt. Naturally, the idea was also rejected in Berlin. In March 1935, Germany announced the existence of its air forces, thus openly admitting that it considered the conditions laid out in Versailles invalid.[88] France, Britain and Italy responded in April by convening in Stresa (Italy) to discuss the sinister omens coming from Germany. The leaders of the three great powers extended the invitation to all the countries mentioned in the French-Italian January memorandum for a meeting to be held in Rome to discuss the prospects of a comprehensive settlement for the Danube region. As Germany again declined the offer, the idea failed; instead, France and Czechoslovakia signed pacts of mutual assistance with the Soviet Union in May.[89]

At the meeting in Stresa, Italian, British and French politicians recommended revision of the military statutes of the Trianon, Saint Germain and Neuilly peace treaties with Hungary, Austria and Bulgaria.[90] This caused grave dissatisfaction from the Little Entente and the Balkan Pact. Publicly, Yugoslavia agreed with its allies and together with them rejected recommendations from Stresa at a meeting in Bucharest in early May.[91] However, recommendations from a seemingly united bloc of the three great powers were a warning to Yugoslavia. To lose support of both France and Britain on such a crucial issue as rearming Hungary and Bulgaria would have been dangerous. At a meeting with Heeren on 24 April, Purić appealed to Germany to participate in the upcoming negotiations in Rome. According to him, if Germany refused, Italy would, with the British and French support, gain a free hand in concluding an agreement to maintain Austrian independence in a way favourable for Rome. Yugoslavia hoped for a general accommodation of great powers which would include Germany. Berlin's participation in solving the Danube region affairs peacefully would for a while prevent any treaty revisions, or so Belgrade hoped. Moreover, for the first time, a Yugoslav official entered the conversation on possible options after the Anschluss. 'If Austria was not viable in this form and Anschluss happened one day, then one would … have to hope that the German pressure on the south would not be towards Slovenia, but rather Trieste.'[92]

Yugoslavia's wish for German participation in a general settlement for the Danube region was unrealistic. Göring visited Belgrade again in June, as part of his second tour of the south-eastern capitals in a year, to 'explain in detail German political aims'.[93] It is beyond doubt that the real purpose of this meeting was talking the Yugoslav government out of participation in the Danube security pact. But although Yugoslavia had no intention to participate in any regional grouping, it did not venture entering into bilateral agreements with Germany either. One difference from the situation a year earlier was that the solution of Yugoslavia's problems with Italy was no longer seen exclusively through the lens of a French-German understanding. Belgrade's belief in France was irreparably shaken; it was still afraid of Italy, insecure about the value of its Little Entente and Balkan Pact partners, mistrustful of the Soviet Union, but still reserved towards Germany.

In June 1935, Milan Stojadinović, hitherto the Finance Minister, became the Prime Minister.[94] The situation in Europe was growing more complex; as the summer progressed, it became obvious that Italy would go to war against Abyssinia. At the Little Entente meeting in Bled in August, the member states agreed on a joint policy: to support whatever sanctions were recommended by Britain and France. Stojadinović's letter to Purić, who had in the meantime become Yugoslavia's Minister in Paris, reveals the former's belief in the necessity to contain Italy: 'Please stress to the English the importance of the role which, for geographic reasons, we could play in that conflict, as well as a common interest with England to inhibit Italian expansion.'[95] At the same time, the Yugoslavs interpreted Germany's attitude towards the conflict from the standpoint of the German wish for improved relations with Britain.[96]

Italy attacked Abyssinia on 3 October 1935 and four days later the League imposed economic sanctions. The following six months were a period of unusual activity in Belgrade. Yugoslavia joined the League's sanctions and was approached by London looking for military assurances in the event of an Italian attack on British forces in the Mediterranean.[97] Military delegations met in February 1936 in order to assess the possibilities for joint military action.[98] Belgrade was excited, as according to the British Minister in Yugoslavia Ronald Hugh Campbell, the Yugoslavs found themselves for the first time during the lengthy period of their problems with Italy alongside more powerful nations.[99] Because of Yugoslavia's position as Italy's eastern neighbour, the British had for the first time taken Yugoslavia's military value seriously into consideration.[100] At the same time, British prestige and influence in Belgrade had risen so much that Heeren expressed fears for Germany's economic position in Yugoslavia.[101] But the lack of British determination to curb the Italian threat for the sake of the stability in Europe, especially after the Germans marched into the Rhineland on 7 March 1936, as no one seriously cared about the fate of Abyssinia, ended Yugoslavia's faith in the League of Nations and the concept of collective security.

Even before the Abyssinian crisis, Germany quickly annulled any, for France or Italy, seemingly positive outcomes of the Stresa conference in April 1935, by signing a Naval Agreement with Britain in June. The Stresa front therefore lasted barely two months.[102] A meeting of Italian, Austrian and Hungarian leaders in Rome in May, pursuing Mussolini's hopes for the consolidation of the Danube region under Rome's dominance, also proved to be a failure.[103] Germany's diplomatic activity contributed to this. Its ministers all over the region were instructed to emphasize that no security pact based on bilateral agreements for mutual assistance was acceptable for Berlin. It was a policy aimed against any grouping of smaller countries under the auspices of some other great power with interests in the region. From this perspective, more worrying for Germany than the fading Italian plans were the newly created links between Berlin's old adversaries in Paris and Prague with the Soviet Union. The alarmed Foreign Ministry instructed Heeren to pass on the message that Yugoslavia should refrain from following in the footsteps of Czechoslovakia in regard to Moscow, as it would be detrimental for mutual relations with Germany.[104]

These fears were exaggerated, particularly as simultaneously to these events the old Yugoslav government of Bogoljub Jevtić fell. Heeren reported that this was due to internal causes and expressed a moderated optimism about Jevtić's successor.[105] Heeren described Stojadinović as a man who was resolved to conduct the foreign affairs of his country purely from the perspective of its national interests. Also, he judged that the new Prime Minister's political inclinations were fully in accord with the views of Prince Paul.[106] Still, Germany was quiet in its relations with Yugoslavia throughout the second half of 1935. Yugoslavia's determination to follow the British lead during the Abyssinian crisis was recognized and accepted.[107] Occasionally, there were some initiatives. In November, in the midst of the Yugoslav-British political and military rendezvous, Colonel Moritz von Faber du Faur, the German Military Attaché in Belgrade, recommended stronger ties with the Yugoslav army through the exchange of junior officers. He also indicated the non-existence of economic cooperation over military equipment and weaponry and recommended a stronger German presence in the processes of mechanization of the Yugoslav field army and in building its air force.[108] At the same time, the German Foreign Ministry started to work in cooperation with Ribbentrop's office and Goebbels's ministry on the creation of the German-Yugoslav Society in Berlin. It was supposed to be a counterpart to the Belgrade based Yugoslav-German Society, founded in 1931 with the purpose of promoting cultural and economic relations between the two nations. The Berlin institution was from the outset supposed to serve a political purpose: 'We have in mind lectures and similar events with the topics chosen to timely correspond [with political developments].'[109]

The year 1936 began with a new initiative for the wider regional groupings, this time stemming from Prague and supported by Paris. With Italy preoccupied in Africa, Austria sought another point of support and found it in Czechoslovakia; in January, the Chancellor of Austria Kurt Schuschnigg visited Prague. Both governments wished a political rapprochement between Austria and the Little Entente in the form of a regional alliance.[110] By that time, Yugoslavia was already disappointed with the lack of any British and French responses to Mussolini's aggression. Frustrated, Belgrade stubbornly resisted any settlement in the Danube region without a proper safeguarding mechanism against the Habsburg restoration. The Austrians even contemplated Schuschnigg's visit to Belgrade, but the Yugoslavs were adamant that such a conference would amount to nothing.[111] The Belgrade government now saw Germany as the only guarantor against the Habsburg restoration, an attitude which perfectly suited Berlin. At the same time, Stojadinović rejected Italy's offer for political and economic cooperation in the Danube region, provided Yugoslavia advocated the ending of sanctions on Italy.[112]

The reoccupation of the Rhineland on 7 March 1936 restored the focus of European politics onto Germany. It was great German political victory and French defeat, as Paris had demonstrated to the continent its inability to successfully defend own interests.[113] Needing to somehow react to the German action in the Rhineland, the French Foreign Minister Pierre-Étienne Flandin advocated the adopting economic sanctions.[114] However, this was badly received in most of Europe. Stojadinović still ordered an analysis on the consequences for Yugoslavia's economy. The Trade and Industry Ministry simply concluded: 'At a time when [Yugoslavia] already apply sanctions to Italy... to agree to sanctions on Germany would mean a true catastrophe for us.'[115] But Yugoslavia's opposition to economic sanctions went beyond purely economic calculations. Since the 1920s, Yugoslavia's foreign trade was oriented towards Italy and Central Europe and not towards Serbia's former war allies and Yugoslavia's anti-revisionist partners, Britain and France. In this regard, Belgrade's foreign trade orientation was disconnected from its foreign policy.[116] Belgrade had willingly supported the Italian sanctions five months earlier, without any regard to the importance which trade with Italy meant for its economy. Simply, Belgrade was not interested in the consequences of Berlin's actions, provided it did not result in closer German relations with Italy.[117] Instead, Yugoslavia advocated for the continuation of sanctions against Italy. On 11 May, Purić spoke to the British Foreign Secretary Anthony Eden in Geneva and insisted that sanctions not be lifted, in a manner that left an impression on the latter that Yugoslavia was even willing to go to war.[118]

Austrian hopes of rapprochement with the Little Entente eventually collapsed when, after securing crucial victories in Africa at the beginning of spring, Mussolini returned to European affairs. While Britain and France were absorbed with their futile attempts to bring Germany to the conference table after the Rhineland affair, Mussolini was ready to focus on the Mediterranean and dreamt of an Italian African empire. A precondition for this policy was a closer relationship with Germany. Since the beginning of 1936, Mussolini had made overtures to Hitler, suggesting that he was willing to withdraw from Austria.[119] Bizarrely, the same Il Duce who had less than two years earlier defended Austrian independence at the Brenner, decisively pushed the Austrians to come to terms with Hitler.[120] The Austro-German Gentleman's Agreement was concluded on 11 July, in the same week as Italian sanctions were lifted in Geneva. Austria acknowledged itself to be a German state and its foreign and internal policies would be coordinated with Berlin.[121]

Events in the summer of 1936 were a turning point in the history of the German-Yugoslav political relations. Mussolini's gamble in Africa paid off; Italy had survived a dangerous economic and political period and returned to Europe seemingly unscathed, swollen with pride and bursting with self-confidence. Worse for Yugoslavia, with Austria finally coming under Germany's wing, Belgrade had lost the common cause which made it Berlin's partner. The danger of a Habsburg restoration was gone, but the main reason for the German courting of Yugoslavia disappeared. From a party playing an active role in the destiny of Austria, Yugoslavia became a mere pawn in the regional power game. Soon, both King Boris of Bulgaria and Gömbös visited Hitler in what seemed to be a demonstration of cordiality between revisionist powers. When the pro-French and vehemently anti-fascist-oriented Romanian Foreign Minister Nicolae Titulescu fell from grace in Bucharest in August, the balance in South-Eastern Europe irretrievably shifted towards the two fascist dictatorships.

## From player to played

It is hard to say whether Yugoslavia gambled and lost by playing on the card of a partnership with Germany against Italy and the Habsburg restoration in Austria in 1933–6. One might assume that the Yugoslavs envisaged Germany after 1933 in the same way as they perceived old Weimar and Wilhelmine Germany: conservative, traditional and only economically aggressive. The very fact that as late as May 1935, Belgrade hoped that Germany might join a wider regional grouping for settling the problems of the Danube region is a testimony of how deluded it was. But Yugoslavia's authorities were aware of the true character of Hitler's regime and its revisionist nature. Even before the assassination of King Alexander, they had enough reports enabling them to estimate properly a very different nature of a dangerous and evil regime in the making inside the Reich. Belgrade probably believed that either Germany would lose interest in the Balkans once it incorporated Austria, or that France and Britain would not lose their interest in the Balkans and leave it entirely to Germany, thus keeping the equilibrium of power in South-Eastern Europe.

There is also a question of whether Yugoslavia had any other choice. Faced with France's courting of Italy due to Paris's obsession with the encirclement of Germany, Yugoslavia needed to find support elsewhere. Britain was possibly the only great power in Europe which honestly endorsed peace in South-Eastern Europe. However, London preferred not to commit itself, hoping that countries of the region would eventually settle their differences themselves. Also, early in the 1920s London developed some opinions about the political situation in the Danube region, manifested in prevailingly negative attitude towards the Little Entente. This continued in the 1930s and was coupled with a continuous British downplaying of Italian danger for Yugoslavia.[122] With both London and Paris obsessed with getting Italian support for safeguarding Austria, Germany was the only remaining outlet of political support for Yugoslavia against Italy, or at least that was how the Yugoslavs saw it.

In the summer of 1936, the Yugoslavs learned another important lesson: great powers had no problem in sacrificing smaller countries for the sake of appeasing other great powers, if it was in their interest. The fate of Abyssinia marked the end of the Versailles order and a symbolical defeat of the League of Nations, which had no means at disposal to prevent great powers in pursuing their own designs, even if it contravened collective security. Once Austria came under the German dominance,

Yugoslavia could have only hoped that Germany would turn its attention away from the Balkans, instead of siding with Italy and other revisionist countries in the region. In accordance with a new reality in the region, Yugoslavia had to adjust its foreign policy. From a proactive regional power with a say in all important problems of South-Eastern Europe, Yugoslavia turned into a country which merely responded to events. To the contrary, 1936 was a breakthrough year for Germany; it took back control over the Rhineland and effectively placed Austria under its control, without any attempts of restraint by France or Britain. With Italy having successfully annihilated Abyssinia, two fascist dictatorships set the pace of political events in Europe.

3

# Economic relations under the auspices of Schacht's New Plan

Earlier historiography used to place German-Yugoslav economic relations within the context of German expansionist aims in the south-east. According to it, Yugoslavia's economic overdependence on Germany was a pre-planned policy, set up to pave the way for achieving political aims. Its implementation would have started with the conclusion of the German-Yugoslav Trade Agreement in May 1934.[1] However, we should make a distinction between the short-term and long-term economic objectives of the Third Reich. The former was determined by the chronic shortage of foreign currency and Germany's indebtedness; the latter referred to the creation of a web of dependent states in Northern, Eastern and South-Eastern Europe.[2] Although the 1934 agreement was important for implementing both short-term and long-term German economic objectives, it was primarily defined by the implications of Germany's short-term economic needs.

After 1945, first Albert Hirschman and then Frank Child asserted that Germany had been using its monopoly position in trade with South-Eastern Europe through bilateral clearing agreements to subordinate it in a political and an economic sense. This theory was in the case of Yugoslavia later reiterated in the writings of Schröder, who used the term 'German informal empire' to describe the mutual relationship between the Reich and the region.[3] However, in the recent past this theory has been challenged. Werner Abelshauser and Albrecht Ritschl emphasized that economic dominance in mutual trade alone was not sufficient to establish massive exploitation of a smaller country.[4] Other authors argue that Germany made use of its trade policies and bilateral agreements in the 1930s for long-term cooperation, which were not necessarily exploitative; instead, they point to a neutralizing effect of the clearing mechanism on otherwise asymmetrical power relationship.[5] John Lampe, a renowned economic historian of the Balkans, also recently questioned the theory of a pre-planned policy which links Nazi trade offensive, Germany's economic hegemony and a resulting political influence, calling it 'the post-war orthodoxy'.[6] So did Marie-Janine Calic in her book on social history of pre-war Serbia.[7] All this brings into question the theory of political subordination by using the economy as a tool. We have to bear in mind that Germany was itself in economic turmoil in the early 1930s and its bargaining power was limited; the new trade agreement with Yugoslavia in 1934 was signed at a time when Belgrade was in a good position to negotiate. What Hitler primarily needed in 1933–6 was economic recovery as a precondition of any political or military advance. Nevertheless, the asymmetrical importance of mutual trade meant that by the early days of 1936, Yugoslavia needed to be careful not to antagonize one of its best customers. With political and economic developments in Europe beyond Yugoslavia's control and the lack of assistance from liberal markets after the outbreak of Abyssinian Crisis, Belgrade's bargaining power was reduced and the choice of options severely limited. But for as long as Schacht was economic master of Germany, German economic relations with Yugoslavia, just like with other countries of the region, served primarily for advancing German economic recovery.

## The transition years 1930–3 in the Danube region

The economic crisis following the New York Stock Exchange crash hit the agricultural states of South-Eastern Europe hard. One consequence was a sharp fall in wheat and corn prices, the region's main export products. The volume of Yugoslavia's agricultural exports in 1932 halved compared to 1929, while their value was a mere 40 per cent of what it had been.[8] In July 1930, representatives of Yugoslavia, Hungary and Romania met in Bucharest to discuss the situation and from there made a plea for preferential tariffs for their agricultural products in European markets.[9] The following month, representatives of all East-Central and South-Eastern European countries (including Austria and Finland) met in Warsaw to demand that the League of Nations put an end to the overproduction of grains in order to stabilize prices on the world market.[10] This was the first example of solidarity between the smaller European agricultural countries since 1918 and it demonstrated their ability, when necessary, to overcome their political differences, unite as a bloc and proactively search for solutions to their economies grievances. Fran Ilešič, lecturer at the Zagreb University, publicly expressed the idea of a political-economic bloc in East-Central and South-Eastern Europe. This would enable mutual economic cooperation based on a market economy and independent political development, serving as a buffer zone between Germany, Soviet Russia and France.[11]

In March 1931, it became known that Austrian and German diplomats tried to negotiate a customs union, which contravened the 1919 Treaty of Saint Germain, according to which Austria was not allowed to enter any political or economic agreement with other countries which could threaten its independence – a provision entered into the treaty in order to prevent some future union with Germany. This provoked international excitement, with France and Czechoslovakia leading the protests.[12] The demise of plans for Austro-German customs union caused other great powers to become distrustful of each other's economic plans for the region.[13] In the winter of 1931–2, every great power presented its own plan for the Danube region and the Balkans. France favoured the Danube federation, a regional economic union between Austria, Czechoslovakia, Hungary, Yugoslavia and Romania based on a system of preferential tariffs – the so-called Tardieu Plan.[14] Germany concluded agreements of preferential tariffs with Romania and Hungary, while Britain advocated a customs union of all countries in the Danube region.[15] Underlying this was an ongoing struggle between France and Germany for control over Austria, which both countries saw as the key to their economic dominance over the Danube region.[16] Both powers pushed for its own concept of the economic and political development, the *Mitteleuropa* in Berlin, that is, the continuation of the French security system through the concept of the Danube federation in Paris.[17] To assist the region, a high-profile conference of the four great European powers met in London in April 1932, where the British and French delegations attempted to push through a deal for lower tariffs among the five Danube states themselves. The conference failed due to German and Italian opposition to any agreement.[18] Five months later, a Conference for Economic Reconstruction of Central and Eastern Europe took place in Stresa. The proposed setting of a fund worth 75 million francs to stimulate agricultural export from Central and Eastern Europe under preferential tariffs and fixed quotas never materialized.[19] The core reason for the failure of both conferences in 1932, in London and Stresa, was German and Italian political interest; Germany opposed any solution seeking to include Austria into some regional organization, while Italy knew that it had no power to control a larger economic bloc and focused on seeking the closer links with only Austria and Hungary.[20]

The problem in 1932 was that mutual trade between the countries of the Danube region was indeed too small to support most of these politically inspired plans. This was not always the case, as old economic links between the newly formed successor states survived the war.[21] In 1925, 54 per cent of their foreign trade was conducted between themselves. However, from the mid-1920s, the politics of tariff protection took over and by 1929 that share fell to 36 per cent.[22] When the economic crisis hit the world at the turn of the decade, mutual trade between the countries of the region was below the level required to help them overcome their problems. By the time of the Stresa Conference in September 1932, protectionism became the dominant economic policy of all great powers, making it almost impossible for the fragile economies of the Danube region to get any help from the international community. At the same time in Yugoslavia, Oto Frangeš, professor at the Zagreb University, former Agriculture Minister and the Yugoslav senator, feared that the most-favoured nation principle had become detrimental to Yugoslavia's economic interests and instead favoured an economic bloc of the South-Eastern European countries which would include Germany.[23] The most important outcome of the general confusion during these years was that the South-Eastern European countries gradually came closer to the German view of a deal based on preferential tariffs and bilateral trade agreements, than to the most-favoured-nation principle on which the French and British proposals rested.[24]

## End of German reparations

There were two important economic issues to be settled between Germany and Yugoslavia immediately after the war. Firstly, it was a problem of the property in western parts of Yugoslavia owned by German nationals before 1918. The Versailles Conference authorized the liquidation and nationalization of any such property in the country, landed or industrial. The Arbitration Court in Geneva in October 1925 ruled that the overall value of these properties would be taken off the reparation share to be paid out to Yugoslavia.[25] Secondly, as Serbia was on the victorious side in war and suffered greatly in the loss of human lives, plunder and material destruction during the occupation 1915–8, Yugoslavia as its successor was one of the recipients of war reparations.

According to the Spa Conference agreement of July 1920, Yugoslavia was to receive 5 per cent of overall value of the amount to be paid through German reparations.[26] In the first few years after the Versailles Conference, German reparations to Yugoslavia were almost exclusively in the form of goods. The Dawes Plan of 1924 settled the mode of Germany's payments to the recipient countries, partly in cash and partly in goods. During the period 1924–9, Yugoslavia was receiving its reparations share regularly, in both cash and manufactured goods, although the government in Belgrade was constantly trying to increase its share of cash payments.[27] In the fifth and final year of the Dawes Plan, Berlin paid a little more than 90 million Reichsmarks.[28] The importance of German reparations for Yugoslavia is clearly visible from the discussion on the Yugoslav budget for the fiscal year 1930–1. It was decided that during the following five years, the annuities provided in German goods would be distributed in the following order: 47 million Reichsmarks to the Ministry of Transport, 31 million to the Ministry of Army and Navy, 19 million to the Ministry of Construction and Infrastructure, 12 million to the Ministry of Forestry and Mines, etc.[29]

The Young Plan of 1929 reduced the total value of German reparations from 132 to 112 billion Reichsmarks, leaving the shares of individual states more or less the same. Still, the application of the Young Plan was confusing. According to recommendations of the Young Report, Yugoslavia was to receive on average 84 million Reichsmarks annually during the following thirty-seven years, which would then be reduced down to 22.7 million annually for the remaining twenty-two years of reparations, scheduled to end in 1988.[30] At the Conference in Hague in August same year, set up to reach an agreement about the Young recommendations prior to its ratification by the national parliaments, German annuities were divided into conditional and unconditional payments. The unconditional German annual payments were limited to one-third of the total annual sum, or 660 million Reichsmarks to be paid in cash each year, out of taxes on the Reichsbahn's revenue.[31] But the lion's share of this amount – 500 million Reichsmarks – was supposed to go to France, leaving Yugoslavia with only 6 million Reichsmarks of cash payments per year.[32] The conditional portion of reparations, which represented two-thirds of annuities, was to be paid only if Germany could afford it without hurting its economy. Important part of conditional portion of annuities were 'deliveries in kind', that is, continued German payments with goods.[33] According to the agreement reached between Germany and Yugoslavia in October 1929, the former was supposed to pay 26 million Reichsmarks in goods for the transitional period of seven months until 1 April 1930, when the first year of Young's annuities started, while the Yugoslav share of German deliveries in kind for the first full year of the Young Plan, that is, 1930–1, was set at 37.5 million Reichsmarks.[34] These were the last payments of the First World War reparations Yugoslavia received from Germany.

By this time, dark clouds had gathered over Germany and its finances. Germany was the most indebted country in the world; between 1924 and 1929, the government in Berlin borrowed 30 billion Reichsmarks, a third of the German GDP in 1929.[35] That year unemployment reached 15 per cent, trade deficit was a constant problem in every year of the 1920s except in 1926 and the net investments ratio never recovered to the pre-war level. The German stock market crashed in May 1927; the level of American credit loans fell sharply in 1928, ceasing completely by the spring of 1929. It was followed by the major capital plight from the country in the remainder of 1929, 1930 and 1931. Any attempt to tackle economic problems caused afresh political crisis and violent attacks on the government from either left or right. The Young Plan only briefly delayed the inevitable and under its provisions Germany paid the reparation instalments only for the year 1930–1.[36] Both Germany's unwillingness to pay and inability to indeed pay its debts led to Hoover's Memorandum[37] in June 1931, proposing a one-year moratorium on all German payments. The motivation behind it was fear for the safety of private investments in Germany, notably those of American bankers. The Hoover Plan thus prioritized private rather than public accounts, greatly benefitting the creditor countries at the expense of war reparations recipients.[38] Following the memorandum, the committee of financial experts from Germany and the former Allied countries met in London in the summer of 1931 to devise a scheme for the suspension of German payments.

The Yugoslav representative was the only one to voice his dissent from the agreement and refused to sign the final report of the Conference.[39] According to the report, delegates 'understood that the suspension of reparation receipts involves a sacrifice both for the budget of the Yugoslav Government and for the foreign exchange resources of the Yugoslav National Bank, which is greater in proportion than the sacrifice involved in the case of other creditor Governments'. However, the only comfort for Yugoslavia was that 'if the monetary position of the Yugoslav National bank were to be seriously endangered, the chief Central Banks and the Bank for International Settlement [in Basel, set up by the Young Plan], in accordance with their habitual practice would take the position into consideration with a view to giving such assistance as might be possible'.[40] Hoover Moratorium was voted on 11 August, meaning that the reparations recipient countries lost both cash and payments in goods.[41] A year later, in June and July 1932, the Lausanne Conference definitely put an end to German reparations. This time, the European powers outplayed Washington by coupling the further postponement of German war reparations after the end of the Hoover year, with the postponement of their payments of war credits taken from Wall Street during the war. The European powers realized that this time Germany was indeed not able to pay reparations anymore. By the summer of 1932, its economy was in chaos similar to the chaos following the end of the First World War. The Europeans acknowledged that if some form of fresh moratorium was not implemented again, the reparations would never be paid.[42]

Immediately after the London Conference which sanctioned the Hoover Moratorium in August 1931, Germany stopped paying war reparations to Yugoslavia. This was officially sanctioned on 23 January 1933 in Berlin, when the German State Secretary Bernhard Wilhelm von Bülow and Balugdžić signed the treaty about the cancellation of German deliveries and payments to Yugoslavia under the provisions of war reparations.[43] The German side took on the responsibility to deliver already purchased goods, the value of which to be shipped to Yugoslavia was set at 20.3 million Reichsmarks. With this agreement, the question of war reparations between the two countries was settled.

## German-Yugoslav economic relations in the wake of Hitler's rise to power

By freeing his government from the obligation of average annual payments of 2.05 billion Reichsmarks in war reparations, German Prime Minister Franz von Papen was now able to reorient German economy from the liberal model, based on a strong export of industrial products and considerable import of raw materials and agricultural products, to the model based on protection and encouragement of domestic agriculture.[44] The fall in prices of agricultural products on the world market severely impacted German farmers and landowners, who urged protection.[45] To achieve this, successive German governments reduced agricultural imports by raising tariffs and customs, abandoning the most-favoured-nation principle and introducing a new system of clearing payments. If these measures were not applicable due to the existing trade agreements, Germany simply renegotiated them by adding new protocols with import quotas in order to bypass the most-favoured-nation principle. Protection of domestic agriculture was also the reason for cancellation of some trade agreements, including those with Yugoslavia, Switzerland, France and Sweden. In this period, Germany concluded agreements based on preferential tariffs with Hungary and Romania in 1931, but the scope and long-term effect of these treaties were limited.[46] The elimination of the most-favoured-nation principle gave Germany greater elasticity in granting import quotas and preferential tariffs for agricultural products when dealing with countries which badly needed foreign markets in which to sell their goods, without the danger that the most-favoured-nation countries would demand equal quotas for their products.[47] Still, concessions given to agriculture by both Papen and the following Prime Minister Kurt von Schleicher did not ease tensions; at the end of 1932, the national agrarian association *Landbund* even accused the government of plundering German agriculture for the benefit of export-oriented industries.[48] On the other hand, measures for agricultural protection left the German industry sector embittered, as reciprocal measures abroad could have been applied to German-manufactured goods.

The existing German-Yugoslav Trading Agreement was signed in 1927. It was a most-favoured-nation treaty with special tariff agreements and had a clause which allowed for its cancellation by one of the contracting sides, provided it was announced six months in advance. During the Great Depression, this clause became a constant threat hanging over the two countries' economic relations. On 6 September 1932, Germany finally announced the agreement's cancellation, effective from 6 March 1933, which caused alarm among the big manufacturers, both importers and exporters.[49] The Yugoslav side had been aware of this possibility. In July 1930, experts in the

Yugoslav Trade and Industry Ministry had already expressed their dissatisfaction with the protectionist measures the German authorities had introduced, which in their view were a violation of the 1927 Trade Agreement.[50] The report on the agricultural fair The Green Week, held in Berlin in February 1932, warned of the atmosphere of protectionism which dominated the exhibition space; the slogan was: 'Germans, buy German [goods]'. The report warned that similar propaganda efforts would continue throughout 1932 and that follow-ups had already been organized in the form of travelling exhibitions and numerous 'German weeks' all over the country.[51] Following this and similar reports, the Trade and Industry Minister Albert Kramer announced that although Yugoslavia had acted liberally in its foreign trade with other countries, '[it] is committed in the future to direct its import trade according to the attitude of certain countries in regard to [Yugoslav] export.'[52]

The cancellation of the 1927 agreement can also be seen from the perspective of new German fiscal policies which started on 18 July 1931. It channelled all transactions in foreign exchange through the Reichsbank, whether foreign currency was held by Germans or by foreign nationals living in Germany, an attempt aimed at preventing the capital leaving Germany. This measure of exchange control was soon copied by many Central and South-Eastern European countries, including Yugoslavia on 7 October.[53] The next step for Germany was to suspend free disposal of any foreign funds, including income earned from goods exported to Germany. In this way, other countries were prevented from using their money earned from trade with Germany, for any other purpose than payments within Germany. This measure was aimed at controlling imports and balancing foreign trade,[54] and it opened the door for introduction of commercial clearing agreements with other countries as of 1932.[55]

In September 1932, the Reichsbank and Yugoslav National Bank reached an agreement regarding the regulation of payment transfers. Its cornerstone was a rule according to which mutually traded goods would in the future be paid in either Reichsmarks or dinars, not in other currencies.[56] This agreement was equally desired by the Yugoslavs, in order to prevent the currency flight from Yugoslavia.[57] It was a necessary measure owing to the country's indebtedness; the total amount of Yugoslavia's private and public debt in 1932 was 40 billion dinars, or approximately 3 billion Reichsmarks; Yugoslavia's annuities were 2 billion dinars. In order to pay annual instalments of its debt, Yugoslavia needed to earn money by exporting more than it imported. Whenever this was not the case in the 1920s and Yugoslavia's foreign trade balance was negative, the annuities were covered by foreign loans and war reparations. But when in 1931 the Hoover Moratorium ended reparations and the world financial crisis halted borrowings, foreign currency reserves in the National Bank started to melt. As stated earlier, in October 1931 Yugoslavia introduced the Act on Regulation of Foreign Exchange Transactions, a set of measures for currency restrictions in order to prevent the capital flight.[58] In June next year, the Finance Ministry in Belgrade introduced price controls on both imported and exported goods, a necessary measure after the introduction of the foreign currency restrictions. Yugoslavia then signed the first clearing agreements with other countries, hoping to improve its foreign trade balance. Before September 1932, Yugoslavia's National Bank already had clearing agreements signed with Austria, Switzerland and Czechoslovakia. Simultaneously to the agreement with the Reichsbank, it reached similar payment agreements with Greece and with the Belgium-Luxembourg Economic Union in October. The implementation of the Yugoslav-Italian clearing agreement started on 1 November, while in December the Yugoslav National Bank reached a clearing agreement with France, which was activated on 30 January 1933.[59] At the beginning of 1933, 72 per cent of Yugoslavia's foreign trade was regulated through some form of exchange.[60] But hopes for an improved trade balance failed as Yugoslavia still maintained a policy of non-restricted imports, while at the same time Yugoslav exports were faced with a wall of protective tariffs and import quotas in other countries.[61] In this way, in addition to Yugoslavia's public and private debts, there was now debt on the clearing accounts, which by the end of 1932 increased to 360 million dinars.[62] Therefore, 1932 can be marked as the year in which Yugoslavia, under the influences and restrictions beyond its control, limited its freedom of payment transfers and when the development of Yugoslavia's financial policy took a course towards exchange in foreign trade.[63]

## The May 1934 Trade Agreement

In 1933, the specifics of Germany's internal political situation and domestic economy made economic cooperation with Yugoslavia complicated. In the 1920s, Germany always had a surplus in trade with Yugoslavia, which at its peak in 1929 amounted to 513 million dinars according to Yugoslav statistics.[64] After the signing of the clearing agreement in September 1932, the Yugoslav payment balance with Germany was negative; in February 1933, Yugoslavia owed goods worth 128 million dinars. Although this debt then started to decrease, mostly as a result of the cancellation of the 1927 agreement,[65] Yugoslavia was still a debtor and at the beginning of 1934, the Yugoslav clearing debt to Germany stabilized at approximately 30 million dinars, or 2 million Reichsmarks. The German announcement of the 1927 treaty's cancellation in September 1932 strongly affected the mutual trade, bringing soon the balance of mutual trade into Yugoslavia's favour; in the first quarter of 1933, Yugoslavia had a positive trade balance with Germany for the first time.[66] This explanation for Germany's declining role as a seller to Yugoslavia was coupled with the new fiscal and trading policies of all recent German Governments since Brüning, which in economic relations with other countries found expression in cancellation of existing trading agreements.[67] All the statistical figures should however be approached with caution, bearing in mind the severe effects of the Great Depression on Yugoslavia's foreign trade. At its peak in 1929, it was worth 15.5 billion dinars; in 1932, Yugoslavia's trade shrank to 5.9 billion.[68] Any improvement in Yugoslavia's trading figures in 1933 was only relative.

At the end of February 1933, Milivoje Pilja and Milan Lazarević, both counsellors in the Yugoslav Trade and Industry Ministry, travelled to Berlin to negotiate a temporary extension of the 1927 Trade Agreement, in order to prevent a state of unregulated trade relations between the two countries.[69] The German side insisted that the period until the conclusion of the new trade agreement was to be regulated under the most-favoured-nation principle.[70] The Yugoslavs could not agree to this and instead demanded the maintenance of existing preferential tariffs for the most important and profitable Yugoslav agricultural exports.[71] No agreement was reached, and on 4 March the negotiations were called off. On 5 March at midnight, all German-imported goods became subject to the maximum Yugoslav custom tariff.[72] The Government in Berlin was aware of these consequences, but at the same time it was the prisoner of Germany's agriculture. In the light of Papen's and Schleicher's continued support to German farmers, which was then continued by Alfred Hugenberg, the Agriculture and Economics Minister in Hitler's government, Berlin had to temporarily sacrifice Germany's industrial interests.[73] This did not mean that the two countries gave up hope of reaching some more preferable form of agreement. Emil Wiehl, economic counsellor in Germany's Foreign Ministry, instructed the Belgrade legation to continue to push to reopen negotiations and to stress that Germany was not seeking a trade war.[74] Negotiations continued throughout the summer.[75] In the meantime, as an example, the import tariff for Yugoslav eggs was raised from 5 to 100 Reichsmarks for 100 kilos.[76]

An agreement was reached at the end of July, on the basis of a temporary four-month treaty which could be cancelled after three months with a month's notice.[77] The Yugoslav press initially welcomed the agreement, stressing its importance for Yugoslavia's fruit exports to Germany, based on the special tariff earlier granted for French fruit exports.[78] But only a few days after its signing, Germany cancelled the trade agreement with France and on 17 August raised import tariffs on plums, the product on which the Yugoslav negotiators had bargained especially hard. The Yugoslav public was furious and questioned the wisdom of the July treaty.[79] In August, Dufour von Feronce reported of a great annoyance towards Germany in Yugoslavia.[80] Lazarević travelled to Berlin again in September and quickly reworked the July agreement; its duration was initially set at eight months, but was later extended to 31 July 1934.[81] German goods would be taxed at minimal Yugoslav tariffs as long as they were not among the goods listed for preferential tariffs granted by Yugoslavia to other countries. The agreement recovered most of the tariff benefits which Germany had previously lost by cancellation of the 1927 Trade Agreement, and some of the Yugoslav losses. Both sides gave way easily, Yugoslavia to Germany in July, and *vice versa* in September. Belgrade probably decided to accept the lesser of two evils – the greater evil being a state of unregulated trade relations with one of its most important economic partners.

In February 1934, the Germans informed Yugoslavia of their readiness to send an economic delegation to Belgrade.[82] In March, Karl Ritter of the Economics Department of the German Foreign Ministry wrote a memorandum for the German embassy in Rome, which revealed the Foreign Ministry's expectations for the upcoming negotiations. German economic aims were to expand and deepen the scope of mutual trade and particularly to increase the value of German exports to Yugoslavia. The political aim was elaborated in more detail. The author acknowledged the failed economic attempts of the previous decade to organize the Danube region according to German needs. This failure had resulted in the formation of two opposed political and economic blocks in the region, the Little Entente and the Rome Protocols between Italy, Austria and Hungary. Ritter hoped that Germany's trade agreement with Hungary signed a month earlier would prevent further Italian intentions in the Danube region, just as the agreement with Yugoslavia should provide Germany's economic foothold in the Little Entente.[83] Although Ritter reiterated that Germany's prime concern was economic benefit for the whole region, German opposition to any attempt of the other great powers to get an economic foothold in the Danube region was clearly outlined.

The Yugoslav side was aware of the economic problems Germany was facing at that time and had no reason to lower its demands.[84] German needs in raw materials, food and fodder and the lack of foreign exchange were no secret. The negotiations dragged on for six weeks, as negotiators attempted to resolve a number of sticking points. During the negotiations, the Germans were on the back foot. The agreement which was taking shape was in contrast to both, attempts to balance the needs of German domestic agricultural production and attempts to maintain German fiscal stability by opposing subsidized imports.[85] It was signed on 1 May 1934 and ratified and came into effect on 1 June, thus replacing the 1927 Trade Agreement. It was a standard most-favoured-nation agreement with the addition of a secret protocol which contained quotas for the Yugoslav agricultural exports.[86] Tariff concessions granted to Yugoslavia were applied to Germany's few remaining most-favoured-nation partners. Yugoslavia got written assurances that its quotas would be respected.[87] Other articles of the treaty covered payment transfer, airline transport, consular issues, as well as the foundation of a Mixed German-Yugoslav Committee which was to meet whenever necessary to settle any problems arising from mutual trade.[88] Yugoslavia granted preferences to some products of the German chemical industry, engineering, steel and textile industries. One of the protocols also regulated tourist traffic.[89] Overall, there was equilibrium in concessions given by both sides.[90]

One of the most important outcomes of the 1934 Trade Agreement – that prices for some of the Yugoslav agricultural products would be paid at higher than world market – is usually used as an important argument for the theory of German imperialist intentions towards Yugoslavia and the region as a whole. However, Yugoslavia itself would not have agreed to anything less than this condition, as internal Yugoslav prices were already higher than world prices. Yugoslavia's Privileged Society for Export of Agricultural Products (henceforth Prizad) was buying wheat from the Yugoslav producers at a higher rate and was also reselling it inside Yugoslavia at higher prices than those on world markets, in order to cover for export losses.[91] The initial idea of the German negotiators was to subsidize import prices of some Yugoslav agricultural products by using German credit in Belgrade. As previously mentioned, at that time Yugoslavia owed Germany roughly 2 million Reichsmarks through clearing accounts. As this money was frozen, meaning it could only be used for German purchases from Yugoslavia, Otto Sarnow, Secretary of Economic Ministry in Berlin and leader of the German negotiating team, suggested that this credit was used for import subsidies from Yugoslavia. This formula was preferred by the German Finance Ministry, as they would not have to pay for subsidies and this was the formula used with Hungary in February.[92] Yet Yugoslav negotiators refused this solution and suggested instead the system of block payments for subsidies which Yugoslavia would then arbitrarily distribute between producers and exporters.[93]

The agreed compromise was contained in the Secret Protocol for the Improvement of the German-Yugoslav Goods Exchange, and was in line with the Yugoslav wishes. Yugoslavia would receive subsidy money in block payment every three months, which would then be distributed to exporters who had already sold their products at the official world market price, therefore at loss. Subsidized exports to Germany were limited to a certain value and volume for each commodity. However, Germany retained control of the way in which the subsidy money was distributed. Also, Germany had the right to decide on the value of subsidies, which would vary according to price changes on the world market.[94] According to the 'Additional Note to Articles One and Two of the Secret Protocol', Berlin kept the right to change the value of subsidies if it caused disturbance on the German market. If the Yugoslav side refused to accept this reduction, the Mixed Committee would meet to discuss the problem until a solution was reached. The only commodities for which the value of subsidies was set for a year-long period were wheat and corn.[95]

The practice of paying higher than the world market prices caused a widespread controversy in the following years about the German intentions and mechanisms for enabling it. However, even the subsequent British analysis of Germany's ability to pay higher than the world market prices for Yugoslavia's goods did not go beyond economic explanations.[96] In November 1938, the Yugoslav economist Gojko Grdjić denied, according to him a widely held opinion, that the Germans were able to pay higher than the world prices by increasing prices of their own exports, thus balancing the account. He claimed that it was a pure economic reasoning by an export-oriented powerhouse, which by this method wanted to increase the purchasing power of the other country, whose population would in turn continue to buy more and more German manufactured goods.[97] Actually, the explanation is much simpler. Since Walther Darré had become the Food and Agriculture Minister in June 1933, one of his most important policies was the protection of agricultural producers by abandoning the market-driven system of price regulation; he instead fixed the prices through the newly established Reich's Office for Food.[98] Prices of domestically produced food were set above the world market price in order to assist German farmers; therefore, all the imported food had to be sold at least at German prices.[99] Besides, despite the objections by the German Finance Ministry, the imbalance in size of the two economies was such that relatively small quantities of Yugoslav agricultural exports would not significantly burden German finances.[100]

As the German Foreign Ministry primarily had political motives in mind, the resulting agreement was described as favourable. It stressed that the agreement provided enough means of pressure to exercise on Yugoslavia. It is not exactly clear how the pressure was to be applied, as the only meaningful tool mentioned was the possibility for the agreement's easy cancellation. It was further acknowledged that benefits for both countries did not perhaps seem balanced enough, but that the agreement's most-favoured-nation character kept an open door for German exports in the Yugoslav market. Germany was also supposed to benefit from the resale of the Yugoslav wheat on the free currency markets, just as the articles regarding the tourist traffic were considered to be beneficial for Germany. Emphasis was further laid on the possibilities for German investment, again without explanation.[101] One sentence of the Secret Protocol suggests a possible reason of German optimism. Article Four read: 'There is a mutual consent that the positive German trade balance with Yugoslavia corresponds to the *natural* ratio of goods exchange of the two countries.' The Germans obviously expected the balance of trade to stay in favour of the bigger nation. It was also a reflection of the historical experience of Germany's favourable trade balance with Yugoslavia. As Berlin expected the trend to continue, it did not ask for the inclusion of any safeguarding mechanisms in the agreement. The German Foreign Ministry expected a positive trade balance, allowing Germany to exercise political and economic pressure on Yugoslavia, indebted via clearing accounts and thus more pliant to German wishes.

## Little Entente's economic cooperation

Yugoslavia did not wait helplessly for an economic miracle at Germany's expense. Belgrade was very proactive in looking for deals everywhere. Together with Czechoslovakia and Romania, Yugoslavia belonged to the Little Entente, a political alliance for defence against Hungary's territorial revisionism. Apart from unifying the foreign policy of the member states, the Pact of Organisation of the Little Entente signed in February 1933 also aimed at coordinating the economic activity of member states.[102] In January 1934, the first meeting of the Little Entente's Economic Council took place in Prague. At the second meeting held in Bucharest in May, the representatives of the three governments agreed that mutual trade between the member states was below the desired level.[103] The first meeting of the governors of the three national banks was held in Bucharest in October 1934, and these meetings would continue regularly from then on.

Neurath assessed that the Pact had no economic importance.[104] But he was wrong; the Economic Council worked out a plan according to which their mutual trade was supposed to increase by 50 per cent in 1934 and by 75 per cent in 1935. The idea of a customs union was never considered due to the opposition of agricultural protectionists in Czechoslovakia, but the move was daring enough to stir up international excitement and cause hostile reactions in Rome and Budapest. Although the expectations were higher than what was realistically possible to achieve, the three countries had an extensive economic cooperation within the framework of what was possible in given circumstances. For example, in November 1936 governments in Belgrade and Bucharest agreed the regular exchange of oil for copper: each year the Romanian side would supply Yugoslavia with 5,500 carriages of petroleum for vehicles, airplanes and industrial use, which would be paid with the regular Yugoslav supply of the equivalent value of copper.[105] The volume of the Yugoslav-Czechoslovakian trade increased significantly; Yugoslavia's import from Czechoslovakia rose by 25 per cent in 1935 (517 million dinars, compared to 417 million in 1934), as did Yugoslavia's export (540 million dinars, compared to 437 million in 1934).[106] The trend continued; according to the Czechoslovak statistics, in 1937 they imported goods worth 410 million korunas from Yugoslavia, compared to 165 million in 1933. In the same period, Yugoslavia's import from Czechoslovakia tripled, from 197 million in 1933 to 597 million korunas in 1937. In 1936, more than 28 per cent of all the foreign capital invested in the Yugoslav banking was Czechoslovakian, or 256 million dinars out of 903 million.[107] The Germans sensed that Prague was their most dangerous rival, particularly as Czechoslovakia was a financially strong and industrially developed country, with the potential to deliver both quantity and quality which matched the German. This was particularly clear in the field of arms and ammunition sales, as well as in Prague's crediting ability, which at that time outstripped German capabilities.[108] Czechoslovakia was politically and ideologically friendly to Yugoslavia, while their mutual trade was also regulated through clearing. In both countries, there were influential advocates of an increased mutual trade and even of some pan-Slavic economic block.[109] Germany would solve the problem of Czechoslovakia's economic rivalry in Yugoslavia only with the use of force, after the Munich Conference.

However, the economic block of the Little Entente never delivered results so optimistically expected by some experts and politicians back in 1933. Some factors which other, more cautious, experts predicted to hinder a closer economic integration proved to be unsurmountable obstacles. Yugoslavia and Romania desperately needed the Czechoslovakian industrial products but could only have paid with their agricultural exports. On the other hand, Czechoslovakia already had a well-developed agriculture which could easily satisfy its domestic needs. Prague also had to be careful when offering preferential tariffs to Belgrade and Bucharest, as these could have detrimental effects on other trading partners.[110] Import of some goods from Yugoslavia, such as lard and pigs, even declined in this period. Export-oriented Czech industry could have benefitted from Romanian oil and Yugoslav copper and other raw materials; however, Belgrade and Bucharest preferred to sell these much-wanted goods to non-clearing countries.[111]

Still, it would be wrong to consider attempts for economic cooperation of the Little Entente countries as a failure. All three governments genuinely tried to stimulate mutual trade. Compensation deals were allowed, enabling Czechoslovakian industry to even sporadically pay higher than market price for Yugoslav and Romanian products.[112] Czechoslovakian industry quickly realized that industrialization of Romania and Yugoslavia was an unstoppable process and made strong attempts to take part in it, either by changing the structure of its export to these countries or by ferociously bidding for lucrative contracts. But this was still not enough; Czechoslovakian market was simply too small to consume all the staple agricultural exports of Romania and Yugoslavia.

## The war economy, Hjalmar Schacht and the New Plan

The first economic programme of the NSDAP was based on the pseudo-economic theories of Gottfried Feder. As the party started to gain ground against the backdrops of the economic crisis in the late 1920s, Hitler realized that they needed a programme which could be realistically translated into politics without antagonizing the leaders of Germany's industry and finance. At the turn of the decade, Hitler brought into the party a number of people who shared his political views and either possessed profound theoretical knowledge, or had the business experience and contacts with influential figures, such as Otto Wagener, Wilhelm Keppler, Walther Funk and Darré. In January 1931, Hitler set up the party's Economic Policy Department in Munich, with the task of preparing the NSDAP for the rebuilding of Germany's economy once the party was in power.[113] The basis for this programme was autarchy within the larger economic area, with the aim of achieving economic self-sufficiency and full rearmament.[114] After the *Machtergreifung*, the outlines of the German economic platform came to be known as the war economy; it implied a complete reorientation of the national economy towards preparation for war, not just granting a special role to arms production within the existing capacities. The economy thus became a tool of Germany's rearmament policy. On 3 February 1933, at the meeting with the War Minister Werner von Blomberg and army commanders, Hitler had announced that the first victim of his economic policy would be German exports, while priority in the relocation of resources went to the army.[115] In early March 1934, Hitler for the first time announced a timetable for rearmament: the army was to be ready for defensive action in five years, and for offensive in eight.[116]

This plan had to be implemented in stages, which required both structural changes to the existing system and the creation of a legal framework which would allow state interventions. This did not necessarily imply a planned economy, but rather what Volkmann calls 'the guided market economy', where the state set up directions in line with its political objectives, but left it to the private sector to accomplish the task.[117] Hitler willingly delegated the economy to Schacht, just as in the sphere of foreign policy in the beginning he opted for more traditional approach pursued by Neurath and the Foreign Ministry.[118] It turned out that the party's economic programme was not suitable for the task, so Schacht – already the President of the Reichsbank – was appointed Economics Minister in August 1934. The first thing he did with Hitler's blessing was to liquidate the beginnings of the corporate system attempted by some party officials. He then fired people like Feder, Keppler and Albert Pietzsch, who was Rudolf Hess's personal economic advisor.[119] However, the Yugoslavs could not be deceived by these changes; in February 1935, the Yugoslav Berlin legation reported that Hitler was and remained 'the absolute master of Germany', who prudently delegated certain powers to Schacht and Blomberg for the sake of reinforcing the particular needs of the regime and the army.[120]

The May 1934 Trade Agreement was thus signed in the period when German economic policy was taking a new direction. The driving force behind it was Schacht, in capacity of the Reichsbank's president. While the war economy was a platform, Schacht's policies provided methods for achieving its aims. They were defined by strict foreign-trade control, allocations of foreign currency only for imports of those goods labelled as priority, manipulations with various payment modalities and a squeeze on all aspects of household consumption.[121] The Nazi regime inherited all the economic problems of previous governments: a foreign currency crisis, rising production costs and falling levels of foreign trade.[122] In 1931, Germany's foreign trade was positive by 2.87 billion

Reichsmarks; in 1934, its trade deficit was 285 million.[123] In trade with South-Eastern Europe, German exports fell from 585 million Reichsmarks in 1929 to 154 million in 1933, while for the same period imports declined from 516 million to 198 million.[124] Another problem was the Reichsmark; since the devaluations of both the pound sterling and the dollar in the autumn of 1931 and spring of 1933 respectively, German exports became too expensive, as most world currencies had lost their value to the Reichsmark. But Schacht refused to devalue the Reichsmark, instead using its strong rate to devalue German foreign debt.[125] Still, the German trade deficit continued to grow and to maintain financial stability, in the spring of 1934 Schacht severely restricted imports paid for in foreign currency, mainly in trade with Western countries.[126] However, the army, undisturbed by scruples over economic or social consequences, insisted on continuous imports of those raw materials necessary for Germany's rearming.[127] Schacht realized that the only way to go ahead with the rearmament was through imports from clearing countries.[128] In March and April 1934 therefore, Yugoslavia was in a comfortable position to negotiate a good deal for itself. Yugoslavia, Hungary, Chile or Brazil were at the moment the needed economic outlets, rather than economic preys.[129]

The New Plan which soon followed was designed by Schacht, now in the role of Economics Minister. It is easiest to describe the changes made by saying that the emphasis was now laid on imports, rather than on exports, which had been traditional German foreign-trade orientation. Previously, Germany had imported in order to be able to export; now, the Reich mainly exported in order to be able to pay for its imports.[130] The isolation of German foreign trade from the international trading system, through the establishment of bilateral trade agreements, was one of the most important strategic aims.[131] Schacht was at first faced with scepticism from leading German politicians and economists, who disliked the bureaucratic complexity of the new system. However, a year later, in October 1935 Karl Clodius of the Economics Department of the Foreign Ministry admitted its benefits.[132]

Implementation of the New Plan on 24 September 1934 was therefore a long-term response towards autarchy and the needs of the war economy; the import of necessary goods was fully modelled in a way to correspond with the needs of the German rearming.[133] When Schacht became President of the Reichsbank in March 1933, he introduced the system of rationing which restricted purchases from abroad for foreign currency; an importer was allowed to buy limited value of goods paid for in foreign currency, equivalent only to a certain proportion of what they had purchased in the period between 1 July 1929 and 30 June 1930, which was taken as the base.[134] The New Plan now also included exports. No company in Germany was allowed to buy or sell goods on the international market without a permission. A distinction was made between essential and non-essential imports; every individual import deal had to be authorized, while foreign currency was not available at all for the import of manufactured goods.[135] Another characteristic of the New Plan was export subsidies in trade for foreign currency, mostly with Western countries.[136] In trade through clearing, Schacht favoured the quota system.[137] While formally the trade agreement with Yugoslavia still had a most-favoured-nation clause, in reality it soon lost its validity.[138]

Germany under Schacht developed a variety of payment methods with different countries and corresponding to it was a monetary system with over half-a-dozen kinds of clearing Reichsmarks.[139] In trade with the countries of Central and South-Eastern Europe, Schacht used the blocked-credit-Reichsmark, which was discounted.[140] Still, Germany quickly developed a deficit in trade with these countries, which led to large accumulated clearing debts. This meant that the national banks of the countries in this region had constantly to be on watch and if necessary ready to intervene, in order to prevent the depreciation of their Reichsmarks blocked on clearing accounts in Berlin. After the New Plan was set in motion in September 1934, the foreign trade in the first two months was relatively balanced, 345 million Reichsmarks of German imports and 355 million Reichsmarks of exports in November. Then the imports exploded; in December, Germany imported goods worth 399 million Reichsmarks, while the export remained the same, 353 million. The following month, imports were 403 million Reichsmarks and exports only 299 million. In February 1935, the ratio was 359 million to 302 million and so on.[141] Both a rise in domestic consumption and rearmament spending kept the pressure for imports high throughout 1935. But Germany still desperately lacked foreign currency.[142] By August 1936, Schacht and the other responsible ministries argued for a return to more traditional economic policies.[143] However, Hitler had other plans and this eventually decided Schacht's destiny.

## German-Yugoslav economic relations after May 1934

Following the general pattern of its foreign trade since the implementation of the New Plan, Germany quickly developed deficit in trade with Yugoslavia and debt on the clearing accounts. At the beginning of 1933, Yugoslavia owed Germany 113 million dinars. This debt at its peak in February was 136 million dinars. Then it started to decline, and in the spring of 1934 it stabilized to 30 million. This rapid decrease of Yugoslavia's debt corresponded with the cancellation of the 1927 Trade Agreement, while its stabilization in early 1934 was a reflection of July and September agreements between Berlin and Belgrade. Then, at the end of May 1934, just after the signing of the new trade agreement, it suddenly fell to 12.75 million dinars, and on 22 June 1934 Yugoslavia became German creditor, for the first time since the two countries regulated their payments through clearing in September 1932; the German debt on that day was 24 million dinars. Yugoslavia's credit then continued to rise dramatically. At the beginning of September, it was 60 million dinars, and by the end of that month it was already 107 million. On the last day of 1934, the German clearing debt to Yugoslavia was 174 million dinars or 10 million Reichsmarks. It kept rising in 1935; at the beginning of April, it was 216 million dinars.[144]

The reason for this development was that the payment balance did not necessarily correspond to the trade balance, which was also in Yugoslavia's favour. In 1934, Yugoslavia was 100 million dinars positive in trade with Germany; but in the same period, overall payments of German importers in Berlin exceeded the Yugoslav payments in Belgrade by 260 million dinars. This imbalance confused economists. In July 1935, the Yugoslav National Bank took the view that the reason for this imbalance was different dynamics of payments in Berlin and Belgrade; while German importers were making their payments for Yugoslav goods promptly, the Yugoslav importers of German goods made their payments with delays of three months and more.[145] This was an unexpected and unpleasant surprise for the Germans as well.[146] At the end of 1934, Germany had a negative trade balance with Yugoslavia of 4.8 million Reichsmarks, but its clearing debt was constantly much higher. By the end of 1935, German deficit in trade with Yugoslavia reached 24.5 million Reichsmarks, while its clearing debt at the beginning of January 1936 swelled to 307 million dinars, or more than 20 million Reichsmarks.[147]

This was not a good development for Yugoslavia, as this credit could not be used in any other way except for purchasing goods from Germany, for which in the first year after the signing of the trade agreement there was not much interest among the Yugoslav importers. One of the explanations sometimes given was the agricultural nature of the Yugoslav economy. But this explanation ignores that before the economic crisis, Yugoslavia imported more than it exported to Germany. The answer should rather be sought in the economic realities of Yugoslav-German relations after the Great Depression and the delayed impact which the crisis had had on the Yugoslav economy. The experts of the Yugoslav National Bank warned in September 1934 that 'the payments [of Yugoslav importers] into the German clearing [account in Belgrade] were not as dynamic as they should have been according to the true state of affairs. For that reason, [Yugoslav] exporters of goods into Germany cannot immediately obtain their claims'.[148] In October, the National Bank applied its first measure attempted to address the problem; it banned Yugoslav exporters from charging their German partners for exported goods before they were shipped.[149] In November, Pilja spoke to the German Trade Attaché in Belgrade Walther Hess, while Balugdžić had a conversation with Schacht in Berlin. The Yugoslavs called for a meeting of the Mixed Committee in order to discuss the situation, but the German side refused and instead called for increased Yugoslav purchases from Germany.[150] Hess further recommended that Yugoslavia should redirect its imports from those countries with which it had a negative trade balance to German exporters.[151] In December, Sarnow approached Pilja and suggested changes in the modality of mutual trade.[152] However, Pilja refused this and pointed out that the priority for the Yugoslav side was the state of the clearing accounts and accumulated German debt.[153] The Yugoslav side was adamant about not entering into any formal or informal talks until the Germans were willing to discuss the existing problems within the Mixed Committee. Berlin finally gave up and the first ever meeting of the German-Yugoslav Mixed Committee was scheduled for February 1935.[154]

The board of Yugoslav representatives in the Mixed Committee met four times in order to discuss its strategy for the coming negotiations. They acknowledged that Yugoslavia had for the first time in its short history developed a positive trade balance with Germany.[155] The most urgent question was that of the German debt on clearing accounts. The debate revealed the confusion among Yugoslavia's experts. While representatives of some ministries preferred the benefits which the German market offered to Yugoslavia's agricultural exports, the Yugoslav National Bank was staunchly opposed to any further increase of Yugoslav exports to Germany, which would only increase German debt. Some board members warned of the grave danger which a possible devaluation of the Reichsmark might do to Yugoslav financial stability and demanded, either a fixed rate for the clearing Reichsmark, or a German commitment to payments in dinars on the Yugoslav account in Berlin.[156] Ultimately, they agreed to demand measures for the stability of clearing accounts and suggested the setting up of a dinar account on the Yugoslav side of the clearing in Berlin.[157]

The first meeting of the Mixed Committee took place in Munich. It was agreed that both national banks speed up future payments on clearing accounts in order to avoid long waits for the exporters' payments. The Yugoslavs agreed to recommend greater imports of German goods, but this point was not further explained and it remained unclear which mechanisms were to be applied. Yugoslavia was liberal economy and the only way in which the government could have stimulated a rise in exports from Germany was by state purchases. Eventually, Germany received no guarantees for its exports.[158] This meeting was important as both sides acknowledged a problem of a German debt. However, the Yugoslav National Bank was not pleased with its outcome, as the question of protection from frequently changing rates of the clearing Reichsmark was not settled.[159] In an article in *Nova Evropa* in June 1935, National Bank's Vice-Governor Ivo Belin was explicit that for this reason Yugoslavia had no interest in further increasing its imports from Germany. Replying to a statement by the former German Minister in Belgrade Dufour von Féronce that Yugoslavia needed to buy more German goods to balance the clearing accounts, Belin bluntly responded that a country should not buy articles it does not need merely for the sake of improving payment accounts.[160]

This was a common problem for all the countries of the region which traded with Germany through clearing. But methods applied by national banks of different countries varied. The Yugoslav National Bank insisted not to pay off its exporters, until it received enough dinars from the Yugoslav importers who purchased German goods by paying for it on the German dinar account in Belgrade. As the more numerous exporters were earning more Reichsmarks blocked on the Yugoslav account in Berlin than importers were spending dinars to buy German goods, this principle led to the devaluation of the Reichsmark on the Yugoslav market and the strengthening of the dinar. Yugoslav exporters were left waiting for months to receive their money for the goods they had already delivered to buyers in Germany. Bearing in mind the waiting period, clearing fees, the loss in interest, etc., once they finally got paid, Yugoslavia's exporters could end up receiving up to 30 per cent less money than the price agreed at the moment of sale.[161] The National Bank tried to help by buying the discounted claims of Yugoslav exporters; this discount was between 3 and 9 per cent in March 1935, depending on how long the exporters had been waiting to be paid.[162] In the second half of 1935, the upper figure was raised to 11 per cent. To stimulate imports from Germany and consequently provide more money for payments to Yugoslav exporters, in April 1935 the National Bank decided to accept the importers' payments for goods purchased from Germany at 8 per cent lower rate for the Reichsmark, for up to one half of the total value of goods.[163] This brought some relief, but only temporarily.[164]

In May, Milan Radosavljević, the National Bank's Governor, urged the Finance Ministry to stimulate state purchases from Germany. For the first time, there were talks about the import controls.[165] In November 1935, the National Bank and Finance Ministry in Belgrade agreed on the introduction of the private clearing.[166] This meant that Yugoslav exporters to German market could sell their demands directly to importers of German goods in dinars at the Belgrade stock exchange. Again, there was no improvement. It seemed that the government measures could only bring temporary improvement, but not a lasting solution. These measures could only be understood in the context of the increased volume of trade with Germany after the signing of the new trading agreement. In 1934, German-Yugoslav trade was relatively balanced – Yugoslav exports to Germany worth 36.3 million Reichsmarks and imports from Germany worth 31.5 million. In 1935, German imports from Yugoslavia almost doubled, while the export increased moderately (61.4 million to 36.9 million).[167] At the same time, the imbalance on the clearing accounts also created problems for German companies. A communication between the Foreign and Economic Ministries in Berlin in September revealed that, although there were millions of Reichsmarks on the blocked Yugoslav account in Berlin, many German exporters were often unpaid for the goods they sold, and sometimes they opted for bonds instead of money in order to recover at least some of their losses.[168]

By now, Hitler was already showing signs of displeasure with the poor results of the New Plan, which was failing to provide the desired pace of German rearmament. In the midst of problems with clearing accounts, Göring visited Belgrade in May 1935, as part of his South-Eastern European tour. Apart from the political importance, these visits to Belgrade, Sofia and Bucharest could also be viewed from the perspective of greatly increased needs for the raw materials necessary for German rearmament.[169] In a year's time, Göring would slowly take over control of Germany's economy from Schacht and was already seeking to create a base for the subsequent exploitation of European south-east.

## Towards import controls

In late December 1935, Radosavljević travelled to Berlin to meet Schacht. The two governors agreed to open a separate dinar account for the Yugoslav National Bank at the Berlin's Golddiskontbank, to which money would be transferred from the existing Yugoslav Reichsmark account and converted into dinars. Yugoslavia agreed to purchase German goods to the full value of the German debt during the following year.[170] In this way, the National Bank wanted to protect the value of its credit in Berlin in the event of the Reichsmark's devaluation.[171] In January 1936, it began to issue clearing cheques for the goods which Yugoslav exporters had already sold, once the money had been paid in Berlin.[172] These cheques were tradable at the Belgrade Stock Exchange and after 15 January the importers were obliged to pay for the goods they imported from Germany by purchasing the exporters' clearing cheques.[173]

These measures were not met with enthusiasm in industrial and trading circles. When private clearing was introduced for the first time in November 1935, the Reichsmark's rate in Yugoslavia fell from 17.65 to 15 dinars. After the introductions of clearing cheques in January, it fell further to 14 dinars.[174] This had harsh consequences for the smaller Yugoslav exporters who had already delivered their goods to Germany months before 15 January 1936. There were many other complaints, especially about the discounted payments offered by the National Bank. In most cases, this was the only way for exporters to get their money, but the discount nullified their profit margin.[175] To settle the old exporters' claims, the National Bank followed chronological order, with the oldest claims being the first for payment. However, the rule was not strictly obeyed – very likely due to corruption – and the National Bank was even taken to the Trading Court in Belgrade by some exporters.[176]

In Berlin, the Germans were desperate to increase the volume of their exports to Yugoslavia. The only successful way to achieve this was if Belgrade abandoned free trade and introduced import controls on the countries which had positive trade balance with Yugoslavia. Hess met Pilja on a couple of occasions shortly after the Munich meeting, but all he could get were evasive answers on that matter. It is hard to say whether at that point Pilja had already developed doubts over Yugoslavia's possible economic dependence on Germany and the political implications which might arise from that. In a meeting between the two officials in April 1935, Pilja hinted that the Yugoslav side would prefer a reduction of Yugoslav exports to Germany as a solution to both, the German trade deficit and clearing debt.[177] At a time when Germany desperately needed raw materials for its rearmament programme, this was unacceptable for Berlin. Correspondence was slow between the two sides during the summer, most likely because Yugoslav measures to stimulate imports from Germany worked temporarily. But when after June the German clearing debt began to rise again, officials in Berlin became nervous.[178] The pressure continued in January 1936, when the German legation complained about the lack of state purchases from Germany, which could reduce Yugoslav credit in Berlin.[179]

At the same time, Yugoslavia was also quick to reject the plan of the Czechoslovakian Prime Minister Milan Hodža, in February 1936, a sequel to the ill-fated Tardieu plan from 1932, suggesting an economic grouping of the Danube countries, based on a preferential system for their agricultural products.[180] The question remains whether such a plan would have been functional in early 1936, as it might have been in 1932. The timing was definitely ill-chosen, as Yugoslavia was seeking a solution to its economic problems with Germany, at the time when it was actively imposing economic sanctions on Italy, upon Italy's attack on Abyssinia in October 1935. To participate in a regional agreement which sought to exclude Germany from Central European economic affairs would have been unwise.

The second meeting of the German-Yugoslav Mixed Committee took place in Zagreb in March 1936. Events leading to its decisions are not exactly clear. It is only obvious that the Yugoslavs gave way to German demands, faced with numerous problems over the previous two years which all jeopardized Yugoslavia's financial stability. Prior to the meeting, Pilja informed other Yugoslav members of the committee that Yugoslavia would be forced to introduce import controls.[181] The Zagreb meeting was indeed a breakthrough for Germany. The very first paragraph of the secret protocol bore the most important conclusion:

> A. The Yugoslav Government will, by the application of the decree of *imports regulation* ... with every means at its disposal endeavour to achieve the reorientation to the benefit of the import from Germany. The Yugoslav governmental committee

estimates that the German exports to Yugoslavia would in this way increase by 20 million Reichsmarks a year.

B. The Yugoslav Government will further, by increasing the value of the state purchases, strive to reduce the imbalance [of the clearing accounts]. The Yugoslav governmental committee will seek to achieve that these [state] purchases reach the value of 10 million Reichsmarks as soon as possible.[182]

It was agreed that only if all these measures did not result in balancing the two accounts in Berlin and Belgrade, the Mixed Committee would consider the reduction of Yugoslav exports to Germany. The German side also demanded an opening of a German bank in Belgrade for bolstering German exports to Yugoslavia, whose start-up capital would consist of unpaid interest rates on the Serbian and Bosnian pre-war loans to the German creditors. This was rejected as the Yugoslav delegation declared itself incompetent to deal with it. However, it was a sinister omen for the Yugoslavs.[183]

What followed was Yugoslavia's import controls, implemented already on 6 April 1936; the Import Committee was set up and began its work on 25 June.[184] Its purpose was to reduce imports from non-clearing countries, to the benefit of clearing countries. In this way, Yugoslavia abandoned its free trade policy of unrestricted imports.[185] The Yugoslavs did not envisage a general reduction in imports, but rather their redistribution. No import quotas, preferential tariffs or import taxes were introduced. The method for achieving this redistribution of imports was supposed to be the control system set up by the Import Committee; a certain number of articles, thirty-three of them listed, which amounted to 35 per cent of Yugoslavia's import, could be imported only after an application had been submitted to the Import Committee and approved. But the National Bank did not only aspire to redistribute Yugoslav imports from the non-clearing to clearing countries; it also hoped in this way to redistribute exports from clearing towards non-clearing countries.[186] The import controls decree almost instantly resulted in a drastic rise in imports from Germany and a decline in imports from non-clearing countries, most notably Britain. At the end of 1936, Yugoslavia managed to reduce its negative trade balance with non-clearing countries from 415 to 104 million dinars – a drop of 75 per cent. On the other hand, imports from Germany almost doubled in value, 1,088 million dinars in 1936 compared to 598 million in 1935. At the end of 1936, the balance of German-Yugoslav trade slightly turned in Germany's favour, as Yugoslavia exported goods worth 1.039 million dinars.[187]

It might seem that Yugoslavia surrendered too easily to German pressure. However, the reasons were purely of economic nature. Some members of the National Bank's Board had suggested import controls as early as spring 1935. The very first paragraph of the letter sent in May 1935 to Stojadinović, at that time still Finance Minister, summarized the way of thinking of the National Bank:

> It is with honour that we present you the reasons which justify the demand that all imports of articles necessary for our state and economy should be from Germany, which represents the most important export market for our country and from which our exporters claim 300 million dinars, and not from the so-called

non-clearing countries, from which [imported goods] need to be paid with free, golden currencies. ... Therefore, not only economic reasons – the maintaining of both our export at favourable prices and the purchasing power of our agricultural producers – but also the currency reasons ultimately demand that our imports have to be from Germany.[188]

At the beginning of September, another letter was sent to Dušan Letica, the new Finance Minister in Stojadinović's Government, repeating the same argument, that imports from Germany should be stimulated, although only for as long as there were unpaid claims of the Yugoslav exporters.[189]

A letter sent from the National Bank to the Finance Ministry just before the start of the Zagreb meeting warned that Yugoslavia could not delay the inevitable anymore. The main reason was Yugoslavia's financial stability. Although the foreign-trade balance for 1935 was overall positive, the problem was in the different methods and dynamics of payments to clearing and non-clearing countries. While in 1935 Yugoslavia maintained a positive trade balance with clearing countries worth 750 million dinars, it was more than 400 million dinars negative in trade with non-clearing countries. In terms of payments, surplus of over 300 million dinars in 1935 was only fictional, as Yugoslavia's money in the clearing accounts was frozen, while the goods obtained from non-clearing countries had to be paid in foreign currencies without delay. The repercussion of this was the weakening of the dinar on international markets, so the National Bank had to sell foreign currency in order to protect the value of the Yugoslav currency.[190]

Lastly, the unfavourable political situation in the world in the winter of 1935-6 had a significant impact on the state of Yugoslav finances. Although the League of Nations' sanctions on Italy had only temporary effects on the Yugoslav economy, as will be seen later, one of the more drastic immediate consequences was a sharp fall in the influx of foreign currency. Yugoslavia and Italy had had their trade arranged by clearing since 1932, but 15 per cent of that trade was still paid in foreign currency. Financially it meant an average influx of approximately 100 million dinars in cash. As the result of sanctions, the inflow of foreign currency dropped from 241 million dinars in the first four months of 1935, to 198 million dinars in the same period in 1936.[191] Although Yugoslavia managed to compensate losses suffered from adhering to the League's sanctions by finding other buyers for most of the products previously sold to Italian market, it was not possible to compensate the portion of cash payments earned from Italy. Yugoslavia needed to save its scarce reserves of foreign currency and in the spring of 1936 import controls were the only viable solution.

In Yugoslavia, there was the feeling of guilt surrounding the decision on import controls and a need to justify its introduction as something inevitable, albeit undesirable and even wrong. In June 1936, Radosavljević held a public lecture in Prague. He used the opportunity to call upon the Czechoslovakian industrialists to increase investment of their profits, made from the capital in Yugoslav joint-stock enterprises, into Yugoslavia's mining and industry, thus helping to solve Yugoslavia's financial problems.[192] This was an unusual timing for such a call and probably revealed fears of falling into deeper dependency on the German market than had been anticipated. The National Bank would have probably rather seen its country falling into Czechoslovakian, or any dependency other than the German. Yugoslavia's commitment to liberalism in foreign trade was a telling testimony about the general atmosphere in the country. Albeit politically not a democratic country, the pre-1914 liberal traditions in economy still stood and were sharply opposed to the German ideas of autarchy.

In admitting the inevitable, the Yugoslav National Bank followed the model set up by Germany.[193] And the creator of the original model soon paid homage to Yugoslavia. Charles Wilson, the American Minister in Yugoslavia, described Schacht's visit from 11 to 13 June 1936 as politically motivated one, with the one goal of increasing economic dependency, which could then lead to political dependency.[194] British Minister Campbell denied that Schacht's visit would be used for making any new arrangements, but was purely to dispel fears about the consequences of German economic penetration and to encourage the Yugoslavs to deepen their trade relations with Germany. He gave credit to Schacht for making a most favourable impression in Belgrade and putting on a great propagandist show.[195] Schacht's visit was part of a larger trip to the Balkan capitals: Belgrade, Athens, Sophia and Budapest. Heeren was right in stressing the importance of the impression which personal contact with the leader of the German economy left on leading personalities of Yugoslavia's economic life. Schacht talked at length about the necessity of deepening economic cooperation of the two countries. In talks with Stojadinović, he hinted that Germany would be ready to invest in the Yugoslav mining industry and that Yugoslavia should place its armament purchases with German companies.[196]

In his own words, Schacht later explained that he undertook this trip in order to consolidate the reciprocal trade position. He remembered the speech he gave at the evening reception in the German Belgrade legation as a stimulus for the industrialization of Yugoslavia: 'It would be quite wrong for the industrial states to set themselves against the gradual industrialization of the agrarian countries ... Such development would not be detrimental to the industrial states – only the nature of the agrarian exports would gradually change.'[197] This was not how the speech was interpreted by contemporaries. Campbell reported that according to his sources, Schacht openly blamed the Versailles system for all the economic miseries in Europe and that relations between states should be based upon their mutual economic needs, not upon 'considerations of sentiment. ... In the interest of self-defence, it was imperative that agricultural countries should endeavour to attain self-sufficiency in the production of war material.'[198] Wilson sent out a similar report, according to which Schacht said at the dinner: 'A peasant country can never make war. Therefore, it is necessary to industrialize it especially for war.'[199]

## Political prey or economic outlet?

The accumulated Yugoslav clearing credit on the Reichsbank's account in Berlin and the complex situations it caused in economic relations between the two countries in 1934–6 were identified by outside observers as a means of applying political pressure, or as Germany's voluntary sacrifice of short-term benefits for the sake of long-term geo-political gains. *Exchange Control in Central Europe* by Ellis and *The Danube Basin and the German Economic Sphere* by Basch, both published during the war, especially influenced the debate on this issue throughout the post-war period. Still, as we demonstrated, Germany already had a positive trade balance with Yugoslavia before the Great Depression, while Yugoslavia's belated recovery slowed down the return to pre-crisis volumes of trade. When the crisis hampered international trade and closed off most of the Western markets, Yugoslavia needed to find an economic outlet for the export of its agricultural products. In this situation, a bilateral clearing agreement with Germany was a way out for the Yugoslavs. In Belgrade, this was seen as a continuation of normal foreign-trade exchange with Germany, as experienced since the 1920s. What the Yugoslavs did not immediately understand was that in the world of free trade of the 1920s, politics and economy had little impact on each other. In the age of autarchy and the bilateral economic agreements of the 1930s, economic overdependence on one country had a dangerous potential to compromise their political mobility.[200]

When questioning German needs for imports, we should first have in mind the needs of German rearmament. It created a demand for food and materials which Germany could not pay in foreign currency. Berlin had no other way but to turn towards the clearing agreements with countries around Europe, including France, Netherlands or Sweden.[201] Furthermore, the May 1934 Trade Agreement did not work to Germany's expectations, as the balance of trade turned out to be in Yugoslavia's favour. Berlin could not exercise any further pressure in its attempt to initiate Yugoslavia's import drive. Within this context, the lesser power maintained its bargaining position throughout 1935. What crucially increased the balance of mutual trade with Yugoslavia in Germany's favour were the import controls which the Yugoslav authorities introduced in the spring of 1936. This was partly the result of the increased importance of trade with Germany after the loss of Italian market, partly of the lack of other, free markets. Still, the decision was not a result of Berlin's pressure, but of fears for Yugoslavia's economic and financial stability. This instability was indeed mainly caused by the effects of the 1934 agreement, but these effects were not something either Berlin or Belgrade could have predicted and both sides needed to deal with the consequences along the way. The search for autarchy which had started in Germany before the Nazi's ascent to power changed the balance of mutual trade in Yugoslavia's favour; the introduction of import controls in Yugoslavia in 1936 restored the trade balance in Germany's favour. Which of the two countries benefitted more in the period observed is hard to judge.

# 4

# In the web of the Axis

After the summer of 1936, Yugoslavia began to politically dissociate itself from Central European affairs. The danger of the Habsburg restoration had gone, but the result was the rise of German prestige and power in the region where it was now unrestrained by any other rival great power. After 1936, the Little Entente became a burden for Yugoslavia's foreign policy, in the light of constant Czechoslovakian attempts to get support against menacing Germany, beyond the framework of the 1933 Pact of Organization of the Little Entente. So were the dying French attempts to restore its position in East-Central and South-Eastern Europe. To the contrary, this was a period of improved political relations with Italy, possibly as both countries viewed mutual cooperation as a safeguard against penetrating German influence, despite Italian ideological closeness to the Third Reich.

Throughout 1936, Germany continued to successfully repudiate the provisions of the Versailles Treaty. After reoccupying the Rhineland in March and placing Austria under its tutelage in July, Germany and Italy signed the friendship treaty in October, which Mussolini referred to as the Rome-Berlin Axis in his speech in Milan on 1 November. Later that month, Germany and Japan signed the Anti-Comintern Pact. Austria and Central Europe were left out of the focus after the summer of 1936 and events in Western Europe and the Mediterranean grasped most of the attention of European public in 1937. The British and French were locked in farcical negotiations with Hitler, searching for some accommodation with Germany. This frantic diplomatic activity which included everything, from economic concessions to colonial offers, in April resulted with releasing Belgium of its obligations under the Locarno treaty of 1925, thus turning it into a neutral state.[1] Further south, the civil war raged in Spain, with the abundant military and financial support to the nationalists from two fascist dictatorships, while the British were simultaneously presented with the rising Italian threat in the Mediterranean and the Near East.[2] In such situation, Western democracies had little time to focus on South-Eastern Europe, leaving the power-vacuum to Italy and Germany. And both were happy to exploit it.

## Germany and Italy in the Danube region

On 8 July 1936, Stojadinović spoke in front of the committee of his party, the Yugoslav Radical Union. He stressed the many problems in modern Europe; calls for a reform of the League of Nations, tendencies towards regional alliances and increased rearmament in countries across Europe were all consequences of the Abyssinian disaster.[3] Although he spoke at length about friendship with England and France, this was probably a basic courtesy towards traditional allies; the Yugoslav Prime Minister no longer trusted anyone and placed his hopes only on the strength of the Yugoslav army as a deterrence against Italy.[4] It is not a surprise that Stojadinović was pleased with Titulescu's removal as Romanian Foreign Minister in August.[5] Seeing him as an exponent of French policy in South-Eastern Europe, the Yugoslav Prime Minister expressed hope in conversation with Heeren that Romania would in the future be more inclined to follow the Yugoslav political line, which implied a distancing from the Soviet Union and friendlier relations with Bulgaria.[6] He wished to restore the Little Entente to its original aim of isolating Hungary and was against any new commitments. Simultaneously the importance of the Balkan Entente grew; Stojadinović tended to see it as a barrier against any great power's encroachment in the Balkans. He was of the opinion that by the summer of 1935 the Little Entente had already completed its historical role; the danger of the Habsburg restoration had long been gone, while new European problems were beyond the power of the alliance and should be resolved by great powers.[7]

The greatest threat remained Italy. Stojadinović assessed that after the Abyssinian affair, Yugoslavia could not count on the help of any great power against Rome; France had lost respect in Belgrade, while there was a fear that the British interests in regard to Italy would never be aligned with Yugoslavia's. Germany seemed to have reached an understanding with Mussolini, which at least gave some hope to the Yugoslavs that friendly relations with Berlin might help in keeping the Italians at bay. Relations with the regional allies were also turbulent. The Bratislava meeting of the Little Entente in September was the beginning of its demise. Differences between Czechoslovakia on one side and Yugoslavia and Romania on the other were insurmountable.[8] Stojadinović was interested neither in upgrading the Little Entente into a single bloc against any unprovoked aggression, as suggested by the Czechs in June 1936, nor into some pact of mutual support between the Little Entente and France, as suggested by Paris and Prague in November.[9] Although the Czechoslovakian President Edvard Beneš probably only had in mind a diplomatic show rather than believing that Yugoslavia and Romania could effectively assist Prague against an attack from the Third Reich, it still represented an unnecessary risk which Belgrade was unwilling to take.[10] The idea of alliance with France was finally rejected at the meeting of the Little Entente in Belgrade in April 1937.

Instead, Stojadinović turned his attention towards the reconciliation with Yugoslavia's neighbours. At the end of October, he met King Boris in Sofia; the two men discussed the Yugoslav-Bulgarian treaty of friendship, an idea already discussed with the Bulgarian Prime Minister Georgi Kyoseivanov. These contacts led to the signing of the Yugoslav-Bulgarian Pact of Eternal Friendship in Belgrade, on 26 January 1937. The idea of a Yugoslav-Bulgarian agreement caused discomfort of Yugoslavia's Balkan allies. It took a lot of diplomatic skill from Stojadinović to get consent from Bucharest and Athens.[11] The Germans were pleased with the signing of the agreement; to them it weakened the position of France and the Little Entente.[12]

Simultaneously, the Yugoslavs worked on the agreement with Italy. In September 1936, Yugoslavia signed an economic and financial treaty with Italy, with the aim of restoring trade relations to the level existing before the sanctions. Relations with Britain were still of higher priority for Yugoslavia, as both countries shared a common political interest, preventing Rome from turning the Mediterranean into the Italian *mare nostrum*. However, the economic agreement with Italy was only a prelude to a political understanding desired by Rome. Seemingly stimulated by Hitler, during his talks with Ciano in Berchtesgaden on 23 October,[13] in December Italy offered talks for the conclusion of a political alliance with Yugoslavia.[14] The negotiations began in January, were tensed and ended with the agreement signed by Stojadinović and Ciano in Belgrade, on 25 March 1937. Yugoslavia rejected the Italian demand for an official alliance and the final wording of the agreement was favourable for Belgrade. It included articles about respecting mutual borders, protection of the Yugoslav minority living in Istria, mutual obligation to respect Albania's independence and the cessation of Italian support for the Croatian terrorists.[15]

Despite the improved Italian-German relations, Mussolini felt that he should reinforce Rome's positions against Berlin in the Danube region.[16] Italian diplomats considered forming a block consisting of Italy, Hungary, Yugoslavia, Bulgaria and Romania. Although such a plan was unrealistic, it illustrated the political atmosphere in Rome. Their territorial ambitions in Dalmatia did not materialize in the past fifteen years; to keep their interests alive, Rome decided to copy German methods.[17] Belgrade remained distrustful of Italy but had its reasons for an agreement; to ease tensions with the 'hereditary enemy' was important, due to Yugoslavia's military weaknesses and the economic importance of the Italian market.[18] Heeren correctly assessed a growing Yugoslav lack of interest in the affairs of Central Europe and the Mediterranean after the Abyssinian Crisis. He understood that Yugoslavia's position in foreign policy was determined entirely by its relations with Italy and that no great power could have offered Belgrade absolute protection against Rome; therefore, Yugoslavia needed to settle the problem itself.[19] At the same time, Berlin suspected that the Italian courting of Yugoslavia was a result of Mussolini's belief that Belgrade needed to be separated from German influence in order to reinforce Italy's position in the Danube region.[20] It is conventional wisdom in historiography that the Yugoslavs kept the French in dark, but informed Germany about the ongoing negotiations.[21] However, the Germans were kept relatively uninformed by both sides for some time. Heeren would occasionally be informed from Berlin about the rare pieces of information which Hassell in Rome managed to extract from the taciturn Ciano. At the meeting with the new Yugoslav Minister in Berlin Aleksandar Cincar-Marković in February 1937, Göring advised the former that Yugoslavia should not go beyond a formal pact of friendship with Rome.[22] By the end of February, the Germans knew that there were no major economic disagreements between Italy and Yugoslavia, but that Stojadinović hesitated regarding some of the political aspects of the proposed agreement.[23]

On the last day of March, Heeren analysed the possible impact of the Italo-Yugoslav agreement on the Yugoslav-German economic and political relations. He dismissed fears for Germany's economic position in Yugoslavia and favoured the political context, as it implied an increased Yugoslav independence from the Little Entente and France in foreign policy. Although not envisaging any sudden brake, Heeren assumed that the agreement reduced a possibility of Yugoslavia's participation in any anti-German coalition and expressed hopes that the agreement with the Fascist Italy would strengthen the 'authoritative and anti-communist tendencies' of the Yugoslav government. Finally, the German Minister optimistically expressed hope that Yugoslavia's agreement with Italy was a way of reducing the once harmful rivalry between Berlin and Rome in the Danube region.[24] But the Wilhelmstrasse was not convinced. There was an unease about ulterior Italian motives. True, the agreement widened already existing cracks in the French security system in South-Eastern Europe and the principles of collective security. But once again, as with the case of Rome Protocols of March 1934, Italian agreement with another Danubian country seemed to have had an anti-German slant.[25] At the end of March, Ciano told Hassell that his next diplomatic move was an approach to Romania, the precondition for which was *modus vivendi* between Budapest and Bucharest.[26] German economic position in the Danube region was strong, but its political position was still not cemented; on the contrary, the Italians appeared to be mounting a full diplomatic offensive. Although Mussolini seemed to have accepted the German-Austrian agreement of 11 July 1936 and was focused mainly on the Mediterranean, the Balkans remained Il Duce's second line of defence.[27] Hitler often reiterated that Germany had no interests beyond the Austrian southern border, thus acknowledging that he understood Italian misgivings about the Anschluss, but he failed to grasp that the Italian interests were not confined solely to the Mediterranean.[28] Still, without as strong an economic presence as Germany and disliked by the elites in most of the countries of the region, Rome could only enjoy a short-term success in South-Eastern Europe. Italian menacing appearance was only temporarily boosted by its recent triumph in Abyssinia, unlike the Germans, who held a dominant economic position in the region, or the British, whose foreign policy still possessed stronger ideological attraction.

Yugoslavia used the agreement with Italy as an excuse to reject any extension of already existing commitments within the framework of the Little Entente during the meeting of its Council in Belgrade in April. The real reasons for the rejection were contained in a comprehensive analysis forwarded to the government by the Yugoslav Chief of Staff in December 1936: an agreement with proposals for the extension of mutual military agreements within the Little Entente and with France would bring German and Italian hostility to Yugoslavia. Berlin and Rome might unleash Hungarian, Austrian and Bulgarian revisionism towards Yugoslavia, instead of restraining it. Such development would involve Turkey and Greece which these countries preferred to avoid. This might even lead to a breakup of the Balkan Entente.[29] Yugoslavia simply wanted to avoid any complications with Berlin and Rome.

The Little Entente meeting in early April was immediately followed by Beneš's visit to Belgrade, in another vain attempt to change Yugoslavia's attitude. By this time, there were rumours in France and Czechoslovakia about Yugoslavia's alleged rapprochement with the Axis; it was not a secret in Europe that Paris and Prague were working together on undermining Stojadinović. The tools were supposed to be the opposition parties from both Serbia and Croatia.[30] From their perspective, the Czechoslovaks were rightly alarmed with what seemed to be Yugoslavia's unilateral attempts to protect itself against the Axis at the expense of the Little Entente. In February and March 1937, the Prague-based *Rude Pravo* published a set of articles warning about the Nazi propaganda in Yugoslavia and that Hitler was working overtime in securing Belgrade's neutrality in the upcoming war with Czechoslovakia.[31] Upon Beneš's arrival, masses of people gathered in Belgrade to welcome him with standing ovations, which could have been taken as a demonstration against the official Yugoslav policy. Heeren predicted that being in such a difficult position, Stojadinović could now expect a frontal attack by Prague and Paris who would both do everything in their powers to undermine him at home. For this reason, the German Minister recommended a restrained reporting in the German press, particularly restraining from praises for Stojadinović, as this might weaken his position at home.[32]

During Neurath's visit to Belgrade in June, Stojadinović was mainly interested in Germany's relationship with Italy, thus showing how unconvinced he was with the latest agreement with Rome. Neurath could sense fear that the German-Italian rapprochement could be at Yugoslavia's expense.[33] Stojadinović tried to advocate for improved relations between Berlin and Prague, but Neurath rejected any discussion on that subject.[34] Throughout 1937, Yugoslavia continued to actively search for a way between its international obligations towards the League and its allies on one side and the changed circumstances in the light of constantly increasing might of Germany and Italy on another. Both Stojadinovic and Prince Paul expressed their desire for Anglo-German rapprochement, seeing it as the only possible solution for European peace. During the meeting of the Little Entente at Sinaia (Romania) in August, the Yugoslav representatives pressured Czechoslovakia to end its attachment to Moscow. The Yugoslavs even tried to mediate between Berlin and Prague, explaining to the Germans that Prague sided with the Soviets only out of fear.[35] In Paris in October, Stojadinović compared the Yugoslav position to one of a mouse caught between two cats.[36]

At the same time, Berlin was anxious to facilitate a rapprochement between Yugoslavia and Hungary. Geopolitically, it would mean further weakening of the Little Entente; ideologically, such an agreement would be another step in dismantling the Versailles system. Budapest was willing to approach Belgrade, as in the meantime the traditional strongholds of Hungarian anti-Yugoslav policy seemed to have lost ground. Despite its internal problems, Yugoslavia did not disintegrate, Germany favoured good relations with Belgrade, Mussolini's hostility towards Yugoslavia was cooling, the strength of Croatian separatism was diminishing and the Habsburg restoration seemed to be a closed chapter after the German-Austrian July agreement.[37] Hungary had been willing to negotiate with the Little Entente since 1935, provided two preconditions were met: improvement of the status of Hungarian minorities and equality of arms with each of the member states.[38] Yugoslavia, Romania and Czechoslovakia were open to conversations about this, provided Hungary first publicly accepted the existing borders, which was unacceptable for Budapest. Throughout 1937, Rome and Berlin encouraged Budapest to negotiate separately with Yugoslavia and Romania, ignoring the Little Entente as a political entity.[39] Both Italy and Germany tried their best in Belgrade, Bucharest and Budapest to encourage Hungary's bilateral agreements with Yugoslavia and Romania.[40] Still, as late as September 1937 the Hungarian Foreign Minister Kálmán Kánya bitterly complained about the impossibility of breaking the monolithic attitude of the Little Entente.[41] During a visit of the Hungarian delegation to Berlin in November 1937, Kánya and the Prime Minister Kálmán Darányi complained that they could not have reached agreements with each state independently, as the Entente only wished to act on this question in concert. Kánya revealed that Hungary was willing to offer final recognition of its border with Yugoslavia, if Belgrade promised to stay neutral in war with Czechoslovakia. Hitler instructed them to focus only on Yugoslavia, without asking for anything more than the cultural autonomy for the Hungarian minority in Yugoslavia.[42] He promised to advocate for an agreement between the two countries.[43]

Such an opportunity came up during his meeting with Stojadinović in Berlin, on 17 January 1938. The Führer claimed that Germany had no interests in South-Eastern Europe other than the economic and wished to see the political consolidation of the Balkans. As far as relations with Yugoslavia were concerned, Germany wished to see it strong and united, emphasizing that his friendship with Italy was not in conflict with his friendship with Yugoslavia. Hitler stated that he would never support Hungarian claims towards Yugoslavian or Romanian territory. Italy had also come to its senses and realized that a strong Yugoslavia was a much better neighbour than Greater Hungary extending to the Adriatic. Alluding to the possibility of Anschluss, Stojadinović asked whether Germany would have any territorial demands towards Yugoslavia if in the future the two countries became neighbours. Hitler denied this saying that German political aims did not extend beyond Austria; also, that good treatment of its German minority was Yugoslavia's best protection. However, to Hitler's insistence that Yugoslavia and Hungary settle their differences themselves, Stojadinović replied that their problems could only be solved within the framework of the Little Entente.[44] Stojadinović held separate talks with Göring; the two men had by now forged a strong relationship. Resulting from these talks was a press and propaganda agreement, arranging a strict control of press publications in both Germany and Yugoslavia against the other country.[45]

The Yugoslav Prime Minister must have been proud of himself upon his return from Berlin. According to one of Campbell's reports around this time, playing a disproportionately important role in European affairs flattered Stojadinović's vanity.[46] The first months of 1938 represented the peak of his self-regard and confidence in his own political acumen. At the end of their meeting in January, Hitler and Stojadinović cordially agreed that 'as Yugoslavia in its relations with Germany had now removed its French spectacles, Germany too, in its relations with Yugoslavia was no longer wearing Austrian spectacles'.[47] In all fairness, in its relations with Germany Yugoslavia never wore French-tinted glasses. It simply belonged to the anti-revisionist camp, like Paris and unlike Berlin. But until the early 1930s, Germany was never a primary factor in Yugoslavia's foreign policy. Therefore, there were not many obstacles to mutual cooperation, provided Germany did not endorse revisionism in South-Eastern Europe. But exactly because of this reason, the two countries were not destined to come closer politically. And there were Germans who questioned Heeren's assurances that patience was needed as Stojadinović was slowly parting ways with both France and the Little Entente. A certain Clemens Diederich, who described himself as a friend of Croatia and who would in 1942 edit a book called *The Croatians*, sent a letter to the Foreign Ministry in Berlin in November 1937, warning its officials that the Serbs would never distance themselves from those powers to whose agency they owed their rise and territorial aggrandizement after 1918. Despite an amateurish analysis and a hyperbolic style of writing, Diederich raised certain points remarkably similar to the analysis of the British Minister in Belgrade, when writing about Yugoslavia's old and new friends.[48] While Belgrade used new friends for commerce and diplomatic show, it was still the old friends with whom the General Staff meetings were organized, political consultations held and from whom armaments were purchased. Diederich concluded that Yugoslavia needed new friends only until it got stronger, but it would never entirely drop its old friends for the sake of Germany.[49]

## Germany comes to the fore

Anschluss was the event which most of Europe considered inevitable and yet it shocked everyone when it happened, as it was not expected to come so suddenly and be executed so efficiently.[50] After the German-Austrian agreement of July 1936, all that was left for Berlin was to prepare the ground for action. The general feeling in the region was that it would be good to postpone the Anschluss for as long as possible, but not to protest once it happened.[51] Stojadinović had no doubts that Anschluss would happen sooner rather than later and at his meeting with Hitler on 17 January 1938 he wanted to get some assurances. According to his own account, he asked for promises regarding the inviolability of the Yugoslav-Austrian border and assurances against any Hungarian territorial demands.[52] Stojadinović had no doubts which of the great powers had the real capacity to protect Yugoslavia's territorial integrity. Although Yugoslavia still insisted it communicated with Hungary only in concert with Romania and Czechoslovakia, it was clear that France and the Little Entente were no longer counted as protection against Hungary, which for Yugoslavia was the very purpose of its post-war alliances. In February, the French government enquired in Belgrade if Yugoslavia was willing to join London and Paris in voicing their concerns about the aggressive German approach to Austria, but was rejected with the explanation that neither Rome, as the power most interested in preserving Austrian independence, nor the government in Vienna itself deemed such an action necessary.[53]

Heeren reported that both Stojadinović and Prince Paul preferred an independent Austria, as long they could be convinced that the country was stable. As this was clearly not possible, the 'German solution' was seen as the most suitable for Yugoslavia's interests. But he was aware that in many Serbian political circles government policy was not popular. Heeren also mocked the tendency of Croatian political leaders to seek hidden motives against Croatia in any political decision made in Belgrade; he confided that Maček allegedly complained to the French Minister about great dangers lying ahead for Croatia which stemmed from the German-friendly policy of the Belgrade regime. Heeren ascribed this to the Croatians' inclination towards the Habsburgs, as well as to the influence of the Catholic church, which feared the national socialism. By far the most hostile reaction to the Anschluss in Yugoslavia was expected in Slovenia, whose people due to historical reasons feared everything about Greater Germany and where for a while the dominant feeling was a fear of 'Swastika on the Karawanks'.[54]

Yugoslavia's attitude was dictated by the inevitability of the Anschluss once its leading personalities understood that no state in Europe was willing to go to war with Germany over Austria. Belgrade's relationship with Vienna remained generally cordial throughout 1937, although at the turn of the year there were some expulsions of citizens from both sides of the border.[55] But this relationship was subordinated to an understanding in Belgrade that German interests came first. In the final phase, the fear of a Habsburg restoration was simply an excuse. Stojadinović did not hide that he went to Berlin to secure Yugoslavia's northern border against Germany. Neither did the Austrian government expect help from Yugoslavia after the meeting between Hitler and Schuschnigg in Berchtesgaden in late February 1938. Right to the end, it looked towards Italy for protection. Some might describe Stojadinović's foreign policy as cynical and shrewd, but ultimately it was in line with the foreign policy followed by King Alexander.

The more the Anschluss appeared to be a reality, the more uncomfortable and nervous diplomats around Europe felt. In February, Ciano contemplated forming a wider coalition of states, which would include Italy, Yugoslavia, Hungary and Poland.[56] In the chaos which overcame Paris that same month, the French experienced a meltdown; there was a plethora of political and military proposals of what to do next.[57] Eventually, the Prime Minister Camille Chautemps resigned on 10 March, two days before the Anschluss. In London, Eden resigned in protest over Neville Chamberlain's meddling in foreign affairs behind his back, much to the delight of the Prime Minister.[58] All this influenced the attitude of lesser powers; at the Balkan Entente meeting in Ankara at the end of February, foreign ministers of the member states agreed to await events.[59] At the beginning of March, Stojadinović instructed Yugoslavia's ministers in European capitals to deny any wrongdoing by Yugoslavia in events in Austria, as Belgrade never wanted or desired the Anschluss.[60] This statement was simply not true.

In Yugoslavia, the Anschluss was seen as an ominous sign by both governmental and opposition politicians.[61] For Stojadinović, it was an internal German affair and any wider European problem stemming from it was a question for greater, not lesser, powers.[62] On the morning of the Anschluss, Stojadinović met the American Minister in Belgrade, Arthur Bliss Lane, and stated that recent events should not be considered as 'an invasion of Austria; the German troops were sent because Austria desired and requested them'.[63] Four days later, Stojadinović commented on the Anschluss in the Yugoslav Senate. He admitted that the Yugoslav Government had received assurances from the Germans that the Yugoslav border would not be violated and insisted that friendly relations with Germany were the best guarantee for the status of the Yugoslav minority in southern Austria.[64] On the same day, 16 March, Stojadinovic spoke to Heeren and expressed his belief that the majority of Yugoslav people reacted positively to Anschluss; he confessed some fears in Slovenia regarding the destiny of the Carinthia Slovenes and a possible German advance towards the Adriatic, but Heeren assured him there was nothing to fear about. The Yugoslav Prime Minister asked humbly if Germany was satisfied with the restrained attitude of the Yugoslav press. Heeren also reported on the impression which the speed and efficiency of the German action had on Yugoslavia.[65]

As much he tried to appear calm in the days after the Anschluss, Stojadinović must have been disturbed by the events. At the national socialist rally in Graz, in the days following the Anschluss, demonstrators shouted slogans about German Maribor.[66] The Anschluss was good only for Germany and no other country in Europe, not even Berlin's friends. When a month later, the fellow revisionist Hungarians asked that some parts of the Austrian region Burgenland, largely inhabited by Hungarians, be ceded to Hungary as goodwill gesture, Weizsäcker bluntly reminded them of Hungary's ethnic structure and the number of Germans living there, with the warning that 'any such comparison [of the number of Hungarians in Burgenland and Germans in Hungary] would only be to Hungary's disadvantage'.[67] During a meeting with Ciano in June, Stojadinović stressed that further German strengthening by the incorporation of 3 million Sudeten Germans would be unwise and reminded his host that Yugoslavia and Italy needed to keep a watchful eye on German foreign policy.[68]

Next on Hitler's list was Czechoslovakia. 'Operation Grün', the plan for military annihilation, had been in place since June 1937.[69] As with Austria, Germany first needed to prepare the stage, so German action would be seen as legitimate and only responding to events. The main role was given to the Sudeten Germans, led by the Sudeten German Party and its leader Konrad Henlein. The context of the Yugoslav-German relations between March and September 1938 was determined by the Yugoslav-Hungarian relationship and touched the very nature of the Little Entente. Budapest never stopped pressuring Berlin about Yugoslavia.[70] Sensing that after the Anschluss it was time for the elimination of the Czechoslovakian problem, the Hungarians wanted to participate in the attack. But worried by the Yugoslav attitude, they sought German support and urged Berlin to advocate on their behalf in Belgrade.[71] In April, Budapest again offered to recognize its border with Yugoslavia as final and unchangeable.[72] Berlin advised that Hungary needed to be patient and wait for Yugoslavia's reaction in the event of a German war with Czechoslovakia. In July, Göring warned the Hungarian Minister in Berlin that he did not mind if Hungary was to grab its share of Czechoslovakia, but they should not rely on Germany 'to pull the chestnuts out of the fire' if something went wrong.[73]

Simultaneously, the Germans continued to advocate for an understanding between Hungary and Yugoslavia, but the reply from Belgrade was always the same: if Hungary attacked Czechoslovakia, Yugoslavia would intervene in accordance to the Little Entente agreement. At the Little Entente meeting in Sinaia in May, Stojadinović and the Romanian Foreign Minister Nicolae Petrescu-Comnen assured the Czechoslovak Foreign Minister Kamil Krofta that Yugoslavia and Romania would honour their commitment in the event of a Hungarian attack; however, in the event of German-Czechoslovakian conflict, they would not offer any military assistance.[74] Stojadinović told the same to Ciano during their meeting in Venice in June.[75] In August, at the height of the crisis, Berlin finally concluded that Hungarian interference would be unwelcome, as it would only provoke Romania's and Yugoslavia's response. As isolation of Czechoslovakia from its Little Entente friends in the event of a synchronized attack by Germany and Hungary had not been fully reached, Berlin concluded that Hungarian help would be of no advantage.[76] The involvement of other powers, whether they liked it or not, could set the whole continent on fire. Thus, instead of a regional conflict, Germany would be faced with a full-scale continental war, for which it was not ready.

The Yugoslavs feared that the partition of Czechoslovakia would spark Hungarian revisionism. The preferred solution for the government was a settlement between Berlin and Prague, with or without the assistance of other great powers, but not for the benefit of any third country. At the same time, the Yugoslav government was actively trying to improve its position where possible. An agreement between Hungary, Romania and Yugoslavia which settled some problematic issues, such as minorities and recognizing the right of equality of arms for Budapest, was signed during the meeting of the Little Entente in Bled, on 23 August, though it left some questions regarding Hungarian-Czechoslovakian minorities to be settled subsequently. Signatories agreed not to use war to resolve disputes in the future.[77] But interpretations of the Bled agreement in Budapest and in the three Little Entente capitals were different. As the agreement was reached during the Hungarian delegation's visit to Germany, this confusion brought great discomfort for the Hungarian leaders; Hitler even interpreted the Bled agreement as openly anti-German.[78] For Berlin, Hungary had reached an agreement with the Little Entente, not just Yugoslavia and Romania, and was irritated with the non-aggression clauses.[79] Romania and Yugoslavia on the contrary were pleased with themselves; they managed to act in concert with Prague, reach an important agreement with Budapest which eased tensions and seemingly acted in accordance with the recommendations from all great powers. But despite the official solidarity with their Czechoslovak allies, both countries wished to avoid any complications.[80] As the Hungarian attitude in the event of war was still uncertain, on the recommendation of Petrescu-Comnen in September, Stojadinović instructed the Yugoslav Minister in Berlin to ask Göring to oppose any Hungarian armed intervention against Czechoslovakia.[81] However, when on 31 August Heeren approached Stojadinović as to whether a German attack on Czechoslovakia from Hungarian territory would be considered a cause for war in Belgrade, the Yugoslav was evasive. Nine days later, the Romanian Minister in Berlin gave an even stronger hint to Weizsäcker that any use of Hungarian territory for an attack on Czechoslovakia would force Romania and Yugoslavia to act. The Romanian Minister asked for assurances that Germany would not make such a move.[82] The Yugoslav and Romanian attitude eventually influenced Berlin to drop any such plan, if it was ever seriously considered.

Internally, the Yugoslav situation was equally unstable. In May, the French military attaché reported growing concerns in Belgrade about German aggressiveness after Anschluss. In his words, the Yugoslavs were disillusioned with Stojadinović's foreign policy of balancing between the two ideologically opposed blocks in Europe.[83] At the end of July, British Military Attaché in Belgrade had a series of conversations with Yugoslav officers and reported his impression that the Yugoslav army was strongly anti-German and, if the situation demanded, would honour its undertakings towards Czechoslovakia against Hungary. In the same dispatch, Terence Shone, the first secretary to the Belgrade Legation, reported on the strong pro-Czech feelings among the population and the difficulty which might arise for the government in the event of not interfering if Hitler attacked Czechoslovakia.[84] According to Heeren, there was a strong feeling of opposition for Stojadinovic's foreign policy among the members of the Serbian middle class, intelligentsia, opposition political parties and junior officer corps. Heeren warned that if the events led to war, the government would be faced with unbearable pressure, most likely resulting in Yugoslavia entering the war.[85]

For these reasons, the outcome of the Munich Conference was a huge relief for the Yugoslav authorities.[86] And despite the shifted balance of political power in Central and South-Eastern Europe after the Munich Conference, Yugoslavia still had some room for manoeuvre. The Hungarian attitude after the conference sparked outrage in Belgrade and Bucharest. Within a week after Munich, both Stojadinović and Petrescu-Comnen complained in Berlin about Hungarian claims to ethnically non-Hungarian parts of what remained of Czechoslovakia.[87] Another cause for concern was Bulgaria. In the past two years, its relations with neighbours had been cordial, which eventually resulted in the signing of the Salonika Treaty between Sofia and the Balkan Entente on 31 July 1938. As a recognition of the peaceful policy of successive Bulgarian governments and supported by the British in order to keep Sofia away from the Axis influence, this agreement removed restrictions on Bulgaria's rearming.[88] However, the Munich Conference almost immediately renewed revisionist hopes in Bulgaria. Fierce anti-government demonstrations broke out in Sofia and students demanded the revision of Bulgarian borders with Greece and Romania. In December, the Bulgarian Minister in Berlin asked for German help in regaining south Dobruja and western Thrace, stating that in this way the Axis would gain an outlet to the Aegean Sea through Bulgaria, although he stressed that Sofia did not have territorial disputes with Yugoslavia.[89] These events brought Yugoslavia and Romania closer together. In an exchange of letters with Petrescu-Comnen, Stojadinović explained that the existing political links between their two countries relied on the Balkan Entente, dynastic ties and mutual political interests.[90]

Left isolated by Paris and London, Prague tried appeasing Hitler to secure its independence. But Hitler was determined to finish Munich's unfinished business; to further weaken Czechoslovakia, he decided to partly satisfy Hungarian revisionist claims against Prague. Following the decision of Ribbentrop and Ciano, the First Vienna Award on 3 November delivered the southern parts of Slovakia to Hungary. The disappointed Hungarians who laid claim to all of Ruthenia, the furthermost eastern part of Czechoslovakia, planned a military occupation of the region, which would give them a common border with Poland. The military action was planned for 21 November, but without Italian support and faced with Hitler's fury upon hearing of the plan, the Hungarians had to back off. The result of this episode was Kánya's removal from the post of the Foreign Minister, while the Germans for the moment even appeared as protectors to the Slovaks and Ruthenia's Ukrainians.[91]

This development was not favourable for Italy, as the Third Reich had become sole arbiter in all political matters in the Danube region. Italy was the weaker partner in the Axis relationship and the only way of bolstering the Italian position was in increasing the numbers on Rome's side. Ciano called this desired alliance the 'Horizontal Axis' and it stemmed from the older idea of a Polish-Hungarian partnership against either German or Soviet domination over East-Central and South-Eastern Europe.[92] At a meeting with the Polish Foreign Minister Józef Beck in March 1938, Mussolini and

Ciano stressed that inaction in the light of German activity in Central Europe would be dangerous. Throughout 1938, Warsaw sought a common border with Hungary in Ruthenia. After the Munich Conference, Poland immediately occupied three districts in the Teschen area and urged Hungary to occupy Ruthenia. But because of its military weakness, Budapest opted for negotiations. Sensing danger for its interests, Berlin made sure to deliver only those parts of Slovakia settled mainly with Hungarians to Budapest in Vienna. The failed plan for a Hungarian invasion of Ruthenia and Kánya's resignation as a consequence marked the end of Hungarian attempts to lead semi-autonomous foreign policy from Germany. After Gömbös died in October 1936, his successors Darányi and Béla Imrédy continued to seek Germany's approval of their foreign policy, but also wished for British, French and particularly Italian support – an approach which irritated Berlin and caused doubts about Hungary's loyalty.[93] Kánya's fall marked the beginning of a firm orientation towards Germany. In February 1939, Hungary joined the Anti-Comintern Pact. This approach rewarded Budapest with Ruthenia in March 1939, after the German annihilation of the remains of Czechoslovakia – but this time on Germany's terms. This ended the Polish-Hungarian-Italian plans for an independent block to contain German influence in Central Europe.

Another blow for Italian policy in the region was Stojadinović's fall in Belgrade. In his diary, Ciano wrote that with his removal 'the Yugoslav card has lost 90 per cent of its value [to Italy]'.[94] In January 1939, the Italian Foreign Minister visited Yugoslavia; he noticed great anxiety in Belgrade over the future aims of German expansionism.[95] During their previous meeting in Venice in June, Stojadinović rejected Ciano's assurances that Germany considered its southern borders with Italy and Yugoslavia as definite and insisted that 'Italy and Yugoslavia, united, always have to be on watch about German foreign policy'.[96] Although commonly accused of steering his country into the arms of Germany, these and other reports from both British and Italian sources indicate that Stojadinović was worried about the escalation of German influence in the region.[97] The Italian plan for the 'Horizontal Axis' and a middle way between Germany, France, Britain and the Soviets was probably appealing to him. After the Anschluss, the Yugoslav general staff warned the government that Germany was now a major potential enemy. As the Anschluss also destroyed the system set up by the Rome Protocols, Yugoslav military believed cooperation with Italy would prevent German penetration south of the Alps.[98]

Stojadinović's meeting with Ciano in January 1939 was the last he had with a prominent foreign diplomat. On 5 February, he was replaced as the Prime Minister by Dragiša Cvetković, while Aleksandar Cincar-Marković, Yugoslavia's Minister in Berlin, replaced him as the new Foreign Minister. The change of government was put down to internal politics, at least publicly, and this was repeated in official and private conversations with foreign diplomats; Stojadinović had not been able to deliver a solution for the so-called 'Croatian question', which had troubled Yugoslavia's internal political situation since the early 1920s.[99] However, Dušan Biber is of the opinion that Stojadinović's growing discrepancy of opinion on foreign policy with the Regent, as well as the latter's increasing mistrust in his Prime Minister's ultimate political motives, equally influenced the latter's downfall.[100] Goebbels in his diary described Stojadinović's fall as a typical Balkan charade, but regretted it as the Germans 'could deal with Stojadinović'.[101] Despite this unease, Berlin took the promotion of Yugoslavia's Minister in Berlin to the post of Foreign Minister as a good omen.[102] Cincar-Marković immediately rushed to Berlin to confirm that German-Yugoslav friendship remained the foundation of the Yugoslav foreign policy, for which the guarantor was the Prince Regent himself.[103] A similar explanation came from Cvetković, during his first meeting with Heeren in Belgrade.[104] Heeren also assessed that in the main, Yugoslav foreign policy would not change.[105]

Following the change of government in Belgrade, there was a renewed approach by some Croatian circles asking for German support.[106] Interestingly, Heeren also asked for a changed approach. While Stojadinović was in power, he supported the authoritarian regime in Yugoslavia, as guarantor of a strong country which was in Germany's interest. Prince Paul decided to solve the internal problem by bringing down the strong authoritarian regime, through what Heeren saw as democratic methods, and weakened the authority of the state. Heeren had therefore come to the conclusion that Germany had no more interest in supporting the regime, but should instead support the Croats. According to him, once internal disputes were settled and the Croats started to participate in the new government, their influence would become stronger. Besides, they would always perceive Italy as their natural enemy and thus seek protection from Germany.[107] Soon, Heeren reported that the mood towards Germany in Yugoslavia had become hostile in the light of German occupation of the remains of Czechoslovakia in March 1939.[108]

To make things worse, Italy occupied Albania in April. Although the March 1937 agreement reiterated Albanian independence, the situation had in the meanwhile changed as the two countries moved closer together in 1938. At their meeting in January 1939, Ciano and Stojadinović had discussed the partitioning of Albania.[109] The Italians had for a while toyed with the idea of occupying Albania, but only in cooperation with Yugoslavia; any Yugoslav hostility might play into the hands of Germany. For the time being, Yugoslavia's friendship, as counterweight towards Berlin, was more important. As a bait for the Yugoslav Prime Minister, Ciano also used the prospect of gaining Thessaloniki sometime in the future. While both Stojadinović and Prince Paul were in agreement that Greece was a friendly country and an ally, thus denouncing the idea of Yugoslavia's occupation of Thessaloniki,[110] the Regent was not interested in any plans for Yugoslavia's territorial expansion on behalf of Albania, as this would increase the already numerous Albanian minority living in Yugoslavia.[111]

With Stojadinović gone and other designs for Italian domination in the region crumbling before overpowering German penetration everywhere in the winter on 1938-9, the Italians returned to the old policy of occupying Albania on their own and flirting with Croatian separatism. Following Prince Paul's instructions, Cvetković had begun secret negotiations with the Croatian leader Maček as early as December 1938, but soon after Stojadinović's fall they broke down. In this atmosphere, during the spring of 1939 the Croats and Italians held secret negotiations. According to some versions of these talks, the Croats were supposed to rise against Belgrade's regime and Italy would march in to restore the peace. The Croatian Assembly would then declare a union with Italy and install an Italian governor, before proclaiming the unification of two countries.[112] These contacts with Rome were probably nothing more than part of

Maček's strategy to assert pressure on Belgrade.[113] However, they marked the end of the Italian policy of cooperation with Yugoslavia; good relations had only lasted for two years and Yugoslavia again had to keep an eye on Rome. When Italy occupied Albania on 7 April, Belgrade had no other choice but to remain calm and hope that Italy would respect Yugoslavia's territorial integrity.[114] Heeren described such passivity as a feeling of helplessness with no influence over events, while Belgrade's relationship with the Axis would from now on be driven solely by fear.[115] Yugoslavia now shared two borders with Italy and one with Germany. London contemplated extending its guarantees to Yugoslavia as it did to Poland on 31 March 1939 and to Romania and Greece on 13 April, but the Yugoslavs sent strong signals that the guarantee would be unwelcome and place them in danger.[116]

Goebbels's visit to Belgrade in mid-April brought a small break for the Yugoslavs; after the talks with Yugoslav officials, he instructed the Propaganda Ministry in Berlin to give Yugoslavia's positive attitude during the events in Albania a special recognition in the German press.[117] Berlin was pleased that Yugoslavia was omitted from the British and French guarantees, which perhaps signalled to Hitler and Ribbentrop that the country was ready for closer relationship with the Axis. On 25 and 26 April, Cincar-Marković visited Berlin and met the two men separately. Hitler again stressed his hopes for an agreement between Yugoslavia and Hungary. He was certain that Hungary was not a threat to Yugoslavia; in his words, Budapest was so saturated with the latest territorial increase in the north that it would take years to adjust the Hungarian economy and social and legal systems to include the newly gained territories. Hitler reiterated that Yugoslavia's greatest defence against Hungary was in a fair treatment of the Yugoslav ethnic Germans. Personally, he was pleased that they were better treated in Yugoslavia than in Hungary and repeated that he wanted to see a strong Yugoslavia, as did the Italians, who would rather have Yugoslavia than Hungary as a neighbour. Hitler emphasized that he was not the one who wished to change borders and that all the borders that needed to be changed were now changed. Germany did not need an outlet on the Adriatic as it already had enough ports on other seas. Hitler even said that if Hungarians had asked him for permission to change the Yugoslav border, he would have replied that in such case they would have Germany as an enemy. Cincar-Marković thanked and replied that Yugoslavia would never allow itself to be drawn into any alliance against Germany. A day later, Ribbentrop repeated that Berlin was very pleased with Yugoslavia's behaviour during the course of two recent crises, in Czechoslovakia and Albania. He hoped that Hungary and Yugoslavia would finally come to an understanding which could lead to a non-aggression pact and the settling of minorities' issues for the benefit of peace in South-Eastern Europe. Ribbentrop then asked Yugoslavia to join the Anti-Comintern Pact. Cincar-Marković repeated his country's loyalty to Germany, but explained that due to Serbian traditional affiliation towards Russia, it was not possible.[118]

On 7 June 1939, it was Prince Paul's turn to meet Hitler in Berlin. Shortly before his visit, on 22 May, Germany and Italy had signed the Pact of Steel, which further demoralized the Yugoslav Regent who nourished hopes that Yugoslavia might balance between the two Axis powers by exploiting their strategic differences in the region. Instead, during the meeting Hitler made it clear that Germany and Italy shared the same policy. Yugoslavia would have to make a gesture of goodwill towards the Axis in order to prove that it was worthy of their trust. Ribbentrop then stepped in, saying that withdrawal from the League of Nations could be such a gesture. Paul stated that withdrawing Yugoslavia from Geneva was not possible at the present moment. Hitler repeated that Yugoslavia needed to consolidate and define its policy towards the Axis, and that such an approach would be the country's strongest guarantee for unity. He confirmed that Italy also desired this, as Rome was confronted with a hostile Britain in the Mediterranean and needed to be clear who were its enemies and who its friends. However, Prince Paul refused to agree on issuing a public statement of solidarity with the Axis. During a separate conversation between Ribbentrop and Cincar-Marković, the former again insisted on Yugoslavia's withdrawal from the League, but the Yugoslav Foreign Minister remained firm. Ribbentrop, obviously annoyed, then questioned the treatment of the German minority in Slovenia, while the Yugoslav complained about the new German Consul in Maribor, whose conduct had inspired some unrest among the Germans there.[119] Overall, despite the great effort put in by the Germans to impress their guests, the visit was a disappointment for Hitler.

It is hard to gauge public opinion in Yugoslavia about the government's foreign policy in the summer of 1939. It is likely that most of the educated people who had an interest in foreign affairs understood the standpoint of their government.[120] Perhaps Heeren's report from June summed it up the best: ordinary people supported Prince Paul's visit to Berlin in an attempt to get guarantees for Yugoslavia's borders, but nothing further than that. Yugoslavia should have intensified its contacts with the Axis, but only in order to reinforce its neutral position, as there was a greater threat for the country's future from that side.[121] Nevertheless, the Germans continued to exercise pressure. On 8 July, the new Yugoslav Minister in Berlin Ivo Andrić was warned that Yugoslavia had to dissociate itself from the Balkan Entente.[122] In the light of British guarantees to Romania and Greece in April, the signing of the Anglo-Turkish Declaration in May and London's constant attempts to reconcile the Balkan Entente with Bulgaria, this regional alliance was increasingly viewed in Berlin with hostility.[123] On 15 July, Ernst Wörmann, the director of the Foreign Ministry's Political Department, renewed the request for Yugoslavia's withdrawal from the League. Andrić replied that the Yugoslav government considered itself already dissociated by not accepting the chairmanship of the League of Nations' Council next meeting in September. Also, it had to some extent dissociate from the Balkan Entente by signing the Bulgarian-Yugoslav communique in Bled at the beginning of July, which expressed the wish for neutral status for both countries; the German disagreed that this was enough.[124] At the end of July, Weizsäcker informed Heeren of the anxiety in Berlin over Yugoslavia's refusal to decisively break with the League of Nations and instructed the German Minister to renew pressure in Belgrade.[125] Heeren met Cincar-Marković in Bled on 10 August. The Yugoslav Foreign Minister clarified that Yugoslavia needed to be allowed to choose its own time and method for leaving the League.[126] Bizarrely, the outbreak of war gave Yugoslavia some breathing space from this immense German pressure and spared it from making uncomfortable decisions demanded by Berlin.

Yugoslavia's attitude annoyed Hitler, who in the last days of peace concluded that Yugoslavia should be regarded as 'an uncertain ally'.[127] Using various excuses, the Yugoslavs refused to join the Anti-Comintern Pact, to leave the League, to dissociate themselves from the Balkan Entente and to publicly endorse the Axis. Belgrade instead attempted active regional policy and in June approached Budapest twice about the prospect of forming an independent block in the region, consisting of Yugoslavia, Bulgaria, Hungary and Romania.[128] In July, Kyoseivanov met with Cincar-Marković and discussed mutual neutrality in the upcoming war.[129] Proof of Yugoslavia's untrustworthiness towards Germany was the shipment of the country's gold reserves to London in May.[130] Then came a mission of General Petar Pešić to Paris and London in mid-July, where he met with Generals Maurice Gamelin and John Gort respectively, in order to find out what Yugoslavia could expect from Britain and France. It was immediately followed by Prince Paul's meeting with the British Foreign Secretary Lord Halifax in London; the Regent wished to enquire personally about the possibility of knocking Italy out of the war early in a conflict which now seemed to be inevitable.[131] Finally, German reports in July stated that the Yugoslav army had begun fortification works on borders with Germany and Italy, assisted by some French officers.[132] Although Heeren kept reassuring Berlin that no matter how much they tried, it was impossible for the British and French to change the mind of the Yugoslavs who were adamant they would remain neutral in the approaching conflict, for Hitler these were all clear signs that German political, economic and propagandist efforts in regard to Yugoslavia could not overcome the country's affiliation towards Western democracies.[133] On 12 August, at the meeting with Ciano in Berchtesgaden, he finally urged Italy to liquidate Yugoslavia as soon as Germany attacked Poland. Hitler claimed that annihilation of Poland and Yugoslavia would strengthen the Axis.[134] Uncertainty over Italian actions lasted more than two weeks, as Mussolini kept changing his mind on a daily basis. Eventually, Yugoslavia was spared only due to Ciano's protests and Italy's unpreparedness to wage a major war. On 1 September, Andrić visited the Foreign Ministry in Berlin and declared Yugoslavia's strict neutrality in the conflict.[135]

## A mouse between the cats

Current historiography calls the development of Yugoslavia's foreign policy after 1936 a retreat to neutrality. This implies that the Yugoslavs had recognized a division of Europe into two ideological blocks and lost any confidence in the system of collective security embodied by the League of Nations. A stance of neutrality also implied that apart from the traditional anti-revisionist line of its foreign policy, Yugoslavia now had to adopt another political attitude as an axiom of its diplomacy – a quest for the constant balancing between great powers with interests in the region and attempts to reconcile with its revisionist neighbours. Relations with Germany remained friendly for most of the time; until March 1938, because there was an independent Austria as a buffer zone between the two countries, afterwards out of fear as Yugoslavia became the Reich's neighbour. Stojadinović tried to preempt dangers from that corner by keeping his country away from any initiative which might have caused German suspicions. In the words of Winston Churchill: 'Each one hoped that if he feeds the crocodile enough, the crocodile will eat him last. All of them hope that the storm will pass before their turn comes to be devoured.'[136]

But this meant the retardation of Yugoslavia's relations with traditional friends, Czechoslovakia and France. Although both Paris and Prague tried to undermine the Yugoslav Prime Minister as early as 1937, Stojadinović would withhold the reins of power for as long as Prince Paul had faith in his political acumen. The British Minister Campbell summed up the situation about the power relationship in Belgrade in the context of Yugoslavia's new and old friends, early in 1938, in the following words: 'If his [Stojadinović's] successor were more pliant in dealing with the old friends, he would almost certainly be weaker in dealing with the new'.[137] The events of 1939 proved him right.

5

# Yugoslavia and the Four-Year Plan

The Summer Olympics in Berlin in August 1936 presented the world an opportunity to witness the scope of German successful economic recovery in only three years. But this was just a façade; behind the glamour of new motorways, rebuilt infrastructure, sport events and parades were serious hardships for the German economy to successfully prepare the army for war. Germany simply could not produce enough goods for the demands of its population, its exports and its army in such a short period. Apart from coal, the Reich was in demand of virtually everything, from food to raw materials. Schacht's model was good for the initial recovery of the economy burdened with debts and unemployment, but for anything more it needed a return to the old liberal model of a powerful export economy. But Hitler could not be less interested; he only insisted on pace of rearmament and from the autumn of 1936, as will be seen, the Nazis took over full control over Germany's economy, setting a Four-Year Plan in action. This was not a beneficial development for Yugoslavia. After the summer of 1936 and the placement of Austria firmly under Hitler's control, the Yugoslavs hoped that Germany might now turn its attention away from the Balkans. But these hopes were badly misperceived. For Belgrade, foreign trade and foreign policy were two separate domains; for the Nazis, they were two sides of the same coin. The resources of Yugoslavia and the rest of South-Eastern Europe were desperately needed for German rearmament. The Germans did not come to the Danube region merely to take Austria and leave; they came there to stay. And the more impatient Hitler and the army were to get ready for war, the more important the resources of South-Eastern Europe became for the Nazi military planning.

As we have seen, the German-Yugoslav economic relations in 1933–6 were set within the wider context of the New Plan, which quickly stabilized German finances, largely by eliminating payments in foreign currencies. The following period, 1936–9, was determined by the Four-Year Plan and the growing needs of the German rearmament. In 1933–6, economic and financial policies of the Third Reich were left to the conservatives of the previous regime.[1] In the period 1936–9, the primacy of German economic decision-making was taken over by the party officials and the army, which resulted in new methods of economic dealings with other countries. As a result, at the end of this period and shortly before the outbreak of war, Germany began to exert political pressure to gain economic benefits. In the light of the new political reality in this part of Europe, the Yugoslavs found it hard to resist.

## The beginnings of the Four-Year Plan

Changes in the world economy in 1933–6 were not beneficial for Germany; the price of raw materials and food recovered by 9 per cent, while overall prices of finished goods fell by the same amount. This meant that by 1936 Germany needed to export 20 per cent more than in 1933 in order to cover for the same quantity of imports.[2] The only way to maintain the ongoing pace of rearmament was at the expense of the domestic consumption. This strained the existing reserves, meaning that by March 1936 the supplies of the most important raw materials fell to a minimum and Schacht insisted on decreased military spending, which was a beginning of his fall.[3]

The New Plan changed the structure of Germany's foreign trade. Imports of food fell in both volume and value, while imports of raw materials increased by 10 per cent in the period 1931–6.[4] However, the problem of depleted foreign currency reserves was not resolved; as a result, frictions between Schacht and various Nazi officials, especially Darré, persisted.[5] One of the consequences of German economic development in the period 1933–6 was increased employment, which in turn increased the level of consumption in Germany. At the same time, increased productivity demanded increased imports of raw materials and increased consumption demanded increased imports of food; this put a pressure on exports in order to balance the trade.[6] Another bone of contention between Schacht and the party supported by the army was an increased rearmament. In the period 1935–8, arms production was responsible for almost half of the growth of the German national GDP. Schacht favoured a limited rearmament at an average rate of 4.3 billion Reichsmarks per year. However, in November 1935 Blomberg had already ordered all the branches of armed forces to ignore any financial limitations. By March 1936, Germany's industrial production, now orientated towards the arms productions, was stretched to its limits. In June 1936, the army was augmented to forty-three divisions instead of twenty-one as envisaged in 1933, three of which were tank divisions and four of motorized infantry. The cost of German armament for the years 1937–41 reached 35.6 billion Reichsmarks, or 9 billion a year, twice as much as envisaged by Schacht. This brought Schacht into conflict with the army, represented by Blomberg.[7]

At the beginning of April 1936, Hitler created the Raw Materials and Currency Office, headed by Göring, tasked with solving the deepening crisis and intervening in the conflict between Schacht and the army.[8] The final issue which moved Hitler to distance himself from Schacht was the latter's doubts about the production of synthetic oil. Being an economist, Schacht could not understand reasons for wasting money on synthetic production when it was cheaper to import petroleum. He advocated increased exports, in order to import necessary raw materials and provide a basis for more comprehensive, albeit slower, rearmament in depth.[9] In contrast, Blomberg wanted to fully equip thirty-six divisions by October. Schacht's opposition to such an accelerated rearmament brought the War Ministry closer to Göring. In this way, the traditional alliance between the army and big business was broken.[10] The problem was also the lack of money for an increased import of raw materials, but Hitler refused to reduce imports of food, thus supporting Darré. In order to find the necessary foreign exchange, Göring ordered the sale of all foreign bonds owned by Germans, despite

Schacht's opposition. By doing so, he gathered 500 million Reichsmarks of private funds.¹¹ By this time, the prices of foreign raw materials had increased due to the recovery of the world market and Germany needed a healthy influx of foreign currency, for which the New Plan was not adequate. The leading industrialists favoured the idea of Reichsmark's devaluation in order to stimulate exports to liberal markets and by the summer of 1936 Schacht himself had come to that conclusion. He contemplated negotiations with the French, hoping to secure a coordinated devaluation of both the Reichsmark and the franc, as confessed in a private conversation with Radosavljević in June, during his visit to Belgrade.¹² This was a common topic for both Schacht and the Finance Minister Schwerin von Krosigk in the spring and summer of 1936 and worked well in misleading many foreign diplomats. In May, the Yugoslav legation reported from Berlin about the crisis of raw materials necessary for the normal functioning of domestic industry and that Germany would seek its old colonies back in order to answer the problem of the material shortages.¹³ However, Hitler had made up his mind and undertook a new economic course, which implied a complete redirection towards the war production at the expense of domestic consumption and the foreign trade, which Schacht could not have accepted.¹⁴ At the Reichstag meeting held on 30 January 1937, Hitler publicly rejected economic theories based in free trade and stated that private capital was there to serve the national economy.¹⁵

At the beginning of September 1936, Hitler published a Four-Year Plan memorandum, which outlined all the measures needed to prepare Germany for war in four years' time. It placed the economy firmly under party control and rejected the idea of increasing exports. The memorandum pointed to the maximization of domestic production and the substitution of import goods such as rubber and oil, with synthetic products domestically made. Until the army and the economy were ready for war, it was the 'temporary easing … within the framework of our present economy' which was to bridge the gap.¹⁶ The biggest problem was that the increased arms production in turn consumed more raw materials than Germany was able to produce or import. The Defence Committee's report from May 1936 warned that increased production, which also involved the export of weaponry and war material to other countries, could only be achieved either by seriously depleting German raw materials reserves, or at the cost of further indebting Germany's clearing accounts.¹⁷ Therefore, the Four-Year Plan was brought in primarily to solve the problems of the German financial and raw materials situation, where the New Plan had failed. But until that was achieved, it was necessary to retain the economic model set up by Schacht, as this still functioned; in the first four months of 1936, there was an increase in trade with countries of Latin America, Africa and South-Eastern Europe, and a sharp decrease in trade with Western countries and the Soviet Union.¹⁸

## Dresden and Berlin meetings

Despite the introduction of import controls in spring 1936, Yugoslav exporters of agricultural products to Germany experienced numerous problems during the summer.

These included limited numbers of import licences for German buyers, deliberate reduction of prices for Yugoslav commodities by various German institutions, deliberate reduction of prices by German buyers once the goods had reached Germany and required payment, and the general mistreatment of Yugoslav goods by the German custom officials who often tended to estimate their value as lower than their agreed price.[19] In July, Göring himself intervened in his new capacity as the head of Raw Materials and Currency Office and overruled a decision by the Foreign Ministry to ban an arranged import of 1,000 heads of Yugoslav cattle.[20]

In August, the Yugoslav Finance Ministry shocked Berlin by announcing that some of the raw materials in demand on the world market would be available for export only if paid for in foreign currency. This referred to hemp, wool, ferrosilicon, lead, zinc and raw hides; much of the material Germany needed for the Reich's war industry. The world market was recovering and Yugoslavia was not willing to miss a chance to earn cash. Its trade balance in August 1936 was 98 million dinars positive, compared to 33 million in August previous year. In the same month, Yugoslavia earned 113 million dinars in foreign currency, compared to 54 million in August 1935. This amount rose to 143 million dinars in September.[21] Berlin was dissatisfied. Feeling that the export of these products to the clearing countries should be exempted from the bill, it rejected to increase the import quotas for some Yugoslav agricultural products, as agreed at the Zagreb meeting of the Mixed Committee back in March. There were also problems with the available funds for German tourists travelling to Yugoslavia.[22] Ivo Belin, the Vice-Governor of the National Bank, travelled to Berlin in September, but despite bluffing on both sides no agreement was reached.[23]

As Yugoslavia's dependency on Germany was caused in the first place by disturbances on the world market, which instigated a need for trade by clearing, it was logical for the Yugoslavs to sell exports for foreign currencies once the world market seemed to have recovered. To solve the dispute, the Mixed Committee met in Dresden in October 1936, ending with concessions done by both sides. The Yugoslavs agreed to allow an unlimited sale of zinc and lead to Germany, with ferrochrome and ferrosilicon in amounts of 250 and 650 tons per annum respectively. In turn, the Germans raised quotas for some Yugoslav exports, while a one-off additional quantity was approved for the whole range of agricultural products. Addressing the problem of Yugoslavia's clearing credit, both sides agreed to take into consideration a reduced volume of exports if the volume of mutual trade caused more disturbances in the functioning of the clearing system in the future.[24] During the conference, in a private conversation with Pilja, Sarnow expressed fears about intensification of economic relations between Yugoslavia, Romania and Czechoslovakia. The latter's reply was that it was only natural for such close political friends to expand their trade relations.[25]

The recovery of the world market was beneficial for Yugoslavia as prices of agricultural products increased and the harvest in the summer of 1936 was excellent. There was an increased demand for dinars on financial markets.[26] In July, the rate of sterling fell to its lowest ever, 238 dinars, which increased the National Bank's buying of the British currency. Devaluation of the French and Swiss currencies in September did not significantly influence the Yugoslav finances; in fact, it reduced the value of Yugoslavia's clearing debt to France and Switzerland. More important for Yugoslavia was the constant loss of the Reichsmark's value, which in August sank to 13.30 dinars.[27]

It is wrong to assume that Yugoslavia simply used the revived world market to coerce Germany into buying more agricultural products, as Grenzebach suggests.[28] Until October 1936, Yugoslavia had an overall negative foreign-trade balance. Only thanks to the strong Yugoslav export on the world market after the Finance Ministry's decision in August, did Yugoslavia end 1936 with a positive balance.[29] The Yugoslav National Bank was not simply pro-French as Grenzebach suggests, but constantly on watch observing the Yugoslav balance of payments, as its fluctuations bore great dangers for Yugoslavia's financial stability. In June 1936, Pilja travelled to London and asked for means to expand mutual trade between Yugoslavia and Britain amidst fears of growing German domination.[30] Then, representatives of the national banks of Little Entente and Balkan Entente countries met in Prague and Athens in November and December 1936 respectively; they expressed hope that import controls and various other forms of state intervention would become unnecessary once the international system of trade and payments recovered. The joint declaration published after the Athens meeting contained a recommendation for the total abolition of clearing as a method in international trade.[31] The Yugoslavs from the outset considered import controls as only a temporary solution, before the world trade returned to its normal currents.

By the beginning of 1937, German clearing debt escalated, while the rate of the Reichsmark continued to fall, sinking to 12 dinars.[32] This was not an unexpected development for the Yugoslavs. In time, they learnt that the clearing balance did not necessarily correspond to levels of trade, as trade through clearing included other items besides visible trade.[33] However, it was still a cause for concern. In January 1937, the Reichsbank received a letter from the Yugoslav National Bank, which emphasized that on 27 October 1936 the Yugoslav credit in Berlin was 14 million Reichsmarks, while in the following three months it rose to 23 million. The Yugoslavs threatened to cancel all the consignments of wheat and maize for Germany. The National Bank demanded that its credit on the Reichsmark account in Berlin be converted into dinars and deposited on a separate account of Berlin's Golddiskontbank in order to protect its value from the changing rate of the German currency.[34]

The problem was aggravated by Germany's desire to import additional quantities of cereals from Yugoslavia, namely 200,000 tons at the world market price and most importantly, above the quotas agreed in Dresden. The decision was made by Göring, as the head of the Four-Year Plan, and prompted bitter protests by Schacht. The latter warned that the purchase of such a quantity would dangerously increase the German clearing debt and cause a disturbance in the sensitive German-Yugoslav trade.[35] Göring could not be moved by these arguments. He had already appointed Erich Koch, *Gauleiter*, the regional party leader, of East Prussia, as his representative in negotiations with the Yugoslavs. Koch travelled to Belgrade twice, in December 1936 and February 1937, and bypassing the German legation conducted his own talks about the import of Yugoslav grain. Göring and Koch envisaged a barter scheme, exchanging maize directly for goods, outside the existing trade regulated by signed agreements. Involved from the German side was the Technical Union, an organization set up by the party to conduct these semi-private trading deals abroad.[36] Eventually the affair backfired at Germans and all the Union's activities came to an end in Yugoslavia, once it became known that the Reich tried to include the Yugoslav fascist organization Zbor in this deal. Reporting on the plot and its outcome, the German Belgrade legation assessed that 'the whole affair has neither helped mutual economic relations, nor raised the Reich's prestige in Yugoslavia'.[37]

The Reichsbank was fearful of any changes in the existing clearing mechanism and considered the Yugoslav request for conversion of the Yugoslav credit in Berlin into dinars alarming. Such concessions could set an example for other countries, but would also be dangerous for the fragile German finances. Still, the problem of German debt could not have been ignored. The Finance Ministry in Berlin partly acceded to Yugoslavia's demands, by recommending a transfer of converted Reichsmarks into dinars on the separate account in the Golddiskontbank, but in stages.[38] Central to these developments from the Yugoslav side was Ivo Belin, determined to limit Yugoslavia's exports to Germany, particularly those which could be sold for foreign currency, including grain.[39] To achieve this, Belin was willing to decrease the overall level of mutual trade. This would have been a heavy blow for Germany. Berlin's counterproposal remained to balance mutual trade by increasing Yugoslav imports from Germany.[40] Meanwhile, German debt rose to 32 million Reichsmarks.[41]

The polemics dragged on for over a month and led to the Berlin meeting of the Mixed Committee in March 1937, usually considered as an extension of the Dresden meeting in October.[42] The agreement was signed in Berlin on 24 March 1937. Yugoslavia agreed to export 50,000 tons of corn and 100,000 tons of wheat by the end of June, ignoring the balance on the clearing accounts.[43] It was agreed that Yugoslavia's monthly exports to Germany would be limited to 90 per cent of its imports; the mutual trade was thus made dependent on payments made by the Yugoslav importers to the German account in Belgrade, which would correspondingly be 10 per cent higher than payments in Berlin.[44] In this way, the value of Yugoslav imports from Germany dictated the volume of trade. The amount at disposal to German importers from Yugoslavia would be divided according to the following formula: 20 per cent (of the value of Yugoslav imports) for the purchase of livestock and animal products, 35 per cent for agricultural products and 35 per cent for the import of other Yugoslav goods. The Yugoslavs also obtained written acceptance that 20 million Reichsmarks from their account in Berlin would be converted into dinars on 1 April 1937. Furthermore, in the note delivered to Clodius on 19 March, the Yugoslav National Bank warned that in case of any problems with the functioning of this agreement, it would further reduce Yugoslavia's exports to Germany.[45] The Berlin meeting was important for several reasons. It took place in the early stages of the Four-Year Plan and demonstrated how sensitive Berlin was to any shortage of food, fodder or raw materials. It is also a fine example of the National Bank's determination to defend Yugoslavia's financial stability. The Berlin agreement meant that Yugoslavia still had the capacity for economic manoeuvre.

## Between Berlin and Dubrovnik

Throughout 1937, the world prices of raw materials and agricultural products continued to rise; by April, they reached 1929 levels. Rearmament throughout Europe significantly contributed to this increase, particularly a decision by the British government to invest 1.5 billion pounds in modernizing its armed forces. By the end of 1936, many governments left the gold standard and devalued their currencies. The consequence was favourable export possibilities for most of the agricultural states of South-Eastern Europe and Latin America. As in the previous year, excellent yields of wheat and corn significantly boosted Yugoslav exports in 1937.

At the May meeting of the National Bank's Board, Belin confirmed that Yugoslavia continued a trend of a strong trade with non-clearing countries. In the second half of 1936, the Yugoslav authorities approved import permits for goods worth 103.5 million dinars and rejected permits for deals worth 88 million dinars. In the first three months of 1937, the authorities allowed the import of goods from non-clearing countries worth 130 million dinars and rejected permits for goods worth only 45 million.[46] Overall, Yugoslavia's foreign trade in 1937 reached 11.5 billion dinars, a 35 per cent increase in international commercial activities to 1936. Furthermore, Yugoslavia's foreign trade was 1.04 billion dinars positive. This was followed by a steady increase in domestic prices, the National Bank's gold reserves and the rate of dinar abroad.[47] The National Bank undertook action to terminate the existing clearing agreements wherever possible, or replace them with new payment system agreements. To this end, Yugoslavia signed and ratified new payment agreements with Czechoslovakia and Poland in April and a new clearing agreement with Switzerland in July, which increased the share of cash payments for Yugoslav goods from 20 to 27 per cent. An agreement with France to abolish clearing in mutual trade was signed in December 1937.[48] Yugoslavia agreed to allow the import of French goods up to the equivalent of 80 per cent of Yugoslav exports to France.[49] Another clearing agreement which was abolished in 1937 was with Belgium. Earlier, in November 1936, Yugoslavia and Britain signed a new commerce agreement. Yugoslavia was experiencing a period of extended financial stability, at the same time expecting the world economy to recover and liberalization of foreign trade. According to a National Bank report in September 1937, 'whenever there is a possibility we attempt to replace clearing with the freedom of payment'.[50] The words of the National Bank's Vice-Governor Jovan Lovčević at the second meeting the national banks' governors of Balkan Entente countries in Ankara in November are testimony to the extent that Yugoslavia was serious in this approach: 'It is desirable to slowly desert the clearing system, or at least make it more flexible.' In the closing protocol of the conference, other representatives expressed their regret that due to the unfavourable international situation Yugoslavia's Balkan partners were still not able to follow Belgrade's example, but recommended to their governments the easing of strict currency policies and more liberalism in foreign trade.[51]

Controlled exports to Germany reduced the clearing debt. Yugoslavia had managed to find the balance Belgrade had sought since the spring of 1936, to import from the clearing and export to non-clearing countries. Germany was also obliged to make payments in foreign currency for some of Yugoslavia's raw materials, such as copper. Another important feature of 1937 was Italy's return to the Yugoslav market. The two countries renewed their economic relations in September 1936. This was formalized with the agreement signed in Belgrade on 25 March 1937.[52] Although confident of Germany's strong position in the Yugoslav market, Heeren warned in April that complications in German-Yugoslav trade might make some of Yugoslav exporters look overseas for new markets; as Yugoslavia's new trade agreement with Italy was also based on clearing, this could have implications for other Yugoslavia's clearing partners.[53] In 1937, Yugoslavia registered a positive balance with clearing countries like Austria, Belgium, France, Hungary and Italy, and a rising free trade with countries such as the United States, Britain, the Netherlands and Denmark. It all helped to partly reduce its dependence on Germany; the German share of Yugoslav exports fell from 23.7 per cent in 1936 to 21.7 per cent in 1937.[54]

After the meeting in Berlin in March, as expected and desired Yugoslav imports from Germany outstripped exports; in the first nine months of 1937, Yugoslav trade balance with Germany was 285 million dinars negative and it kept growing. This nearly halved the German clearing debt, but caused further loss of the Reichsmark's value in Belgrade, which in turn threatened to fuel imports from Germany over the limit. Since 1934 and the signing of the trade agreement, the Yugoslavs had come a long way in learning about the instability of trade through clearing and the hardships of predicting the fluctuations of accounts. In time, they learned that in order to keep German clearing debt at the minimal possible level, but not to become a debtor, Yugoslavia needed to keep its trade with Germany negative by some 300 million dinars; not much more and not significantly less.[55] As we can see, in September 1937 Yugoslavia's trade balance with Germany had almost reached this desirable balance. But the problem was the uncertainty over the rate of the Reichsmark in Belgrade. An illustration of how tricky it was to make even a short-term analysis, let alone a long-term, is a report of the Yugoslav Coordination Board for Foreign Trade in late October 1937: 'Last week the clearing Reichsmark was steadily rising and approached the rate of 14 dinars for one clearing Reichsmark. This was an utter surprise and contradicted earlier expectations and predictions about the fall in the Reichsmark's rate.'[56]

During the preparations for the next meeting of the Mixed Committee, to be held in Dubrovnik in September, Pilja and Belin summarized their views of the situation: it was necessary to balance mutual trade between the two countries, prevent further fluctuations of the Reichsmark whose rate was too dependent on the frequently changing nature of trade and decide on the type of goods, apart from maize and wheat, which best suited both Yugoslav export and German import demands. Pilja recommended the limitation of both imports and exports from Germany in order to orient Yugoslav trade towards other countries. He described dependence on Germany as damaging to national interests. The problem now was uncontrolled imports from Germany, which threatened to have a detrimental effect on Yugoslavia's own industrial production. The solution was seen to be the specified maximal value of goods permitted to enter the country from Germany and to continue to bind exports to Germany to that value. This became the crux of Yugoslavia's strategy for the Mixed Committee meeting in Dubrovnik.[57] Wishing to limit its dependency on Germany, Belgrade ended with contradictory attempts to centralize and control its trade with one country, while at the same time liberalizing trade with the rest of Europe.

Pilja was pleased with the result of the Dubrovnik meeting in September 1937. In talks with Campbell he regarded it as a success; the Yugoslavs set limits to some of its export commodities in demand in the world market and provided for better distribution, that is, obliged Germany to import less of those products which Yugoslavia could sell elsewhere.[58] But the Germans remained firm on many Yugoslav demands and managed to increase the existing quotas for imports of Yugoslav raw materials. According to the new distribution of German imports from Yugoslavia, 50 per cent of it would go on agricultural products and live animals, 11 per cent on wood and 39 per cent on industrial products and raw materials.[59] If any of these limits were not reached, the difference could be redistributed elsewhere, meaning that Germany would probably try to circumvent this rule to the benefit of import of raw materials. Export to Germany remained limited by the payments of Yugoslav importers in Belgrade, but Yugoslav import was now allowed to exceed export to Germany by only 5 per cent if the Yugoslav credit in Berlin exceeded 10 million Reichsmarks.[60] The Yugoslavs hoped that this last provision would both limit excessive imports from Germany and keep the German clearing debt under control. In October 1937, the Finance Ministry and the National Bank recommended a halt to the policy of state purchases from Germany and wished a rise of the Reichsmark's rate in Yugoslavia, to further reduce imports from Germany.[61] In the summer of 1937, Germany's share of Yugoslav imports was 36 per cent, and by the end of that year it was reduced to 32 per cent.[62]

Berlin was worried that its imports from Yugoslavia slowed down after March 1937. As it was unrealistic to expect rise in domestic production of raw materials from the onset of the Four-Year Plan, it was important to maintain the steady pace of rearmament by continuously importing necessary material. The rising costs of food and raw materials in the world market meant that Germany needed to export in order to pay for them. Then in the summer, world trade slowed down again; German foreign trade in 1937 recorded a considerable rise – 30 per cent more imports and 24 per cent more exports compared to 1936, but most of this was achieved in the first half of the year.[63] In 1938, both imports and exports sharply declined and the foreign trade balance turned negative. Schacht's worries, that the German economy would be put at risk for as long as domestic purchases were prioritized over the export deals, proved right.[64] Still, Göring continued to prioritize purchases for the Four-Year Plan, with no regard to the fact that German industry did not possess enough productivity to satisfy both, export and rearmament demands.[65] An early warning was the decision to ration steel for the domestic consumption, introduced in February 1937.[66]

In July 1937, Hitler founded Reichswerke 'Hermann Göring', which forcibly acquired German domestic iron mines owned by the leading Ruhr industrialists, followed by the building of Salzgitter steelworks, which was set to produce 1 million tons of steel annually from domestic ore. Despite these measures, German strategic plans suffered; it was unrealistic to expect the army to be ready for war until 1943.[67] In the summer of 1937, Schacht and Göring had an exchange of letters in which the former warned that any further pressure for increased imports from the countries of South-Eastern Europe would be counter-productive as the Reich was already heavily indebted through clearing. He warned that the continuing use of raw materials purely for rearming, instead of for the production of exportable consumer and production goods, would inevitably lead to the halt of imports into Germany.[68] Finally, Schacht resigned his post of Economics Minister in November 1937. After Göring's short spell there, the Ministry was given to Walther Funk. But he could not exercise any authority in his new post; Göring circumvented him, declaring in July 1938 that the Economics Minister was only in charge of legal aspects of the war economy.[69] Thus, Göring became Germany's economic dictator, with the final say over any question on the economy or foreign trade.[70] He stood for a self-sufficient state economy, able to provide for all the needs of an aggressive foreign policy – at which the German economy had failed in 1914–18.[71] The officials in Belgrade and other East-Central and South-Eastern European capitals were fully aware of these power struggles for the control of German economy and had no illusions as to what the purpose of the Four-Year Plan was.[72]

In November 1936, the German legation in Belgrade faced a new problem when Göring appointed one of his confidants, Franz Neuhausen, to be a representative of the Four-Year Plan in Yugoslavia. Although Neuhausen himself was amicable towards the Belgrade legation officials, this challenge to the official representatives of the Reich caused tensions, as there was confusion over the extent of Neuhausen's jurisdiction.[73] Neuhausen was already active in Yugoslavia as the chairman of the German Travel Bureau in Belgrade and the representative of Rosenberg's Foreign Policy Office of the NSDAP for Yugoslavia, making him effectively a political leader of all the Reich's nationals residing in the country.[74] However, it was his confirmation as Göring's representative which gave Neuhausen's mission in Yugoslavia its most important purpose. Throughout 1937, both War and Foreign Ministries in Berlin attempted several times to get rid of him from Belgrade. However, Neuhausen was safeguarded by his personal friendship with Göring.[75] He would later have the title of Consul General and increasingly take over the reins of all economic and military negotiations in Belgrade. Neuhausen's task was to provide concessions for the research into and exploitation of Yugoslavia's mineral wealth. This was not easy, as since the early 1920s the Yugoslav mineral wealth was largely managed and exploited by the Western capital.[76] Still, political events in Europe worked for the Germans.

## Economic relations after the Anschluss

The Anschluss brought numerous economic advantages for the Third Reich in terms of Austrian industrial capacities, the possession of Austrian deposits of iron ore and various important raw materials, Austrian electricity supplies, its wood production capacities and half a million unemployed Austrian workers for the chronically understaffed German industry.[77] Germany gained possession of Austrian gold reserves worth 362 million schillings. These advantages helped Germany to overcome its rearmament problems at the most critical period of the Four-Year-Plan, maintaining existing levels of arms production for nine more months.[78] Austria was less lucky;

it quickly experienced many of the Reich's restrictions, including food rationing.[79] Importantly, the Anschluss provided Berlin with direct access to the Balkans and its economies with raw materials. For Yugoslavia, bearing in mind the significance of Austria for the economy of South-Eastern Europe, the Anschluss brought significant economic and financial difficulties. Both the country itself and private importers had debts towards Austria totalling 325 million dinars. Although clearing accounts in Belgrade and Vienna were immediately closed down and their balances merged with the German accounts, it was of essential importance to agree on the schilling/dinar rate, in a way which would not artificially inflate the Yugoslav debt.[80] The Yugoslav payment transfer with Austria functioned only via private clearing, so the National Bank had no immediate evidence of which Yugoslav importers owed money to their Austrian partners at that moment; it was only assumed that this debt was in the region of 200 million dinars.

To discuss the consequences of the Anschluss for German-Yugoslav relations, the Mixed Committee met in Berlin in May 1938. Belgrade managed to preserve some of the concessions and tariffs previously granted by Austria, and the rate of the schilling was kept low until payments of the Yugoslav importers were regulated. Trade with Austria was now regulated under the provisions of the 1934 German-Yugoslav Trade Agreement, which remained the basis of mutual economic relations.[81] The two countries agreed the same modality regarding the transfers of payments and goods after the secession of the Sudetes from Czechoslovakia, at the meeting of the Mixed Committee in Berlin in February 1939.[82] However, the old clearing agreement with Czechoslovakia remained in effect after the establishment of the Protectorate of Bohemia and Moravia and all the mutual payments were to continue through accounts in Prague and Belgrade. With some changes, the previous trade agreements between Czechoslovakia and Yugoslavia remained the base of mutual economic relations, as agreed at the meeting of the Mixed Committee in Cologne in June 1939.[83] Importantly, the Anschluss did not hamper Yugoslavia's trade interests in Austria, as the Berlin meeting mostly preserved the most important Yugoslav concessions, now extended to the territory of the whole Reich. This is understandable as according to one estimate, after the incorporation of Austria, the Greater Reich could only produce 87 per cent of its needs in food and the need for imported raw materials was greater than ever.[84] Furthermore, Yugoslavia's clearing debt to Austria reduced the value of its clearing credit in Germany, which the National Bank considered a favourable development.[85]

Still, the reality of the post-Anschluss economic relations was that Yugoslavia was now in a more difficult position *vis-à-vis* Germany than ever before. Any possibility of avoiding economic dependence on Germany, which the Yugoslavs had hoped and worked for throughout 1937, disappeared after the annexation of Austria. Germany's share of the Yugoslav foreign trade, which decreased in 1937, was now enlarged by the Austrian share, amounting to 39 per cent of Yugoslav imports and 42 per cent of Yugoslav exports.[86] The Yugoslavs were fully aware of all the dangers of becoming a part of an economic area dominated exclusively by Germany. In May 1938, the government and the National Bank decided to give a stimulus to exporters to Britain, by granting them a higher rate of exchange to the sterling.[87] In June, Stojadinović openly asked Campbell for British economic assistance in the form of credit.[88] By the end of 1938, the British share in Yugoslav trade rose and Britain climbed to the second position in Yugoslav exports, with 9.6 per cent and the third in Yugoslav imports, with 8.7 per cent, slightly behind Italy.[89]

Worldwide, 1938 was the year marked with a sudden fall in economic activity, in both trade and foreign investments. One of the most important signs of the crisis was sharply fallen prices of raw materials and agricultural products, particularly those important for the Yugoslav exports, such as wheat, maize and copper.[90] Yugoslavia's economy was still fragile and sensitive to any changes in the world market. Political events leading to the Munich Conference in September caused more uncertainty which affected the markets, while large quantities of gold and capital were transferred from European countries to the safety of the United States. The Finance Ministry in Belgrade reacted by expanding the import controls to another nineteen products whose importation from the non-clearing countries was banned, while it simultaneously increased the list of products which could only be exported for foreign currency.[91] At the same time, the National Bank frequently intervened in order to keep the rate of sterling at the highest and the rate of Reichsmark at the lowest allowed level.[92] Keeping the high rates of non-clearing currencies on the Yugoslav market to stimulate exports to these countries was the National Bank's main preoccupation in the winter of 1938–9. The German side was not happy with many of the Yugoslav measures. At the meeting of the Mixed Committee in Berlin in February 1939, they expressed their annoyance with the Reichsmark's low rate in Yugoslavia, which at that time stood at 13.80 dinars, almost unchanged since the summer of 1937. Belin however made it clear that Yugoslavia would keep a low rate of the Reichsmark for as long as Germany owed Yugoslavia money on its clearing account in Berlin.[93]

Political events abroad and falling prices on world markets caused Yugoslavia's foreign trade to decline after the summer, but overall 1938 was again a good year. Yugoslav exports to non-clearing countries were the highest since 1933, while the overall balance of trade with the clearing countries was negative for the first time since 1932 and the introduction of clearing as a payment method.[94] Yugoslavia's imports, although slightly decreased in value, were significantly higher in volume.[95] And the officials still favoured a return to liberalism in foreign trade. In August 1938, the National Bank proudly concluded in its monthly report that 'the Kingdom of Yugoslavia is one of rare countries in Europe which, despite the changed circumstances in the world, more and more implements the currency regime closest to the regime of free trade, thus applying recommendations made by various committees and departments of the League of Nations'.[96] This positive development continued in 1939.[97] Exports to non-clearing countries kept rising as the year progressed; the share of Yugoslav exports to the clearing countries fell to 60 per cent in August, while imports from these countries rose to 77 per cent.[98] In order to stimulate exports to non-clearing countries, the officials sometimes subsidized exporters' prices.[99] The unstable political situation in Europe and rearmament of the great powers further benefitted Yugoslavia, and in the first five months of 1939 exports of metals increased by 50 per cent, especially the export of copper, aluminium, ferrochrome and lead.[100]

But the business of selling to one group of countries under one set of rules and buying from another group of countries under a different set of rules was a delicate matter. Yugoslav officials constantly had to be wary of two dangers; running out of foreign currencies and the increase of other countries' clearing debts. In order to further control foreign trade, the National Bank and the Finance Ministry in Belgrade set up a Currency Committee in July 1939. Its main task was to direct and regulate the import and export of goods. At the recommendation of this committee, on 12 September 1939 the Finance Ministry finally made all imports from non-clearing countries subject to prior approval by the National Bank.[101] That month, the Trade and Industry Ministry founded the Department for Foreign Trade, with the task of regulating the import and export of goods between the clearing and non-clearing countries.[102]

After the Anschluss with Austria and the annexation of Sudetenland, exports to Germany again rose above the required level and with it came the old problem of an excessive German clearing debt.[103] At the end of 1938, it was 30 million Reichsmarks.[104] As the Anschluss increased Yugoslavia's dependency on Germany in foreign trade, Belgrade faced the possibility of relying too much on trade with the country which was seen as politically dangerous. In May and June 1938, Stojadinović held meetings with Campbell and openly asked for British economic support, in the form of either loan or a greater trading activity between the two countries.[105] Despite the changed political reality in South-Eastern Europe at the time of the Munich Conference and afterwards, Yugoslavia persisted in keeping all options open. In late September, Belgrade asked for a new trading agreement with Britain, similar to that already in place with Germany, and for the purchase of British arms. But the British response was lukewarm. Then, a million-pound credit was approved for Yugoslavia in London in December, under condition that it was not used for arms purchases.[106] Simultaneously, the French began to increase their interest in the Yugoslav economy. During the summer of 1938, Trade and Industry Minister Milan Vrbanić visited Paris and was promised increased French imports from Yugoslavia.[107]

At the same time, despite political successes, the German economy continued to struggle. In the early summer of 1938, the Four-Year Plan was revised into a New War Economy Production Plan. Aware of their economic limitations, the Nazi leaders placed an emphasis on mineral oils, synthetic materials and explosives, in order to make quick conquests feasible, which would in turn create a base for an increase in German industrial capacities in war conditions.[108] This made an unrestrained influx of raw materials even more vital. In July 1939, the Economics Ministry in Berlin compiled a lengthy report on economic relations with foreign countries in the first three months of 1939. It emphasized that both Romania and Yugoslavia feared the growing German economic domination over the region after the political events of 1938 and had therefore tried to maintain their freedom of movement in economy by regulating mutual trade with Germany. The report touched on the issue of the Reichsmark's rate in the Balkans and stressed that if this was solved, the south-east would become an enclosed and exclusive economic domain of the Third Reich.[109]

This was all known in Belgrade and it was slowly becoming clearer to wider economic circles. Even the traditionally liberal *Narodno blagostanje* supported the National Bank's policy of controlling the Reichsmark's rate at the lowest possible level, stressing that any increase in its value could dangerously increase German clearing debt.[110] A British report from May 1938 praised the role which the National

Bank played in constantly manipulating the Reichsmark's rate to benefit Yugoslavia's trade with Germany.[111] But at the Mixed Committee meeting in Cologne in June 1939, the Germans pushed hard for an increase in the Reichsmark's rate in Yugoslavia to at least 15 dinars. Berlin wanted to raise its imports from Yugoslavia, as Germany was experiencing higher than ever demand for raw materials vital for military production. It is important to stress that by the decisions of the second Mixed Committee meeting in Zagreb in April 1936, the Yugoslav side agreed to keep the Reichsmark's rate above 14 dinars, while at the same time the official rate in Berlin was set at 17.70 dinars for one Reichsmark. As we have seen, the rate of the German currency had soon afterwards fallen in Belgrade below this agreed level.[112] In 1937 and 1938, Yugoslavia resisted the German pressure and managed to keep control of its trade with Germany mainly through manipulating the rate of the Reichsmark to its benefit. But eventually the Yugoslav side gave way in Cologne in June 1939 and the Reichsmark rate was set at 14.50 dinars. According to reports, this was done after the approval from the Finance Ministry.[113] Most probably Yugoslavia found it too hard to resist pressure from Berlin. With the creation of Bohemian Protectorate, the Reich now controlled almost 50 per cent of Yugoslavia's foreign trade. Germany used the rise of its political power in South-Eastern Europe for economic gains. Fear of Germany, politically powerful and territorially enlarged after the Anschluss in March 1938, the Munich Conference in September and the creation of the Protectorate in March 1939 forced Yugoslavia into making economic concessions.[114] Still, despite the higher rate of the Reichsmark after June 1939, overall Yugoslav exports to the Third Reich were lower in 1939 than in 1938.[115] One German report before the outbreak of war acknowledged the fall in Yugoslav exports to Germany of almost 200 million dinars for the first six months of 1939 and blamed the political pressure from France and Britain for this. It acknowledged a prevailing feeling in Yugoslavia that the country should maintain its economic independence, not only among the officials of the National Bank and the Finance Ministry, but also among financial experts and in business circles.[116]

## Armament deliveries

The bleak outlook for German finances and deficiency in the most urgently needed raw materials moved Hitler in 1935 towards the decision to start exporting war materials to any country willing to buy it.[117] The protest of the Foreign Ministry, that the Reich might arm some states whose conduct in the future conflict would be doubtful, was rejected. The Export Society for Military Equipment[118] was set up in October, to properly organize the sale of German weaponry.[119] It was only in July 1939 that Hitler banned these deliveries, allowing further sales only to countries which did not represent a direct danger to Germany, such as Latin America, the Baltic States or Bulgaria. During this period, the Reich sold and delivered armaments worth some 250 million Reichsmarks. This constituted only a small portion of overall German exports and from that perspective the expectations were not fulfilled.[120]

However, the sale of armaments became part of Germany's political agenda in regard to countries which traded with Berlin via clearing. At first, the share of payments done in foreign currencies was small and delivery deadlines short and swift. In exchange, Germany purchased vital raw materials which would otherwise have had to be paid for in cash. The German Foreign Ministry insisted on defining these sales as political, rather than economic, matters and recommended different terms for different countries. In the Balkans, Yugoslavia and Romania were considered untrustworthy.[121] However, Germany maintained negative clearing balance with the Balkan countries and the economic logic dictated using these sales for reducing Germany's debt. Expanding German clearing debt had, by late summer of 1935, forced Berlin to approach Belgrade and suggest the balancing of clearing accounts by supplying Yugoslavia with war material. A couple of visits by Yugoslav army representatives to the company Rheinmetall followed in the winter of 1935–6, but no deals were agreed; the Yugoslav military representatives favoured Škoda and did not conceal it.[122] At the same time, Yugoslavia reached an agreement with Prague for military credit worth 450 million korunas.[123]

In total, before 1939 Yugoslavia purchased armaments worth barely 13 million Reichsmarks from Germany, for thirty-six Dornier light bomber aircraft, sixteen Dornier hydroplanes, eight patrol boats and various signalling and listening devices, but the supply of the Yugoslav ground forces remained the domain of Czechoslovakian producers.[124] During the negotiations for the sale of aircraft to Yugoslavia in 1937, Berlin insisted on payments in cash. Yugoslavia reacted by demanding payments in foreign currency for some of its export goods needed by Germany, hitherto traded via clearing and the Germans backed off.[125] In general, methods of payment for German armaments were not different from other Yugoslav state purchases from Germany. For most purchases made before 1939, Yugoslavia managed to secure payments, at least partly, from the clearing account. The general rule was that the German government would have guaranteed such deals to its exporters for up to 70 per cent of the agreed price.[126] Most importantly, these were all relatively minor purchases for the Yugoslav air forces and navy. This could have changed in the winter of 1936–7, when Koch arrived in Belgrade, privately as chairman of the Technical Union and by Göring's authorization, and met Yugoslavia's War Minister Ljubomir Marić and Stojadinović, to conclude an agreement for the purchase of Yugoslav maize in exchange for German armaments. The subsequent affair already described meant that no deal was made.[127]

Apart from Czechoslovakia, Yugoslavia also favoured the ideologically closer French and the British. In November 1937, the British aircraft supplier Bristol delivered two Blenheim bomber airplanes, which immediately became 'the pride of the Yugoslav air-force'.[128] In October 1937, the Yugoslavs expressed a wish to test and eventually buy twelve Hawker Hurricane or Spitfire fighters.[129] But after the Munich Conference, it was clear that Yugoslavia needed more options for purchasing armaments. In November 1938, Stojadinović informed the Finance Minister Letica of the Italian offer of credit worth half a billion liras, for the purchase of weapons, ammunition and war material. But the latter judged its terms as unfavourable and advised some changes.[130]

In less than two months, Stojadinović was out of the office and for a while there was no more talk of the Italian offer. The talks were renewed at the beginning of April 1939, when the special Italian representative Schmidt di Friedberg visited Belgrade.[131] The new Yugoslav government raised the same objections as before and the talks were prolonged for six weeks. Yugoslavia managed to secure slightly better terms than initially. The credit was to be used for the purchase of airplanes, artillery, ammunition, armed vehicles, etc.[132] However, on 27 September 1939 the Italian legation in Belgrade informed the Yugoslav Foreign Ministry that this deal was off.

German companies were still losing contracts for the Yugoslav armament purchases to Škoda in 1938. Heeren recommended patience, as Yugoslavia's army was still suspicious of Germany and was concerned about the quality of German weapons.[133] But the situation changed after September. Political developments in Europe were worrying and the Yugoslav army was deficient not only in weaponry and ammunition, but even in the most basic technical material. The September 1937 military exercise in Croatia was praised in the official press, but behind the scenes it revealed all the weaknesses of a poorly equipped army.[134] Furthermore, political developments in Europe reduced the willingness of many countries to sell weapons, as domestic needs had become priority. The War Ministry in Belgrade warned that as the political situation in Europe was deteriorating, it was getting harder to reach favourable deals for buying weaponry.[135] For these reasons, at the beginning of 1939 Yugoslavia and Germany began talks about the sale of German armament to Yugoslavia on the terms of a large credit.

In January 1939, Prince Paul and his Chief of the General Staff Dušan Simović approached Carl von Schönebeck, the German Air Attaché in Belgrade, with a plea for credit of 200 million Reichsmarks to be used for the purchase of German aircraft, anti-aircraft guns and armed vehicles. This plea caused excitement within German diplomacy. Neuhausen asked of Göring and Funk to confirm the authority of the Four-Year Plan, while Ribbentrop thought of it as a good opportunity to reassert the control of the Foreign Ministry. He frequently visited Hitler at that time and it is likely that the question of the Yugoslav loan was mentioned.[136] The Italian offer of credit, which was known about in Berlin, caused further irritation. Clodius warned that Italy and Germany needed to avoid mutually harmful competition in the region of greatest interest for the Axis.[137] The problem was also the attitude of major manufacturers, such as Krupp, as they demanded a 100 per cent guarantee from the Reich's government, probably because they distrusted Yugoslavia's ability to refinance such a large purchase. In connection to this was another problem, overinflated prices offered by the private German companies. The Yugoslav military officials clearly stated in their conversations with German air and military attachés in Belgrade that no agreement was possible unless the prices were lowered. Wiehl tried to explain the significance of a breakthrough on the Yugoslav armament market to all interested sides in Berlin, reminding them how inferior German producers had been hitherto.[138]

On 22 April, Clodius of the Foreign Ministry, Gramsch of the Four-Year Plan and Neuhausen met in Berlin to agree the outlines for the upcoming Göring's negotiations with the Yugoslav Foreign Minister. Clodius made it clear that the Foreign Ministry wished to limit the credit to 100 million Reichsmarks.[139] For his ministry, this was an opportunity to exercise political pressure which they did not want to miss. At the meeting between Göring and Cincar-Marković on 26 April, the former did not specify the amount of German credit. According to a report by Erich Neumann, the Secretary for the Four-Year Plan, Göring suggested that it would depend on the German ability to fulfil Yugoslavia's order list, but Neumann clarified that it would actually depend on Yugoslavia's political attitude.[140] Germany also attempted to link oil concessions in Croatia to the armament deliveries. Heeren discussed this with the Yugoslav Foreign Minister on 4 May, when delivering Germany's proposal for a credit agreement. The German Minister considered this to be a good opportunity to settle all remaining questions, but Cincar-Marković did not commit to this statement.[141]

In Belgrade, informal negotiations with the principal German negotiator Neuhausen began early in March in the offices of the Finance Ministry. The Yugoslavs insisted on payments through clearing and in raw materials, preferably tobacco and iron.[142] Neuhausen agreed to all the Yugoslav demands, but because of events in Berlin, any agreement was delayed. The Yugoslavs insisted on a conclusion and, unaware of the internal German frictions, became annoyed. In late April, the Yugoslav Finance Ministry reminded Neuhausen that no armament purchases were possible before the financial terms for the credit were agreed.[143] The German proposal, finally delivered by Heeren on 4 May, was inspired by the agreement signed with Romania in March, the so-called Wohlthat Treaty, which enabled Germany to equally participate in the research and exploration of the Romanian mineral riches.[144] Particularly questionable was the seventh article of the German proposal: 'The Yugoslav government agrees to explore new sources of raw materials suitable for exploitation, with the participation of German experts. German industry will be the first to exploit these new sources of raw materials.' The article was phrased to appear as a sign of German goodwill and stated that the German government had decided not to demand a part of the payments in foreign currency, contrary to its usual dealing with other countries.[145]

The proposal assumed a ten-year repayment period for an unspecified value of credit with the interest rate fixed at 6 per cent, but only for weaponry, ammunition and technical material, excluding aircraft, which were to be covered under different terms. The German proposal also empowered the government in Berlin to choose with which raw materials Yugoslavia would pay off this credit. As many of these materials were valuable sources of foreign currency for the Yugoslav treasury, the Finance Ministry ruled it as unacceptable. At the meeting in Cvetković's office on 11 May, the new Finance Minister Vojin Djuričić suggested a counter-proposal: Yugoslavia would set the amount of credit in the region of 200 million Reichsmarks, aircraft would be included under the same terms as the rest of the material and credit would be paid partly from the German clearing debt, partly in Yugoslav deliveries of raw materials determined by the agreement. He rejected the seventh article by explaining that to accept such a demand 'would have harsh consequences on Yugoslavia's independent economic and industrial development, as well as on the political situation'.[146]

Negotiations based on the Yugoslav counter-proposal were led first in Berlin, in late May, and then in the backgrounds of the German-Yugoslav Mixed Committee meeting in Cologne. Yugoslavia was represented in Berlin by Sava Obradović, a senior official of the Trade and Industry Ministry and renowned economist, who was joined by Belin when the talks continued in Cologne. Agreement was reached on 3 June and was left to be approved by both governments before the official signing. However, it caused more disagreement in Berlin. The Finance Minister Krosigk insisted that German negotiators had failed to obtain guarantees against the risk of the Reichsmark's devaluation during the repayment period, which might cause private German contractors to turn to the government for the compensation of their losses.[147] However, Germany desperately needed Yugoslavia's raw materials and the Finance Ministry's conservative officials were easily sidelined by more powerful competitors in the decision-making process.

More than a month passed after reaching the agreement, before it was signed in Berlin. The German air attaché in Belgrade warned that to further prolong the signing would be detrimental to German political influence in Yugoslavia and that the delay had already caused doubts about Germany's goodwill. Schönebeck reported rumours regarding the Yugoslav interest in getting a licence for production of the new type of Blenheim aircraft and linked them with the delayed German credit.[148] He then reported rumours that the French had allegedly offered armaments credit to Yugoslavia worth a billion francs.[149] In the last week of June, Cvetković verbally assured Neuhausen that Yugoslavia would award Germany with oil concessions; this prompted the latter to join the chorus of those who demanded urgency in signing the Cologne protocol.[150] Schönebeck warned that any further insistence on coupling political demands with economic matters could eventually rebound on Germany and it seems that he was heard. It could also be argued that the Yugoslavs played their cards well. As long as they had the possibility of choosing between more suppliers, they could still manoeuvre to protect their interests. The problem for the Yugoslavs was that their space for manoeuvring depended on others, that is, the Western democracies and their willingness to keep their interests in the Balkans alive.

The Cologne protocol was finally signed by Heeren and Djuričić in Belgrade on 5 July 1939. According to the wording of the agreement, the value of armaments credit to Yugoslavia was left unspecified, the repayment period was set at ten years, the interest rate at 6 per cent and the repayment period for aircraft at six years, shorter than for the rest of the material. Yugoslavia remained firm about the article seven; the text only stated that 'the [Yugoslav] government would timely examine the German wishes and fulfil them if possible'. It was agreed that the annual quotas of certain raw materials and of wood, which were already regularly traded through the clearing, would increase by 50 per cent.[151] But the unspecified value of credit, which was 'left to be decided', opened it to the potential for German political pressure on Yugoslavia and depended on the level of Yugoslavia's political cooperation with Germany.[152]

There were more problems. Belgrade wanted to include new purchases from Škoda and other Bohemian suppliers within the provisions of the German credit, but Berlin opposed this. There were also problems with the armament purchased from Czechoslovakia back in March 1936, worth 57 million korunas, paid for and not yet fully delivered.[153] But soon after the signing of the protocol, Göring banned any export of the German aircraft. Then, on 18 July Hitler ordered that only a limited supply of weapons to certain countries would be allowed, which especially applied to Yugoslavia.[154] According to the short instruction sent from the High Command of Wehrmacht:

Regarding Yugoslavia, the Führer decided the following: 1) The demands of the German Army come first, [therefore with the delivery of] 200 pieces of 3.7 cm anti-tank artillery from Škoda for Yugoslavia not to proceed. 2) The 7.5 cm anti-aircraft artillery, which should be ready for the delivery by Škoda in the next months should first be offered to Italy and only then to Yugoslavia.[155]

Yugoslavia had no more luck in buying German aircraft. At the meeting with Heeren on 22 April, War Minister Milan Nedić mentioned that Göring himself had promised him a delivery of more than 130 bombers, fighters and training aircraft for the Yugoslav air forces and demanded urgency. According to his words, this delivery was supposed to be a part of the German credit.[156] Three months later, Andrić complained about the lack of response to Yugoslavia's appeals.[157] The Yugoslavs continued their pressure through every possible channel of communication. In order to appease them, on 20 August Göring approved the delivery of five Messerschmitt fighters. On 10 September, officials from the Air Ministry in Berlin informed Yugoslavia's Air Attaché that no modern German fighters or bombers could be delivered in any circumstances.[158]

## Elusive freedom

After 1936, Yugoslavia's economy remained tied to the German market with the clearing system of trade and payments and was primarily seen a source of raw materials vital for the military production under Göring. But the German economy slowed down in this phase, because its productive capacities were used for non-profitable military expenditure. This deliberate neglect of consumer industries reduced growth, renewed the problem of financing through exports and reduced domestic consumption, which the government was happy to cut down, as it was seen as a hindrance to the increase in military production.[159] Germany needed food and raw materials from Yugoslavia; Hitler's and Göring's least worry was the problem of clearing accounts in Belgrade and Berlin.

The problem with Yugoslavia was that despite its dependence on the German market during the most of this period, its economic ideology was oriented towards the free markets and the maintenance of existing financial and economic relations with the Western powers. Yugoslavia's economic decision makers considered any form of exchange as only a temporary deviation in international trade and much to Germany's annoyance were persistent in limiting trade with Germany whenever it threatened to jeopardize Yugoslavia's financial and economic stability. Also, Yugoslavia's productive capacities were not organized to suit German needs. Belgrade pursued economic policies which were designed in accordance with the needs of Yugoslavia's industrialization, as will be seen in the following chapter. The future of this tense economic relationship now depended on political developments, which were largely beyond Yugoslavia's control.

One has to sympathize with tremendous efforts the Yugoslav economic experts and officials invested in defending Yugoslavia's economic interests and autonomy against the pressing German demands, as well as with their devotion to economic liberalism and free trade. And just as Yugoslavia's foreign trade was gathering momentum in detaching itself from the danger of becoming an exclusively German trading domain in the winter of 1937–8, a political event in the form of the Anschluss placed it back under the Third Reich's commercial dominance, with all the familiar economic consequences stemming out of it. It is also important to stress the autonomy of economic motives, which were strictly separated from the realm of Belgrade's diplomatic relations with Berlin and which the leaders of Yugoslavia's economy had demonstrated in dealing with their German counterparts. When they finally had to give way in some instances, for example in regard to the problem of the Reichsmark's rate in Belgrade in June 1939, it was only out of understandable fear and realization that any further opposition was futile and even dangerous; to insist on pure economic reasoning in the early summer of 1939 could have easily placed the country in grave political danger. Also, only in 1939 Germany was for the first time presented with an opportunity to abuse mutual economic cooperation, in regard to armament deliveries, for purely political gains. Yugoslavia had a misfortune of being too important for the German war economy. However, if there was anything called 'German informal empire', it was forged only after the great German political successes in 1938–9.

6

# The Third Reich and the industrialization of Yugoslavia

Any research on Yugoslavia's industrialization in the 1930s has to take into account the wider economic context of Yugoslavia's relations with the Third Reich, the country's most important trading partner. By trying to connect the two, some Yugoslav historians in the 1980s promulgated the view that by adhering to the so-called Agrarian Block of Central European and South-Eastern European countries in 1931, Yugoslavia placed itself inside the German-dominated agricultural zone and doomed its economy.[1] This is opposed by Alice Teichova, who argued that even if true, such a situation was not always unbeneficial for the countries of the Danube region and the Balkans and necessarily favourable for Germany. She suggests that apart from its strong economic presence in these countries, Germany did not play a crucial role in their industrialization, which was more a result of the specific economic development of the region.[2]

This chapter welds together two processes which have so far been mostly observed separately in the existing literature. One is the industrialization of Yugoslavia during the aftermaths of the Great Depression, its scope and achievements.[3] The other is the significance of the increased momentum of Yugoslavia's mutual trade with Germany after 1934. This is set into the wider context of Yugoslavia's place in the Nazi New Order, which has been well covered in historiography.[4] The underlying idea follows the thread set out in previous chapters, that the German economic approach to Yugoslavia was not linear in following a specific programme, but was instead pragmatically changing as the situation demanded. These adjustments, mostly according to the needs and problems of the German economic development, sometimes created situations which were eventually contradictory to the Reich's interests.

## The consequences of the Abyssinian Crisis

Did the Abyssinian Crisis damage Italy's positions in the Yugoslav market to an extent which cleared the way for Germany to fill the void? Such a statement is made by many historians, including Sundhaussen, Cvijetić, Avramovski and others.[5] It is indeed hard to contradict this opinion in the light of statistical data, as the value of German trade with Yugoslavia increased by 60 per cent in 1936 compared to 1934, while the overall value of the Yugoslav-Italian trade in 1936 shrank to a mere

23 per cent of what it was in 1935.⁶ However, firstly, such change also pointed to the adaptability of Yugoslavia's economy; secondly, Yugoslavia's foreign trade with both Italy and Germany should be analysed from more angles, as the statistics may blur some less visible developments.

The world economic crisis hit Italy particularly hard. Between 1929 and 1932, Italian industrial productivity shrank by a third and its gold reserves were depleted by 3 billion liras; the number of unemployed workers increased from 200,000 to 730,000.⁷ Just as in other countries at this time, Italy chose to deal with the crisis by applying protectionism, various trade controls and the clearing method in trade with other countries. The crisis had severe consequences on trade with Yugoslavia. In 1930, Yugoslavia was 1,135 million dinars positive; this shrank to 705 million in 1931, to 343 million in 1932 and to only 265 million dinars in 1933. This was a reflection of a generally reduced volume of trade between the two countries; in 1932, Italian imports from Yugoslavia sank to a mere third of its 1929 level, while its exports to Yugoslavia halved.⁸ In order to increase the sale of its industrial goods on the Yugoslav market, Rome approached Belgrade with the offer of a new economic agreement. Yugoslavia accepted and the new agreement, based partly on clearing, partly on payments in cash, was signed in April 1932. However, it did not solve the problem of Italy's trade deficit, which was even aggravated as Yugoslavia lacked foreign currency to pay for its purchases from Italy. The two countries then signed a new payment agreement in October 1932.⁹ But Italian share in Yugoslavia's foreign trade was steadily declining, one of the reasons being the constant increase in Italian taxes on Yugoslav products. The signing of Rome Protocols with Hungary and Austria in March 1934 further damaged Yugoslavia's exports to Italian market; Hungary became the chief beneficiary of Italy's needs for grain and meat, while Austria replaced Yugoslavia as the principal exporter of industrial wood. Data about the Yugoslav export of industrial and firewood to Italy, which was Yugoslavia's chief export market for this commodity, are important indicators of this declining relationship: in 1929, Yugoslavia exported 1.3 million tons of wood, while in 1935 this amount fell to 590 thousand tons.¹⁰ The same applied to Yugoslavia's exports of meat and live animals to Italy, which by May 1935 nearly halved from the previous level.¹¹

In February 1935, Italy introduced a quota system, which brought further obstacles for the sale of Yugoslav products in the Italian market.¹² Although it was still one of Yugoslavia's principal trading partners, these trade conditions were clearly not as favourable as before, and in 1935 the Yugoslav export to Italy sank to 672 million dinars, the lowest since 1918.¹³ The value of Yugoslav imports from Italy declined from 555 million dinars in 1934 to 373 million in 1935.¹⁴ Another serious problem in 1935 was the Italian clearing debt to Yugoslavia, which kept rising at a dramatic pace: in March 1935, it stood at 12 million dinars; in May, 30 million; in June, 42 million; in August, 75 million; and in September, 105 million dinars. In the month of Italy's aggression on Abyssinia, when economic sanctions were imposed by the League of Nations, Italian clearing debt was 139 million dinars. To put this into perspective with German debt: in March 1935, the value of the Italian debt was a mere one-sixteenth of the German clearing debt to Yugoslavia (199 million dinars), while in October it was 60 per cent (Germany owed Yugoslavia 242 million dinars that month).¹⁵

Yugoslavia was not an exception; by 1934 Italy had a huge payment deficit with the rest of the world, which at the end of that year stood at 2,617 million liras.[16] This brought Yugoslavia into the position of being an Italian creditor, with all the familiar negative consequences which the country was already facing in trade with Germany.[17] For this reason, the National Bank had to extend to Italy a policy of buying off the claims of Yugoslav exporters, the same measure it used in the case of exporters to Germany. It is no surprise that when the Abyssinian Crisis began with all its economic consequences for the two countries, the Yugoslav National Bank concluded that the difficulties in trade with Italy had existed for a while already and that even before the sanctions were introduced, Yugoslavia was forced to actively search for new markets and new trading partners for certain export products, due to the large volume of Italian debt and the instability of the lira's exchange rate.[18]

Despite the loss suffered in trade with Italy, Yugoslavia's overall exports in 1936 surpassed the 1935 exports by more than 300 million dinars (4,376 million to 4,030 million dinars). Hitherto dominant exports to Italy were redistributed to other states, namely to the Near East and the Danube countries, while the total value of the export of live cattle in 1936 surpassed that of 1935.[19] Particularly important was the increased export of pigs into Austria, Czechoslovakia and Germany. The share of live animals and processed meat in Yugoslav exports rose from 27 per cent in 1935 to 32 per cent in 1936, equivalent to an increase of 317 million dinars of export income. The fall in income from the export of wood was smaller than feared, due to increased exports to Britain and Germany.[20] The German legation in Belgrade reported in February 1936 that the decline of Italian-Yugoslav trade was not a consequence of sanctions on Italy, as it had started as early as the beginning of 1935.[21] Even the import of goods which were traditionally purchased from Italy, such as silk and silk products, rose in 1936 (3,245 tons to 2,506 tons in 1935), as well as the import of cotton, another traditional domain of Italian exporters on the Yugoslav market (33,000 tons to 32,000 tons in 1935).[22] A British report from Belgrade in late December 1935 also predicted such a development. According to it, many larger Yugoslav exporters to the Italian market had already reorganized their sales to Germany, while Belgrade and Zagreb had been flooded with the Spanish traders, who offered to supply local businesses with the cheaper Spanish yarns and fabrics. Large timber exporters continued to supply Italian customers using their branch offices in Austria, with payments being made in schillings through the private Austro-Yugoslav clearing. Yugoslavia's agricultural products quickly found their way onto the Italian market via Albanian ports, while Hungarian traders purchased large quantities of other Yugoslav goods, acting mainly as intermediaries for Italian buyers.[23] This swift Yugoslav recovery from the shock caused by the League's sanctions on Italy resembled pre-war Serbia's victory in the trade war with Austro-Hungary in 1906–10 and later served as an argument for the view that despite its overdependence on the German market in the late 1930s, Yugoslavia could still have detached commercially from Germany without a lasting damage to its economy.[24]

Avramovski claimed that Yugoslavia's strict adherence to the League's sanctions on Italy created immense opportunities for German economic ambitions in Yugoslavia and supported it with numbers: in October 1935, Germany's share of Yugoslav exports was 21.2 per cent, in November it slightly rose to 23.1 per cent and then it sharply increased to 29.1 per cent in December and 37.3 per cent in January 1936.[25] However, he failed to notice that already in February, the German share of Yugoslav exports had fallen to its pre-sanctions level, 21.5 per cent.[26] This rise and subsequent fall of German trade in the winter of 1935–6 fitted rather within the wider seasonal character of the German trade with Yugoslavia. Also, earlier Yugoslav exports to Italy were redistributed among many countries after October 1935, not only merely redirected to Germany.[27] The rise of the German share of Yugoslav exports in 1936 compared to 1935 was significant, but not drastic, from 18.7 per cent to 23.7 per cent.[28] The rise of Germany's share of Yugoslav imports in 1936 was due to Yugoslavia's import controls introduced in April that year, as already explained.

Strict enforcement of economic sanctions on Italy did initially shake Yugoslavia's economy and caused disruption to smaller exporters who were not able to reorient quickly to new markets. The psychological effect was equally important; the British analysis of the Zagreb meeting of the Mixed Committee in March 1936 stressed that, apart from reducing the amassed German clearing debt to Yugoslavia, the Yugoslavs would also do everything in their power to expand their export basis to Germany to compensate for the losses which Yugoslavia had sustained through the application of sanctions on Italy.[29] These were the immediate consequences of the Abyssinian Crisis on Yugoslavia's economic decision-making. Still, bearing in mind that the volume of Yugoslav-Italian trade in 1935, before the imposition of sanctions in October, had already had a downward trend, we could argue that even without the Abyssinian Crisis, Italian long-term prospects as the major Yugoslavia's trading partner were not promising. Even though the signing of the new Yugoslav-Italian trading agreement in September 1936 contributed to the normalization of economic relations between Belgrade and Rome, the position which Italy had previously held in Yugoslavia's foreign trade was lost.

Another dimension of this issue revolves around the structure of Yugoslavia's foreign trade. The emphasis of Italian exports to Yugoslavia was on the products of light industries, mostly textiles and agricultural products. Italy's share of Yugoslavia's import of cotton yarn was 62.8 per cent, as well as 44.2 per cent of the silk yarn. Yugoslavia imported 31.6 per cent of cotton fabrics from Italy, as well as 17.9 per cent of silk fabrics and 12.4 per cent of wool. Italy covered 80 per cent of Yugoslavia's need for rice and half of Yugoslavia's imports of citrus fruits.[30] The structure of German trade with Yugoslavia was completely different. In 1935, Germany exported goods worth 36.9 million Reichsmarks, of which 92 per cent was export of finished goods: chemical and pharmaceutical products, glassware, ironware, copperware, various machinery, electrical and communicational devices, cars, bicycles, etc.[31] Between 1925 and 1931, Germany's share of the overall Yugoslav import of machinery, tools, electronic devices and vehicles was in the region of one half and two-thirds, reaching its peak in 1929. During the Great Depression this share declined, but after 1933 it started to rise again.[32] In 1937 and 1938, German share of these imported commodities was around 60 per cent, and in 1939 it rose to a staggering 69 per cent of all the machinery Yugoslavia imported that year.[33] Although this drastic rise in imports of Germany's machinery after 1935 could be attributed to import controls introduced by Yugoslavia, and in

1938–9 to the addition of Austria, Bohemia and Moravia to the Third Reich, it is easy to notice that the figures were only restored to the 1920s level. Again, the high figures for the pre-crisis period could equally be attributed to the war reparations for which Germany was paying mostly in goods. Still, the dominant position which German-made machinery held in the Yugoslav market in the inter-war period cannot be denied. It stemmed from the traditional links and business partnerships, which was a result of a long-term German economic presence in the countries which joined together in 1918 to form Yugoslavia. The German Finance Ministry concluded in its report from March 1933 that 'the main German export into Yugoslavia consist of namely those products which are essential for the industrial development of the country. … Numerous Yugoslav industries were created with German machine industry products and their further development depends on the export of [German] machinery'.[34] In the long run, Italy could not have competed with Germany for dominance in the Yugoslav market, as it was the latter which had the capacity to answer the problem of modernizing needs of Yugoslavia's economy.

## German investments in Yugoslavia

It was normal for a rural country, rich in ores and with fertile soil, but depleted of significant financial means, to develop slowly and in stages. The greatest problem for Yugoslavia's economic progress was the lack of capital. For this reason, Yugoslavia depended on foreign investments; this dependence was evident in the spheres of mining, banking and electric infrastructure. The share of foreign capital in other branches of the Yugoslav industry was much smaller. After 1918, circumstances for foreign investments in Yugoslavia's economy seemed favourable and it was encouraged by successive governments. But many foreign investors misinterpreted the initial need for Yugoslavia's post-war reconstruction as a sign of the strong absorbing power of the Yugoslav market, often ending with investments in unprofitable enterprises. Already by 1922, the National Bank was warning against unplanned investment in those industries for which there were not enough preconditions for profitable existence.[35]

In order to protect domestic industrial production, in 1925 the government introduced import tariffs for foreign manufactured goods which ranged between 21 and 25 per cent and were at that time some of the highest in the world.[36] This measure accelerated the pace of foreign investments, and in the period 1926–31 the share of foreign capital invested in Yugoslavia's industrial enterprises reached 35 per cent of the overall capital of joint-stock companies, compared to 23 per cent before 1925. In sum, 3.5 billion dinars of the foreign capital was invested in Yugoslavia's economy before the crisis, excluding the purchase of government bonds.[37] The French and the British capital was mainly involved in Yugoslavia's mining industry; Austrian, Hungarian and Czechoslovakian money in banking and insurance; and the Swiss and Swedish capital in the energy sector and electrification. But the Great Depression put a halt to foreign investments. And when the international economy began to recover in the early 1930s, the world of international financing looked radically different to the times before the crisis: investors became cautious, new regulations were introduced in countries which tended to import capital and in countries which exported capital earlier belief in liberal capitalism was replaced with economic protectionism and a drive towards the self-sufficiency. Nevertheless, positions taken in the 1920s were preserved and in 1935, 20 per cent of all the foreign capital invested in Yugoslavia, comprising both the ownership of shares in joint-stock companies and loans granted to the Yugoslav economy, was French; 16 per cent was British, 14 Swiss, 9.5 Czechoslovakian, 8.3 Italian, 7.4 American, 5.7 Austrian, 4 Hungarian, 3.6 Belgian and only 1.35 per cent was German capital.[38]

Foreign capital was mostly invested in mining. Most of industrial enterprises in this sector were joint-stock companies in the hands of the British (copper, lead, zinc, chrome, manganese, antimony, oil), French (brown coal, copper, bauxite, magnesium), Swiss (bauxite), Belgian (hard coal, brown coal, copper, magnesium) and to a smaller degree American (oil and gas), Hungarian and Italian capital; the German share was negligible.[39] At the outset of the Second World War, the value of foreign capital invested in Yugoslavia's mining was 88 per cent, or 763 million dinars out of 877 million.[40] Thirty out of sixty-six mining companies were joint-stock companies with the foreign capital, but their overall value was 781 million dinars; the value of the remaining thirty-six purely domestic companies was only 96 million. The British share was 40.7 per cent, the French share was 28 per cent, while other countries with invested capital in Yugoslav mining were far behind. The Germans invested 6.85 million dinars, less than 1 per cent. If we add the value of all credits in Yugoslav mining granted by foreign investors, the German share tripled between 1935 and 1937, but only from 1.26 per cent to 3.75 per cent. This was still far behind the value of British credits granted to the private mining corporations in Yugoslavia, worth 142 million dinars or 43 per cent of all the foreign credits in mining. In 1935, these thirty joint-stock companies with the participating foreign capital were in control of 61 per cent of the overall Yugoslav mining and smelting production.[41]

The Germans got a partial foothold in Yugoslav mining only in the late 1930s. One field where they felt the options were still unexploited was gas and oil production. In 1937 German capital purchased Rudokop, the oil and gas research company, soon after it was established with purely Yugoslav money.[42] The company's capital in 1939 increased from 1 million to 25 million dinars and the name changed to Jugopetrol. In 1938, the Germans pushed to buy oil concession for an area in Medjumurje (Croatia) from Radomir Pašić, son of the former Serbian and Yugoslav Prime Minister. However, they faced stiff competition from the American company Standard Oil, who pushed hard to obtain concessions for research and exploitation for the next fifty years for a larger area in the same part of Yugoslavia, which completely surrounded the part covered by Pašić's concession. There were fears within the German legation in Belgrade, the Foreign Ministry and private organizations of German capital, such as the Central European Economic Council, *Mitteleuropäischer Wirtschaftstag* (henceforth MWT), that this would lower the value of Pašić's share. But Göring personally ordered the go ahead for the German purchase of Pašić's concession. Some members of the Yugoslav government favoured the deal with Standard Oil, while Stojadinović personally urged the Germans to sign. The contract with Pašić was to be signed at the beginning of 1939 at the insistence of Neuhausen.[43] However, no contracts were signed before Stojadinović's fall.

There were only two larger mining corporations in Yugoslavia owned by German capital before the outbreak of war, Montania and Lisanski rudnici. They owned antimony mines in Lisa, near Ivanjica and Zajača, near Loznica (both in Serbia). These companies came under the umbrella of MWT in 1937.[44] In 1940, they merged into a single enterprise called Antimon. German capital was indirectly involved in the Yugoslav bauxite production; the largest investor in this field was the Zurich based Bauxit-Trust, controlled by the Vereinigten Aluminium-Werke from Berlin.[45] In 1939, Montangesselschaft founded Jugomontan, while in 1940 MWT initiated the founding of Jugohrom. The two companies which jointly invested in Jugohrom were Krupp and Reichswerke 'Hermann Göring'.[46] Jugohrom and Jugomontan were both set up with the task of searching for new deposits of chrome and zinc in Yugoslavia. In 1937, MWT initiated the foundation of Society for Exploration of Foreign Ore Deposits, *Gesellschaft für Erforschung ausländische Erzvorkommen* (henceforth GEaE); the most important German electronics companies such as AEG and Siemens took their part in this venture. In January 1938, again under the auspices of MWT, IG Farben founded Ore-Society for Exploration of Non-Ferrous Metals, *Erzgesellschaft zur Erschließung von Nichteisenmetallen*.[47] These two associations were founded with the task of purchasing shares in Yugoslav mining corporations. Krupp actively participated in some of these enterprises, although their only individual investment in Yugoslavia was a small chrome mine near Skopje.[48] Finally, after the fall of France Germany took over the French-owned Bor copper mine. As Pétain's government was fiercely opposed to this takeover, the negotiations lasted five months before the sale was finally agreed at the beginning of February 1941. The main German negotiator was again Neuhausen, acting on Göring's behalf and the price agreed was 108.5 million Reichsmarks. Documents show that the Germans paid this in part from the money they received from the war contributions imposed on defeated France.[49]

Although Germany arrived late to participate in the exploitation of Yugoslavia's mineral wealth, this did not mean that the officials in Berlin were content with the existing state of affairs. More details about the MWT, its origins, structure and aims will follow later. For the moment, it is important to note that it worked independently in pursuing the aims of the German businesses in South-Eastern Europe, but mostly in accordance with the official institutions in Berlin. To prepare the ground, in November 1934 MWT founded the German Chamber of Commerce for Yugoslavia, *Deutsche Handelskammer für Jugoslawien*, which worked towards promoting the commercial cooperation between the two countries.[50] At one of MWT's meetings in December 1936, Helmuth Wohlthat of the Reich's Economics Ministry and the person directly responsible to Göring and later Funk in the economic affairs of South-Eastern Europe insisted that the balance between the imports of raw materials and unnecessary goods from South-Eastern Europe was not favourable; he stressed that in Yugoslavia, although its foreign trade was dependent on the German market, Germany participated with a mere 5 per cent of the total invested foreign capital.[51] Obviously, it was the task of MWT to increase this proportion.

At one point, the leading men of the organization faced a dilemma of which strategy to follow. A riskier and cheaper one meant obtaining concessions for building new enterprises in areas where researches pointed out to possibly profitable mineral deposits. The other option, safer but more expensive, was the financial takeover of already existing mines. This dilemma was never decisively resolved, just as MWT was not always successful in achieving its goals. In 1937, a decision was made to place an offer for the purchase of two mines, in Srebrenica (Bosnia, lead and zinc) and Slatina near Zaječar (Serbia, copper), both owned by private Yugoslav individuals and corporations. The GEaE was to be instrumental in these operations, but it did not happen until 1941, due to unfavourable estimates of the profitability of these mines.[52] Therefore, despite such an aggressive approach and certain gains in the later 1930s, Germany overall failed to get a stronger foothold in the Yugoslav mining. This was indirectly admitted by MWT's chairman Tilo von Wilmowsky, who in November 1938 realistically described their first successes in the Balkans merely as a result of annexations of that year; these 'only slightly opened the blocked doors of the south-east. It will take more years of a tough, proper economic effort in order to open the doors wide.'[53]

No other sector of Yugoslavia's industry experienced any significant participation of German capital at this time. This also referred to banking, where the situation changed only after the Third Reich began to expand. Unlike Germany, Austria and Czechoslovakia possessed significant capital invested in Yugoslavia's economy. In this way, Berlin used the back door to increase its presence in Yugoslavia and other countries of South-Eastern Europe.[54] In February 1938, Göring's confidant for economic affairs of the south-east, Hermann Neubacher, arrived in Belgrade, where with Stojadinović he discussed the opening of a German bank in Yugoslavia. Within days after this meeting, German army marched into Austria and any such plan became superfluous.[55] The acquisition of Austrian and Czech banks gave Germany the control over many industrial enterprises in sectors of metal, textiles, wood-processing, food industries and particularly in banking.[56] In 1939, the German share of all the foreign capital invested in eighteen Yugoslav banks, enlarged by the capital which was previously in possession of Czechoslovakian and Austrian institutions, reached almost 36 per cent.[57] The most important was their control over the Creditanstalt-Bankverein from Vienna, founded in 1934 by the merger of the troubled Creditanstalt with the Wiener Bankverien. Through this financial institution, the Deutsche Bank entered Yugoslavia's market. Creditanstalt-Bankverein operated in Yugoslavia mainly through two important financial institutions: Yugoslav United Bank, whose large portion of shares was previously controlled by the Creditanstalt, and the General Yugoslav Bank Union Zagreb-Beograd, founded by the Wiener Bankverein after the merger of its Zagreb and Belgrade branches. Deutsche Bank then purchased shares in the General Yugoslav Bank Union previously held by some Belgian and Czechoslovakian banks; at the outbreak of the Second World War it controlled 92 per cent of the General Yugoslav Bank Union. Its capital was then increased from 60 to 100 million dinars, making it the largest financial institution and creditor in Yugoslavia and the leading German-owned bank in South-Eastern Europe.[58] By getting into the possession of Austrian and Czechoslovak financial institutions, with bank loans worth 335 million dinars in 1940, of which barely 46 million were loans granted by the banks located in the old Reich, Germany became the leading creditor in the Yugoslav economy. The second phase of this process followed after the military occupations of France and Benelux.[59] German capital then spread quickly to other forms of non-industrial enterprises, and by the end of 1940 Germany was already in control of the capital worth 370 million dinars invested in Yugoslavia.[60] As Wendt puts it, the Third Reich in a short period of time outplayed the Western powers in South-Eastern Europe, taking over their positions carefully built there over the previous two decades, at the same time overcoming its own financial and economic weaknesses.[61]

But this development alarmed the Yugoslavs. In October 1939, the Finance Ministry published a decree about the control of foreign capital in Yugoslavia. It referred to all, companies owned by the foreigners, joint-stock companies with either majority or minority stocks owned by foreign individuals and institutions and foreign loans to domestic companies. Every Yugoslav enterprise had to report any form of presence of the foreign money; the official explanation was the lack of foreign currency in Yugoslavia.[62] This was an unlikely reason as the control referred not only to the outgoing, but especially to incoming foreign capital in Yugoslavia. The real reason was openly discussed by the National Bank, in a letter sent out to the Finance Ministry in September 1940:

> There were many cases of bringing the capital into the country recently, especially via certain clearing accounts. In the beginning, these were mostly firms conducting various researches in our country, but recently it is often the case that the capital is imported [in Yugoslavia] via clearing accounts for the purpose of creating various trading companies. The method used implies that a domestic company, which had hitherto represented some foreign corporation, apply [to Yugoslav authorities] for the approval to concede part of its capital to foreign investors from a clearing country, who then bring the capital in via clearing [to pay for the ownership of the Yugoslav company].[63]

Although no country was mentioned in particular, the wording referred to Germany. Germany's new role as major capital investor in Yugoslavia differed from Western investments in the years before the crisis, as the Germans did not invest in Yugoslavia's productive capacities. The purpose of these new trading companies founded with German capital was to steer the sale of the Yugoslav metals and ores towards German buyers.

## Yugoslavia's state purchases in Germany

Stojadinović fully understood that political developments in Europe would result in increased rearmament on all sides, which placed his ore-rich country in a favourable position. At the same time, developing the domestic metal and machine industry was a guarantee of a cheaper domestic rearmament. The problem was that the production of metals, a necessary precondition for the development of domestic machine and goods-producing industries, was significantly delayed by technological backwardness, particularly the lack of metalworks, although Yugoslavia possessed mines with some of the highest percentage of metals in Europe. To solve this problem, the government prioritized capital investments in mining, metallurgy, electrification and infrastructure. The largest state investments of this kind were the rolling mill in Zenica (Bosnia) and the plant for aluminium production in Lozovac near Šibenik (Croatia).[64] Much work was done in electrification. Priority was always given to those areas with significant industrial and mining capacity; the power stations were connected by power lines with networks of mines in their geographic areas, supplying them with electricity. Particular attention was paid to investments in mining, for adaptation of existing structures and modernization of the work process.[65] But this was still a modest development in terms of the size and industrial backwardness of the country. Yugoslavia did not achieve its industrial take-off before the outbreak of war, as it failed to make a decisive shift from the production of consumer goods to the production of machinery.[66] The main problem for Yugoslavia's governments in the second-half of the 1930s was the lack of money, despite some skilfully developed financial schemes for domestic financing in industry and infrastructure, in the absence of foreign credits after the Great Depression.[67] This opened the door for German investments, despite Berlin's own financial troubles, as Germany was flexible in offering different investment modalities. These methods, usually in the form of Yugoslav state purchases paid from the German clearing debt, became one of the outlets for Yugoslavia.

The most important German investment in Yugoslavia was in the Zenica Steelworks. In August 1935, German coal and steel giant Gutehoffnungshütte offered to build a rolling mill in Zenica and be paid from the Yugoslav money on the clearing account in Berlin: 'The German-Yugoslav clearing account offers at the moment an unusually favourable opportunity to settle the debt, purely from the perspective of Yugoslavian economic interests, as a result of the build-up of the [German] debt.'[68] This deal, worth 8 million Reichsmarks, was of such importance that it was part of the discussions at the Zagreb meeting of the Mixed Committee, where it was officially decided that its construction would be financed by the Yugoslav clearing credit in Berlin.[69] In March 1936, Yugoslavia signed a contract with Krupp for the construction of rolling mill in Zenica, which started in June the same year and finished in October 1937. The purpose of modernizing the Zenica Steelworks was to render it capable of producing steel and rolled iron of high profiles, which Yugoslavia had to import. This was a step towards supplying the domestic market, although only small, with much-needed domestic steel and also a way to save up to 200 million dinars a year in imports.

The construction of the rolling mill was not supposed to be the only investment in Zenica, as the Yugoslav government also contemplated the building of a coking plant, the plant for petroleum extraction from coal, weapons manufacture and some other smaller installations. The total cost of all these planned works exceeded 600 million dinars. In addition to three already existing Siemens-Martin open hearth furnace, the construction of the fourth was completed in April 1938 and Zenica began to produce steel in the following month. The capacity of the fourth furnace was 30,000 tons of steel per year, while the earlier three already possessed a combined capacity of 20,000 tons. With further improvements to be made, it was expected that Zenica steelworks could reach annual production of 80,000 tons of steel.[70] It was anticipated that in 1938, Zenica would produce 35,000 tons of railway tracks for the needs of the Yugoslav Railways, as opposed to 9,150 tons of tracks imported in 1936.[71]

Although the largest of its kind, Zenica was not the first major deal agreed to be paid from the German clearing debt. In April 1935, the Siemens representative in Belgrade sent an offer to the Transport Ministry for the sale of equipment for Yugoslavia's telephone network. The recommended sale was worth 3.625 million Reichsmarks and was to be paid from the Yugoslav credit in Berlin. The letter contained a reminder that the existing system was manufactured by Siemens; therefore, an investment into its modernization with the effect of increasing the number of telephone subscribers in Yugoslavia would become a necessity sooner or later.[72] Later that year, Yugoslav government bought the machinery and installations for the partly state-owned gold mine in Slišane village, near Leskovac (Serbia). The sale worth 800,000 Reichsmarks was agreed with the German company Humboldt-Deutz Motoren.[73] These compensation deals corresponded with the Yugoslav modernizing needs and the country overall benefitted from these investments. It could be seen as a kind of capital importing, and according to Božidar Jurković there was nothing wrong with it, as long as Yugoslavia was able to use it rationally.[74]

The idea of using Yugoslavia's credit in Berlin for financing large infrastructural works was not very different to the use of German deliveries in kind in the 1920s, before the war reparations ended in 1931. In both situations, Yugoslavia was trying to get what Germany owed and use it for modernization purposes. Zagreb-based *Yugoslav Lloyd* pointed to this when, in the words of Vladimir Skerl, the head of the Economic Department of the Central Press Bureau, it stressed that it was natural for Yugoslavia to use the funds which it already had at its disposal in Berlin. Skerl tried to calm down some fears from abroad that such a practice facilitated German economic penetration. In his words, this was 'our own capital which [in this way] we merely returned to the country. ... At the moment [the government] sees no other way of returning our capital frozen on clearing accounts in Germany.'[75] This was true; Yugoslavia had no capacity to buy as much of German finished and semi-finished products, as Germany was buying Yugoslav food, fodder and raw materials. This was clear to most of the decision makers, but also to the National Union of Yugoslav Industry for Iron and Metal Works. At their annual meeting in February 1936, the industrialists supported the idea of eliminating Germany's clearing debt in this way, but not at the expense of domestic industry. They understood that with each rise of Germany's clearing debt the Reichsmark's rate fell, which made German exports cheaper. However, they insisted on a planned and careful approach, to avoid a mistake of placing state purchases with German companies at any cost, even when there was a capacity of domestic industry to deliver the product or service.[76]

The idea of compensation deals for Yugoslav state purchases was also slowly developing in Berlin throughout 1935. As early as January 1935, Sarnow listed a number of projects in which German industry would be especially interested. The first on the list was a call for supply of railway carriages to the Yugoslav Railways, worth 2.1 million Reichsmarks and was to be concluded as a compensation deal for deliveries of Yugoslav tobacco. Secondly, the company named Klöckner

Reederei und Kohlenhandel from Duisburg was said to be interested in exporting 20,000 tons of coke worth 8.5 million dinars for the iron mill in Vareš (Bosnia) and in further deliveries for the Yugoslav War Ministry. Julius Pintsch, a Berlin-based company, was interested in the export of lightning equipment for trains, worth 3 million Reichsmarks. There was a bitter contest over delivery of a cable-railway for the quarry in Rakovac near Novi Sad; although there was a tough competition from many European companies for this job, Sarnow was hopeful that it could be given to German companies Pohlig from Cologne and Bleichert Transportanlagen from Leipzig. The biggest prize of course was to be a construction of the iron mill in Zenica, which lined up numerous German companies under the Krupp banner.[77] In September 1935, in correspondence with Sarnow, Hess of the German legation in Belgrade also recommended compensation deals as a solution to the problem of German clearing debt.[78] By that time, compensation deals were already a reality, as in July the Yugoslav Railways had concluded a deal for the train carriages paid with the delivery of Yugoslav tobacco.[79] There were many more agreements reached between Yugoslavia and various German manufacturers from 1935 on.

But the German side was still not satisfied with the pace and scope of these business deals. In March 1935, Heeren complained to the then Finance Minister Stojadinović that the conditions for state tenders were set up in such a way as to be unattractive for German bidders.[80] In September that year, Fritz Reinhardt, State Secretary of the Reich's Finance Ministry, made the assumption that German bidders at the Yugoslav tenders for public infrastructure works had been deliberately circumvented despite, in his opinion, them submitting the best offers. The case was raised of the company Vögele, which had lost couple of bids for railway and tram works in Yugoslavia to Czechoslovakian Vítkovice.[81] Bizarrely, at the very same time the Yugoslav manufacturers were complaining about the opposite, that the German firms were given preference in public tenders after recommendations from the National Bank. While some companies simply complained that, given another devaluation of the Reichsmark since the introduction of the private clearing in November 1935, the Yugoslav bidders could not compete in prices with the German companies, the Union of Yugoslav Industry for Iron and Metal Works specifically complained about the National Bank's prioritizing of German firms.[82] This was not far from the truth, as in May 1935 the Yugoslav National Bank asked of Finance Ministry that all the ministries and local and regional authorities be instructed to 'make all public purchases in Germany, which is demanded by the economic and financial interests of our country'; at that time, German debt was already 300 million dinars.[83] In February 1937, leading Yugoslav industrialists blamed the government for its 'tendency to acquire large quantities of material from abroad, which could be produced domestically and to offer large construction works, which could be done by domestic firms, to foreign companies'. The state officials were accused of changing legal procedures as it suited them in order to give tenders to foreign bidders; couple of examples of such practices were listed.[84] Any favouring of foreign capital was legally problematic, as since July 1934 the Yugoslav authorities had brought in a set of measures to protect domestic industry. According to it, any foreign bidder at the public tender had to make an offer at least 15 per cent lower than a Yugoslav company in order to be successful.[85]

At first, it was thought that setting up import controls in June 1936 would change this situation. In October 1936, the National Bank urged the Finance Ministry to terminate the prioritizing of state purchases from Germany, as it was expected that the German clearing debt would shrink.[86] As we have seen, these hopes failed and the National Bank had no other solution than to suggest further prioritization of state purchases from Germany whenever purchases from abroad were necessary. As late as December 1938, the argument was the same: in order to eliminate money trapped on the Yugoslav clearing accounts, it was necessary to make all state purchases, either by the government or by regional or local councils, whenever possible, from the clearing countries, which effectively meant Germany, 'for the sake of financial and economic interests of our country'.[87] In January 1936, the instruction came from the highest level. In a letter to Vrbanić, Stojadinović suggested that the former should 'give an order to [Vrbanić's] subordinate officials who are in charge of state tenders, to pay special attention to offers made by German industry'. The Prime Minister had previously explained that this was the way in which to reduce the German clearing debt which dangerously threatened to halt the mutual trade.[88] Stojadinović's letter did not specify whether this should always be the case, or only when tenders did not include domestic bidders. For Yugoslavia's authorities, favouring German bidders temporarily eased Yugoslav financial situation, but in the long run was harmful for domestic industrial development. At the same time, the balance of payments with Germany became too dependent on state purchases, as the purchasing power of Yugoslavia's economy was still too weak for such a large volume of mutual trade.

According to a communication between the National Bank and the Trade and Industry Ministry in Belgrade during the Munich meeting of the Mixed Committee in February 1935, the German side made their purchases of Yugoslav tobacco conditional upon the placement of Yugoslav state purchases with German companies.[89] However, at this time both sides spoke only in general terms and no binding regulation emerged from it. Within a year, things had changed and at the Zagreb meeting of Mixed Committee in April 1936, the Yugoslav side presented a list of purchases to be paid from the Yugoslav credit in Berlin. The War Ministry placed orders amounting to between 6.5 and 8.3 million Reichsmarks, which included a steel pontoon bridge, military terrain vehicles, various military equipment, signalling devices and forty-five hydroplanes. The Transport Ministry ordered railway material and between seventeen and twenty locomotives of unspecified value, to be paid in six annual instalments. The Communications Ministry ordered telephone cables worth between 8 and 9 million Reichsmarks, the Agriculture and Trade and Industry Ministries placed orders for construction of a silo and a flax mill worth over 2.5 million Reichsmarks and the Constructions Ministry ordered forty-five stone crushing machines worth 350,000 Reichsmarks.[90]

The question remains why the Yugoslavs agreed to both, placing large state purchases with the German companies and introducing import controls at the same time in the spring of 1936. As we have seen, the import controls were agreed to correct the imbalance on clearing accounts in trade with Germany. But this was far from being the only Yugoslav economic problem. The other measure, placement of large purchases with German companies, was directly linked to Yugoslavia's urge to industrialize and simultaneous impossibility of getting favourable international loans for this purpose, which implied the lack of working capital. The government was already heavily indebted to the National Bank and due to a budget deficit, it became impossible to pay claims of various government contractors. Yugoslavia also had to pay regular annual interest to its foreign creditors, which in 1932 amounted to 26 per cent of total government spending.[91] The country struggled to finance its modernization and every help from any corner was welcome. If Germany was willing to do compensations, or pay its debt by getting its companies to undertake large projects in the Yugoslav infrastructure, which Britain and France were not, then it made sense to use that possibility.

## Germany and modernization of Yugoslavia's agriculture

Stojadinović's government favoured industrialization but did not neglect the modernizing needs of Yugoslavia's agriculture. It targeted the increasing in production of those crops which could best be used for the needs of domestic industry. Yugoslavia possessed favourable conditions for the development of those branches of industry which were closely related to agriculture, such as textile and food and drinks industries. But this potential was never fully exploited as agricultural production was traditionally concentrated on wheat and maize, while many industrial crops, which could have been grown domestically, were imported.[92] A big problem was the intrinsic conservatism of the Yugoslav peasantry, stemming from having little knowledge of the modern techniques of land cultivation, poor education, but also from a distrust in state institutions and their policies which they felt did not benefit farmers.[93]

Modernization in this field primarily meant increased exports of those products which could get higher prices outside Yugoslavia and were already known to its farmers. Again, this is where the German market came to the fore. Hemp is a good illustration of how the 1934 Trade Agreement with Germany stimulated an increased cultivation and export of those plants which were already traditionally produced in the country. In 1932 and 1933, hemp export was worth approximately 40 million dinars a year, with the German share being one third of it. In 1934, hemp export doubled to 90 million, while German share rose to 41.5 million dinars.[94] The following year it doubled again, to 180 million dinars and exports to Germany increased to 57 million.[95] But this was only the beginning. In the summer of 1934, the German side warned Yugoslav representatives that their long-term export of wheat on the German market could not be guaranteed and suggested an adjustment of Yugoslav agricultural production more in line with the German needs.[96] This meant increased growing of soybeans and other industrial crops.

However, it would be an overstatement to ascribe the rise in production and export of some industrial crops solely as responding to German pressure. Also, in general terms the figures were relatively modest. The growth and export of soybeans to Germany increased eightfold in the period 1936–8, but in reality this was a modest increase from 685 hectares in 1936 to somewhat less than 1,700 hectares under soybeans in 1937, and 6,100 hectares in 1939.[97] Although this increase seems drastic, these numbers are very small. The Yugoslav production of soybeans was insignificant compared to Romanian and Bulgarian and especially with regard to German requirements: in 1939, Yugoslavia exported 3,200 tons of soybeans out of 89,000 tons Germany imported from South-Eastern Europe, or a mere 3.6 per cent.[98] The same goes for other industrial crops. Overall, apart from the increase in hemp production in the period 1932–8 (21,000 to 55,000 tons), other industrial crops for the same period either experienced modest increase, or even decreased, such as tobacco (17,000 to 15,800 tons).[99] The mentality of Yugoslav farmers, who had rarely opted to change the crops they had cultivated for generations, remained a stumbling block.[100] Overall, the area of land where industrial crops were grown increased by 45 per cent in the period 1934–7, from 115,000 to 165,000 hectares, but this was still an increase from a mere 1.6 to 2.7 per cent of the total area of cultivated land in Yugoslavia.[101] And this increase even slowed down in the period 1937–9, from 165,000 to 195,000 hectares.[102] Importantly, this modest increase coincided not only with the existing German pressure, but also with the growing need in Yugoslavia for hemp, linen, tobacco, poppy, hops, sugarbeet, cotton, etc.

German capital was active in stimulating agricultural exports from Yugoslavia. In October 1935, the Agriculture Ministry in Belgrade regarded favourably an application by a number of German manufacturers from a consortium led by the Society for Cereal Trade[103] from Berlin, to set up a joint-stock company for export of oilseeds from Yugoslavia. The idea was to bring under its umbrella all the domestic oil refineries and cooperatives of oilseeds farmers, with the main purpose of promoting and assisting the production of oilseeds. The move was authorized by the National Bank, provided that the money for Yugoslav share in this venture was taken from the Yugoslav credit in Berlin.[104] Increased cultivation of oilseeds in Yugoslavia had already been discussed at the Munich meeting of the Mixed Committee earlier that year. In June 1935, the German side sent a nervous letter to Pilja, warning him that it had been waiting far too long for the two sides to finally agree on the modalities of oilseeds production in Yugoslavia. It was stated that any further delay of necessary actions might jeopardize the yield of the 1936 harvest.[105] Two German initiatives, one official for promoting cultivation in Yugoslavia and another one private, for promoting exports to Germany, went hand in hand. Berlin continued to encourage Yugoslavia's efforts to modernize its agriculture with various inducements for Yugoslav export. After the meeting of the Mixed Committee in Dubrovnik in September 1937, Germany revoked its previous quota of 12,000 tons for Yugoslav hemp and allowed its unrestricted import; it was now limited only by the overall condition of the clearing accounts.[106]

German initiatives were not different from the wishes of the Yugoslav officials and the public opinion regarding the needs for agricultural modernization. Government's decree in June 1936 aimed to increase the land cultivation for oilseeds in order to reduce the importation of crops which could be grown successfully in the country.[107] This measure seemed justified, as there was an increase in production of oilseeds in 1936, namely a quadrupled rise in production of both rapeseed (2,300 wagons compared to 544 in 1934) and sunflower (1,400 to 343 in 1934).[108] Another reason was an increasing domestic need for cooking oil, which was one of the products Yugoslavia was importing.[109] The decree gave a minimum price, which in a short period of time did bring a sustainability of Yugoslavia's oil production and consumption, and even a surplus of oilseeds and cooking oil for export. A similar decree referring to cotton production was introduced in October that year. It resulted in a rapid increase in area under cotton, though still small; it doubled from 1936 to 1937, from 1,000 to 2,000 hectares and quintupled by 1939. In the same period 1936–9, the production of ginned cotton increased sixfold, from 200 to 1,200 tons.[110] Another two bills before the end of 1936 regulated silk and wool production. These bills guaranteed the price to be paid to farmers, but were not meant to have a detrimental effect on Yugoslav industry, as manufacturers were guaranteed preferential prices with the difference being paid from a special fund set up by the Agriculture Ministry.[111] Importers were not granted import permits before the whole domestic yield had been purchased. Another innovation was that industry now had to buy these materials directly from the producers, usually small farmers. In this way, a whole range of middlemen was wiped out.[112] The government also prided itself on investing more than 3 million dinars in the period 1935–7 in training the personnel and modernizing regional and local stations to control and maintain the quality of a number of sorts of fruits, vegetables, grains and industrial crops. Similar measures were applied in animal husbandry. By the order of the Education Ministry, the Faculty for Veterinary Medicine was founded in 1936 as part of the Belgrade University.[113] In April 1937, Agricultural Ministry provided a credit of 700,000 dinars to buy cattle of high-quality breading stock, mostly at the agricultural fairs around the country, to be distributed among secondary vocational schools for agriculture.[114]

Whether the German policies had stimulated these new initiatives in Yugoslav agriculture is hard to judge. Terzić disagreed that they had and concluded that the reason for this modernizing trend in Yugoslav agriculture was unstable world market prices of wheat and maize.[115] It also fitted the overall modernizing tendencies and activities of Stojadinović's government. Also, any increase in Yugoslavia's production of industrial crops was modest and insufficient for German needs. Despite all the efforts in Berlin and Belgrade in that direction, Germany remained the most important foreign market primarily for traditional Yugoslav agricultural products.

## Mutual importance

Yugoslavia's industrialization, although instigated by internal drives, needs of domestic market and wishes of Yugoslavia's elites, was significantly accelerated by the peculiarities of the German-Yugoslav trade relationship in the 1930s, not only by German capital investments in Yugoslavia, but also by the import of German-made machinery which kept fuelling Yugoslavia's industry. Two-thirds of the overall Yugoslav importation of machinery, tools and vehicles in the late 1930s was import from Germany. It would be superficial to ascribe this development merely to German wishes to subordinate Yugoslavia politically by using the foreign trade, or to explain it by the consequences of the Abyssinian Crisis; the figures for 1938 represented an increase in the overall import of machinery of 26 per cent to 1937. Clearly, there was an economic need in Yugoslavia which Germany was fulfilling.

In 1936, the Yugoslav statistics indicated that the import of machinery for the textile industry rose from 49 million dinars in 1935 to 73 million. In the following years, Yugoslavia maintained a steady import at this level and before the outbreak of war Germany supplied Yugoslavia's textile industry with three-quarters of all imported machines. To the contrary, in 1933 Yugoslavia imported textile machines worth 31.8 million dinars, of which Germany's share was only 4.5 million, or 14 per cent.[116] The same applies to Yugoslavia's import of motor vehicles, which doubled from 1,655 in 1936 to 3,217 in 1937, of which 2,366 vehicles, almost three-quarters, were cars and trucks imported from Germany.[117] Overall, 60 per cent of all Yugoslavia's imported machinery, tools and means of transport in 1937 were manufactured in Germany (463 million dinars out of total import of 734 million), while in 1939 goods of this kind manufactured in Germany covered a record 69 per cent of Yugoslavia's import (569 million dinars out of 826 million).[118] Industrial machinery contributed to 32 per cent of all the German exports to Yugoslavia in 1938.[119]

The progress Yugoslavia made in modernization of its economy is visible from changes in the structure of Yugoslavia's foreign trade. In the period 1937–9, Yugoslavia especially reduced its import of cotton fabrics, raw cotton and cotton yarn, pig iron, oilseeds, glassware and, to a lesser degree, ironware. What increased was the import of machinery, crude oil, anthracite, railway tracks, medicines, aluminium, vehicles and raw materials such as magnesium. At the same time, there was a steady increase in the export of smelted metals and the rise of income from their export. The sale of metals and ores reached 1.15 billion dinars in 1937, breaking the previous sales record from 1929, this time also including products such as crude lead, calcium carbide, sodium carbonate or ferromanganese.[120] Yugoslavia also became an exporter of some finished goods previously not in the list of its export commodities, such as chemical and pharmaceutical products. Simultaneously, the export of coal nearly halved in the period 1930–8; exports of pyrite, zinc and lead ores and their concentrates, chrome ore and raw copper also significantly decreased by the end of the 1930s.[121] Trade with Germany followed this pattern. In 1935, only 8 per cent of total imports from Germany belonged to the group of raw materials and semi-finished goods. Three years later, when the German share of Yugoslavia's foreign trade was significantly higher, it rose to 12 per cent.[122] However, the overall export of Yugoslav-finished goods also declined in the late 1930s. The explanation provided by German experts was the increased demand of domestic Yugoslav market, another development which feared the Germans.[123]

After the political events of March 1938 and March 1939, it was inevitable that Yugoslavia's foreign trade would end up overly dependent from the aggrandized German market, as the world market and free trade never fully recovered for some products after the Great Depression. At the same time, a constant increase in Yugoslavia's mining production in the period 1936–9 and the rise of domestic metallurgy, coupled with the foreign-political development in Europe in 1939, made Yugoslavia one of the leading European exporters of metals and material necessary for waging war. Germany was happy to exploit its hardly won position of Yugoslavia's most important customer, by being the principal buyer of Yugoslavia's metals and raw materials. In the period 1936–9, German share of Yugoslavia's export of raw materials reached 52 per cent.[124] The example of bauxite is illustrative. In 1934, Germany purchased 70 per cent of Yugoslav bauxite for export; in 1935 and 1936, this share rose to 90 per cent, and in 1937 it reached 99.99 per cent.[125] In the first six months of 1937, Yugoslavia covered 44.3 per cent of the German import of bauxite, 21 per cent of its need for lead ore, 14.35 per cent of magnesium, 8.7 per cent of copper and 6.4 per cent of ferrochome.[126] In 1938, Yugoslavia covered 20 per cent of German needs in building timber and was the second largest European supplier of hemp and flax, after Italy.[127] In the period 1932–9, Yugoslavia exported 19,000 tons of ferrosilicon and more than 60 per cent of this was exported to German and Austrian markets. Germany was also the main customer of the Yugoslav ferrochrome; of 4,250 tons of ferrochrome which Yugoslavia exported in 1935–9, almost 65 per cent was exported to Germany.[128] Yugoslav annual production of antimony reached 1,000 tons by 1940 and Germany was the major customer. The Yugoslav production fulfilled one quarter of Germany's overall need for this material.[129] In October 1939, Yugoslavia doubled exports of lead to Germany from 1,500 tons to 3,000 tons monthly, as well as exports of copper, from 1,000 to 2,000 tons.

At the same time, Germany remained one of the most important importers of Yugoslavia's grain and other agricultural products. Much to the annoyance of Berlin, the nature of these exports depended on Yugoslavia's ability to sell its wheat and maize for cash in the world markets. For example, in 1937 Britain imported the Yugoslav maize worth 202 million dinars, or more than 40 per cent of all the maize Yugoslavia exported that year.[130] According to an agreement reached with France in November 1936, Yugoslavia exported 150,000 tons of wheat for cash on favourable terms, although at that time the two countries still regulated their mutual trade via clearing.[131] However, these were occasional demands and in 1938 almost all Yugoslav wheat for export went to Germany. After the Anschluss and the creation of the Protectorate, the Greater Reich absorbed terrifying proportions of some Yugoslav agricultural export products: 72 per cent of all Yugoslav hemp, 70 per cent of cattle, 99 per cent of pigs, 68 per cent of poultry, 92 per cent of fresh meats, 98 per cent of bacon, 99 per cent of lard, 51 per cent of eggs, 52 per cent of fish, 83 per cent of wool, almost 100 per cent of feathers, 94 per cent of fresh fruit, etc.[132]

According to a secret report for internal use during the preparations for the state visit of Prince Paul in June 1939, it was of particular importance to secure this existing share of the Yugoslav exports to Germany and to provide concessions for exploitation of Yugoslav oil.[133] This illustrates the principal value which Yugoslavia had in German geo-strategic planning and how sensitive Germany was to any change in this delicate relationship. In 1938, the Yugoslav share of the overall German bauxite imports fell to 29 per cent, from 44 per cent a year earlier, a result of the beginning of Yugoslavia's own production of aluminium in Lozovac.[134] This was a dire reminder to Berlin of the dangers which industrialization in South-Eastern Europe bore for Germany's war economy.

## The deployment of Germany's soft power

The beginnings of Germany's economic offensive in South-Eastern Europe coincided with Germany's economic recovery in the mid-1920s, the conclusion of important political agreements with the Western powers, such as the Dawes Plan in 1924, Locarno Pact in 1925 and German adherence to the League of Nations in 1926, but also with the setting up of some big industrial conglomerates, such as IG Farben in December 1925 and the United Steelworks[135] in 1926.[136] The Danube region and the Balkans were areas where France had already established its economic dominance, exerted mostly through the capital state loans to regional governments, and political influence through a series of military agreements. Because of its political and military weakness, the only way for Germany to combat French dominance in the region was through the economy. There were voices among the economists, industrialists and diplomats who urged Germany to work in partnership with its European rival. These voices grew louder after the Locarno Treaty and the French initiative for a tighter political cooperation in Europe through the so-called European Customs Union. Interested in cooperation with Western partners were representatives of light industries, the chemical industry and the electrical industry. Leaders of these sectors of German industry saw the opportunity to sell their products on French- and British-controlled markets.[137] They faced a strong opposition from the representatives of heavy industries, who insisted that Germany still possessed enough economic capacity to match and eventually overpower France. In 1926, leaders of the Union of German Iron and Steel Industries described any aspiration towards the European customs union as a utopia, as collective agreements of such nature were detrimental to the national sovereignty. Instead, they favoured mutual agreements with other countries based on custom tariffs, which was in their opinion the only way to militarily rearm Germany and regain a position of power. Eventually, the representatives of the heavy industry came out victorious from this conflict of ideas.[138] The most important problem which they all faced was the destroyed network of Germany's trade representations in East-Central and South-Eastern Europe. Without the proper information, it was hard to establish strategy or to direct the trade. Even the largest corporations suffered heavily in this regard during the early 1920s, let alone the small firms without any knowledge of the local markets.[139]

The confrontation between political and economic arguments was a constant cause of friction in German internal political dialogue in the 1920s. Getting answers to these dilemmas and creating a common strategy for both politics and the economy were an important motivation behind the MWT. It was actually first organized by two non-German economists, Elemér Hantos and Julius Meinl in Vienna in 1925.[140] The initial motivation for its founders was the speed of Germany's economic integration with East-Central Europe. They claimed that any sudden dissolution of borders and tariffs would dangerously expose fragile Central European economies. Instead they suggested economic integration of the region based on tariff agreements and modelled after Locarno. Initially, MWT focused broadly on the region of Central-Eastern Europe.[141] The establishment of an organization concerned with the political and economic structures and problems of the Danube region in a German-speaking country was not unusual in the 1920s, which saw proliferation of similar institutions across Germany, such as the East-European Institute in Breslau, Research Society for Central and South-Eastern Europe in Berlin, Central-European Institute in Dresden, or the Institute for the Economic Research of Central and South-Eastern Europe in Leipzig.[142] The one thing they all had in common was their denial of the *status quo* in post-1918 Europe, which was widespread across all levels of German society.[143] What was different about the MWT was its strong links with German industrial circles. Although founded in Vienna, MWT had its branches across Central Europe. By 1931, its German section completely took over the organization and reshaped its agenda. From then onwards, it lost its international character and despite its name, the focus of the organization turned solely onto South-Eastern Europe.[144] In 1938, Tilo von Wilmowsky, the new president of MWT, described it as a society for building private economic links with South-Eastern Europe.[145]

The question is where the MWT fitted inside the decision-making process of the German economic and political life in the 1930s. An earlier view, particularly from the GDR historians, saw MWT as an instrument of German imperialism for making contacts with conservative circles in South-Eastern European countries, with the aim of steering their economies and foreign policies towards Germany and this viewpoint cannot be contradicted.[146] Big challenges for German economy at the turn of the decade, in the form of the Great Depression, the drive towards autarchy, the Creditanstalt affair and failure of the planned Austro-German customs union, combined with the first preferential tariffs agreements which Germany reached with Romania and Hungary, all brought the German section of MWT to the fore of an interest of Germany's largest associations of heavy industry and large business, such as *Langnam-Verein*, RDI and the Association of German Chambers of Industry and Commerce.[147] They saw MWT as a useful tool for their own political-economic drive towards the south-east and a weapon against the French influence.[148] Their understanding of the future development of German foreign trade was best described by Carl Duisberg, the chairman of the RDI and one of the leaders of IG Farben in October 1930: an economy oriented towards exports such was Germany's could not be allowed to depend on the moods of the world market. It should seek to create its own economic area for the sale of German industrial products, from which any competition would be excluded. It should consist of two zones, the industrial core of Germany, Austria and Czechoslovakia and the agricultural periphery of South-Eastern Europe. These two zones would gradually increase their mutual trade. According to Duisberg, the agricultural periphery should be prevented from industrializing.[149]

In a rapid takeover in 1930–1, the old leadership of MWT had to step down and all the opponents of the German line in the Vienna headquarters were replaced by more cooperative representatives. Georg Gothein, the first leader of the German section, remained a pro forma co-president, but the real power was now with the representatives of the Ruhr industries: Max Schlenker; Max Hahn; Wilmowsky; the companies such as Siemens, Krupp, and IG Farben; and the biggest German banks, such as Deutsche Bank and Dresdner Bank.[150] Wilmowsky later claimed that in 1930 representatives of the German industry, largest banks and the most influential families from the Ruhr decided to reorganize MWT and downgrade its scope to South-Eastern Europe. In his own words, Hahn explained at the time the reasons for this twist in one sentence: 'German foreign trade with the south-east was a tragedy.'[151] Wilmowsky himself described the method for correcting this state of affairs in the talk he gave in November 1938: 'A successful policy for obtaining raw materials in the south-east could only happen when the German economy grasps in its hands the development of [the region's] mining.'¹⁵² Another contemporary, Alfred Sohn-Rethel, a research assistant for MWT in its headquarters in Berlin, later described MWT as a vehicle for reunification of German big business on the basis of a common policy.¹⁵³

MWT was opposed to the narrow interpretation of the autarchy and favoured the idea of one large economic space in which Germany could trade with the countries politically and economically dependent on it. Their own weekly publication, *Mitteilungen des MWT*, in March 1936 analysed the economic situation in the Danube region and insisted that neither the Little Entente nor the countries of the Rome Protocols possessed enough economic capacity to reach sustainability, as they were both burdened with political aspirations which determined their economic activities. Only Germany could have absorbed the region's production surpluses, provided it matched German needs.¹⁵⁴ Such ideas not only stemmed from the economic reasoning, but were also inspired by the laws of physics and astronomy which were popular at that time, particularly by the notion of gravitational attraction of stars and their planets.¹⁵⁵ The most suitable policy for such a concept was not free trade, but mutual trade agreements with other countries. Already at this time the concept of a greater economic area implied a planned production in dependant countries of only those goods which would be needed by the German market.

The Nazi seizure of power in January 1933 was in a way a setback for MWT, as many connections built up with the officials of previous administrations lost their value. Wilmowsky and Krupp quickly realized how difficult it would be to work with the likes of Hugenberg or Göring. Wilmowsky, being an advocate of modernization in agriculture, had to withstand fierce attacks by Darré, while other Nazis were particularly spiteful towards Schlenker. Hahn had no such problems and in April 1933, at the first meeting of MWT after Hitler's ascent to power, he stated that the conditions were still favourable for the organization to continue towards its aims. However, he struggled to impose his view on representatives of heavy industry, who were disturbed by the anti-capitalist rhetoric used by the Nazis. On the other hand, MWT never managed to get a clear confirmation from the Nazi leadership as to what exactly its task was in the new circumstances. There were of course common interests between the two and MWT leadership greeted Hitler's government as a force against communism. Most importantly, as South-Eastern Europe was of little interest to Hitler, MWT had freedom to pursue their goals throughout the 1930s.¹⁵⁶ But even then, there were struggles and MWT had to withstand criticism that investments such as the one in Zenica damaged German exports.¹⁵⁷ At the beginning of 1940, the South-Eastern European Society, *Südosteuropa Gesellschaft* (henceforth SOEG), was founded in Vienna under the auspices of Walther Funk. Its presidency consisted of the leading Nazi and SS officials in Austria, while the person who appeared in public to front the organization was August Heinrichsbauer, Funk's personal contact with the leading Ruhr industrialists well before the Nazis took power in Germany. MWT soon realized that the SOEG was a rival organization, set up by the party for conducting the Reich's policy in the south-east. The two organizations remained locked in a struggle for influence throughout the war.¹⁵⁸

Most of the time, MWT and Schacht were on the same side against the overly rigid and aggressive Nazi politicians. It was Schacht's success in obtaining a free hand from

Hitler in all economic matters which abated the political pressure exercised by various Nazi officials on leaders of German business society.[159] However, the most important difference between Schacht and the proponents of the so-called Drive to the South-East, *Drang nach Südosten*, was that the former's policy prioritized imports and required only sufficient exports as it was enough to pay for imports; the other side was oriented towards turning South-Eastern Europe into an exclusively German export market. While Schacht in this area mainly cared about short-term interests for the sake of the German economic recovery and rearming, the MWT had developed a broad platform of long-term relationship with South-Eastern Europe, based on increasing the average purchasing power and living standard of their population in order to increase sales of German-manufactured goods there. Nevertheless, Schacht's demand that the largest corporations search for the foreign buyers themselves in non-industrial countries of Latin America and South-Eastern Europe and sell their goods in compensation deals enabled many of them to find a sustainable base for their own raw materials needs. In this way, the largest German companies became part of the official policy as defined by the New Plan.[160] But not all companies were successful; for example, Siemens struggled to get adequate exchange allocations in its purchase of materials such as copper or lead from South-Eastern Europe.[161]

The attitude of MWT in regard to the industrialization of the European south-east changed before the war, towards the greater reciprocity in mutual relations between the Reich and the Balkans. This was mostly due to Max Ilgner's obsession with transforming South-Eastern European states by providing the German technical and financial assistance in developing regional agriculture, investing in new industries and transportation and in general improving the standard of living. Ilgner spoke as both the vice-president of MWT and one of the IG Farben leaders. However, any change in the general direction of the German political or economic planning was out of question and this situation shows the political naivety of some of MWT's leaders.[162] The main purpose of the increased direct foreign investment in the region's industries after 1938 was to fight off the competition, not to serve as a basis for further industrialization. Taking IG Farben as the example, this meant that the protection of its export interests still remained the most important feature of their strategy. The same is true for the company's participation in various projects in cooperation with MWT, with the aim of raising local populations' purchasing power. But this was only to be done if it was complementary to the needs of the German economy and in order to protect the company's export positions on the local markets.[163] Siemens was also opposed to industrialization in South-Eastern Europe and, like IG Farben, was willing to directly invest in industrial production only when that meant fending off the competition.[164]

In a speech held in Vienna in September 1940, Ilgner called for stronger German engagement in the development of South-Eastern European economies. He pointed out that in the past there had been some confusion regarding the term 'industrialization' in this area, and instead he suggested the phrase 'intensification' of economy. By this he meant the focus of each country on their *natural* production capacities. According to Ilgner, the concerns of German exporters would be justified if the intensification of economies in question was unorganized, as strong industrial development was not a characteristic of those countries based in agriculture. Only great powers with large and wealthy populations were predestined to reach full industrialization.[165] Ilgner stated that the future of the south-east lay in a parallel and mutually complementary development with Germany. Such economic collaboration also implied political coordination, and combined together these two were the foundations of the *Wirtschaftsraum*, which excluded any drive towards economic autarchy of individual countries belonging to this economic area. One of the tasks of German policy was to increase an average purchasing power of their populations, so that they could buy more German products. As this was a long-term objective, it was first necessary to satisfy the most basic needs of these people by improving agricultural production. The main task in this sense was to increase the average yield per hectare with the use of fertilizers and modern agricultural machinery. The second stage required the construction of modern infrastructure, energy supply systems and the improvements in mining. The final stage would be the development of domestic consumer industries. As mechanized agricultural production increased, more peasant would become unemployed, meaning some would need to retrain to work in industry, while others could be used for the needs of the German economy. Parallel to this process, those workers who remained in agriculture would gradually improve their living standard and purchasing power. In due time, this process would increase the national income of South-Eastern European countries by a third. Finally, Ilgner expressed his strong belief that such a development represented the best guarantee of a continuous progress in South-Eastern Europe. As an example, Ilgner mentioned the British Empire and the economic solutions reached at the Ottawa Conference in 1932.[166]

However, any parallel with the British Empire was ill-suited, as the Ottawa Conference ended with the agreement between Great Britain and eight autonomous governments. And in his speech, Ilgner denied the expression of a national political and economic free-will to other member states of the German economic area:

> Guidelines for future German economic relations with the states of the south-east are wrapped up simply in the framework of the foreign policy of the Great German Reich and indeed within the position which Greater Germany holds today within the European economy ... This framework is clearly outlined and naturally comprises of the intensification of agricultural production and acquisition of raw materials to a degree which covers German needs.[167]

Despite their declared interest in an increase in general living standards in the southeast, the leading men of MWT hardly differed much in the scope of their strategic thinking from the Nazi elite. The difference was in the method: Nazi *Lebensraum* implied hard-power and physical subjection of the conquered people, while MWT's approach implied soft-power tactics with the aim of dictating orders to dependent governments. But both sought to control and denied free-will to the objects of their policies.

The same could be said for other similar institutions which were nothing more than tools for the deployment of German soft power in the region. In the period 1939–41, under the presidency of Walter Lörch, the Central-European Institute in Dresden steered away from advocating an export offensive towards the south-east and instead began propagating a hierarchically structured New Order. The Institute sought to ideologically justify German hegemony over South-Eastern Europe.[168] One might argue that people like Lörch and Hahn, although perhaps personally not devoted to Nazism, changed their views and hardened their approach with every political and military success Hitler had. Also, it should not be forgotten that they all belonged to the era they lived in. They grew up in a time when Friedrich Ratzel first made public the definition of *Lebensraum*, while people like Ernst Jäckh and Karl Helfferich popularized the idea of a liberal *Weltpolitik*, an approach which favoured the creation of an economic block under the German control, without formal annexation.[169] The period which followed, when they established themselves as successful business leaders, was politically defined by the ideological crisis and chaos of the Weimar Republic and culturally with Social Darwinism and popular receptions of Nietzsche's ideas, despite how those ideas were brutally vulgarized to make them more receptive to the conservative elements in interwar German society. At the same time, Karl Haushofer announced that the natural German living space was in *Mitteleuropa*.[170] The gap between the concept of the Nazi's *Lebensraum* and the MWT's and similar institutions' concepts of informal economic empire was only as wide as was the class difference between their main proponents.

The influence of MWT's propagandist efforts and its cooperation with other institutions in charge of imposing German soft power in Yugoslavia are exemplified by conclusion presented in Ivan Crnić's book *Yugoslavia's Iron Industry in the Framework of the Yugoslav Economy*, published in Germany in 1938. In the final chapter, one about Yugoslavia's iron and steel industry, the author recommended a *rational* development of the Yugoslav metal industry, with focus on those sectors of industrial production which could best serve everyday needs in Yugoslavia, namely the consumer industry: 'The production of ... machinery is not worth it in Yugoslavia due to a small market; it does not make sense to build up an entire industry for the sake of barely a hundred machines.' In his opinion, Yugoslavia's industry should only make products of mass consumption and not 'factory machines, the products of high quality and above all refined and complicated products'.[171] The author obviously did not take into consideration the possible export value of such products. This book was Crnić's converted PhD dissertation, submitted at the University of Cologne, for which he received a scholarship by the MWT-DAAD in 1936.[172] In a report on his progress, Crnić thanked MWT for the scholarship and his professors who 'made it easier [for Crnić] to understand various problems of German economic and cultural life'.[173]

The 1930s Germany witnessed a proliferation of books, reviews, newspaper articles and periodicals about the political, economic, demographic, cultural, geographic and other characteristics and problems of South-Eastern Europe; some were discussed in the first chapter of this book. All these publications reiterated that Germany was a natural partner for the agricultural states of South-Eastern Europe and reminded their readers of important political changes which occurred with the foundation of the Great German Reich; at the same time, they constantly emphasized the region's richness in mineral wealth and natural resources. This fitted well into an argument that Germany needed to create an economic area under its control and it all led towards the formulation of the theory of complementary economies. While the official political and economic approach provided the basis for *Drang nach Südosten*, it was the theory which offered an ideological justification for it.¹⁷⁴ This was necessary in order to provide Germany with an ethically higher ground, the one which excluded any German political intentions and insisted on purely economic cooperation for the benefit of all sides. Yugoslavia's or any other regional country's economic cooperation with another great power was immediately stigmatized as political in nature. Accordingly, other great powers with economic and political interests in the region were often referred to as powers alien to the region, *raumfremden Machte*.¹⁷⁵ Milan Ristović analysed the ideas of the Reich's leading experts about the changes in economic and social structures of South-Eastern European countries in the period after the outbreak of war and their adjustment to the German economic needs. The theory of complementary economies continued to be the focal point of any such study, in pretty much the same manner as it was before September 1939. Ristović pointed out to a discrepancy between the theoretical thinking and a lack of any practical approach towards the implementation of such ideas. Without any systematic plan in the context of European wartime day-to-day, big plans for harmonization between the German industrial core and its agricultural periphery turned into a straightforward plunder of the latter's natural resources and a brutal dismantling of already existing industries, of both allied and conquered nations.¹⁷⁶

Andrej Mitrović pointed to a significant difference in the content of earlier and later publications in the 1930s, which was a consequence of some important political developments in Europe: the tone, phraseology and the use of more aggressive statements after 1938.¹⁷⁷ Ian Innerhofer pointed to Germany's opposition to both modernizing tendencies of regional economies and their industrialization, in an article about the German obsession with the term 'agrarian overpopulation' in this period.¹⁷⁸ The context was fear of shortfalls in foodstuffs and raw materials necessary for German economic recovery and rearming, due to excessive consumption by the enlarged population of exporting countries, which led directly to German economic planning for South-Eastern Europe. This planning, as already explained, meant the establishment of a united economic block of an agrarian periphery and the German industrial core, while industrialization of the periphery was possible only if it suited German needs.¹⁷⁹ It points out to the greatest pitfall in the theory of complementary economies and Yugoslavia's place in it, namely the theory's dislocation from the reality of the region's *own* industrial development.

## Yugoslav reaction to German economic theories

Some Yugoslav experts adopted the German position. While in conclusions of Ivan Crnić we may recognize traces of ideological indoctrination during the course of his stay in Germany, other more established Yugoslav experts simply adjusted their views over the time and possibly because they were impressed by German political and military achievements. In the summer of 1939, Croatian economist Rudolf Bićanić was very critical of Yugoslavia's economic orientation towards Germany. He numbered four important reasons against it: the first two revolved around the fact that Germany was much stronger partner in the mutual trade; therefore, it would be easy for Berlin to sacrifice trade with Yugoslavia for the sake of greater political and economic aims. Then, German economy was centralized and organized; therefore, it would have been easy for Berlin to direct the development of Yugoslavia's economy towards German import needs. And lastly, as Yugoslavia's economy was not organized in the same way, at some point Yugoslavia would probably have to either follow the German model or allow Germany to administer it to its own benefit.[180] A year later, Bićanić changed his views and spoke more optimistically about the prospects for the Yugoslav economy when oriented towards Germany. In this argument, stronger cooperation with Germany would enhance Yugoslavia's agricultural production, likewise its industry. Leaning towards Germany would quadruple Yugoslav mining production which would ease the problem of agrarian overpopulation. In turn, this would increase the purchasing power of Yugoslavia's population, which would lead to increased sales of German products on the Yugoslav market. In order to achieve this, Bićanić agreed that Yugoslavia should not develop heavy industry, but focus on consumer goods and light processing industries, while Germany would supply all domestic needs for machinery and chemical products.[181] Sava Ulmanski, professor at the Faculty of Agriculture in Zagreb and former Yugoslav senator, praised the Greater Economic Area as a reality and in January 1941 called for complete reorientation of the Yugoslav economy towards German economic needs, as Yugoslavia needed to coordinate with the centre of the New Order.[182] The former Agricultural Minister Oto Frangeš and Mirko Lamer, the editor of the Zagreb-based monthly economic magazine *Ekonomist*, also favoured stronger economic connections with Germany.[183]

Somewhere in between was Vladimir Bajkić, professor of political economy at the Faculty of Law in Belgrade and the founder and editor of *Narodno blagostanje*.[184] In 1934, he had a polemical exchange with the German economist called Hasselbach. Bajkić opposed the latter's accusations, published in *Berliner Börsen Courier*, that the agricultural countries of Eastern Europe abused clearing agreements with Germany by not purchasing enough of German goods. The two economic experts disagreed fundamentally on everything; the Yugoslav dismissed moving towards planned organization of the Yugoslav economy based on the German model and insisted that mutual trade should be the domain of private deals, not that of state regulations. He also disagreed that increased Yugoslav imports of German goods regulated by the state would do any good, as the purchasing power of the average Yugoslav was low. Bajkić claimed that the only lasting solution for Yugoslavia's economy was a more equal distribution of national wealth across all sectors of Yugoslav society and not just increasing the purchasing power of the peasantry, as '[other social classes] were better consumers of the German goods'.[185] And yet, after September 1939 *Narodno blagostanje* became more receptive towards the prospect of increased trade with Germany. It referred to Germany's increasing interest in the south east, which was more than mere economic exchange. In June 1940, the magazine praised the conclusions of the MWT's annual meeting in Vienna and spoke positively about the organization's attempts to increase the technical skills of the people in the southeast through organized training in modern agricultural methods.[186]

Ljubomir Kosier, another distinguished Croatian economist, spoke at length about mutually complementary economies, of Yugoslavia as a natural market for German industrial products and *vice versa*. The Anschluss was beneficial for Yugoslavia, as it finally ended Vienna's mediatory role and the common border increased mutual trade as Yugoslavia 'did not have to deal with two custom areas anymore, but with only one'. But talking about the importance of South-Eastern Europe as only complementary space to the German economy, Kosier cautiously expressed doubts regarding awarding a similar role to Yugoslavia. He pointed out that the German success was a result of the inability of Western powers to maintain their positions in the region. Kosier's conclusion was somewhat ambivalent: 'In these chaotic and stormy times, it is a requirement of each government to achieve the coordination of both its economic and its foreign policy in relations with other countries, in the way which does not contradict the requirements of national defence.'[187]

It is important to stress that although a proportionally larger number of Croatian economists and businessmen supported stronger economic cooperation with Germany than their Serbian counterparts, no particular ideological or political standpoint should be read from it. From the first days of Yugoslavia, industrially more developed western and northern parts of the country continued to nurture hitherto existing economic ties with their Central European partners. After the Anschluss and incorporation of Bohemia and Moravia into Germany, most of their business contacts and contracts were merged into the Reich. It was only natural that the Croatian business elite favoured the economic policy which would best protect their interests. At the same time, many holders of the highest national offices from Croatia were vehement opponents of the closer Yugoslav integration within the *Grosswirtschaftsraum*. These included Ivo Belin, who persistently championed Yugoslavia's orientation towards the international markets and published articles in the Yugoslav press along those lines; Edo Marković, the director of Prizad since 1931; a group of liberal intellectuals gathered around the Zagreb-based journal *Nova Evropa* and others.[188]

On the other hand, members of the Serbian economic elites still remembered how easily Germany's hard power had trumped soft power and the liberal 'informal empire' approach during the First World War, for which pre-war Serbia paid a hefty price in material destruction, loss of human lives and economic plunder.[189] Berlin was seen as a fair and good business partner in times when German strength and influence were balanced, but as a hard master in times when it was politically and militarily unrestrained. Being used to cultivate a liberal economic policy in foreign trade, Serbian elites were opposed to economic and ideological concepts coming from Germany. In an article published in *Jugoslovenski ekonomist* in June 1936, Jovan Mihailović blasted the concept of economic autarchy and claimed that autarchic tendencies in the European economy only created a gulf between industrial and agrarian Europe. He saw the increase of the purchasing power in the Balkans only as the first step towards further industrialization and emphasized the need for increased international trade. Mihailović accused the Germans of putting an equation sign between the terms 'free trade' and 'international trade' and considered the latter necessary for European economic recovery.[190]

In September 1938, Vladimir Djordjević held a lecture in the premises of the Serbian Cultural Club where he spoke about the historical and contemporary links and interaction between the nation-state and its economy. He favoured the 'socio-economic' model as he named it, which tended to cultivate individual rights of citizens, political liberalism and free economic initiative, but which at the same time allowed the state to interfere wherever and whenever it was necessary to provide a fair and equal treatment for those individuals who were 'weaker in economic and social terms'. He also regretted that 'some countries recently left this teaching ... and wandered either into communism or fascism, thus extending the state authority to economic life according to the principles of the so-called planned economy'.[191]

Two months later, the Serbian Cultural Club organized a lecture by Gojko Grdjić, counsellor in the Trade and Industry Ministry, whose PhD in economics was awarded in Berlin in 1936. Grdjić praised Germany for its strong contribution to the development of the Yugoslav economy, for two reasons: Yugoslavia's independence from the unpredictable fluctuations in prices on the world grain market and the role which the importing of German machinery and tools played in Yugoslavia's industrial development. But he then questioned what the German motives were. In his opinion, they were for a stronger attachment of Eastern and South-Eastern European economies to Germany, which would eventually lead to the customs union. The ultimate motive was maintaining the existing character of economic relations, the one in which Yugoslavia and other similar countries were kept in the role of suppliers of food and raw materials to Germany. It was true, Grdjić continued, that Yugoslav agriculture and mining would benefit from such a relationship, but he questioned its usefulness for the further development of Yugoslavia's industry. In the final outcome, Yugoslavia would remain nothing more than an agricultural country renowned for its mineral wealth; its economy would be one-dimensional and vulnerable to the wishes of its customer. In his words, only strong industry, strengthened by a developed agriculture, was able to truly provide national independence. Finally, he suggested the maintaining of existing economic partnership with Germany as it was still beneficial for Yugoslavia, for as long as Germany needed resources. But he also called for stronger economic relationships with Italy, Britain and France. Grdjić concluded his lecture by calling for the creation of an economic block of all states of the Balkan and Danube regions, which would deny Berlin the advantage of negotiating independently with each one of them.[192] In 1940, Sava Terzić, with a PhD in economics from Vienna, also opposed the concept of *Grosswirtschaftsraum*, which he described as a union of industrial Germany and agricultural states to its east and south-east, by arguing that developments in European economy during the 1920s clearly showed that the exchange of goods between highly industrialized states was greater and of higher value than between an industrialized and an agrarian state.[193]

It was not only the experts who favoured an industrialized economy based on the doctrines of liberalism and free trade. At the meeting of the Central office of Industrial Union in Belgrade in February 1937, Trade and Industry Minister Vrbanić and the National Bank's vice-governors Lovčević and Belin had to listen to harsh criticisms by industrialists who accused the officials of 'abandoning the doctrine of free trade in sectors of production and goods exchange and [also accused them for] constantly strong state interference in economic life'.[194] *Industrijski pregled*, a journal which specialized in the problems of Yugoslavia's industry and a staunch advocate of industrialization, was opposed to the official policy of import controls and demanded free export to and import from the free currency markets, particularly since 1939, when it started to appear that Yugoslavia might have to choose between two economic blocs.[195] The Yugoslav press was sceptical about German motives. An article in *Trgovačke novine* from Belgrade after Schacht's visit in June 1936 accused Germany of manipulating the clearing mechanism in order to force agricultural states of the south-east to buy as much German goods as Berlin needed to sell, without regard to their real needs. Writing about Schacht's warmongering during his state visit, the article spoke of Schacht's need to sell old German weaponry to the Balkan states, as new ones needed to be produced and wondered whether Yugoslavia would finance its own occupation in that way. The author concluded: 'One day, when these countries so nicely advised [by Schacht] adjust their production and foreign trade to the needs of the German market, the diplomacy of the Third Reich will come up with the new demand: "Do it, they would say, otherwise we would not buy anything anymore".'[196]

## Conflicting directions

In March 1939, a memorandum for internal use made it clear that the Romanian, Yugoslav and Greek oil, iron, bauxite, copper and other ores should be secured for the German use. As part of these plans, Berlin decided to tolerate independent industrial development in these countries, but only to the extent that it would not impede its own interests.[197] However, by this time Yugoslavia's economic development took another course, the one which in the long term steered towards the building of the country's own heavy industry; and this was partly stimulated by increased Yugoslav imports of machinery from Germany and German capital investments in Yugoslavia's industry. Teichova argues that 'the larger Germany's share [of the foreign trade] ... on the bilateral basis grew, the more the industrialization of the region was threatened'.[198] From a political perspective, the statement is correct. The Reich penetrated slowly and in stages, adjusting its approach to the circumstances and with every political and military success was getting more aggressive and assertive towards the South-Eastern European countries.

But Yugoslavia was politically far from being Germany's pawn in the Balkans and might be excluded from being a part of the German 'informal empire', as described by Schröder and Grenzebach, unless the term is corrected to the 'informal *trading* empire'. Germany could have directed Yugoslavia's economic development, namely the direction of its industrialization, only if Berlin gained decisive political influence, which was not the case before the fall of France. Still, industrialization demanded machinery and tools and this is what Germany provided. Berlin's position was thus paradoxical; it contributed to Yugoslavia's industrialization, however limited it was, at the same time when it wanted to set boundaries to the region's economic development.

Teichova was right in suggesting that industrialization of South-Eastern Europe was a result of specific circumstances of the region's own economic development. The Yugoslav government had a decisive influence on industrialization of its country; it simultaneously appeared as capital owner, investor and main buyer.[199] Industrialization was thus more a result of the specific conditions of Yugoslavia's own economic structure, which involved measures such as public works, domestic market protection, state intervention in economy and a planned foreign trade policy.[200] However, would most of these measures have provided results if the German market had not been there to ease the problems of post-crisis economic recovery, as both importer from and exporter to Yugoslavia? Especially at the time when Western powers were unable to or disinterested in assisting Yugoslavia's economy. We also need to be clear that any success in Yugoslavia's industrialization in the second half of the 1930s should be viewed in the context of poor initial growth rates; also, that Yugoslavia's industry employed less than 10 per cent of the overall workforce and throughout the 1930s remained unable to absorb the rapidly growing working-age population.[201]

Given the circumstances, the theory of complementary economies would have been wasted on Yugoslavia in the long run without Germany's hard power to implement it. Constant referring to the Ottawa Conference, which was a common theme of German press and various economic analysis of the late 1930s, should have created the illusion of a *bona fide* agreement between Germany and its *natural* sphere of interest in the east and south-east. The smooth talk of German economic experts, advocates of the *Grosswirtschaftsraum* and some business leaders was brutally unmasked once the Nazi leadership lost patience, while the true nature of the New Order was exposed in the reality of German occupation. The problem for most Yugoslav economic experts who embraced Germany as Yugoslavia's ultimate and irreplaceable economic partner was that their sole argument rested on emphasizing the German share of Yugoslavia's foreign trade. Such a one-dimensional approach simply restricted the Yugoslav economic prospects merely to the role of supplier of agricultural products and raw materials to Germany. In essence, it was the role of a colony and fitted perfectly into the German economic theory; these experts failed to recognize the alternative directions of Yugoslavia's own economic development. Yugoslavia's future was thus seen only from the standpoint of a foreign-trade relationship, frozen in a specific moment in time, and not from the standpoint of sustainable economic development. This development, in the form of building a domestic heavy industry, was continued after the Second World War. The foundation of socialist Yugoslavia's industrialization after 1945 was laid out in the last years of life of capitalist Yugoslavia and in that respect, there is a clear continuity between the two.

7

# Ideological traps in the Nazi decade

Nothing in Hitler's antisemitism was new or original; it was built on layers of earlier German and European antisemitic traditions. He blindly believed in a proven forgery, *The Protocols of the Elders of Zion*, and the Jews became his obsession and the central motive of his world vision. Once in power, the new racial antisemitism of the Third Reich's ruling party became one of the most important axioms of Germany's daily politics. Consequently, it also influenced Hitler's understanding of foreign policy; he saw the Jews as constituting a ruling class in Paris and Moscow, having influence on politics in London and Washington, while for him one of Mussolini's great virtues was his ability to firmly keep the Jews in place for the benefit of his country's interests.[1] As such, once in power, the antisemitism of the Nazis affected Germany's relationship with other countries. Everything related to Jewry abroad was important and German legations across Europe regularly reported on every change in regard to the Jews in the countries of their placement, as well as on local reactions to the Reich' antisemitic policies. The complexities and implications of the Nazi antisemitism have been well researched so far; what is more important for us here are the implications the Reich's antisemitic policies had on Berlin's relations with Belgrade. All the countries of the region sooner or later had to adapt their attitude towards their Jews and to fascism as ideology once Germany became a dominant power in the European south-east. It is however important to determine the character of these changes. Were they made voluntarily or under pressure, and were they political or ideological in character?

Another cornerstone of national socialist ideology was the concept of the *Volk*, referring to both the people and the race. But *Volk* was anything but a monolithic model to which all Germans outside the Reich's borders equally belonged. Details such as which dialect of German was spoken, local customs, the distance of their historical area of residence from Germany or the level of mixing with other ethnic groups could in some cases confirm, in others deny, an ethnic German group full access to the Germanness, *Deutschtum*.[2] Despite these academic and ideological dilemmas within Germany and the ruling party, which largely remained unresolved until 1945, unfortunately for a wide swath of countries with numerous German minorities from the Baltic to the Balkans, ethnic Germans outside the Reich in any case played a role in the Nazi foreign policy. But there was a difference in the Nazi approach towards ethnic Germans from those areas which were destined to become parts of the *Lebensraum* and the ethnic Germans living outside the projected living space. In

Eastern Europe, the very existence of the *Volksdeutsche* offered legitimization for the murder of millions of Slavs, Jews and Roma, while it was Germans, either local or resettled, who subsequently became the prime beneficiaries of the property and land taken from the former.[3] South-Eastern Europe was not perceived as part of the living space, but the German-speaking people in the area represented valuable leverage for the Third Reich in political dealings with their home countries. Hitler himself did not have any set ideas about what the role of the ethnic Germans there would be and was generally uninterested in either South-Eastern Europe or ethnic Germans there. He regarded them mainly as an instrument for promoting German political interests.[4]

By the end of the 1930s, German power and influence in the region began to put pressure on the decision-making in the home affairs of South-Eastern European countries regarding some ideological issues. For Berlin, the way the state authorities treated these cornerstones of Nazism was a test of their attitude towards Germany and of their readiness and willingness to become part of the German-dominated New European Order. Although questions of antisemitism, native fascism or the place of the German minority in Yugoslavia seem to fall outside the scope of this book, it is important to revisit them in order to examine whether these highly sensitive issues eventually influenced Yugoslavia's decision-making in regard to its relationship with Germany; and if they did, to what extent and from when?

## Antisemitism in pre-1941 Yugoslavia

Antisemitism is a very basic ideology; it occurs on the level of emotions and does not have any deeper theoretical interpretation. Its only function is to create the image of an imagined enemy. In socio-economic terms, antisemitism is usually a response to difficult situations and occurs mainly when a society is in lack of means, or faced with some form of suppression which burdens its members. Then it has the function of a tool to relieve the pressure, by passing it down to others.[5] The Bolshevik Revolution of November 1917 added a missing political ingredient to the modern antisemitism of the twentieth century; it was the event which decisively linked Jews with leftist revolutionary tendencies in European minds.[6]

It is easy to see how it was possible for such a primitive political ideology, with simple but aggressive messages, to permeate societies in the interwar period, which was marked by economic depression and poverty in many corners of Europe, by using the extreme nationalism raging throughout Central Europe and the Balkans and the omnipresent fear of communist revolution identified with the Jews. Of course, antisemitism predated Nazism and interwar politics; for example, hatred towards the Jews was strong in some antirevisionist countries such as Poland and Romania. In the Balkans, antisemitism mainly stemmed from economic or religious prejudices. Still, it was the racial antisemitism of the Nazis which eventually influenced the other types of antisemitism, enabling an important transition towards the political antisemitism in South-Eastern Europe in the 1930s. Of Yugoslavia's neighbours, Hungary and Romania institutionalized antisemitism before the outbreak of war,

Austria was part of the Greater Reich after March 1938 and shared its policies, Italian Fascism came closer to the Nazi racial ideology in 1938, although in general Italian society was tolerant towards Jews, while Greece and Bulgaria, albeit not institutionalizing antisemitism, brought in some anti-Jewish measures before the outbreak of war, mainly pragmatically, in response to the stronger German influence in the Balkans.

Approximately 70,000 Jews lived in Yugoslavia in the interwar period, divided between themselves into an older and larger Sephardic community, living in central and southern parts of the country since the early Ottoman era, and a smaller Ashkenazi community in the north, mainly having settled there following the expansion of the Habsburg Empire.[7] Jews were not an important factor in Yugoslavia's economic life, but as elsewhere their economic power was disproportionate to their population size; the most prominent Jewish community was a rich and well-organized one in Zagreb.[8] When antisemitism in Yugoslavia became loud and aggressive in the 1930s, some intellectuals felt obliged to respond to it. They viewed antisemitism as an expression of the political and cultural regression of the modern world, describing antisemitic practices in Nazi Germany as part of the 'bloodiest reaction [to progress and modernity] of the post-1918 period, which surpassed even the Middle Ages'.[9] They claimed that political antisemitism affected mainly small-town philistines, distant either from the world of capitalist production, or from the working class, thus preventing them from understanding the deeper meaning of political events and battles for the transformation of society. For these intellectuals, antisemitism was purely a catalyst of political and economic dissatisfaction of the class of small craftsmen and traders, whose profits were jeopardized by industrial mass production.[10] Determined to confront emerging indications of antisemitic paranoia in Yugoslavia, two Belgrade journalists, Mića Dimitrijević and Vojislav Stojanović, edited in 1940 a collection of various discussions by a number of distinguished Yugoslav public figures on the place of Jews in contemporary Yugoslav society. This book is of especial importance in light of the date of its publication, which is an excellent example that, despite the increasing dangers to the country, Yugoslavia's intellectual elite still considered it important to emphasize its contempt for antisemitism. Two distinguished Jewish lawyers, Lavoslav Šik from Zagreb and Samuilo Demajo from Belgrade, both insisted that Yugoslav Jews felt safe and equal with Serbs and Croats, praising Yugoslavia's political leadership for refusing to bow to the antisemitic trends of contemporary European politics.[11] Others pointed to the basic illogicality of most antisemitic theories, which all viewed Judaism as a unity, with no regard for economic and social differences among the Jewish people themselves.[12] Mihailo Kujundžić of the Democratic Party, former deputy chairman of the National Assembly, pointed to the difficult living conditions of many Jews in Vardarska province (comprising Macedonia, Kosovo and southern Serbia), where they shared the impoverished destiny of all the other non-Jewish residents of that province, one of the poorest in Yugoslavia.[13] Derviš Korkut, a Muslim and curator of the Sarajevo museum, warned about attempts to turn Muslims against Jews and denied that there were any problems between the two religions.[14] Finally, Juda Levi, university professor and another distinguished Yugoslav Jew, numbered numerous artists, poets and writers of Jewish origin whose work and creativity flourished in Yugoslavia.[15]

However, most of these publications made a basic mistake in suggesting that antisemitism was something alien to the Yugoslav nation, an imported ideology imposed on the lower classes by foreign propaganda.[16] As elsewhere in Europe, it already existed, utilizing religious themes, the problems of local economies and the inclinations of national politics. Antisemitism was part of European history for centuries and Serbs, Croats and Slovenes were not exceptions. In the nineteenth-century Serbia, there were legal bans directed against Jews in the 1840s and 1860s, influenced by an emerging class of Serbian urban traders and craftsmen who viewed them as rivals.[17] Jews were granted full Serbian citizenship under the 1888 Constitution, which marked the beginning of a dynamic integration of Serbian Jews into the economic, social and cultural life of the country and their political emancipation. However, belief in Jewish occultism directed against Christians still persisted in a predominantly illiterate peasant country, while stereotypes about the generic Jewish looks and behaviour were widespread. The same prejudices existed in the formerly Austro-Hungarian parts of Yugoslavia, especially in northern Croatia and Vojvodina, where some of the most notable representatives of both Croats and Serbs did not hide their dislike for Jews, such as Ante Starčević, founder of the Croatian Party of Rights; Stjepan Radić, leader of the Croatian People's Peasant Party; or Jaša Tomić among the Vojvodina Serbs in the late nineteenth century. Among the Slovenes, Janez Evangelist Krek, one of the founders and leaders of the Slovene's People Party, was known for his antisemitism before his death in 1917; antisemitism was also present in Korošec's political activities. Mehmed Spaho, political leader of the Yugoslav Muslims, was not friendly towards the Jews, although his attitude was politically inspired, as in the second half of the 1930s Yugoslavia's Muslims sympathized with the cause of the Palestinian Arabs, which affected the relationship with their Jewish neighbours.[18]

During the interwar period antisemitism was stronger in the former Austro-Hungarian parts of Yugoslavia, but it was also present in eastern parts of the country. In general, the relationship between the Jews and the Orthodox church was more cordial than their relationship with the Catholic church in Croatia and Bosnia, especially after the death of the moderate Zagreb Archbishop Antun Bauer in 1937. His successor Alojzije Stepinac was by that time already in control of some influential clerical newspapers which preached antisemitism.[19] Also, the Jews of the pre-1918 Serbia more eagerly embraced Yugoslavia as their new homeland than the Jews over the Danube, Sava and Drina rivers. This was a sensitive issue as after 1918, the Jewish nationalism – Zionism – started to spread among Yugoslav Jews, challenging their sense of belonging to Yugoslavia. In general, economic form of antisemitism was dominant among the Serbs south of the Danube and Sava rivers, while antisemitism amongst the Croats, Slovenes and the former Austro-Hungarian Serbs took religious form.

Mainly focusing on the well-known national and political problems of the new country after 1918, Yugoslav historiography did not consider antisemitism in the interwar period as a serious issue in Yugoslavia's political and social life. It is true that Serbia's pre-war policy of full Jewish equality also became official policy towards Jews of the new state.[20] However, in the years immediately following the Great War, there were some very serious antisemitic incidents, both from embittered masses blaming the Jews for allegedly causing the war and from the authorities occasionally attempting the expulsion of some Jews from Croatia and Bosnia, only to be prevented by a strong pressure from both inside and outside the country at the time of the Versailles Conference. In Vojvodina, Jews were mainly accused of harbouring pro-Hungarian sentiments, by both Serbs and Croats. Throughout the country, they were associated with events in Russia and the authorities were quick to restrict the number of visas given to the Russian and Polish Jews fleeing the atrocities of the Russian civil war and the ensuing Soviet-Polish conflict, afraid of communist propagators and spies posing as refugees. Also, because of their unclear citizenship status, Jews were not allowed to vote in Yugoslavia's first elections in 1920 in Vojvodina and some parts of Croatia.[21] Things calmed down later in the decade and sporadic incidents directed against Jews could be considered marginal events. The censorship which followed the proclamation of King Alexander's dictatorship in January 1929 further contributed to turning Yugoslavia into a quiet and safe place for Jews.[22]

*The Protocols of the Elders of Zion* was published in Yugoslavia for the first time in Dalmatia in 1929, although some newspapers published parts of the pamphlet during the 1920s. The following year, it was published in Zagreb at the time of a Eucharistic congress. *The Protocols* was first published in Belgrade in 1934, secretly, with no publisher's name. This disturbed the public and in March 1935 it was banned in Yugoslavia.[23] But this marked an important transformation in the character of antisemitism in Yugoslavia, a transition from the traditional religious and economic antisemitism of the 1920s to political antisemitism in the following decade.[24] It thus became an integral component of a homegrown extreme right-wing political ideology in the 1930s. Unlike the previous decade, which mainly witnessed occasional isolated incidents and the publication of antisemitic articles in the fringe right-wing press, manifestations of antisemitism now became visible in the streets. Although there were no violent incidents, anti-Jewish graffiti and distributions of flyers with antisemitic messages became common all over the country and occasionally similar sentiments were even published in the mainstream press. Bearing in mind the conventional prejudice about the economic activities of Jews, it is safe to assume that antisemitism in Yugoslavia was partly aggravated by economic crisis in the early 1930s, partly by the Nazi takeover of power in Germany in 1933 and partly by political changes in Yugoslavia after 1934.

The proliferation of anti-Jewish publications at first alarmed the authorities, who occasionally issued bans on the most extreme ones. However, such publications kept re-emerging, either by changing their name and starting afresh after each individual ban, or by moving to underground printing and distribution.[25] The situation deteriorated after 1938, when Yugoslavia and the Reich became neighbours. In articles whose main purpose was unmasking the Jewish danger, some propagators of fascism began to threaten openly. The authorities continued with bans, often confiscating the whole printed editions of some journals. However, as the decade went on, they were more concerned about the political attacks on the government and its policies, rather than about the antisemitic character of some articles in such publications.[26] The police became visibly less zealous in preventing the dissemination of antisemitic material when Korošec became the Interior Minister in Stojadinović's government in 1935.[27]

Of journals and magazines which oriented their editorial policies to disseminating antisemitic views, *Hrvatska straža*, *Mlada Hrvatska* and *Nezavisnost* were especially notorious for their anti-Jewish propaganda in Croatia, while in Sarajevo *Večernje novosti* frequently printed accusations against the Jews. *Balkan* carried the torch of antisemitism in Belgrade, occasionally the mainstream *Pravda* and a number of newspapers and periodicals published by the fascist party Zbor. In Slovenia, *Slovenec*, a news organ of the leading Slovene People's Party, was not sympathetic to Jews, to say the least.

Despite the poisonous rhetoric in the press and at some public events during the 1930s, there were no manifestations of physical violence towards Jews in Yugoslavia until the outbreak of war.[28] Also, no mainstream political party in Yugoslavia had antisemitism as a cornerstone of its programme.[29] But this does not mean that major parties were immune to antisemitic prejudices, let alone their membership. In Zagreb, on the evening of 19 July 1935, celebrating Maček's birthday, the crowd roamed the streets demanding a boycott of shops whose owners publicly supported the government, especially targeting Jews.[30] The Catholic church also struggled to keep some of its distinguished members under control. It was part of a well-documented Catholic antisemitism, strong across Europe, even inside the very heart of Catholicism, in Vatican, where periodicals such as *La Civilta Cattolica* had been attacking Jews in the most violent and abusive way for decades.[31] In Yugoslavia, the most notorious individual was Janko Šimrak, a priest and the editor of *Hrvatska straža*. Also known for their antisemitic attitude were the religious newspapers *Nedjelja* (Zagreb) and *Katolički tjednik* (Sarajevo).[32] However, these were journals with small circulation and influence compared to liberal and influential mainstream papers, such as *Obzor*, *Jutarnji list*, *Novosti* and *Hrvatski dnevnik*, which mainly remained in opposition to the rising antisemitism in Croatia. Finally, *Jugoslovenska reč* (Zagreb) was the newsletter of the fascist organization Yugoslav Action and a staunch supporter of Yugoslavia, whose editorship opted for the third way, by insisting on the existence of a specific Yugoslav racial type, to which only purebred Serbs, Croats and Slovenes belonged and which also toyed with antisemitic ideas.[33]

In 1936, at the meeting of the Union of Jewish Communities in Yugoslavia, its chairman David Albala for the first time mentioned his worry over the increasing levels of antisemitism in Yugoslavia. Although Prince Paul expressed his personal sympathies towards Jews at the meeting with Albala in April 1936, the government continued to relax its attitude towards extreme right-wing movements, in accordance with Yugoslavia's careful foreign policy in the second half of the 1930s. An extremely violent attack on Jews happened in *Erwache*, one of the Zbor periodicals printed in German. The Union of Jewish Communities pressed charges against Milorad Mojić, the editor of the paper in 1937, but the court decided to take no action with the explanation that the newspaper assaulted Jews as a race, not as a faith or nation; therefore, *Erwache*'s writing was not subject to Yugoslav laws.[34]

After 1933, Yugoslavia became the destination for many Jewish refugees from Germany, which further alarmed not only the right-wing extremists, but also the authorities. Neither Stojadinović's nor Cvetković's governments were especially friendly towards these newcomers, as creating the image of Yugoslavia as a safe-haven for Jews could have strained political relations with the powerful German Reich in the second half of the 1930s.[35] For most of Jewish refugees, Yugoslavia was anyway only a stop along the transit route. Overall, around 55,000 Jews from Germany, Austria and Czechoslovakia entered Yugoslavia in 1933–41, mainly on the way to Palestine. Their sheltering was costly for the government, which usually tried to swiftly escort them out of the country; for this purpose, two small transit camps were set up near Niš and Kuršumlija (Serbia), while the largest camp was in Šabac, on the bank of the river Sava. When the war broke out, the British halted further immigration to Palestine, while the Romanians banned the use of the Danube for these purposes. Thousands of Jewish refugees from Central Europe thus ended up stranded in Yugoslavia at the dawn of the war in the Balkans and shared the sad destiny of the Yugoslav Jews during the upcoming occupation.[36]

The increasing power of Germany played its part in Yugoslavia's attitude towards Jews. Stojadinović was not an antisemite, but was politically pragmatic and wanted to avoid any unnecessary confrontation with Berlin. In the month of the Anschluss, Yugoslavia's government refused to issue credentials to the Albanian honorary consul in Dubrovnik, due to his Jewish origin. In July 1939, the government stopped giving Yugoslav visas to foreign Jews.[37] The situation worsened after the fall of France in June 1940, when official newspapers started attacking Jews; this would not have been possible without clear government instructions.

It is worthwhile mentioning the reaction of Yugoslav Jews to Nazism in Germany. Reasonably, the Nazi *Machtergreifung* caused great excitement in the Jewish community all over the world. Numerous and well-organized Jews from Zagreb soon contemplated a boycott of German-made goods.[38] This was part of a worldwide Jewish boycott movement, first started in New York immediately after Hitler's rise to power.[39] In March, the Union of Jewish Communities in Yugoslavia indeed voted for the boycott. Of course, action by such a small group could not have a major impact. Still, the German legation and consulates occasionally reported problems which German businesses experienced in Yugoslavia due to cancelled purchases and lost partnerships. A list of companies which dared to confront the Reich include the textile factory Fako from Subotica (Vojvodina), Daruvar Brewery (Slavonia), Zagreb Paper Factory and others.[40] Especially noble was a telegram sent by the management of the Daruvar Brewery on 9 June 1934, curtly informing their business partners in Munich that 'out of a consideration for our Jewish, Marxist, Catholic, Liberal and other customers, management and employees, we will not be purchasing any German goods in the foreseeable future'.[41] It is hard to tell whether these cancellations were mainly down to the Jewish ownership of some Yugoslav businesses, or to the awakening of the Christian consciousness of non-Jewish Yugoslav businessmen. There were situations where the management of a Yugoslav company opted for pulling out of a deal with German partners as a result of the pressure from their Jewish customers. Sometimes rival Jewish-owned foreign companies stepped in, deliberately trying to outbid the Germans. These examples testify that Yugoslavia's Jews still had the will and agency to strike back the only way they could, by harming German economic interests, despite finding themselves in increasingly hostile surroundings at home.

## Native fascism in the 1930s

The story of antisemitism inevitably leads to that of the reception of fascism in Yugoslavia. There were far-right organizations in the interwar period and many held views close to fascist ideology. What most of them had in common were their extreme nationalism; intolerance towards other nations, ethnicities, political opinions or ideas; and the use of violence. There is a problem of classification of far-right organizations operating in Yugoslavia in the interwar period; it was not enough for a political group to be authoritarian in the traditional sense to immediately stigmatize it as fascist or pro-fascist.[42] This is especially challenging, as it was rare for any political grouping in Yugoslavia to openly preach fascism, yet many toyed with profascist ideas, sentiments and organizational structure. We will mention those which came closest to the definition of the term; some were pro-Yugoslav, others supported the cause of ethnic chauvinism.[43] We can define four attitudes towards Italian Fascism and German National-Socialism in the Yugoslav public: leftist/communist rejection, democratic/liberal criticism, nationalistic/conservative indifference and extreme-nationalistic approval.[44]

The first Yugoslav nationalist organization, Orjuna,[45] was founded in Dalmatia in 1921; not surprisingly as Italian territorial aspirations towards Yugoslavia's coastline after 1918 stirred anti-Italian and pro-Yugoslav sentiments here more strongly than in other parts of the country. It was also very popular in Slovenia.[46] Orjuna possessed some fascist characteristics, it was antisemitic and pan-Slavic in character and its members firmly believed in the unity of the three Yugoslav nations; they were frequently involved in violent street brawls with members of the rival Serbian and Croatian nationalist organizations.[47] Orjuna was dissolved in 1929 and Yugoslav Action was founded the following year. Even more extreme than Orjuna, it stood for corporatism, a planned economy and was anti-parliamentary. It was abolished in 1934. Of the others, mention should be made of the Patriotic Youth Front, the Organisation of Yugoslav Students and National Defence, but there were many smaller ones. They were all Yugoslav in character and supported the regime in carrying out its centralism.[48] The problem for most of them was that, albeit enjoying government funding and support, they rarely enjoyed the support of the rural population. This lack of popularity among the members of the most numerous social element in Yugoslavia crippled them politically. Although small in membership, these organizations were very active, thus making themselves more visible to the public than their influence should have allowed.

Unlike Orjuna and similar pro-Yugoslav organizations, Serbian and Croatian far-right groups stood for their own national traditions. Greatly influenced by German and Italian examples and building on national foundations, a peculiar version of fascism was created at the turn of the decade, in both eastern and western parts of Yugoslavia. It combined religious elements with the glorification of the peasantry as the most heroic element of a nation.[49] Admiration for a strong nation-state and its predominance over individual rights was an inspiration drawn from the Italian model. At the same time, this version of extreme right-wing ideology was related to Nazism by insisting on antisemitism. Politically, the majority of its followers became supporters of Nazi Germany in Yugoslavia.[50] Aleksa Đilas's description of an ideological mishmash of influences which eventually contributed to the programme of the Croatian Ustaše movement could equally be ascribed to other Yugoslav fascists. Following the examples of their Italian and German role models and unable to create an original doctrine of their own, these organizations combined modern totalitarianism and conservatism with elements of Social Darwinism, antisemitism and racism, the glorification of religion and archaic peasant democracy, all mixed with the corporatism of the modern fascist state.[51] The most important ones were Serbian National Youth, Croatian National Youth, Organisation of Catholic Nationalists, Muslim National Youth, Union of Slovene Soldiers and others.[52] But politically the most significant of all Yugoslavia's chauvinistic organizations and the ones that were explicitly fascist in character were Zbor in the Serbian parts of the country and Ustaše in Croatian.

Serbian extreme nationalism before the war was grounded in rejection of democracy, liberalism and cities as bearers of modern culture. All three elements were seen as integral parts of a system opposed to traditional Serbian patriarchal values. As opposed to urban culture, the countryside and peasants were mythologized, romanticized and idealized, often by twisting the past in an attempt to glorify the lost ideal of a once allegedly harmonious society of peasants and town dwellers, which was ruined by modernity and industrialization. The West was seen as old, waning, materialistic and as such its culture was a bad example. Serbian nationalists denied that any inequalities existed among the pre-1918 'purebred' Serbs, insisting that social stratification happened only afterwards, as a result of damaging external influences.[53] These would become central elements of the political programme and ideology of the 'rump' Serbian puppet government of Milan Nedić during the German occupation, 1941–4.[54]

Although such ideas remained confined to a relatively small and politically insignificant circle of followers, some very prominent Serbian intellectuals were sympathetic to them, namely Nikolaj Velimirović, an influential bishop of the Serbian Orthodox Church; Vladimir Velmar-Janković, a renowned novelist; Svetislav Stefanović, doctor and poet, founder of the Yugoslav Medical Society; Miloš Crnjanski, a renowned writer and poet; Danilo Gregorić, journalist; and others. Velimirović was full of praise for Hitler, while in an interview for *Völkischer Beobachter* in May 1937, Serbian Patriarch Varnava expressed his admiration for the Führer and his role in the defence of Europe against the communist peril – all this, despite the fact that the full range of Germany's viciously antisemitic actions and violence against political opponents of Hitler's regime were well known to the Yugoslav public.[55] Stefanović and philosopher Branimir Maleš were pioneers of eugenics in Yugoslavia. They sought to determine a pure Yugoslav racial type, from whom all physical and anatomical deviations were to be eliminated through correct 'racial hygiene', by selection, segregation and, if necessary, sterilization.[56]

The official umbrella movement for all the political extremes in Yugoslavia by the mid-1930s became the Yugoslav National Movement Zbor, its name being an acronym for United Combatting Labour Organisation,[57] founded in 1935 by lawyer and former Justice Minister Dimitrije Ljotić. Zbor was a Yugoslav party and its leadership consisted of members of all three Yugoslav nations; however, the membership mainly came from the Serbs, with very few Croats and Slovenes joining it. The party was Christian, antisemitic, anti-capitalist and anti-communist, opposed to democracy and firmly supporting planned economy, corporatism and the racial purity of the Yugoslav nation, with a militarized internal structure. Ljotić was inspired by the programme of Action Française and its leader Charles Maurras in France. He established cordial relations with the Serbian church and Velimirović's religious movement, thus combining religious mysticism with political extremism.[58] In its newspapers and political rallies, Zbor propagated a vision of a Jewish enemy responsible for Yugoslavia's economic and political problems. In October 1939, Ljotić toured Yugoslavia giving a lecture entitled 'The Drama of Modern Mankind' in more than twenty cities, accusing the Jews of causing the Second World War. Throughout 1940, the Zbor leader expanded on this theory; metaphorically, the war was drama and the Jews its directors. As such, they manipulated all of the ideologically opposed sides, including Hitler, who turned out to be an unwitting engine of war, while its true steering wheel was the Soviets – who were not even engaged in the war at the time.[59]

Still, these ideas failed to fall on fertile soil. Although antisemitic prejudices existed in every corner of Yugoslavia, antisemitism was not ingrained in the everyday thinking of the average Serb, Croat or Slovene. There were regional deviations between eastern and western parts of the country; in general, there was a sense among the Yugoslavs that Jews lived next door, that they were newcomers and that they were different. But they were seldom seen as foreigners and this awareness of a Jewish presence rarely went beyond the most basic form of the binary opposition of 'us' and 'them'. True, this opposition is responsible for some of the worst crimes committed against 'others' throughout human history. But in general, Jews in Yugoslavia were rather seen as tolerable tenants than undesirable neighbours.

And Zbor learned this the hard way in the two Yugoslavian general elections in which they participated, in 1935 and 1938, both times suffering crushing defeats. In 1935, out of 2.9 million people who cast their votes, fascists received only 27,000, or less than 1 per cent. In 1938, they improved slightly, winning 31,000 votes out of a turnout of 3.04 million. As a comparison, the far-right, pro-German Arrow Cross Party in Hungary won 15 per cent of the votes in the elections held in May 1939. It is true that in Yugoslavia both times the elections were unfair and strongly favoured the ruling party. But, compared to the 1.4 million people who in 1938 voted for the united opposition of Croatian and Serbian conservative and liberal parties, it is hard to ascribe these fascist failures purely to a distorted electoral system. The narrative of the Zbor leadership rarely went beyond attempts to construct and spread the image of an omnipresent enemy whose central character was always the Jew. But this 'siege mentality', which called for a defence against an *imagined* enemy, was badly misplaced in those years when Yugoslavia was in *real* danger from all the revisionist political forces in South-Eastern Europe. Their links to Nazi Germany, known to the public, further damaged Zbor's prospects among the dominantly Germanophobic Serbs.[60]

There were no mainstream parties with fascism as a cornerstone of their programme in Croatia during the interwar period. However, the idiosyncrasies of Croatian political life after 1918 contributed to widespread grievances against the new country it was now part of and consequently an inclination towards extremism among those feeling oppressed and embittered. The Catholic church was very influential and there was a strong tendency among the clergy to monopolize Croatian nationalism. There were extreme organizations of Catholic youth with significant membership, dedicated to fighting liberalism, communism and 'Great Serbian' political tendencies in Croatia. These were the Eagles Union in the 1920s and the Crusaders in the 1930s. Both sought to re-Christianize the public sphere and impose Catholic values onto civil life.[61]

After 1920, Radić's Peasant Party proved to be the true representative of the majority of Croats and the bearer of their political wishes. The party drifted between demands for an independent Croatian republic and support for federalist Yugoslavia. Its supporters mainly came from the countryside and lower urban classes, leaving the members of the pre-1918 upper and middle classes from the ranks of military, intelligentsia, bourgeoisie and landed elite feeling unrepresented.[62] Sections of the Croatian intelligentsia, petite bourgeoisie and students turned towards the Party of Right, known for its animosity towards Serbs and opposition to any cooperation between the two nations. Originally founded by Starčević in 1861 as the Party of Croatian Rights, in time it developed all the elements of extreme nationalist ideology: a denial of any national consciousness but the Croatian within what they considered the historical borders of Croatia, seeing others as racially inferior and morally corrupt and being intolerant and violent. It later went through changes; at the turn of the century, it was reorganized by Josip Frank and renamed the Party of Pure Right.[63] But from having once been the most popular political entity in Croatia, it was on the fringes of Croatian political life after 1918, winning less than 11,000 votes in the 1920 elections.[64] The party's leaders Ivica Frank and Vladimir Sachs were exiled and from abroad, where they joined a cohort of Croatian emigrants consisting mainly of officers and soldiers of the former Austro-Hungarian army, they schemed and conspired against Yugoslavia with ex-emperor Karl I of Habsburg, representatives of the Italian secret services and from November 1922 with the Fascists.[65] Back home, the party's leader was Ante Pavelić, a Zagreb lawyer born in Bosnia.[66]

After the incident with shooting in the Yugoslav Parliament in 1928, which resulted in mortally wounding Radić and the killing of three other Croatian politicians by a Serbian member of parliament, Pavelić left the country and with the support and under the protection of the Italian police and secret services founded the new organization of Croatian resistance from abroad named *Ustaše* (insurgents), choosing terrorism as a method of struggle. Through a carefully established network, the new organization drafted people from the ranks of a number of Croatian diasporas in Western Europe and the Americas and from among political refugees from Yugoslavia. The first training camps were in Italy, and in 1931 one was founded on a farm at Jankapuszta in Hungary, close to the border with Yugoslavia. The early 1930s in Yugoslavia were marked with Ustaše terrorist attacks all over Croatia and in Belgrade, to which the police responded with brutality and repression, further widening the gap between Serbs and Croats.[67] The murder of renowned historian Milan Šufflay by two members of the Zagreb police in 1931, who then escaped to Belgrade, stirred international reaction and accusations against the Yugoslav authorities for the killing. One such protest letter was signed by both Albert Einstein and Heinrich Mann.[68] The climax of Ustaše terrorist activity was the assassination of King Alexander in Marseilles, on 9 October 1934, in coordination with the Bulgarian Internal Macedonian Revolutionary Organization, and with financial and logistical support from Italy.

From late 1936 on, Yugoslavia and Italy came closer politically. Although Il Duce never extradited Ustaše's leadership to be prosecuted for their role in King Alexander's assassination, most of them were interned on the island of Lipari for the rest of the decade. Back in Croatia, things became calmer and violence largely ceased after 1934 and then especially after 1937, when the government allowed the return of Croatian emigrants not implicated in terrorist activities against Yugoslavia.[69] However, there were still some social clubs of far-right intellectuals and student groups calling themselves Frankists, who sympathized with Ustaše. Pro-fascist students of Zagreb University were members of two organizations, 'August Šenoa' and 'Domagoj', demanding the purging of the Jews from the university.[70] After the August 1939 Agreement between Cvetković and Maček and the creation of Croatian province (Banovina) within Yugoslavia, the political climate in Croatia became more violent, especially towards the local Serbs. Ustaše propaganda was freely disseminated through their newspaper *Hrvatski narod*, although the group was at the same time becoming increasingly opposed to Maček and his party. The Catholic church headed by Stepinac also distanced itself from Maček and come closer to Ustaše. Eventually, after some terrorist acts in Zagreb, the Banovina authorities banned *Hrvatski narod* in February 1940 and made a number of arrests, pushing Ustaše back underground.[71]

## The Third Reich and Yugoslavia on ideological crossroads

In September 1932, a small Ustaše group secretly entered Yugoslavia's territory and after a few skirmishes with the Yugoslav army manged to escape to the city of Zadar, at the time the Italian territory. The so-called Lika Uprising was nowhere near a proper uprising, but was still massively used as propaganda by Italy a month later, at celebrations of the jubilee of The March on Rome, to illustrate the alleged expansion of the Fascist revolution throughout Europe. In a way, this event marks the beginning of a competition between Italian Fascists and German Nazis, over who would be the leader of the far-right, revisionist and totalitarian movements across the European southeast. While Fascists played the card of their ideological seniority, Nazis at first focused on members of German minorities spread along the Danube basin. However, in time German political might overshadowed Italy's and the Reich became the gravitational centre for all the far-right political groups in South-Eastern Europe. It is not surprising that Pavelić only incorporated antisemitism as part of his programme in 1936, when Ustaše turned to Berlin for support.[72]

As previously mentioned, Hitler initially supported the Wilhelmstrasse in their clash with Rosenberg's Foreign Policy Office regarding the treatment of Croatian émigrés in Germany. However, other interested power structures still considered them a useful future asset. From 1935 on, the Yugoslav authorities often complained about the presence of a number of Ustaše leaders in Germany. In October, the Yugoslav legation in Berlin passed down the information that Andrija Artuković, a notorious Croatian emigrant, was planning a journey from Stettin to the United States and demanded that any such trip be prevented.[73] In June 1936, the Yugoslavs complained again about the presence of Branimir Jelić, another high-profile person in the Ustaše hierarchy. Foreign Ministry denied any knowledge of it, but after conducting an internal enquiry, learned that the Yugoslav information was correct – in May that year Jelić was indeed allowed, by discretion of the Gestapo, to enter and remain in Germany under surveillance.[74] Another high-profile Ustaše leader with a Berlin address was Mladen Lorković, considered to be Pavelić's German connection. Following Yugoslav demands, Wilhelmstrasse frequently urged the Gestapo to put a halt to the underground activities of Croatian emigrants in Germany.[75] In December 1936, Busse, a Foreign Ministry counsellor, met two Gestapo officials and discussed the situation. The former recommended the removal of any person associated with the Ustaše movement from Germany, in order to avoid accusations that the Reich was involved in the Marseilles assassination. However, the Gestapo men disagreed, with the pretence that once on the loose, the Croatian extremists might retort to violence.[76] The Foreign Ministry admitted that its views differed from those of the secret police, but was powerless to impose policy changes. During Stojadinović's visit to Berlin in January 1938, the question of Germany sheltering Ustaše was brought up in talks with Göring. As a result, Germany reinforced its control over the activities of Croatian emigrants, but refused to extradite Jelić, while the Gestapo still used Ustaše members in Germany as a source of information on Yugoslavia.[77]

The Nazis were equally industrious in supporting political groups which sympathized with Hitler's Germany inside Yugoslavia. This was another area where the Foreign Ministry experienced problems with its numerous competitors set up by the party to unofficially support the Germany's cause abroad. In February 1937, the Renewal Movement, *Erneuerungsbewegung*, an organization of young Yugoslav ethnic Germans, united with Zbor, which caused outrage in Yugoslavia. An alleged motive for the amalgamation was their common struggle against Bolshevism; however, the government's immediate reaction was to ban the Zbor youth movement.[78] This was a clumsy and untimely move by both, the Yugoslav fascists and the young Yugoslav ethnic Germans, as barely a week prior to this, the pages of Yugoslav newspapers had been filled with stories of Zbor being accused of developing a scheme to receive financial support from Germany. Involved from the German side were both Rosenberg and his office and the Technical Union, an organization for pursuing German economic interests abroad, set up by Göring in the winter of 1936–7. Part of the profit from its trading activities with a number of business partners, members of Yugoslavia's sections of the Technical Union would then be paid over to Zbor as a subsidy.[79] From 1937, German propaganda activity in Yugoslavia shifted into a higher gear; it included the distribution of newspapers, books and pamphlets, often free of charge, with Nazi and antisemitic content, printed in Germany in both languages.[80] Much of this material was banned by the Yugoslav authorities, but it was hard to control its flow, especially when it was aimed at the Yugoslav Germans. Having had enough of this, Stojadinović called upon Heeren and unusually openly expressed his displeasure with the aggressive interference in Yugoslavia's internal affairs from certain quarters in Germany. He explained clearly that his supporters were politically conservative, but in no way ready to follow any extreme ideology, whether communist or fascist.[81]

Still, with deeper German penetration in the region, the political situation worsened for Yugoslavia and the authorities began to adapt to a new political reality by changing their attitude towards the Jews, especially after the change of government in 1939; possibly because Cvetković was meeker than his predecessor in his dealings with Berlin. New army Minister Nedić distrusted Jews and after September 1939 slowly removed most of them from high office in the army.[82] However, the major changes coincided with the German offensive on the western front and the fall of France. In May 1940, the government allowed the former editors of the currently banned *Balkan* to start a new paper, renamed *Novi Balkan*. It immediately recommenced its antisemitic campaign and its praise of Germany. In July, the government replaced the old, liberal and pro-Western management of Radio Belgrade and appointed a new editor, the former Zbor chief of propaganda, novelist Stanislav Krakov. Radio Belgrade thus became a powerful tool for spreading German propaganda in Yugoslavia. At the same time, Gregorić was made the director of *Vreme*, giving a voice to all pro-German Yugoslavs and immediately starting with a campaign against the Jews and Masonry in numerous articles. In August, all the masonic lodges in Yugoslavia were closed down by Cvetkocić's direct order and Masonry was outlawed.[83]

These were only preparations for introducing discriminatory measures against Yugoslavia's Jews in autumn 1940, known in historiography as *numerus clausus* – a denial of basic human rights to the Jews, restricting their access to certain professions, offices and educational institutions by instigating quotas proportional to their statistical representation in the overall population. These measures were unconstitutional, but this was possible as the Yugoslav Parliament was dissolved after the creation of Croatian Banovina in August 1939 and new elections were never held; as a result, the government ruled by decrees until its end in March 1941.[84] On 5 October 1940, the government introduced two decrees, one banning Jewish wholesalers from trading in foodstuffs, another introducing *numerous clausus* for Jews in high schools and universities. Both were issued after the long and persistent pressure by Korošec, now in the capacity of the Education Minister;[85] there were no protests and every minister in the government signed these bills which violated Yugoslavia's constitution. Four days later, Croatian Banovina confirmed these measures in its territory. These were obviously rushed decisions, as there was no agreed definition of a Jew; this caused great confusion and the decisions were left to the discretion of local authorities.[86] Korošec now demanded new bills for restricting Jews' access to cultural institutions, publishing and media; he also sought ways to limit the autonomy of universities, using communist infiltration among the students as an excuse. He did not hide his pleasure upon hearing the news of the attack on the students of Belgrade University by an armed mob of Zbor youth later in October. Soon, Korošec's secret links to Zbor and the Germans were revealed and other members of the government led by Maček and the Justice Minister Konstantinović confronted him regarding the new set of anti-Jewish measures. After the brawl at Belgrade University and in the light of Germany's menacing presence in the Balkans, in order to prevent a fascist turmoil inside the country, the government banned Zbor on 28 October. Numerous arrests were made and Ljotić went into hiding. It was now known that the Slovene leader was the main proponent of the German line in the government, which explains Prince Paul's hesitation to replace him. Eventually, Korošec did everyone in the government and court a favour and died on 14 December, ending all the speculation about new anti-Jewish measures in Yugoslavia.[87]

Although both antisemitism and domestic fascism were getting increasingly more vocal in the 1930s, they remained fringe occurrences in pre-war Yugoslav society until the summer of 1940, while public support for ideas of liberalism and democracy was much stronger. In Croatia, Maček, the undisputed leader of Croatian politics was opposed to antisemitism, as well as those leading Croatian intellectuals associated with the daily newspaper *Obzor*, edited by Milivoj Dežman, and the periodical *Nova Evropa*. Among the Serbs, politicians opposed to the government, such as Živko Topalović and Adam Pribićević, as well as the leading opposition party, the Democrats led by Milan Grol, were vehemently opposed to antisemitism and German influence. Within the government, many Serbian ministers did not hide their contempt for antisemitism and fascism, such as Konstantinović, Branko Čubrilović, Srdjan Budisavljević or Djura Janković. The most important Belgrade daily newspaper *Politika* remained devoted to the ideas of liberal democracy throughout the decade. When the director of the Rostock University Dental Clinic and a renowned professor Hans Morel was fired due to his Jewish origin in April 1933, he was immediately offered a post at the Belgrade Medical Faculty.[88] At the opening ceremony of the Berlin Summer Olympics in 1936, the Yugoslav team members refused to salute with the raised right arm when passing before Hitler and instead only nodded their head at the Führer.[89] Early in September 1939, Božo Banac and his stepson Vane Ivanović, the owners of Yugoslav Lloyd, the largest Yugoslav shipping company, placed their ships in the service of the British war effort. When the Yugoslav authorities protested on the ground of Yugoslavia's neutrality in war, the latter told them that the government might be neutral, but he was not.[90] Although there were priests who preached antisemitism, the Serbian Orthodox Church did not hide its friendly feelings for Yugoslav Jews, especially after the death of Patriarch Varnava in 1937. His successor Gavrilo invested a lot of effort in emphasizing the traditional harmony between the Serbs and the Jews, by frequently and cordially meeting with spiritual leaders of the Jewish community, even after the outbreak of war, in Vukovar (Croatia) in November 1939, in Priboj (Serbia) and Sarajevo in September and Kumanovo (Macedonia) in October 1940. Although the official press was understandably restrained in commenting on the government's anti-Jewish measures, the Jewish press in Yugoslavia reported eagerly on every example of support for the Jews and contempt for the government's decisions upheld in small provincial newspapers. According to Milan Koljanin, this was mostly the case in eastern parts of the country and the Jewish press insisted that among the Serbs, traditionally friendly feelings towards the Jews were untouched by recent events.[91]

What was then the reason for the change of policy in October 1940? On 26 July 1940, Cvetković spoke to Heeren; after formal assurances that Yugoslavia would not take any anti-German political course, the Prime Minister went further in announcing his intentions of closing down all the masonic lodges.[92] Although not mentioning the Jews or the Jewish question, a few weeks later Cvetković indeed banned Masonry in Yugoslavia. It is clear that this and the measures on 5 October were by their character political, not ideological. The Yugoslav authorities cracked under the fear of the Third Reich after the fall of France. It does not excuse the government for the cowardice which prompted it to violate its own constitution, but with the exception of Korošec, there were no other passionate antisemites in the Cvetković cabinet. And despite the cautious approach of Yugoslavia's government, many officials, especially diplomats abroad, worked on their own in assisting Jewish refugees from Germany, Austria, the Protectorate and Poland, by granting them visas unconditionally, even when they had clear instructions from Belgrade not to do so.[93] Perhaps the prevailing attitude of the majority of Yugoslavia's officials was demonstrated by Živojin Simonović, Deputy Minister of the Interior, when in Berlin in October 1940 he coolly responded to Himmler's question about the number of Jews in Yugoslavia, that he would not know the answer as all Yugoslavs were considered equal by the law.[94] It needed a lot of courage to say this directly to the face of the second most dangerous man in continental Europe at that moment.

## Yugoslav *Volksdeutsche* between homeland and fatherland

The term *Volksdeutsche* was used to describe people who were German in culture and language, but who were not German citizens. Yugoslavia had a considerable German minority, living mainly in northern parts of the country, but Yugoslavia's ethnic Germans were not a coherent ethnic body with a unique historical experience and the same socio-economic development. We can identify four different groups of Yugoslavian *Volksdeutsche*, living in Vojvodina, Slavonia, Slovenia and Bosnia.

Germans had lived in Slovenia since the Middle Ages and were mostly a privileged and dominant urban class, compared to the rural and underprivileged Slovenian Slavic majority. They represented the southernmost fringes of a coherent German ethnic population stretching all the way to the Baltic and the North Sea. In contrast, the origin of the Vojvodina and Slavonia Germans comes from state-organized migration after the end of the Austro-Turkish War of 1716–18, into the areas spread along the Sava and Danube rivers, bordering Ottoman territory. The Viennese court insisted on the settlement of Catholic German-speaking peasants and craftsmen from Bavaria, Swabia and Rhineland, although in the process many German-speaking and other Protestants also moved in. However, while Germans who migrated to present-day Banat moved in as free men and settled in individual model villages built especially for them, separating them from the indigenous population, Germans in Slavonia, Bačka and Srem were often settled on the landed estates of the old Hungarian and Croatian nobility, as people dependent on their feudal lords. While Slovenian Germans were a privileged group which encouraged Germanization of the lower Slavic masses, the Vojvodina and Slavonia Germans were disempowered after the Austro-Hungarian Compromise of 1867, and exposed to Magyarization in Vojvodina and Croatization in Slavonia. Finally, there were groups of Germans living in Bosnia after the Austro-Hungarian occupation in 1878, either through organized settlement, voluntary internal migration or following the insertion of professional Austrian-German administrators and professionals.[95] At the same time, ethnic Germans in Yugoslavia were divided by sectarianism, with the majority of their Catholic priests being suspicious of any German political or cultural organization in Yugoslavia headed by Lutherans.[96] Overall, around 500,000 ethnic Germans lived in Yugoslavia before 1941, or about 4 per cent of the total population: 340,000 lived in present-day Vojvodina; 110,000 in present-day Croatia; a little less than 40,000 in Slovenia; and others in Bosnia, Central Serbia and Belgrade. About 20 per cent of Yugoslav ethnic Germans were Protestants.[97]

In Vojvodina, the organized settlement pattern prevented the integration or assimilation of ethnic Germans with other ethnic groups, with the minor exception of Hungarians after 1867, thus preserving the German language and culture of these people. At the same time, the agricultural and provincial lifestyle in Slavonia and Vojvodina largely prevented them from aspiring towards higher education; consequentially, they developed political self-awareness relatively late, not before 1900, later than Slavs, Romanians or Hungarians. Being mainly farmers and craftsmen, Germans in Yugoslavia lacked both traditional aristocracy and intelligentsia, one explanation as to why they became receptive to the political appeal of Nazism in the 1930s.[98] The foundation of the state of South Slavs in 1918 accelerated the creation of a distinct German national identity in Vojvodina – until then, they had mainly viewed themselves as the Danube Swabians. Yugoslavia's government unintentionally helped this process by sponsoring state education in the German language and by tolerating cultural associations throughout the interwar period, hoping in this way to earn the loyalty of ethnic Germans and use them as a bulwark against Hungarian territorial pretentions.[99] However, during the interwar period the Croatization of local Germans in Slavonia went on, while the regional authorities in Slovenia pursued a policy of revanchism towards ethnic Germans.[100] Overall, a respectable 80 per cent of German-speaking children in Yugoslavia attended schools in their mother tongue.[101] Germans were also the minority with the most developed press activity in Yugoslavia; there were a multitude of weekly and monthly publications, while the daily *Deutsches Volksblatt* from Novi Sad was the largest selling newspaper with a circulation of 12,000 copies and distribution in German communities all over Yugoslavia.[102]

From early on, the German minority largely accepted Yugoslavia as their new country. However, there were problems on the other side. The Slavic people, both north and south, tended to see the minorities in their newly founded state as a foreign element, an inheritance from the previous era stained by historical injustices towards the Slavs and a relic of the old regimes, of which the Germans, Hungarians, Turks and Albanians were the privileged part before the wars of 1912–18. Like all other minorities, ethnic Germans were excluded from the post-war land reforms. According to the wording of the peace treaties, Germans and Hungarians could opt for voluntary relocation to Austria and Hungary by 1922 at the latest; until this deadline, the government suspended some of their civil rights and restricted them from participation in the first post-war Yugoslav elections. Yugoslavia's Germans therefore needed to react quickly and to organize themselves. In April 1921, thirty representatives of ethnic Germans from all over the country met in Jimbolia (present-day Romania since 1924, Yugoslavia between 1918 and 1924, Hatzfeld in German) and founded the Party of Germans, *Partei der Deutschen*. At a politically sensitive moment, it stood for the economic, cultural and educational prosperity of the German minority, but remained uninvolved in questions of national policy. In the 1923 elections, the party won eight seats in the parliament, its biggest success during the interwar period.[103] Although banned in 1929 as a result of the introduction of King Alexander's dictatorship and never restored in the 1930s, it played an important role in the initial homogenization of the hitherto disparate groups of Yugoslavia's ethnic Germans.

In order to facilitate the development of their cultural and national identity, Yugoslavia's Germans also set up the Cultural Association of Danube Swabians (henceforth Kulturbund),[104] in Novi Sad in 1920. Throughout the interwar period, it remained the most organized and influential association of Yugoslavia's ethnic Germans and the one which eventually claimed primacy in all matters relevant to their lives, including politics.[105] Its most prominent leaders in the 1920s were Stefan Kraft and Georg Grassl, who would later become a Yugoslav senator. Still, Kulturbund was banned twice; first in 1924, when the government accused it of political activity; the second time in 1929, at the start of King Alexander's dictatorship, when all nationalist organizations in Yugoslavia were banned. Kulturbund was again allowed to operate in 1931, but only after the government had insisted on changing the organization's statute; its president throughout the 1930s was Johann Keks. In 1922, Kraft founded *Agraria*, an economic cooperative of Yugoslav Germans, providing credit and other forms of financial support to German farmers; it was also successful in promoting economic cooperation with Germany.[106]

After 1918 and the dissolution of the Habsburg Empire, Berlin began showing interest in the Danube Germans. Stresemann and successive German conservative governments advocated the cause of Yugoslav ethnic Germans at the turn of the decade. Because of the Weimar Germany's economic importance for Yugoslavia, Berlin's pleas carried weight; for example, in 1931 the authorities allowed the restoration of Kulturbund.[107] The response from the other side was manifested in a greater political affiliation of Yugoslav Germans with Berlin, which was increasingly seen as the new gravitational centre of the *Volksdeutsche* spread along the lower Danube. The main German organization for cultural work with the *Volksdeutsche* was the Association for Germans Abroad, *Verein für das Deutschtum im Ausland*. It was founded in the nineteenth century and after 1918 it became the main promoter of German culture among the Danube Germans in order to prevent assimilation to other nations. In 1933, it changed its name to the People's Association for Germans Abroad, *Volksbund für das Deutschtum im Ausland* (henceforth VDA). Although there were some changes in personnel, VDA remained relatively non-political and kept its focus on supporting the cultural development of various ethnic German groups abroad; later in the 1930s, its chairman was Karl Haushofer. The most powerful German organization working with Germans outside the Third Reich in the 1930s and the one directly under the control of Himmler and his chief lieutenant Reinhard Heydrich was the Central Office for Ethnic Germans, VoMi. After 1937, it coordinated the political activities of all German minority groups and was headed by the SS officer Werner Lorenz.[108]

Events in Germany in the 1930s predominantly influenced the political development of ethnic Germans in Yugoslavia. The Nazi *Machtergreifung* in 1933 was seen differently among various German groups in Yugoslavia. In Slovenia, this event split the loyalty of the Catholic German minority between the local pro-Austrian and the pan-German Nazi sentiments. Slovenian Germans identified themselves by German language and culture, but equally strongly by their Catholicism, thus inclining predominantly towards Roman-Catholic Austria, rather than sympathizing with the Nazi version of German nationalism. This split lasted for years and remains uncertain to what extent Slovenian Germans were receptive to Nazism before 1941.[109] At the same time, Roman-Catholicism and a sense of belonging to Austria were not such strong bulwarks against Nazification among ethnic Germans in Vojvodina where, unlike in Slovenia, many of them were Lutherans. Throughout the 1930s, approximately 10 per cent of Yugoslavia's ethnic Germans were members of Kulturbund; therefore, the organization's growth after 1939 through either coercion, statistical manipulations by its leadership or as a result of admiration for German military successes should not be taken as ultimate proof of their Nazification.[110]

The second half of the 1930s brought fierce internal clashes within the Kulturbund. The younger generation of more agitated Yugoslav ethnic Germans challenged the old leadership and demanded the reshaping of the organization according to national socialist ideals. They were influenced by the National Renewal Movement of Romanian Germans, *Erneuerungsbewegung*, founded by Fritz Fabritius in 1934. The Renewers among the Yugoslav Germans were led by Jakob Lichtenberger and Jakob Awender in Vojvodina; ideologically close to them was Branimir Altgayer, who founded a similar organization in Slavonia. They all gathered around them a group of like-minded young people, mainly former students at German universities, where they were indoctrinated with Nazism.[111] The problems with their merger with the Zbor movement in 1937 have already been mentioned. Germany's Anschluss with Austria then further radicalized these youngsters. In 1938, Altgayer took his place at the NSDAP congress in Nuremberg.[112] Yugoslav police and secret services successfully tracked these and similar activities among Yugoslav ethnic Germans, but prosecution was rare. This does not mean that the authorities were not alarmed by the threat which the rise of Nazism among ethnic Germans posed to Yugoslavia. In February 1938, Stojadinović's government passed a law which effectively banned land sales to members of the German and Hungarian minorities.[113] In general, the position of the German minority in Yugoslavia worsened under Stojadinović; and yet, after being instructed to by the VoMi for foreign policy reasons, Yugoslav Germans voted overwhelmingly for the ruling party in the December 1938 elections.[114]

For as long as Stojadinović was in power, the old leadership of Yugoslavia's German minority enjoyed the support of the Reich's institutions and of the German legation in Belgrade. The most important advice they received was not to antagonize the Yugoslav authorities in any way.[115] But with the fall of Stojadinović and the looming war in Europe, the VoMi changed its approach towards the Yugoslav Germans. The old leadership fared better among the dominantly agricultural and conservative masses of their compatriots, than the younger and relatively unknown extremists within their ranks did. Nevertheless, with the help of VoMi and after many clashes within the Kulturbund, sometimes even ending with physical violence, a young lawyer from Vojvodina, Josef 'Sepp' Janko, finally took over the leadership of the organization in the summer of 1939; prior to that, Keks was summoned to Berlin in April and hardly pressed to resign. Janko thus become the undisputed leader of Yugoslav ethnic Germans; as of March 1940, he held the title of the People's Group Leader, *Volksgruppenführer*, and introduced the 'Heil Hitler' salute.[116]

This event marked an abrupt break with the hitherto politically benevolent attitude of the German minority towards Yugoslavia, and steered the loyalty of its political representatives towards Nazi Germany. With the outbreak of war and the first German military successes, the ranks of Kulturbund swelled with new members. In Croatia, after the summer of 1939 many ethnic Germans left Maček's party and joined Kulturbund, causing tensions between themselves and the Croat majority.[117] The best opportunity for young, enthusiastic ethnic German Yugoslavs to express their new-found loyalty to the *Volk* occurred between August and November 1940, during the resettlement of 100,000 ethnic Germans from Ukraine and South Russia, along the Danube. The Yugoslav government set up two transit camps on the river, in Zemun and Prahovo (Serbia). While the administration of these camps was given to the Reich's Germans, members of the VoMi, staffing and outside help came from the Yugoslav Germans, mostly young volunteers. The SS used this opportunity to secretly give basic military training to about 300 volunteers inside the camp, who were then smuggled into Germany for further training. Some were enlisted in Waffen-SS units and fought across Europe in the war; others returned to Yugoslavia to carry out a variety of tasks.[118]

At the same time, faced with the menacing German presence in South-Eastern Europe, the Yugoslav government was becoming more acquiescent to the German minority. As early as 5 September 1939, Cvetković pardoned 2,300 ethnic Germans from Slovenia and Vojvodina who had mainly been fined for Nazi salutes and similar provocations.[119] At the same time, upon establishing the new Croatian province, Maček promised Altgayer full German equality in education with Croats.[120] Within weeks after the defeat of France, Cvetković allowed the opening of private schools for Yugoslav Germans, from the school year 1940–1; this immediately became a tool for disseminating Nazi ideology among the youngest members of Yugoslavia's Germans. In September, the Yugoslav Prime Minister made a number of political promises to Yugoslavia's German minority, allowing ethnic German administrators in those boroughs where they constituted a majority and lifting the ban against ethnic Germans purchasing land.[121]

Despite this conciliatory attitude of Yugoslavia's political leadership, the Yugoslav police doubled its activities to curb a growing challenge to the authority of the state by the leadership of the ethnic Germans. And they had their hands full. Events, parties and lectures in the national socialist spirit, even simulations of military exercises in the settlements where ethnic Germans represented a majority, became commonplace from 1939 on.[122] The choreography, messages and atmosphere of these events seemed rather as if they were staged somewhere in the Third Reich.[123] Increasingly there were more violent incidents and fights, mainly with the Serbian youth in Vojvodina.[124] In a speech held at the meeting in Novi Kozarci (earlier Heufeld, Vojvodina) on 28 December 1940, Gustav Halwax, one of the most extreme new leaders of the Kulturbund, said:

> Our country is Greater Germany ... The German Führer cares about us ... We, here, have to be united, to work and be disciplined; for discipline, work and order are preconditions of our victory. Therefore, to reach our goal [you have to] listen to your superiors. Make arrangements and be quiet; because you live among our *enemy*, who cares to learn about our cause. Let our password be – *Schweigen* [Silent]![125]

These words are a good illustration of the mindset of a young ethnic German Yugoslav indoctrinated with Nazism in 1940.

On 31 December 1940, *Deutsches Volksblatt* demanded the right for the German minority in Yugoslavia to legally organize itself in accordance with national socialist principles.[126] At the same time, Janko asked for a large quantity of guns and ammunitions to be secretly supplied to the Yugoslav Germans from the Reich. Both the Foreign Ministry and VoMi refused this, judging that good political relations with Yugoslavia were the paramount need at the time. Furthermore, after Ribbentrop's pressure early in January, the SS had to stop with recruiting young ethnic German Yugoslavs to its ranks.[127] The Reich's Foreign Ministry then toyed with the idea of a minority protection treaty, similar to those already signed with Slovakia, Hungary and Romania, but at the dawn of the war with Yugoslavia, it was already too late for that.[128]

During the subsequent demonstrations upon the signing of the Tripartite Pact on 25 March, there were many violent clashes and attacks on ethnic Germans in Serbian parts of Yugoslavia, as they were increasingly seen as the Third Reich's fifth column in Yugoslavia. After the military coup two days later, VoMi ordered Yugoslav Germans to avoid mobilization in the Yugoslav army, while Hungarian authorities were requested to allow free entry into Hungary to any Yugoslav German who was fleeing the country. In order to prepare the German public for an imminent attack on Yugoslavia, the Reich's Propaganda Ministry used the plight of ethnic Germans there. Just as prior to the Munich Conference and the attack on Poland, the alleged terror and violence against the German minority in Yugoslavia were once again used as the excuse for an attack on another country.[129]

## Limited fear

Prejudices and racial stereotypes about Jews existed in the area long before the creation of Yugoslavia and continued thereafter. Albeit not as strong as in some other European countries, it intensified in the 1930s as a consequence of the economic crisis, the implications of internal Yugoslav politics and especially after Hitler's rise to power in Germany. But unlike in some other countries of the region, such as Romania or Hungary, where the role of the Jews in the economy was stronger, their number and presence in Yugoslavia were small and their significance in the social, economic and cultural life of the country limited. Antisemitism in Yugoslavia, in both east or west of the country, was different from Nazi racial antisemitism; to say that overall Yugoslavia was a tolerant country and a safe place for Jews throughout the interwar period would be an overstatement, but to stigmatize it as antisemitic would be wrong. The same applies to native fascism in Yugoslavia, which, albeit becoming louder and more aggressive as the 1930s went on, remained only a minor element of Yugoslavia's political life. Its appeal to Serbs, Croats or Slovenes was limited to small segments of society. Despite their differences and basic political culture, all three nations preferred to leave their fate in the hands of mainstream parties. Finally, a similar transformation in the 1930s gripped Yugoslavia's German minority, which was rapidly Nazifying as the war approached.

Unlike the Yugoslav people, the government had no luxury of freely expressing its wishes or passions. Responding to increasing German political pressure, Yugoslavia's authorities became more tolerant towards these phenomena, but never allowed them to grow out of proportion and become threatening to Yugoslavia's internal stability. Some decisions made by the Yugoslav authorities, such as measures against the Jews or a tolerant attitude towards Zbor in the late 1930s, were purely political, not ideological – and that is the point this chapter is making. Two antisemitic decrees from October 1940 and a growing acquiescence towards the Yugoslav *Volksdeutsche* in the autumn of the same year were clearly the result of fear of seemingly invincible Germany in the time after the fall of France. And yet, even then, the government had had enough of fascist provocation and on 28 October 1940 it banned Zbor, making numerous arrests. Of course, the ban came more as a result of fears for the government's own internal position and the stability of the country, than as a demonstration of Yugoslavia's attitude against the Reich's political order, or even a measure of disgust towards fascist ideology and propaganda. But the Zbor ban reflects very vividly that the Yugoslav authorities understood the scope of the danger coming from the direction of the German-sponsored proxies in Yugoslavia and the Third Reich itself. And that Yugoslavia's fear had limits.

# 8

# Bringing Yugoslavia in line

The outbreak of war placed Yugoslavia in the favourable position of an exporter to both camps and economic relations with all countries continued as normal. In the first war year, Germany needed a good economic relationship with Yugoslavia and wished to avoid any complications. Before September 1939, German army officials led by General Georg Thomas, the head of the Wehrmacht's Defence Economy and Armament Office, were concerned about the capacity of the German war economy to wage a long war. There were fears that Britain and France combined, supported by the United States, outperformed Germany's war production. Britain's maritime blockade was efficient from the start. The truth could not be hidden from officials: German raw materials imports had been reduced by 80 per cent by the beginning of 1940 and they got through the critical first ten months of war only thanks to draconian government measures. The two Western allies made a combined order of 10,000 aircraft from the United States, which lifted its ban on armament sales in November 1939, to be delivered by the end of 1940; this was more than Germany's annual production. Combined British and French foreign currency assets outmatched Germany's by a ratio of ten to one.[1] Germany resembled a large armoury of weapons and war material ready for use, while its industry and agriculture could not produce sufficient food and consumer goods for its population. According to Vladimir Vauhnik, Yugoslavia's Military Attaché in Berlin, reliable sources in the Defence Economy and Armament Office claimed that Germany simply had no economic potential to wage war beyond October 1942.[2]

This chapter follows German-Yugoslav economic relationship in its final stage, after the outbreak of war in September 1939 and before Yugoslavia's demise in April 1941. The relationship is divided in two phases, before and after the fall of France. In the first phase, Yugoslavia was still one of the crucial countries for supplying Germany with the commodities necessary for waging war. More importantly, in the light of the Reich's chronic shortages and high demand of food and material, Yugoslavia maintained a strong bargaining position to Germany, while selling goods to all sides in war. But Yugoslavia's agenda of balancing as a supplier of material in demand for waging war between all sides fell apart in the summer of 1940. The balance of power which was necessary for such an approach was gone and after the fall of France, Germany remained the only political power in South-Eastern Europe, unrestrained by any scruples in imposing its wishes. The second phase of this relationship is thus marked with the quick settlement of many existing economic problems on Germany's terms.

## German armament deliveries after September 1939

With the outbreak of war, Yugoslavia's priority was to modernize its army. It lacked everything, from uniforms and basic war material to modern artillery, tanks and aircraft. Because of the slow development of its own war industry, the situation necessitated buying from abroad. According to Elisabeth Barker, the British were aware that Yugoslavia and other Balkan countries needed armaments which they could not provide and lamented the fact that Germany could do so.[3] However, this claim is exaggerated. In July 1939, the British government responded positively to Yugoslavia's plea for aircraft deliveries and offered credit worth 1 million pound sterling.[4] There were some sticking points between the two sides, but negotiations for this agreement went on uninterrupted until 11 January 1940, when Halifax and the Yugoslav Minister in London Ivan Subotić signed the secret agreement; Yugoslavia received credit worth 1.5 million pounds sterling, repayable over the next twenty years in forty instalments, with a 5 per cent interest rate. London agreed to deliver Hawker Hurricane fighters and Bristol Blenheim bomber aircraft Yugoslavia had asked for, with spare engines, spare parts and weapons.[5] The first aircraft were delivered within a few months of the contracts being signed with the manufacturers: twelve Hurricanes in March and twenty Blenheim bombers in April 1940.[6]

In contrast, Yugoslavia had many problems with Germany. Avramovski suggests that the export of weaponry was the ultimate tool of German foreign-political pressure.[7] This was true in the summer of 1939; however, with the outbreak of war Berlin's attitude had to adjust. In the changed circumstances, Germany could not impose strong political pressure in the south-east as it had before September 1939, until decisive victories were gained on the western front. Berlin also knew that Yugoslavia would be courted by Germany's enemies and therefore it had to moderate its tone. Secondly, Germany was struggling with shortages of supplies and inefficiencies in its own production and the requirements of its war effort.[8] The first months of the war were marked with tensions in German-Yugoslav relations over the delays in armaments and war material deliveries which were agreed in July. A transport of antiaircraft guns from Bohemia was returned to the factory just before reaching Yugoslavia's border; however, a shipment of weaponry for Bulgaria was delivered normally.[9] Wiehl informed Heeren that in the changed circumstances, Germany could not honour the July agreement and would instead ask for a barter arrangement – a direct exchange of German weaponry for Yugoslavia's raw materials.[10] Nothing was said about the political conditioning of the deal, although the episode with the returned transport indicated that Yugoslavia was not trusted. According to Wiehl, the leading role in this matter was in the hands of the Aviation and War Ministries in Berlin and the Foreign Ministry was at pains to address Belgrade's complaints.[11] Displeased with the German attitude, the Yugoslavs informed Neuhausen that the previous promise of oil concessions to Germany was suspended.[12] Still, needing urgently to modernize its army, Belgrade had no choice but to comply with German demands. On 19 September, the two sides reached an agreement for further exports of Yugoslav zinc, copper, lead, tin and hemp to a total value of 34 million Reichsmarks over the next eight months, in exchange for German weaponry, 100 Messerschmitt fighters, some training aircraft and hundreds of anti-aircraft and anti-tank guns.[13] The story of German credit that was dragging since January was thus closed; instead of paying for weaponry through its clearing credit in Berlin, Yugoslavia agreed to pay for imports of aircraft and guns with the equivalent exports of metals and raw material. This was ratified in the so-called Landfried protocol,[14] signed on 5 October in Belgrade, which specified the prices and amount of Yugoslav raw materials to be dispatched monthly to Germany and according to which German armaments and war material were to be delivered to Yugoslavia by July 1940.[15] The agreement was a setback for Yugoslavia, as some of the raw materials Yugoslavia was obliged to deliver to Germany represented a valuable source of foreign currency.[16] Despite the agreement, the German manufacturers hesitated in signing contracts. On 17 October 1939, Andrić's combination of complaints and threats seemed to have worked and the agreement with the Messerschmitt aircraft company, worth 19 million Reichsmarks in aircraft and spare parts, was finally signed on 23 October.[17]

In the meantime, the German War Ministry banned a delivery of anti-tank guns and Heeren was instructed to inform the Yugoslavs that only part of the agreed war material could be delivered.[18] Heeren's protestations and warnings that any confidence in Germany would be lost and that no real danger to German military interests existed as Yugoslavia was determined to remain neutral in war were futile. On 30 October, Nedić accepted the reduced delivery of anti-tank guns, provided other equipment and types of aircraft were sent in exchange.[19] On 8 November, Heeren and Pilja exchanged letters which contained a summary of these changes to the Landfried protocol.[20] Germany thus got away with serious breaches of two agreements made with Yugoslavia in less than five months. Berlin then insisted that previously agreed and partly paid armament purchases from Škoda would be treated as part of the October agreement. In this way, Germany obtained more Yugoslav raw materials than the amount of armaments the factories from the Old Reich needed to deliver. The Germans continued to ignore delivery deadlines and frequently changed the previously agreed types of armament. In the words of Vauhnik, 'for barely 100 fighters and 40 bombers [aircraft], it took as many official visits, negotiations and diplomatic actions, always alongside new concessions the Germans demanded, which in reality all represented a form of blackmailing'.[21] By the end of 1939, Germany was supposed to deliver armaments worth twice as much as the raw materials it received from Yugoslavia, but in reality, they dispatched less than half of what the Yugoslavs had paid for.[22]

Yugoslavia occasionally responded with halting deliveries of copper which annoyed Berlin. Also, Belgrade actively negotiated elsewhere. The new German Military Attaché Rudolf Toussaint reported bitterly in October that Italy had offered a deal to Belgrade, consisting of Savoia bomber aircraft, various transport and light armoured vehicles and what seemed to be the Škoda guns, previously purchased by Yugoslavia, but after Hitler's orders in July delivered to Italy.[23] The offer referred to Yugoslavia's decision to undertake mechanisation of its units and the Germans were preparing to get one more deal done under the provisions of the October agreement. But Italy seemingly offered better terms, and more worryingly for Berlin Italy asked for payment partly in deliveries of Yugoslavia's lead and copper.[24] German diplomats were warned to intervene and Yugoslavia formed a military committee to investigate the pros and cons of both offers, which in January ruled in favour of Italy. Apart from a number of trucks, automobiles and light armoured vehicles, the two sides also agreed on delivery of forty-five Italian Savoia bombers, which were all dispatched in 1940.[25] Yugoslavia did not rely only on great powers for armaments deliveries; in April, Yugoslavia made a deal with Spain for the delivery of anti-tank guns which would be paid for with 30,000 tons of Yugoslav wheat.[26] All this news alarmed the Germans, forcing them to speed up their deliveries; in March and April 1940, Berlin dispatched most of the Yugoslav purchases made in October. Only twenty-seven Messerschmitt fighters remained undelivered before the deadline at the end of June. However, the events on the western front in June meant that these remaining aircraft were never delivered.

Overall, by January 1941 the Yugoslav War Ministry had purchased aircraft, artillery, various technical and marine equipment worth 114 million Reichsmarks, of which 80 million worth were delivered. In addition to the delayed deadlines, the Yugoslavs rarely ended up with what they had purchased; anti-aircraft guns were delivered without the vehicles to move them, anti-tank guns without sufficient ammunition, vehicles without tyres and instead of modern fighters and bombers, Yugoslavia once received fifty harmless Bücker training aircraft.[27] Finally, in December 1940 the Foreign and Aviation ministries in Berlin agreed to ban aircraft deliveries to Yugoslavia as they no longer saw economic reason for them; Yugoslavia's economy was subordinated to Germany and 'even without [the armament deliveries], we [Germany] are receiving the war material deliveries important for us'.[28] In February 1941, the Germans for the last time before the April attack refused to deliver the remaining twenty-seven Messerschmitt fighter aircraft.[29] German military successes elsewhere brought the Yugoslav economy in line. The fact that Germany considered hitherto all the unresolved matters solved by the sheer force and felt no need to respect signed agreements anymore speaks volumes about the place of the smaller European nations in the future German New Order.

## Before the fall of France

The war affected all European economies and disrupted international trade. The British blockade restricted trade of overseas countries with Germany, affecting the prices of grain and some raw materials worldwide. The drain of European gold to the safety of the United States increased daily. Regulations restricting payments with foreign currencies became a rule in every country, as did various financial bills and decrees for preventing the black market, obtaining new loans or issuing government bonds to cover the costs of war, or preparations for either war or defence, etc. Yugoslavia was not an exception. On 18 October 1939, the Finance Ministry banned payments of dividends to foreign shareholders of joint-stock companies without prior approval of the National Bank. A month later, the same ministry authorized the issuing of bonds up to a sum of 700 million dinars with an interest rate of 6 per cent, for the needs of Yugoslavia's defence and public works requirements.[30] At the beginning of November, despite British and French protestations, the Yugoslav government forced the management of the French-owned Bor copper mine and British-owned Trepča lead and zinc mine to sell their total production to the state, in dinars at the official international price.³¹ The German legation reported late in November that '[the war] gave strong impetus to plans and attempts to increase a domestic production [of hitherto imported goods] by using the favourable climate and richness of [Yugoslavia's] ore deposits'.³² Yugoslavia's increased deliveries to Germany alarmed the Western allies, resulting in the signing of new favourable trading deals with both France and Britain in December 1939 and January 1940, respectively. The deals regulated the export of Yugoslavia's metals and raw materials to these countries in exchange for the products Yugoslavia needed and would otherwise have to pay for in cash.³³

Still, 1939 was another good year for Yugoslavia's economy; it ended with a foreign-trade surplus of 764 million dinars, ten times more than in 1938, while exports increased by 10 per cent. More importantly, Yugoslavia had a surplus of 700 million dinars in trade with non-clearing countries.³⁴ In September, there was a fear that hitherto favourable economic development would change under new circumstances. Still, the outbreak of war did not hinder trade with Western Europe, nor decreased the influx of foreign currency. True, the overall volume of trade decreased by approximately 15 per cent in October compared to August, but for the first time since the introduction of the import controls, Yugoslavia's trade with non-clearing countries surpassed 30 per cent of overall foreign trade, imports declining by 37 per cent, but exports rising by 23 per cent on 1938. Yugoslav exports to Germany continued to decline, falling by 17 per cent from 1938, but imports from Germany grew by 16 per cent.³⁵ Including the Protectorate, the Reich now provided a staggering 47 per cent of Yugoslavia's imports. However, its share of Yugoslavia's exports fell to 30 per cent, even after the inclusion of Bohemia. For Belgrade, this represented a 'healthy' negative trade balance of 500 million dinars which kept the clearing account stable.³⁶ Furthermore, Yugoslav exports increased in value, but decreased in volume, due to the increased price of food and metals in the world market, thus justifying the efforts for the modernization of Yugoslavia's economy in previous years. Consequently, the National Bank could limit and for some periods even entirely stop the sale of foreign currencies, as through exports alone Yugoslavia earned enough to cover the market's demand.³⁷ But not all was positive; inflation grew rapidly and visibly affected the population's purchasing power. By April 1940, prices had grown on average by 33 per cent since September 1939. Despite all the efforts of the Finance Ministry and the National Bank, the war psychosis was taking its toll.³⁸ Another reason for this rise in prices was an increased domestic demand for raw materials. The urgent need to improve Yugoslavia's defensive abilities, coupled with the need to export under favourable terms, increased a demand which domestic production could not satisfy.³⁹

Toussaint's analysis of the German-Yugoslav economic relations before the end of 1939 was unfavourable. After listing all the metals important for Germany's import, he objected that '[altogether] Germany does not use all the benefits Yugoslavia offers. Roughly, in all sectors there is a possibility for doubling or tripling [of Yugoslavia's exports to Germany]'. Toussaint then stated that Yugoslavia saw no interest in shipping its metals to Germany, as there were customers willing to pay in gold, cash or weaponry. Political neutrality in the present conflict contributed to this attitude: 'If sometime in the future Germany was forced to rely predominantly on the Yugoslav export of raw materials, and simultaneously was not able to pay with its war material, then the vital matter would be [securing] Yugoslavia's further crediting of Germany.'[40]

Being neutral, Yugoslavia was caught between the two sides, experiencing the pressure from both. Upon the news that the British had warned Belgrade against any increase in trade with Germany above normal, a warning was sent from Berlin that Germany would 'have to consider any commitment entered into by a neutral country with England restricting normal trade and transit of goods between Germany and that country as aid to enemy countries and thereby as a violation of neutrality against which we reserve the fullest freedom of action'.[41] Yugoslavia quickly realized that in order to manage its position of exporter to both sides, a necessary precondition was balance between them; for as long as there was a balance, there was room for manoeuvre. Britain and France were delivered a serious blow with the Yugoslav decree which established a state monopoly on ore production in the Trepča and Bor mines. For Yugoslavia, this was an enforced move, as the only way of paying for the necessary armament deliveries from abroad was in goods. In October 1939, the Trade and Industry Minister Ivan Andres advised the British Minister that if London wanted to help, Britain should open a clearing account in Belgrade. Typically, the British stalled, probably as a result of the weakness of their war economy.[42] London sent a negotiator to Belgrade late in November, who joined the French team which had already arrived, to discuss the problems arising with Yugoslavia's decision to acquire the complete production of Bor and Trepča mines.[43] As previously mentioned, the agreement for the aircraft delivery was signed in London in January 1940; Yugoslavia also aimed to obtain a million pounds credit for the purchase of other material necessary for war production from Britain'.[44] Yugoslavia's favourable position of exporter of goods in demand at the market also worked to its benefit in negotiations with France. Apart from other provisions regarding armament and other goods, the agreement gave Belgrade the privilege of paying off its significant debt to France with the export of goods.[45] In October 1939, Yugoslavia and Romania agreed the exchange of 300,000 tons of petroleum for iron and copper.[46]

In addition to official contacts, after September 1939 Britain increased its unofficial economic offensive and Yugoslavia became a battleground for British and German economic agents. London attempted a policy of pre-emptive purchasing, with the primary aim of hurting Germany's economic requirements. The Germans reported various examples of British purchases of Yugoslavia's goods at unusually high volumes, or even attempts to buy the businesses important for trade with Germany.[47] This policy culminated in April 1940, when the Economic Warfare Ministry in London established the United Kingdom Commercial Corporation, with the official task of conducting trade with the Balkans neutrals, but in reality for waging economic war on Germany.[48] More worrying were attempts and acts of British sabotage in Yugoslavia, aimed at industrial and mining plants. The most adventurous were plans for blocking the Iron Gates gorge on the Danube, by sinking cement-filled barges.[49] This plan, known to the Germans, was even more disturbing as the vast majority of Russian ores, metals, foodstuff and fodder for Germany were transported via the Danube.[50] Yugoslavia shared German worries and in December the War Ministry organized additional protection of the most important mines, oil fields in Croatia and factories, such as the aluminium plant in Lozovac.⁵¹ The Germans considered this measure as inadequate and from the beginning of 1940, organised by the *Sicherheitsdienst*, the SS agency for foreign intelligence, began protecting those industrial plants in Yugoslavia which were of interest for the German war industry, disregarding if these plants were owned by the German capital or not.⁵² German intelligence work in Yugoslavia was systematically organized since the arrival of Gestapo's Hans Helm to the Belgrade legation in December 1937, to officially work as a liaison with the Yugoslav police. Maintaining close relationship with Milan Aćimović, the Belgrade City Administrator, a policeman number one in Yugoslavia and Stojadinović's confidant, and enlisting Dragi Jovanović, the chief of the Belgrade Police and later an advisor in the Interior Ministry in his payroll as an informant, Helm built strong positions for Germany's espionage in Yugoslavia. These were reinforced in 1939, when Helm was joined by Karl Kraus of the *Sicherheitsdienst*, officially employed by Neuhausen's German Travel Bureau in Belgrade. German military attaché Toussaint, who was at the same time the head of the German military intelligence service *Abwehr* for Yugoslavia, worked independently from them.⁵³ By 1940, this intelligence network was ready to efficiently confront the British and the French in an underground war on the Yugoslav soil. In January and February 1940, the Germans purchased all the available dinars on the Zurich currency market. This move caused an unease in both London and Belgrade, as it was unknown how these resources would be used. The British first guess was for financing the network of German agents in Yugoslavia.⁵⁴

Still, the most important issue for Berlin was securing regular supplies of Yugoslavia's raw materials. The meeting of the German-Yugoslav Mixed Committee was held in Belgrade in October 1939; during this meeting, the two sides merely confirmed the existing state of affairs with minor modifications. More important was the secret meeting, previously mentioned, held against the backdrops of the Mixed Committee sessions, which discussed the precise quantities of the German armaments and Yugoslavia's raw materials. These two simultaneous negotiations resulted in exempting Yugoslav copper, lead, lead concentrate, zinc concentrate, pyrite, aluminium, antimonies, hemp and some other non-metals from the existing system of trade through clearing and placing them under the rules of barter exchange for German armaments.⁵⁵ For this purpose, a third account was created, separate to the Reichsmark and dinar accounts in Berlin and Belgrade. The Landfried protocol turned out to be unfavourable for Yugoslavia. Its main flaw was the clause which as a basis for exchange set the average prices for metals and raw materials Yugoslavia would deliver, at the rate they were traded at the London Stock Exchange in July 1939. But there were not the same stipulations for the price of German armaments, as no deliveries had been made before September which could be taken as a basis. This meant that except in the case of copper, Yugoslavia traded at loss, as prices of other metals rose after September 1939. The Commissariat for Ores and Metals at the Yugoslav War Ministry was in charge of buying domestic ore and metals at the current daily prices, which was afterwards shipped to Germany at the lower July prices. Also, the protocol never determined the responsibility for transport and various other taxes and the Germans felt no obligation to share these expenses.⁵⁶ Upon realizing the problem, the Yugoslavs tried to negotiate. In February 1940, Belin spoke to the German representative and the latter agreed to a price increase of 13 per cent, but refused to negotiate about the transport expenses, which would have increased the July 1939 prices on average by 22 per cent per ton.[57]

The Yugoslavs had a few strong cards in their hand. The first one was continued sale of ore and metals for foreign currency; the second card was delayed deliveries to Germany. Berlin urged Radovan Jeftić, the head of the Commissariat for Ores and Metals, to make sure that Yugoslavia honoured the agreed monthly deliveries of 2,000 tons of copper.[58] But Neuhausen's frequent visits to Jeftić were futile, as on 30 November 1939 the Yugoslav Trade and Industry Ministry asked Nedić to 'given our need to be careful of the feelings of these sides [French and British], instruct the commissar for ores not to rush too much with belated deliveries for Germany'.[59] The increased Yugoslav deliveries to France, Britain and everywhere where foreign currencies could be earned, or materials Yugoslavia needed obtained by exchange, are proof of how little influence Germany could exercise in Belgrade before the summer of 1940.[60]

Another issue which continuously irritated Germany was the ever-present problem of the Reichsmark's rate in Yugoslavia. Although slightly raised after the Cologne meeting in June 1939, at 14.50 dinars it was still lower than what the Germans wished. In December, Clodius sent an angry letter to Belgrade, instructing Neuhausen to remind Belin of the necessity of correcting the currency rate. He asked the German Consul to convey the message that Germany tolerated the Reichsmark's low rate only because of understanding the damage the imbalance of payments in Berlin and Belgrade was doing to Yugoslavia's finances. Clodius believed that the October protocol would restore stability to the clearing accounts, thus removing the main excuse for a strong dinar. He gave the example of the dollar. The National Bank kept its rate deliberately high; in Germany it was 2.50 Reichsmarks, but in Yugoslavia it was 55 dinars, meaning that in Belgrade one could buy 3.80 Reichsmarks for one dollar. Clodius rejected the argument provided by the Yugoslavs, that the higher Reichsmark's rate would reduce Yugoslav imports from Germany, or lead to inflation in Yugoslavia. Instead, he mentioned that Romania had already increased the Reichsmark's rate by 22 per cent: 'As in Romania, we will take more vigorous actions than [ever] before, against undervaluation of the Reichsmark in all the south-eastern countries, in order to oppose English attempts to limit German purchasing opportunities by artificially driving the prices up. The issue is therefore of crucial importance and goes beyond [the wishes of] Yugoslavia.'[61] The National Bank however did not raise the rate above 15 dinars per Reichsmark until autumn 1940. Furthermore, on 1 April Yugoslavia increased export and import customs charges for a large number of goods, of which new, higher export taxes hit German imports of Yugoslav linen, soybeans, lard, eggs and poultry particularly badly.[62]

It is important to stress the determination with which the Yugoslav officials such as Milan Radosavljević, Ivo Belin, Milivoje Pilja, Milan Lazarević, Sava Obradović and many others stood up for their country's best economic interest. Belin was especially notorious with the Germans, who considered him a tough and strongminded negotiator. Experts at the National Bank, Economics Department of the Foreign

Ministry, Finance Ministry and Trade and Industry Ministry rarely allowed their decisions, recommendations and analysis to be blurred by political sentiments, or interests other than economic. However, their firm attitude was frequently negated by the compliance of Yugoslavia's political authorities. Thus, on 11 January 1940 Belin informed the Germans that Yugoslavia's deliveries of raw materials would stop until the augmented Yugoslav credit on the new account was balanced by German armaments deliveries.[63] Simultaneously, the same message was passed on to Neuhausen's associate Karl Gemünd in the Commissariat for Ores and Metals in Belgrade; Jeftić said firmly that he did not care who was right or wrong, but he had strict instructions from the War Ministry and the National Bank to follow.[64] However, ten days earlier Cincar-Marković told Heeren how all the relevant political authorities, the Prime Minister, War Minister, Interior Minister and himself formed a united front, 'fully endorsed from the highest place', which was an obvious reference to Prince Paul, to remove any obstacles to closer economic cooperation between the two countries – without any reference to or complaint about German delays in armament deliveries.[65] In April, Cincar-Marković told Heeren that Yugoslavia needed to maintain good economic relations with Germany, which were by itself natural, as opposed to economic relations with 'England and France, artificially constructed on the political foundations'.[66]

In such circumstances, it was hardly surprising that the Germans decided to prepare the political ground prior to the next meeting of the Mixed Committee in May 1940. It was vitally important to secure the existing levels of imports from Yugoslavia, as in 1940 these were not threatened just by the activities of German enemies. The new problem was shortages in Yugoslavia, of metals, raw materials, grains, meat and lard, all vital German imports.[67] At the beginning of May, Clodius arrived in Belgrade and discussed German-Yugoslav economic relations with the Yugoslav officials. Cvetković was more reserved than the mealy-mouthed Cincar-Marković and Prince Paul and refused to unconditionally back German demands for increased exports, stating that Yugoslavia's own needs were a priority. Pilja and Belin stressed that despite German fears, the British were not attempting to interfere in Yugoslavia's foreign trade.[68] Clodius left Belgrade with unfavourable impressions. Talking to the Italian Minister in Sofia two days later, he stressed that of all the Balkan countries, Yugoslavia 'had the greatest potential to [unpleasantly] surprise'.[69]

The German economic team arrived in Belgrade five days later for the meeting of the German-Yugoslav Mixed Committee. The reason for this meeting was the established customs unity of the Third Reich on 31 March, meaning that the Protectorate was merged with the Reich and all the prior trading agreements and regulations between Yugoslavia and Czechoslovakia lost validity. Regulating the trade with Bohemia was important, as since September 1939 Yugoslavia's balance of trade was positive over the limit which could allow regular payments of Yugoslav exporters from the clearing account in Belgrade. Not surprisingly, the Yugoslavs used the opportunity to point out to the problem of delayed deliveries of German armament and the Germans acknowledged it. The question of the Reichsmark rate was not discussed and the meeting ended on 31 May.[70] To further reinforce their position, the Yugoslavs also looked east and in June, upon establishing diplomatic relations with the Soviet Union, two national banks opened accounts in dollars for mutual trade.[71]

At the moment when the Yugoslavs believed the situation was under control, France fell and on 15 June Wiehl instructed Heeren to convey the following messages in Belgrade: Yugoslavia would from now on sell of all its export goods to Germany and Italy; trade with France would return to its pre-war levels and all the copper hitherto sold to France would be redirected to Germany. The instruction ended: 'It would be very useful if you clarified to the Yugoslav government their utter economic dependence on the Axis'.[72] Yugoslavia lost its economic independence.

## Pre-1914 credits

In June 1938, Funk made an angry speech at the meeting of German chambers of commerce in Berlin. He denounced the existence of German debts which, even if there was some foreign crediting in the past, were political in nature. Funk claimed the same about the Austrian debts; demands that Germany honoured them were to him unfounded.[73] However, the Germans were more diligent in the matter of money owed to them, that is, their nationals, or Austrians after the Anschluss, anytime in the past. The problem of pre-1914 debts of the lands which formed the state of South Slavs in 1918 arose silently and continued to grow as German political power in the region grew, pressing the Yugoslav authorities into the realization that one day the question would have to be resolved. Altogether, there were seventeen major and many smaller loans, granted before 1914 to governments of pre-war Serbia and to local authorities and institutions in the territories of Austro-Hungarian Bosnia and Herzegovina, Vojvodina and Croatia.[74]

The matter was mentioned first during the negotiations for the conclusion of the May 1934 Trade Agreement. The Yugoslav side acknowledged its obligations, but no details were discussed. The excuse was Yugoslavia's economic difficulties. In an analysis after the Anschluss, the National Bank assessed that the German demands were justified, as their bondholders were excluded from the settlements made in the 1920s with the French, British and Swiss bondholders of Serbian pre-war government loans. Regarding the infrastructural loans, granted mostly across the Yugoslav territories of the former Austro-Hungary, the National Bank stated that 'the investments made from loaned money still bring income, therefore to use the depreciation as an excuse would be invalid'.[75] In December 1935, the German legation asked the Yugoslav government to organize a meeting with representatives of the German bondholders in order to resolve the problem.[76] After this, the Germans kept pushing for a resolution at every meeting of the Mixed Committee. Each time, the Yugoslav team declared itself not competent to discuss the financial matters.[77]

At the meeting of the Mixed Committee in Cologne in June 1939, the German pressure reached a climax; its side delivered a memorandum calling for an urgent resolution of the problem. According to the report of the Yugoslav Foreign Ministry, 'in the light of our country's present relationship with Germany, [the Yugoslav] side was afraid and unable to prolong the matter again ... To reject, in the present circumstances, is not an option anymore'. Germany demanded the setting up of a special committee to resolve the problem by 1 August.[78] However, the Finance Minister Djuričić refused to discuss this and reprimanded the Foreign Ministry for receiving the German memorandum without his prior approval. 'Such an act represents a precedent unusual in negotiations. ... Without going into details whether the German demand is valid, it is doubtful that our financial and economic situation allows us to venture into such a solution, which would additionally burden our budget and economy.'[79] He remained adamant ignoring renewed German demands and it only took the change of government on 26 August, after the Cvetković-Maček Agreement, to break the deadlock. New Finance Minister Juraj Šutej formed an inter-departmental committee to prepare the Yugoslav case before the meeting with the German side set for 15 November 1939 in Belgrade.[80]

Earlier Yugoslav decision to ignore the pre-war German bondholders was based on the Section B of Article 297 of the Versailles Treaty: 'Subject to any contrary stipulations which may be provided for in the present Treaty, the Allied and Associated Powers reserve the right to retain and liquidate all property, rights and interests belonging at the date of the coming into force of the present Treaty to German nationals, or companies controlled by them.'[81] Since then, international law practice had become more disposed towards the creditors rather than debtors, as opposed to the judgements in international courts immediately after the war. The members of the Yugoslav committee understood that pushing the matter for international arbitration would probably mean losing the case. Yugoslavia fared better regarding some old Bosnian loans given just before the outbreak of war, therefore mostly unused.[82]

At the beginning of the meeting, the Germans made it clear that the least they expected was the reimbursement of the interest lost by the German bondholders in the period prior to 1939. In three sessions held over the following two weeks, there were many circumventions and attempts by both sides to outsmart their opponents.[83] The protocol was signed on 29 November, after each side moderated its initial position. Yugoslavia acknowledged the same right to German bondholders as previously granted to the holders of pre-war Serbian bonds from other countries. It was agreed that 27 million dinars would be paid to them for their lost income in the past twenty-five years, in instalments until March 1942. Yugoslavia also committed to pay belated bonds' interest for two 1914 Bosnian loans, in five instalments until February 1942. However, it managed to get favourable rate of 1.50 dinars to the Austro-Hungarian krona, although the Germans initially insisted on 4 dinars. Other thirteen credits in dispute were also settled. Altogether, Yugoslavia agreed to pay 150 million dinars in instalments over the course of the following two and a half years through its clearing account. As the Germans had started with a demand for 1 billion dinars, Yugoslavia managed to get relatively favourable agreement for settling its debt. Upon the last payment, all seventeen loans would be considered repaid and bonds would be destroyed.[84] The committee met three more times throughout 1940, discussing the method of settlement of the remaining, minor and private loans. This referred to every loan, no matter how small it was, granted to any institution or individual residing on the pre-1918 territory of what was to become Yugoslavia, unpaid after the war. However, the Yugoslavs were mostly satisfied with the terms agreed. The Committee also agreed an amount of 1.5 million dinars to be paid by the German government to Yugoslav nationals who had owned the Graz water supply company, sold it to the city in 1911, but never received their money.[85]

Bizarrely, the fall of France in June 1940, which had caused the severest change of the German-Yugoslav economic relationship, detrimentally for Yugoslavia, had one positive effect for the Belgrade government. In October, the Department of Yugoslavia's State Loans received a letter from the Berliner Handelsgesellschaft, who offered to buy pre-1914 Serbian government bonds held by French bondholders. Following the French military defeat, there was a widespread crisis of confidence in Paris in the value of the franc and many bondholders wished to get rid of their bonds. This presented an opportunity for Yugoslavia to buy back the bonds issued by Serbian governments before 1914 at favourable price. The Berlin company offered to provide as many bonds as possible from France and resell them to Yugoslavia at the price of 250 dinars per 500 francs bond, from December 1940 to 31 December 1941.[86] As this price meant that Yugoslavia would pay less than the interest being paid to French bondholders, the Finance Ministry accepted the offer and signed a protocol on 29 October.[87] Yugoslavia thus briefly before its own demise benefited from the misery of its old war ally.

## Economy and politics become one

In a special report published by MWT in February 1940, Wilmowsky warned about the extraordinary measures needed to be taken in trade with South-Eastern Europe if Germany's war effort was to be successful. He reiterated that MWT had been warning since 1938 that South-Eastern Europe had reached its capacity for covering German import needs from the region, which was confirmed by the foreign-trade statistics for the previous six months. Since September 1939, domestic consumption, stockpiling for domestic needs and the requirements of their own industries increased in all these countries, meaning there was less surplus to export. There was also the problem of increased prices on the world market and finally that of reduced German deliveries of those goods imported by these countries due to Germany's own needs. Therefore, Germany's position in trade with South-Eastern Europe at the beginning of 1940 deteriorated. Wilmowsky mentioned the examples of Romania and Yugoslavia, which had both adapted their foreign-trade policies in order to increase exports to those countries paying in cash or with gold. Wilmowsky's solution to the economic problems was a political one – to threaten with delayed or cancelled deliveries of German armaments. In his words, this solution had already been successfully applied in Yugoslavia, reminding of its government's earlier decision regarding the production of French and British mines. The solution for the whole region was to use new approaches, because purely economic solutions did not bring success. Such an approach implied increasing political pressure with the aim of 'economic occupation' of the south-east, camouflaged by customs union.[88] Everything was pointing towards the serious hardships the German war economy was experiencing after barely six months of war. The policy towards the south-east essentially failed and the only solution the MWT's president could think of was political pressure.

But Germany could not exert pressure as long as France and Britain stood undefeated. At the same time, Germany could not allow a long war as it did not have the resources to wage one. Three individual estimations, Wilmowsky's, Vauhnik's and General Thomas's, independently from each other all pointed to the same conclusion: Germany needed to end war decisively and quickly, or its economy would crumble. Hitler could have been aware of this, as immediately after the Polish conquest he demanded an assault on France, even setting 12 November 1939 as the date for the attack. It took a lot of effort by Halder and Walther von Brauchitsch, Commander-in-Chief of the Army, to dissuade Hitler by explaining that the German army was still not adequately prepared and equipped for a major offensive in the West.[89] The relative passivity of both sides during the winter of 1939–40 created the impression in Yugoslavia that the war would last, with both Britain and France focusing on the blockade, thus slowly exhausting the German economy.[90]

The fall of France in June 1940 was a shock for the Yugoslavs.[91] However, there was no time to recover from it. Italy's entry into the war meant that most of Yugoslavia's trade routes were now severally cut off; the problem was finding ways to import the necessary raw materials for the Yugoslav economy.[92] But more importantly, the bleak reality of Yugoslavia's new geo-political situation meant making severe economic concessions.[93] At the meeting of the Yugoslav-Italian Economic Committee in June, the two sides agreed a significant increase in Yugoslav deliveries of industrial wood, meat and live cattle, but also of copper, at the expense of Britain and France. Italy promised to increase its deliveries of fabrics and yarn but did not make commitments for Yugoslavia's needs for petrol, tin and rubber.[94] Yet the main pressure was coming from Berlin. In early May, Berlin and Belgrade signed a secret protocol which amended some of the quotas of the Yugoslav export of copper and lead agreed by the Landfried protocol.[95] But this was still less than what Berlin wanted and needed for its war economy; it was the victory over France which finally gave Berlin the opportunity to settle the problem of Yugoslavia's deliveries. The Yugoslavs were still hesitant and on 5 July Heeren concluded that 'the attitude [of the Yugoslav government] was expressed by the tendency to satisfy German wishes only to the level necessary to keep the Germans away from exerting political pressure'.[96]

Berlin did not waste time. An emergency meeting of the Mixed Committee demanded by Germany was held in Berlin at the end of July, barely two months after the previous regular meeting was held in May. It regulated Yugoslavia's trade with the Netherlands through the Berlin clearing office, at the rate of 17.82 dinars for the Reichsmark.[97] More importantly, the Germans made it clear that following the fall of France, Yugoslavia had to coordinate its economy with that of the Reich. The demands spanned from insisting on cutting off the Yugoslav deliveries of goods to the defeated countries, over the issue of adjusting Yugoslavia's production to Germany's needs and the taking over of all the Yugoslav export surpluses, to a ban on signing any trading agreement with a third country without prior German approval and an increase in previously agreed volumes of raw materials' deliveries to Germany.[98] The Yugoslavs rejected the last two demands, but it was clear that they would in the future have to comply, without delaying or withholding deliveries. It was too dangerous to reject the demand to cut off Yugoslavia's deliveries of raw materials important for armaments production to Britain and on 1 August the Yugoslavs signed a letter confirming the reduction of their deliveries to German enemies.[99]

As a result of these events, Yugoslavia's dealing with the free trade zone rapidly diminished over the summer and by the end of September exports to non-clearing countries fell to 14 per cent of total exports.[100] There were still reports in Berlin that ships were dispatched from Thessaloniki or trains to Turkey via Bulgaria, carrying lead or lard for British customers. However, the bigger problem for Yugoslavia from Heeren's protestations throughout August was a rapid melting of Yugoslavia's clearing credit in Berlin; by October, Yugoslavia had become Germany's debtor again, for the first time since 1934. This was a result of increased payments by Yugoslavia's importers, partly as a panic response to frequent rumours about the impending rise of the Reichsmark's rate. The National Bank had to increasingly sell Reichsmarks in order to cover the higher demand in the market. There were other problems, such as shortages of metals and raw materials for domestic production. Inflation continued to rise and after only one year of war, prices in Yugoslavia were 60 per cent higher than in September 1939. During the summer, the government set up the Directorate for Foreign Trade, with power to control all Yugoslavia's exports and imports, hoping in vain to control events. The stockpiling of food across the country was ordered in September.[101]

The next meeting of the German-Yugoslav Mixed Committee was held between 20 September and 19 October 1940 in Belgrade. The most important decision was reached already at the beginning – raising the Reichsmark rate in Yugoslavia to 17.82 dinars for trade with the Reich and all occupied or dependent territories and countries in Europe.[102] As with the Netherlands, Yugoslavia would in future trade with Belgium, Denmark and Norway in Reichsmarks, through one clearing office in Berlin.[103] More complex was the question of unpaid goods the Yugoslav importers owed; it was agreed that all the deals concluded before 25 September would be paid at the old rate of 14.80 dinars for a Reichsmark, with the deadline for payments set for 31 March 1941. Purchases agreed with German exporters after 25 September would be charged at the new rate of 17.82 dinars. However, until all the delayed Yugoslav payments were settled, German importers of Yugoslavia's goods were to pay only one third of the agreed price at the new rate on the new Reichsmark's account; the rest would be paid at the old rate of 14.80 on the old Yugoslav account. The Yugoslav exporters would thus initially receive their payments at an average Reichsmark's rate of 15.80 dinars. Belgrade promised not to disrupt exports to Germany with any of the decisions of its Directorate for Foreign Trade. Above the agreed quotas for Yugoslavia's foodstuff and raw materials, Germany obtained the right to import all additional Yugoslav surpluses. After 1 April 1941, Yugoslavia would lose all preferential tariffs for its export goods.[104] Finally, agreement was reached between the two committees on the setting up of an Industrial Committee. Its task would be to promote industrial cooperation between the two countries, by 'determining in which ways German and Yugoslav industrial production within the new European economic order could mutually be coordinated to achieve an increased goods exchange. This implies paying attention to *natural* and *organic* preconditions of industrial production [in both countries].'[105]

Weakening of the dinar should have stimulated exports to Germany, as hoped in Berlin. As already mentioned, Yugoslavia had by this time become Germany's debtor on clearing accounts; its debt to Germany on old clearing account surpassed 62 million Reichsmarks in January 1941.[106] The reasons for this drastic development were not clear to contemporaries and the demise of Yugoslavia soon after these events denied us the opportunity to see further progress of mutual economic relations. It seems that Yugoslavia did not have enough goods for export due to its own rapidly growing needs.[107] This was confirmed by a series of decrees of the Trade and Industry Ministry in December 1940, which imposed strict control on exports of Yugoslavia's cattle and industrial wood.[108] The first months after the signing of the October 1940 protocol were confusing; it was a transitional period and there was a plethora of different clearing accounts and payments under the different conditions and currency rates on both sides. The payments of Yugoslavia's importers rose again after October 1940. However, these were not payments for new imports, but predominantly for earlier purchases, as importers wished to take the advantage of paying their debts at the old, lower Reichsmark's rate. If only payments for purchases made after 1 October 1940 are considered, Yugoslavia quickly became a creditor again; as on 25 January 1941, its credit in Berlin stood at 10.5 million Reichsmarks.[109]

German-Yugoslav economic relations now rested upon the provisions of the Secret Protocol of the Mixed Committee meeting in October 1940. In this way, Germany managed by force to finally break Yugoslavia's resistance. But this was still far from the mutual economic relationship the Wohlthat treaty with Romania gave Germany. The reason why the Germans did not push harder for a more defining agreement during the meeting in Belgrade was beyond economic reasoning. On 8 October, the Italian Foreign-Trade Minister Raffaello Riccardi was scheduled to visit Berlin. Because of his forthcoming talks with Funk and Hitler, German Economic and Foreign Ministries instructed their Mixed Committee representatives in Belgrade not to push for 'a strong underlining of the German-Yugoslav economic agreement', as at that moment it was not politically desirable. Wiehl instructed Landfried, the leader of the German deputation, not to discuss the *Europäische Grossraumfragen* in Belgrade. To reveal any such conversation with the Yugoslavs might have turned Riccardi's visit into an uncomfortable episode and instigate Italian suspicions over Germany's intentions.[110] Berlin's rivalry with Rome over the economic hegemony in Yugoslavia temporarily saved Belgrade, although it was clear that Germany desired the rewriting of the 1934 Trading Agreement in line with the new political reality in Europe.

On 22 June, the day the armistice was signed at Compiegne, Göring charged Funk with the task of developing plans for the economic unification of Europe under German guidance.[111] In an interview with the Viennese *Südost-Echo* the following month, Funk talked at length about the new economic reality in Europe. It could be summarized by its ending statement: that the European economy as a whole had to provide economic stability for the German Reich and welfare for German people.[112] The urge to keep South-Eastern European countries predominantly agricultural in character was now openly revealed and Berlin did not hide its wish to tailor the economies of South-Eastern Europe to its needs. This referred to all of them, allied, trusted and untrusted countries of the region alike. It also suggested a type of economic relationship based on the total authority of Germany, as discussed by Wilmowsky six months earlier. Even the more politically cooperative countries like Hungary had by this time realized that any economic relationship with Germany would end up being only a dictated cooperation.[113] It was the model of a centralized relationship between one dominant core and submissive periphery. German economic bloc would be based in a currency union, where other European currencies would be tied to the Reichsmark as a reserve currency and trade regulated through multilateral clearing, with one clearing office in Berlin set for the whole continent, excluding Britain and Italy.[114]

In March 1939, Germany and Romania had signed the previously mentioned Wohlthat treaty which was to serve as a template for German relations with other countries of the south-east. Unlike the older agreements of more conservative German Foreign and Economic Ministries, aiming at establishing a dominant trading position for Germany, the Wohlthat agreement defined the means by which Romania was forced to internally regulate its economic development as Germany wished. It stated that Romania had to develop its agriculture and its wood processing industry according to German needs, while Germany was granted rights to research and exploit Romanian oil, copper, chrome and manganese. Berlin undertook the obligation to supply Bucharest with machinery and to deliver armaments.[115] The means were set up for Germany to control Romania's development along these agreed lines; the agreement turned Romania into an economic satellite of the Reich.[116] In January 1940, following the pressure from Berlin, Hungarian National Bank restored the exchange rate of its national currency pengo to hard currencies to the pre-war level; Budapest also signed the commercial agreement and promised to economically help German war efforts with its resources. Then in July the same year, at the time when Budapest was hoping to get territorial concessions in Romania, Germany and Hungary signed another commercial agreement, bringing in further benefits for the Third Reich. These implied considerably increasing export of agricultural products to Germany, improvements in Hungarian cattle breeding, a shift from growing grains towards industrial and fodder crops, etc.[117] During 1940, Bulgaria increased its yields of oilseed, cotton, linen and hemp and their export to Germany. This was discussed at the two trade conferences in October 1939 and May 1940, with the aim of securing and increasing Bulgarian exports to Germany; they resulted in turning Bulgaria into a German economic satellite with little freedom in decision-making.[118] The improvements in industrial and agricultural production of all three countries were done with the help of German experts and technology.[119]

Until the autumn 1940, Yugoslavia was the only country in the region where the economy was still not fully in line with German requirements. Mutual economic relations were still regulated by the 1934 Trade Agreement, which by this time was considered as inadequate in Berlin. The October 1940 Protocol was the closest Berlin came to the Wohlthat treaty in its economic relations with Yugoslavia, but despite giving Germany hitherto unprecedented influence, the protocol did not regulate the specifics of Yugoslavia's industrial and agricultural production. Belgrade still enjoyed the freedom to navigate its own economic development and this was mentioned at the meeting of the German Trade Chamber for Yugoslavia in Berlin in December 1940. Yugoslavia's internal economic problems such as rising prices of consumer goods and failing wages and purchasing power were disturbing. Such conditions were hardly corresponding to the doctrine of *Ergänzungswirtschaft*. It was actually the situation which terrified the Germans – a country which by pursuing an independent economic policy got into difficulties, thus restricting Germany's share of its food and raw materials. Questions were asked whether Yugoslavia was able to produce enough goods for export. The meeting ended with the conclusion that Yugoslavia required a closer cooperation between its politics and its economy, modelled after the Wohlthat treaty, to secure German interests in Yugoslavia's mining industry.[120]

On 25 January 1941, Neumann drafted a memorandum entitled 'Towards the Question of the Future Economic Policy in the South-East'. He asserted that in previous years Germany had sacrificed itself in order to increase the purchasing power of these countries by paying higher prices for their exports. The penetration of the German capital and industry for Neumann was natural. Although Germany overall had an interest in improving the living conditions of its neighbours, any increase in standard of living and purchasing power was not to be allowed in the future if it came at the expense of the surplus exports of the goods on which Germany relied. The only reason why those countries could provide an export surplus of the goods which Germany needed was their low average consumer spending, which in Yugoslavia was seven times lower than in Germany. The average consumption of meat and bread in Yugoslavia was one-third of that in Germany, and according to Neumann it should stay that way. The German task was not to increase the living standard of the region, but to help with technical improvements which could increase production and yield. Any independent economic development of these countries was to be prevented, they should be kept in the status of raw materials and foodstuff suppliers to the Reich, and their surplus population used as migrant workers in Germany. Such a policy would 'keep [the Germans] from danger ... that the consuming power of the people from the south-east grows faster than their production abilities, which would leave only smaller and more expensive leftovers for our import needs'.[121] However, none of this mattered to the Kingdom of Yugoslavia anymore; less than three months after Neumann's memo, that country would not exist anymore.

## Economy of fear

Two diametrically opposed economic ideologies which drove developments in the Third Reich and the Kingdom of Yugoslavia in opposite directions throughout the 1930s significantly contributed to the friction between the two countries. The Third Reich invested more effort with Yugoslavia than with any other country in South-Eastern Europe to bring it in line with Germany's economic needs, plans and wishes. And yet, this process was still not done before the military annihilation of Yugoslavia in April 1941. The 1934 Trade Agreement remained legally binding framework of mutual economic relations until the very end. The question remains what would have happened if it was not for political events which led to the destruction of Yugoslavia in the spring of 1941, especially in the light of the Reich's military failure in eastern front. Provided the country was not territorially forcibly reshaped according to the wishes of Yugoslavia's revisionist neighbours, as it had already happened to Czechoslovakia in

1938 and Romania in 1940, it is safe to conclude that all the ideological and structural differences between the German and Yugoslav economies would have, sooner rather than later, forced the Nazi leadership to intervene and direct the development of Yugoslavia's economy according to the needs of the German war economy. Yugoslavia's supplies of raw materials, foodstuff and fodder were so important for Germany's war efforts, that to allow its independent economic development, whether it eventually joined the Tripartite Pact or not, was not an option for the Nazis.

9

# Yugoslavia commits suicide

The final chapter of this book unintentionally bears an identical name to the title of Danilo Gregorić's 1942 book *Samoubistvo Jugoslavije*. This is an unfortunate coincidence, as this book points out all the opposite reasons of Yugoslavia's demise in 1941 than those emphasized in the memoirs of one of the leading Yugoslav Germanophiles. Gregorić's reasoning is superficial and never goes beyond insisting that Yugoslavia needed to seek friendship with Hitler's Germany at any price, stemming out of his political prejudices and a conviction that Germany would come out victorious from war, while Yugoslavia's catastrophe was to be blamed on – who else than – the British, Jews and Masonry. However, one line where the author of this book agrees with the former director of *Vreme*, at the time when this newspaper pursued the fiercest antisemitic and pro-fascist campaigns in Yugoslavia, was that the Yugoslav officials indeed doomed the country by their own deeds and poor judgement of situation at the most critical moment.

Paradoxically, the outbreak of war eased German political pressure on Belgrade. The symbolism of Yugoslavia's adherence to the Anti-Comintern Pact, or leaving the League of Nations, as the Germans had demanded in the summer of 1939, lost its importance in September. The profiling of the two enemy camps in Europe and their struggle for economic, political and ideological supremacy over the Balkans restored the balance of power in the region to the benefit of its countries. According to Martin Broszat, the period before the fall of France can be described as the retardation of German hegemony in South-Eastern Europe.[1] The situation changed after the fall of France in June 1940, when Germany's political might and military prestige put the whole region under firm domination. To a superficial eye, South-Eastern Europe seems to have been agonizingly close to avoiding the war and it was only the Italian failure in Greece in autumn 1940 which created a need for Germany to militarily intervene, thus setting the whole region on fire. However, Germany had already had a military foothold in South-Eastern Europe, in Romania, from October 1940 on, in order to protect the oil fields there. Secondly, political pressure for the whole region to join the Axis was immense and unrelated to the Greek-Italian war. Thirdly, even without the war, state borders in the region had already been changed twice, by the decisions of two Vienna Awards, in 1938 and 1940. And fourthly, being an integral part of Germany's war machine as its suppliers, Yugoslavia and other countries of the region were by 1941 already heavily implicated in this conflict.

This final chapter argues that Yugoslavia made a deadly mistake of bowing down before the German pressure and that signing the Tripartite Pact on 25 March 1941 was a mistake. Until February, Belgrade played the waiting game and played it relatively well. It was rather the particularities of Yugoslavia's internal affairs and the national question, combined with a reasonable fear of the menacing German military presence in the region, which eventually led to a series of blunders ending with the short April war with the Axis. Nevertheless, demonstrations in the Serbian towns of Yugoslavia in support of the military coup on 27 March against the government which had signed the Pact with the Axis remained one of the most dramatic turnarounds of the Second World War, a notable redemption of the nation's repressed feelings and an unprecedented spit to Hitler's face in the moment of his greatest might. Of course, we now know that out in the streets, people celebrated a death sentence to their country.

## Uncomfortable neutrality

Within the first week of war, Prince Paul asked of Raymond Brugère, French Minister in Belgrade, that the French forces immediately land in Thessaloniki, assuring Yugoslavia's exit to the sea.[2] Under certain circumstances, the Yugoslavs supported the idea of Yugoslavia's military cooperation with the British and French and even asked for military contacts between the Yugoslav and French armies.[3] Because of various reasons and opposition from both Paris and London, nothing came out of it, but obviously the Yugoslav government considered the status of neutrality as only temporary and benevolent for the Western allies.[4] The same could be said for the Yugoslav public, which mainly tended to see the war as a conflict between one side which stood for the liberty and freedom of small nations, and the other which struggled for their own interests and living space.[5]

However, in order to survive until the moment when the Allies' victory seemed obvious, Yugoslavia needed protection from Italy. As Britain and France did not seriously consider the military operations in the south-east and Germany was bound to Italy with an alliance, the only remaining great power was the Soviet Union. Prince Paul acted quickly and already in October 1939, Strandtman, the former Charge d'Affaires of the Russian embassy in Belgrade, who acted as a representative of the non-existing Tsarist Russia in Yugoslavia, made public that he no longer performed his duties. In May 1940, after the end of the Soviet-Finnish war, the Yugoslavs and the Soviets signed a trading agreement in Moscow; diplomatic relations were established the following month and Milan Gavrilović, a liberal and a democrat, the leader of the opposition Serbian Agrarian Party, became the first Yugoslav minister in Moscow. His primary aim was to voice a danger for Yugoslavia coming from the Axis and to seek Moscow's military help in case of aggression. Unfortunately for the Yugoslavs, at the time of signing the agreement of mutual recognition with the Soviet Union, the western front seized to exist and Yugoslavia's comfortable position between all the great powers never materialized as the balance shifted towards the Axis.

In the light of the French and British inability to support Yugoslavia due to their preparations for the battle on western front, Yugoslavia had no other way but to rely on German protection against Italy. During the meeting with Heeren in April, Prince Paul reminded the German Minister of his personal and his country's friendship with Germany, expressed his hopes for a possible understanding between Germany and Britain, but did not miss the opportunity to voice his distrust of Italy.[6] In general, political relations between Belgrade and Berlin were quiet throughout the first nine months of war; the Yugoslavs tried hard not to make any move which might have antagonized Hitler. However, June 1940 brought in the first problem in mutual relations, partly sparked by the affair of Stojadinović's house arrest. Fearful of his influence, in April the Government interned him away from Belgrade. Heeren first explained this with Stojadinović's intentions to set up a new political party.[7] However, two months later the German Minister described the harsh conditions of Stojadinović's internment as a proof that the Yugoslav Government was still doubtful that the final victory would be German. He even saw it as a direct challenge to the Axis powers and warned that it lowered the German prestige, as Stojadinović was seen as the future Yugoslav Quisling. Therefore, he recommended expressing astonishment in German press of unchanged political attitude of Yugoslavia.[8] By the beginning of July, the Germans were increasingly annoyed that the Yugoslav government was still allowing the freedom of press, which to them was just a euphemism for spreading the Francophile feelings over the general population.[9] To make things worse, Yugoslavia established diplomatic relations with the Soviet Union and on 7 July, Viktor Plotnikov, the first Soviet Minister ever arrived in Belgrade. Heeren reported renewed Russophile emotions that swiped over the Yugoslavs – not only the Serbs, but also many non-Serbian parts of the country. While peasantry was in general ignorant of politics and had romantic memories of the old Tsarist Russia, the intelligentsia simply supplanted the old Francophile feelings for the hope that 'Russia' might step in as an ally. There was an impression in Yugoslavia that war between the Soviet Union and Germany was inevitable and that such a development was the only thing that might bring political relief to the Balkans.[10]

In April, Heeren spoke to Cincar-Marković about the failure of the Yugoslav police to stop the spreading of the Western allies' propaganda; on the other hand, the police were very efficient in proceedings against the Reich nationals living in Yugoslavia. He even questioned if secretly, at heart, anti-German feelings were behind the alleged Yugoslav neutrality.[11] A month later, Heeren expressed fears that the increasing Yugoslav chauvinism might turn against the German nationals living in Yugoslavia.[12] At the end of May, in a report on Yugoslavia's reaction to the German military successes, Heeren described a panic which took over the large sections of population, especially in the light of Italian strengthened position. There was a fear of a combined Italian attack from both north and south, towards Dalmatia and Macedonia, and furthermore this might be adjoined by the German attack from the north. A result was an atmosphere of deep mistrust towards anyone who resembled the fifth column, which brought visible presence in the public of various national organizations, such as Sokols, Četniks, or National Defence. The police actions and military measures had also taken anti-German character, which made it all easier for the Western propaganda to fall on the fertile soil. The government was aware of the negative consequences of such a propaganda but at the same time it was not free from certain mistrust towards Germany.[13]

The second half of 1940 brought two successive crises to the Balkans – the Romanian-Soviet one in the summer and the Greek-Italian at the end of the year. In June 1940, the Soviets demanded a return of Bessarabia and Bukovina from Romania. Bucharest appealed to Berlin for protection but being involved in the last stages of the battle for France, Hitler did not consider it wise to politically antagonize Moscow and refused to interfere. After all, the return of Bessarabia to the Soviet Union was part of a secret annex of the non-aggression pact signed between Ribbentrop and the Soviet Foreign Minister Vyacheslav Molotov in August 1939.[14] According to the impressions of German Minister in Sofia after talks with King Boris and the leading Bulgarian politicians, the Soviet occupation of Bessarabia came as a shock to the Bulgarian public, but once it recovered from that shock, there would be violent incidents and requests for urgent occupation of South Dobruja. The King was even worried that the situation might escalate to an extent where the government might be at risk. For this reason, he asked if Germany might try to persuade Bucharest 'to correct the injustice done to Bulgaria in 1913' and if the similar gesture could have been done towards Hungary at the same time, while the remainder of the Romanian territory could be guaranteed by all three: Germany, Italy and the Soviet Union; this would at the same time prevent further Soviet advance in the region. King Boris blamed Yugoslavia for trying to bring 'Russia' back to the Balkans for the sake of its own protection. The German Minister suggested that Bulgaria deserved some kind of support as it was an honest and faithful friend of Germany, who had in the past resisted all the tempting offers to join the Balkan Entente.

A few weeks later Hitler and Ciano met with the Hungarian representatives and told them that the Axis' interest was peace in the region, suggesting that Budapest solved the problem of their border revision in direct negotiations with Bucharest, but not to be unreasonable in its territorial demands. Rome and Berlin recommended the same to the Romanian government. The same applied to Bulgaria. On 16 July, Hitler sent a letter to King Carol, suggesting him to solve the Romanian problems with Hungary and Bulgaria in a friendly way.[15] Ten days later, Hitler and Ribbentrop met the Bulgarian Prime Minister Bogdan Filov in Salzburg and advised conciliation and quick diplomatic solution.[16] Despite Hitler's reassurances, continued Romanian, Hungarian and Bulgarian appeals to him and offers of various favours to Germany, resulting in the signing of new trade agreement with Hungary and expending of the existing trade agreement with Bulgaria, helped Berlin to cement its positions in this region. Romania was in the weakest position; in a vain attempt to gain support from Berlin, King Carol brought a set of measures during the summer, such as the introduction of his personal dictatorship, walking out of the League of Nations and political reconciliation with the Romanian fascist organization Iron Guard, which all destroyed any remaining democratic potential of the country, but increased Romanian internal instability.

Yet Germany wanted to avoid Romania ending in war with Hungary and Bulgaria, as such a development would have probably involved Yugoslavia, Italy and the Soviet Union into the conflict; more importantly, war in the Balkans would endanger the safety of Romanian oil wells. After futile negotiations between the Romanians and Hungarians during the summer, all parties met in Vienna on 30 August 1940, where Ribbentrop and Ciano bluntly dictated the conditions of the new territorial settlement between Hungary and Romania. According to this so-called Second

Vienna Award, Romania was forced to surrender two-thirds of Transylvania and more than one million Romanians to Hungary.[17] Simultaneously to Romania's negotiations with Hungary, Bucharest began talks with the representatives of Bulgarian government in Craiova in August and after an increased German pressure on the new Romanian government of Ion Antonescu, on 7 September the two sides agreed the return of South Dobruja to Bulgaria.[18] This success sparked hopes for new territorial gains in Bulgaria.

## War comes to the Balkans

Much bigger problems for the government in Belgrade arose with the crisis in Greek-Italian relations. At the beginning of June, the Greek Prime Minister General Ioannis Metaxas warned Berlin that Greece was going through an increased pressure from both Italy and Britain in terms of offers for guarantees to Greek neutrality. He asked from Berlin for the public announcement of the neutrality of Greek territory, which both the Greek government and people would have accepted; Ribbentrop denied any possibility of giving such guarantees.[19] Later in August, the German Minister in Athens reported of greatly changed mood in Greece, influenced by an aggressive writing of the Italian press about the alleged Greek involvement into the murder of some Albanians in Epirus and the alleged Greek oppression of the Albanian minority which lived next to the border. There was also a general feeling in Greece that the German press copied the tone of the Italian press in accusations towards Greece. At the same time, the Greek Minister in Berlin complained about the Italian behaviour, expressing his fear that the Italians were heading towards the war and warning that such a war could set the whole Balkans on fire. The Italians in turn accused Greece of allegedly offering shelter to the British navy. The Germans replied that they would rather rely on the reports of the situation in the Mediterranean from their ally; therefore, it was ridiculous if the Greeks expected the German press to publish Greek version of events.[20] The last weeks of August were hectic in Greek conciliatory moves towards the Italians, despite the increasing Italian provocations, one of which included the sinking of the Greek frigate, but also in desperate attempts to obtain German protection. The German attitude towards Athens was summarized in Ribbentrop's tirade to the Greek minister in Berlin on 27 August. He accused the Greeks of siding with Britain and advised them to immediately seek ways to come to an agreement with Italy and fulfil Italian demands. Ribbentrop also reminded the Greeks of the destiny of Romanians and he warned that once when war ended, the attitude of small countries towards the Axis during the war would determine their destiny.[21]

At the same time, the Italians had simultaneous plans for Yugoslavia. Ever since January 1940, Mussolini had been toying with the idea of an attack against Yugoslavia, combined with the Croatian revolt supported by Ustaše terrorists harboured in Italy. German action against France and Britain temporarily turned the Italian attention towards west, but once France was defeated, Yugoslavia was again in Il Duce's mind.[22] At the meeting with Hitler in Berlin on 7 July, Ciano insisted that since France had fallen, the time was ripe to eliminate Yugoslavia. Clear Italian territorial pretensions in

Dalmatia were poorly masked by the ideological reasons: Yugoslavia was a Versailles creation and as such could never be friendly towards the Axis. Also, in the new Europe, once the war was over, Yugoslavia should never exist in the present form. Hitler was patient to explain reasons of his disagreement: any attack on Yugoslavia at present would only set the whole region on fire; Hungary would attack Romania, which would most likely involve the Soviets who, despite the change of ideology, still nurtured the old strategic goals of the Tsarist Russia – Constantinople. Soviet armies might cross Danube and probably cause pro-Russian revolution in Bulgaria, where the position of King Boris was not stable. At the moment when Germany was importing 140,000 tons of petroleum a month from Romania, any change of hands or the destruction of Romanian oil wells would have been dangerous for both Axis countries.[23] For the moment, Hitler was satisfied with strong German political and economic positions in the region which, after the French defeat, had no other way but to listen to Berlin's wishes. Of course, he did not wish to protect Yugoslavia because he favoured it; a year earlier he urged Italians to finish with Belgrade as an 'unreliable neutral'. But while contemplating a war with the Soviets now that France was knocked out, any disturbance in the Balkans was undesirable. He did not mind Italy having its way with Yugoslavia, but it had to be at the time more favourable for the Axis.

Hitler's attitude however did not dissuade the anxious Italians. At the beginning of August, the Deputy Chief of Staff of Italian Army General Mario Roatta discussed preparations for a possible conflict with Yugoslavia with Enno von Rintelen, the German Military Attaché in Rome. The Italians hoped to advance into Yugoslavia through Austria, as the geography of terrain from the side of the Yugoslav-Italian border was not suitable for a massive attack by motorized forces. Roatta emphasized that Italy did not intend to start a war immediately, but simply to have plans at hand in case of war. Italians required 5,000 vehicles for such an attack, as most of their vehicles were in North Africa. He also asked for a conference of the highest representatives of the two armies in order to discuss this question. Rintelen replied that momentarily German attitude was that peace in the Balkans was a common interest of both countries. According to a further explanation from Berlin, Hitler was 'completely uninterested in Italian wishes about the attack on Yugoslavia. He wished peace on Germany's southern border and warned against giving the English an opportunity to establish their air force in Yugoslavia.'[24] Moreover, German High Command decided not to share its intelligence reports on Yugoslavia's borderline fortifications with the Italians.[25]

During August, the Germans again meddled in Italian affairs. Ciano had previously decided to mediate between Moscow and Ankara and tried to reach an understanding between Italy and the Soviet Union.[26] Ribbentrop again warned that such an approach was unnecessary, as it would not bring any gains for the Axis in the Balkans. Germany would welcome some form of closer relations between Rome and Moscow, but any agreement was out of question. Ribbentrop then commented on a conversation between Roatta and Rintelen; the High Command of Wehrmacht insisted that before any staff talks, the political aspects of the problem needed to be clarified. According to Ribbentrop, at the moment, there was a life and death struggle with Britain; therefore, all efforts by the Axis should concentrate on that battle. From the military perspective, the Yugoslav problem should not be taken too easily, as the Serbs proved themselves to be good soldiers in the past. There was also a possibility that the British aviation came to their aid, which would imply further commitment of the Luftwaffe, already stretched across the continent. Such a conflict would only spark a general war in the Balkans, with unknown consequences and attitudes of neighbouring countries. Also, it might easily bring in the Soviets, having in mind newly established relations between the two countries and the old affiliations between the two nations. This would in turn imply German commitment in the east. Therefore, the High Command suggested the postponing of any General Staff talks for the times when Britain was defeated. When the Italian Ambassador in Berlin Dino Alfieri asked about the Greek problem, Ribbentrop pointed out that the German attitude to this problem was the same as towards the question of Yugoslavia.[27] At the same time, Belgrade was aware of the Italian itchiness for war. Heeren had an interview with Cincar-Marković on 26 July and the Yugoslav passed on the message that in case of any Italian hostility, Yugoslavia would fight to the end.[28] A month later, Prince Paul warned Heeren that because of the Italian behaviour, there was a mistrust towards Germany in Yugoslavia.[29]

On 28 October, despite all the German warnings, Italian army invaded Greece from Albania. Mussolini probably opted for Greece, rather than Yugoslavia, as the former was smaller, less populated and was considered militarily weaker.[30] A badly prepared operation, based on the assumption of a quick campaign and perhaps even an immediate Greek surrender, turned into a fiasco. There were many reasons which influenced Italian action, from Mussolini's vanity and a need for reasserting the value of Italian arms, to more complex geo-strategic reasoning. Ever since September 1939, Italy's stake as an influential power was waning. Mussolini's hopes to appear as mediator and a decisive factor in the balance between Germany, France and Britain proved to be an illusion. Despite Italy's neutrality, the British blockade locked it inside the Mediterranean; in March 1940, British fleet even cut off neutral Italy from the shipments of German coal from Rotterdam. After Germany's victory in northern France, Mussolini declared war on France and Britain on 10 June, but this did not improve Italy's standing. Instead, the Germans treated Italy's interest on an equal footing with Franco's Spain and even with Petain's France, out of fear of losing French colonial administrations in Northern Africa and their deflection to the British if France was humiliated over the limit. At the same time, the Germans were wiping out Italian influence everywhere in South-Eastern Europe. Berlin then prevented Italian understanding with the Soviets, whose interests in the Balkans were not opposed to Rome's, as this could have instigated Moscow to step into the Balkans. The final straw was Hitler's decision to transfer German troops into Romania on 10 October, for the purpose of securing Romanian oil wells and Antonescu's new pro-German regime. However, a week earlier at their meeting on the Brenner pass, Hitler did not inform Mussolini of the forthcoming action. It also did not help that, afraid of the information leakage, the Germans never told the Italians about their plan for war with the Soviets in 1941.[31] From the Nazi viewpoint, stability was the key for success in that upcoming war, particularly on the flanks and in the rear of such a massive operation. For this reason, Hitler tolerated a stable Finland, despite its democratic constitution which he despised, but was forced to intervene in shambolic Romanian internal affairs, although the nature of the new regime in Bucharest was personally favourable to him.³² Unaware of the incoming war against the Soviets, the Italians could not properly comprehend the importance of peace in South-Eastern Europe.

Hitler's decision to go to war with the Soviets followed the fall of France. At the conference with the army commanders in Berghof on 31 July 1940, he announced his decision to attack the Soviet Union the following spring. The idea slowly matured over July, simultaneously as the prospects for intended invasion of Britain appeared less and less favourable.³³ On 27 September, Germany, Italy and Japan signed the Tripartite Pact, which divided spheres of interest between the three. In November, Hungary, Slovakia and Romania joined the Pact. After some hesitation, fearful of the Yugoslav and Turkish reaction and out of concern for traditional pro-Russian feelings of its people, Bulgarian government adhered to the Pact on 1 March 1941.³⁴ During the ceremony of Hungarian signing in Vienna on 20 November, Hitler told Ciano about the idea of an 'alliance with Yugoslavia'. According to Ciano, he was excited about the new prospects in the Balkans.³⁵ While Yugoslavia managed to stay out of German focus for much of the first year of fighting, the Italian failure in Greece brought it back at the table.

Yugoslavia's diplomacy, both official and unofficial, did not help. Upon the news of the Italian attack on Greece, the Yugoslav Crown Council met to discuss Yugoslavia's attitude. No decision was reached; Prince Paul insisted on mobilization in southern parts of the country, but was opposed by the War Minister Nedić for military and Cvetković for political reasons. However, they all agreed that the fall of Thessaloniki into Italian hands was not an option, as the port was Yugoslavia's only open outlet towards the Western allies.³⁶ What followed was a strange episode of unofficial diplomacy which misfired badly on the Yugoslavs. On 1 November, Nedić instructed Vauhnik to approach the German military authorities in Berlin with the question regarding the future of Thessaloniki – thus bypassing the established procedure which demanded Vauhnik's communication only with the General Staff. However, Gerhard Weinberg was wrong to conclude that these were the signals coming from the Yugoslav government.³⁷ Events were dynamic and an entangled web of unofficial diplomatic messages and meetings occurred between proxies; therefore, it is unclear who was the first to bring the question of Thessaloniki out in the open. Based on a documented informal communication between some Germans and lower-ranked Yugoslav officials in Belgrade, Dragan Bakić believes that the initiative still came from the Germans, who were for a while well aware of the Yugoslav interest in the port.³⁸ But it is more important to stress the nature of Yugoslavia's interest in Thessaloniki. Before 1914, it was a port of special economic and geo-strategic importance for landlocked Serbia, located in a friendly country, and it was perceived in the same way after 1918. Even such a staunch Germanophile as Danilo Gregorić told Rirrentrop during their meeting in November 1940: 'Regarding Thessaloniki, Yugoslavia does not mind if it stays in Greek hands. Of course, the situation changes if any other [power] would lay its hand on it. If Greece should lose Thessaloniki, then it is only natural for Yugoslavia to take it, as it is of vital importance for us.'³⁹ Greece was a friendly and allied country, but in case of war with Germany, its odds for keeping possession of Thessaloniki were slim. However, the offer of Thessaloniki alone was not enough in attracting Yugoslavia to join the side of the Axis, as the Germans soon learned. The first consequence of this amateurish diplomacy through unofficial channels was Italian bombing of Bitolj (Macedonia) on

5 November, upon hearing of Yugoslavia's enquiry about Thessaloniki.[40] Consequently, Prince Paul had Nedić replaced by General Petar Pešić, already on 6 November.

This was the second time in a couple of days that Vauhnik learned outside the official channels about his own country's interest in Thessaloniki, as he had already received an information from his contacts in the Gestapo that some members of the Serbian Cultural Club asked Germany's approval for Yugoslavia to take Thessaloniki when King Peter comes of age the following September.[41] At the same time, powerful Court Minister Milan Antić sent one of his confidants, Belgrade lawyer Vladislav Stakić, to Rome, thus bypassing the official Yugoslav representative, to sound out Ciano if Italy still considered the 1937 agreement with Yugoslavia valid.[42] On 11 November, Ciano went a step further and offered the official alliance between the two countries. A few days later, Gregorić arrived in Berlin and met the Director of the News Service and Press Department of the Foreign Ministry Paul Schmidt. Saying that he was sent by Cvetković, but was speaking his personal opinion, Gregorić suggested that Germany should offer Thessaloniki to Yugoslavia, as the port falling into Italian hands would be a rope around Yugoslavia's neck. According to Gregorić, in such case the Yugoslavs might consider some gesture towards Italy and in return would expect German and Italian guarantees. Asked about his opinion on the matter, Heeren was undecided, but replied that some kind of a deal might have been forged with Belgrade.[43] Prior to becoming the director of *Vreme*, Gregorić was a member of Zbor, was close with Cvetković, was a Germanophile and was convinced that it was the Free Masons who had exercised a decisive influence in Yugoslavia wishing to tie the country's destiny for Britain. Seeing the old democratic constitution as outdated and leading to nothing other than chaos, Gregorić and people with similar mind-frame firmly believed that Europe had to choose between national socialism and communism, ideologies of the future.[44] Gregorić suggests in his memoirs that he had himself offered his services to Cvetković, who agreed that it would be useful to unofficially examine the German attitude towards Yugoslavia.[45]

Using the secret channels of communication meant that Yugoslavia's leaders gathered around the Crown Council bypassed the country's official representatives, Yugoslav diplomats in Rome and Berlin. Yugoslavia was unprepared for war and the only way of preserving its independence, until the time would come for Yugoslavia to come to the assistance of the Allies, was through a careful and skilful diplomacy. Rushing into haste and imprudent combinations with the Axis would only have given Berlin the excuse for exercising even stronger political pressure. And this was exactly what happened; enquiring about Thessaloniki had left an impression in Berlin that Yugoslavia was willing to bargain hard, but could be lured. Hitler was probably honest in wishing peace with Yugoslavia while preparing for war in the east, but he still insisted on guarantees for Yugoslavia's behaviour during the Greek campaign. Maček wrote in his memoirs that Yugoslavia's entire foreign policy became a race against the time.[46]

Another axiom of Prince Paul's policy touched the essential question of internal stability. Throughout the interwar period, Italy had been trying to use the so-called Croatian question for its own benefit; numerous Italian designs for the breakup of Yugoslavia all had in common stirring up a revolt in Croatia against the Belgrade government, which would have eased Italy's military action. The August 1939

Agreement between Cvetković and Maček seemed to have put aside the problem of Croatian dissatisfaction by setting up the self-governed Croatian province, thus removing an internal problem which could have had significant external consequences. Maček entered the government as a Deputy Prime Minister, alongside four other Croatian ministers and continued to support Prince Paul's foreign policy together with his Serbian colleagues within the government.[47] But solving one problem created another. By giving to Croats more territories than ethnically seemed justifiable, Prince Paul and Cvetković caused dissatisfaction among the Serbian elites, who regarded the Croatian province being a state within a state. The last nineteen months of Yugoslavia's independence were internally burdened with what Dejan Djokić calls the Serbian Question.[48]

Serbian portion of the Yugoslav people and the army, both traditionally Francophile, was for a while displeased with the policy of what publicly appeared to be closer ties with the Axis. The August 1939 Agreement only caused more discontent. After the Great War, it was generally considered that the Serbian national question had been settled – all Serbs now lived in one country, although it was called Yugoslavia. The setting up of the self-governed Croatian Banovina in 1939 left most of the Serbian elite frustrated. One of the manifestations of this irritation was the reorganization of the Serbian Cultural Club. Organized in 1937 by some of the leading Serbian intellectuals to contemplate over the question of integration of Serbian culture with the Yugoslav idea, after the Agreement in 1939 the Club became a think tank for defining Serbian national interest inside or outside Yugoslavia.[49] It started to publicly push strongly for setting up the Serbian province. The Serbian Orthodox Church actively supported this new trend among the Serbs.[50] This unrest alerted other nations to question their own place within the country, namely the Yugoslav Muslims. At the same time, situation in Croatia was not as calm as it could have been expected after the Agreement. The Croatian nationalists considered the setting up of the province as only a step towards full Croatian independence and there were many incidents directed against the local Serbs, police and the army.[51] The idea of integral Yugoslavia was dead, but more importantly, Prince Paul, preoccupied with external perils, seems to have failed to grasp how deep divisions inside the country were even after reaching the Serbian-Croatian Agreement.

The Italians have in the meanwhile suffered a series of defeats in Greece. Italian failure and uncertainty over Bulgarian claims on Yugoslavia's territory made a great impact on the Yugoslav army, resolved to fight if necessary. The government's attitude towards Italy had also stiffened. During the first months of fighting in Greece, Yugoslavia secretly supplied the Greek side with artillery and ammunition.[52] Furthermore, war in Greece opened the door for British involvement, as the Greek government asked London for naval and air support against Italy, but not the dispatching of land corps as it feared Hitler's reaction. More importantly, London contemplated a united front of other Balkan countries with Greece against the Axis, namely Turkey and Yugoslavia.[53] At the beginning of November, the British landed on Crete and Lemnos, making Hitler believe that the oil wells in Romania were within the reach of the RAF.[54] Furthermore, Stalin was treating his pact with Hitler very seriously and demanded the explanation about the presence of German troops in Romania.

The Soviets' suspicions alarmed Sofia; true, the Bulgarians rejected Soviet proposal for a Mutual-Assistance Pact, but also decided to stay out of the Tripartite Pact in November, which further complicated situation in the Balkans for Germany.[55] On 12 and 13 November, Hitler had two uncomfortable meetings with Molotov in Berlin. While the Führer insisted that the war was already won and as usually spoke only in general, Molotov was determined to get clear answers and stressed the Soviet interests in Finland, Bulgaria and the Straits.[56]

Initially, both Hitler and Wehrmacht were inclined to settle the Greek crisis peacefully, but the British involvement and an increasing mistrust towards the Soviets forced Hitler's decision. On 13 December, Hitler issued a directive for the plan to attack Greece under the code name Marita, to increase the number of German troops in Romania and to transport some of them via Bulgaria towards Greece as soon as weather conditions allowed it.[57] These troops were not initially supposed to get involved against Turkey or Yugoslavia; but it was still imperative to line up all the Balkan countries together with Germany.[58] However, things would not go easy with Yugoslavia. At the end of November, Belgrade sent clear signals that it would oppose the use of Yugoslavia's territory for any military purpose, including the transport of troops, war material and food.[59] On 25 November, Heeren speculated that a guarantee of the Yugoslav integrity in new European order after the war, and perhaps an offer of Thessaloniki, might have influenced the Yugoslavs to join the Reich's camp.[60] Eventually, the situation in the Balkans turned out to be too complex, just as Hitler feared, as he described it in a letter to Mussolini on 20 November.[61] In such an atmosphere Cincar-Marković was invited to secretly meet Hitler and Ribbentrop, which he did in Berghof on 28 November.

It started as usual, with Hitler's long tirade; the pretext was the failure of Italian aggression in Greece. Hitler stated that for the sake of the balance of power in the Balkans he wanted a strong Yugoslavia. Another reason was the economic one, as both countries supplemented each other, Yugoslavia benefitting from German industrial exports and Germany from Yugoslavia's agricultural surpluses. He emphasized that Germany at the moment had 230 divisions and that Yugoslavia should make a strong position for itself in the future. This should be achieved by reaching an understanding with Italy. Hitler then went on to excuse Italian failure in Greece as a result of underestimating the lesser power, the same mistake done by the Soviet army with the Finnish, or the Austro-Hungarians with Serbian armies. He blamed the British for setting a foothold in Greece, using it for sinking Italian ships and destroying its submarines; however, the good thing in Italian failure with Greece was that some sanity had come out of it in regard to Yugoslavia and that now some Italians who had always shared Hitler's positive views of Yugoslavia had again come to the forehead in Rome. According to him, Germany now needed to come to the Balkans to intervene, which placed Berlin in a position to impose circumstances to Rome and Hitler said his first request would be Italy's accommodation with Yugoslavia. The Führer further assessed the situation as follows: regarding the German intervention, it would not be against the Greeks, but against the British in Greece, and Berlin could easily spare even 180 divisions for that task. In terms of territorial changes, Bulgaria would be rewarded with the outlet to the Aegean Sea at Greek expense, but not with the Yugoslav territories. Hungary on the other side was so saturated with its recent gains in the north and the east that it could hardly even consider asking for more territories in the south. Hitler said he wished to see Yugoslavia in the future European coalition, which would be beneficial for the country, and he did not ask for anything in return. He also expressed dissatisfaction with the Soviet penetration in the region. Moscow wished the old goals of the Tsarist Russia and for this reason it supported Bulgaria's revisionism against all its neighbours. Russian aim was to establish a military base close to the Dardanelles; however, Italy was anxious to see Russia in the Balkans, as Russian influence could easily spread onto Yugoslavia. In such a case, Rome would be looking at another great power across the Adriatic. For this reason, Hitler recommended that Belgrade demilitarized Dalmatia, in order to rest Italians assured that there was nothing to be afraid of from that side, and in exchange Yugoslavia could count on Thessaloniki. He then offered a conclusion of a non-aggression pact between all three – Germany, Italy and Yugoslavia – and warned that if Belgrade did not respond quickly enough to such a favourable offer, it might not come again. Ribbentrop then spoke about the Golden Age of peace in Europe which was about to come once Britain was defeated, as London was the greatest cause of disturbance in Europe with its policy of balance of power.[62]

Aware of its reduced manoeuvrability, the Yugoslavs were eager to improve mutual relations with their neighbours. As Hungary was facing similar dilemmas despite its adherence to the Tripartite Pact in November, on 12 December the two countries signed the Treaty of Eternal Friendship. This agreement was recommended by Hitler on the day of Hungary's signing of the Pact in Vienna; it fitted well within the German political agenda of reducing tensions in South-Eastern Europe.[63] But the agreement with Hungary caused suspicion in London and Washington and the Yugoslav Minister in the United States Konstantin Fotić had troubles to explain that it did not change Yugoslavia's attitude towards the Axis.[64] This is a good illustration of how carefully Yugoslavia had to tread in its relations with great powers in the winter of 1940–1. The agreement with Hungary indeed did not mean that Yugoslavia was getting friendlier towards the Axis. On 7 December, Cincar-Marković informed Heeren of Yugoslavia's rejection to allow the right of passage for Italian vehicles on the way to the front in Albania, as Belgrade insisted to remain strictly neutral in the present Greek-Italian conflict. He even expressed his astonishment that Germany could have supported such a request from Italy. According to Cincar-Marković, the Yugoslav side considered the agreement of 25 March 1937 as a foundation for mutual relations with Italy, although Italy had violated some points of that agreement with the occupation of Albania. More importantly, the Yugoslav Foreign Minister informed Heeren that Yugoslavia was willing to accept the signing of non-aggression pact with Germany and Italy, as mentioned by Hitler during their talks.[65]

The first reply from Ribbentrop to the Yugoslav rejection of the Italian plea was to immediately, the very same day, ban the delivery of aircraft material to Yugoslavia.[66] Then, after analysing the Yugoslav reply together with Hitler, Ribbentrop instructed Heeren to convey the message that the non-aggression pact was not enough anymore; it would not have strengthened the Yugoslav case and some issues, such as Yugoslavia's adherence to the Tripartite Pact, still remained open.[67] Cincar-Marković was surprised as none of this was mentioned during the meeting at Berghof.[68] It seems that the

Yugoslav Foreign Minister attached too great importance to one of Hitler's statements during their meeting in November, which the Führer had probably mentioned along the way, without himself giving serious considerations about such an idea.

By the end of December, Mussolini finally asked Hitler to intervene in Greece. With every hope that the Italians would get themselves out of the mess gone, German military entry to the Balkans meant that Yugoslavia would be soon pressed hard to reach crucial decisions. Metaxas understood well what the movement of the German troops meant. In January, a few weeks before his death, he sent a personal letter to Prince Paul and asked him of remaining firm in refusing the German army a right to passage through Yugoslavia.[69] The Greeks began to prepare for defending their border with Bulgaria, namely the Struma valley, where they anticipated German attack. At the same time, Paul was well aware that Hitler would intervene in Greece; both Germany's concentration of divisions in Romania and uncertainty about the future Soviet moves made him a nervous man. He described Hitler as 'the most cunning German one could ever think of'.[70]

Yugoslavia also tried to get some benefit from the recently established relations with the Soviets. However, Moscow rejected Yugoslavia's pleas for help in modern weaponry and equipment twice, in December 1940 and March 1941. In February, Gavrilović reported from Moscow that no assistance could be expected from that corner; according to him, 'the Russians' were primarily interested in Bulgaria and the Straits, but were generally unprepared for war and hoped to avoid it themselves. Still, the Yugoslav Minister assessed that Stalin would not mind chaos in the Balkans, provided it led to Germany's defeat and opened the door for Red Army to enter South-Eastern Europe.[71] At the same time, Mussolini sent a message for the Yugoslav government through Stakić; it was imperative for Yugoslavia to choose wisely, but before the German troops entered Bulgaria – afterwards, Yugoslavia's relations with the Axis might be settled under much less favourable terms.[72] With the options seriously limited, Belgrade had no other way but to negotiate and Cvetković arranged to meet Hitler secretly at Berghof on 14 February.[73]

Before Cvetković left, Konstantinović had compiled a memorandum for his Prime Minister. He analysed three possible German demands; the first one, transfer of German troops through Yugoslavia's territory, was deemed unacceptable. The second was a demand for Yugoslavia's adherence to the Tripartite Pact. Konstantinović foresaw that Hitler might agree to Yugoslavia's exemption from some military provisions of the pact, but he still recommended a firm stand against it; in case of Germany's urgent need, no guarantees could be taken for granted from Hitler. 'The Tripartite Pact means to tie one's destiny for the destiny of three Axis powers. Adherence to it inevitably leads to a conflict with Britain and the United States.' Konstantinović predicted the breach of any German promise already during the conflict with Greece, disregarding the promises they might make, as Berlin would soon realize how easier it was to use the Vardar valley, rather than the Struma valley, for penetration into Greece. The third option was a possibility for non-aggression pact with Germany, which would shame Belgrade in case Germany attacked some of the countries friendly to Yugoslavia, but also might not be guarantee enough against any future German hostility. Konstantinović instead recommended Yugoslavia's mediation for the termination of Greek-Italian conflict, which would be followed by mutual consent of all the Balkan countries to prohibit the use of their territories for military operations by any foreign power.[74] With this recommendation in mind, the Yugoslav Prime Minister met Hitler.

Berlin demanded urgency in negotiations with Yugoslavia due to problems with the deployment of German divisions for operations against Greece. Wehrmacht was aware of all the difficulties of transporting fourteen divisions across the country with such a bad infrastructure as Bulgaria ever since December 1940, when two missions sent to Sofia returned with the same bleak report.[75] Another problem was political, as the news of possible German crossing into Bulgaria alarmed Stalin, who in mid-January warned Berlin that the Soviet Union considered Bulgaria and the Straits its interest zone. Sofia panicked frightened of a possibility of the Soviet attack on their Black Sea coast; Bulgarian hesitation further prolonged the German advance towards Greece.[76] Even before the crossing of the Danube from Romania on 1 March, the date which was also constantly delayed, the problems were augmented by unfavourable weather conditions. This instigated General Wilhelm List, the commander of the Twelfth army in charge of Marita, to ask for political pressure on Yugoslavia, as the transport of some units was easier by Yugoslav railways.[77] He again pressured the high command with the same demand in February.[78] In preparations for the meeting on 14 February, Ribbentrop was forwarded a memorandum by the military with demands to be put before the Yugoslavs; in essence, a transport of everything but the troops and weaponry at the pace of ten trains a day.[79]

But Cvetković never even allowed his hosts to come out with such demand. Instead, by immediately suggesting that Yugoslavia and other Balkan countries guarantee peace in the region, he let them know that diplomacy is the only option possible for Belgrade. Hitler was unimpressed. He referred Cvetković to Mussolini in regard to the Greek-Italian conflict and expressed doubts that the British would ever leave the Balkans on their own will; instead, he went on to speak about the danger of Bolshevism in the Balkans. Hitler said that Molotov himself told him that Moscow wished for a pact of mutual assistance with Bulgaria, and in return would support Sofia in obtaining large areas of Yugoslavia's Macedonia. The Führer then proceeded to again explain the new reality in Europe once after the war was over and a unique opportunity for Yugoslavia to find a place for itself. He repeated an offer of Yugoslavia's adherence to the Tripartite Pact and suggested that instead at the Adriatic coast, the Yugoslavs should contemplate building a strong naval port on the Aegean Sea. Once it joined the Tripartite Pact, Yugoslavia would receive guaranties by both Italy and Germany.[80] The meeting left the Germans with the feeling that the Yugoslavs were not interested in annexation of Thessaloniki.[81]

## The end

Two days after this meeting, Heeren was instructed to arrange a meeting between Hitler and Prince Paul. During this secret meeting in Berghof on 4 March, Hitler more or less repeated everything already said to Cvetković. He stressed that Greeks would not be able to maintain Thessaloniki and that German troops would one day have to withdraw from the Balkans; therefore, he asked if it was in Yugoslavia's interest to leave such an important port in the hands of a third power. Paul said honestly that his sympathies were on English side and that the Greek origin of his wife obliged him to reject the offer. Speaking about Italy, he stated that he could not have offered a handshake to the people who were responsible for the murder of his first cousin. Paul also stated that should he follow Hitler's advice, in less than six months he would no longer be in power; therefore, it was in Yugoslavia's best interest to remain neutral.[82] After this meeting, Halder entered in his diary: 'no positive results. No intention to join the Tripartite Pact.'[83]

Yugoslavia in the meantime became fully isolated by the signing of Turkish-Bulgarian non-aggression pact on 17 February. This was a huge success of German diplomacy; one of the two countries which could have posed a danger for the German troops in Bulgaria was now obliged to remain neutral. Any British hope that Turkey could have been lined up against Germany was gone. The pact also left a bad impression in Yugoslavia, as it was now known that Turkey would stay neutral if Germany attacked Yugoslavia from Bulgaria. The Yugoslavs then tried to gain time by negotiating with Italy. Stakić was again sent to Rome on 24 February with an offer of extending the 1937 Italian-Yugoslav agreement and the explanation that the Yugoslav public would be more receptive to it than the adherence to the Tripartite Pact. Although Mussolini was receptive to the idea of the mutual Yugoslav-Italian agreement, the moment Germans learned about these contacts, they warned the Italians against any further discussions.[84]

On 6 March, Crown Council met to discuss Hitler's demands. Cvetković recommended rejection, but the War Minister Pešić left an impression by estimating that in case of war Yugoslavia would not last longer than few days in border area, although troops which would withdraw to the mountains of Bosnia might last up to six weeks, before they run out of food and ammunition.[85] The following day, Cincar-Maković called Heeren and asked for the promise that Yugoslavia's territorial integrity would be respected, as well as its interests regarding Thessaloniki, in terms of a free corridor between the Yugoslav-Greek border and the port; also, that no military assistance or the request for passage of neither material nor troops would be asked of Yugoslavia.[86] The Yugoslavs probably purposely put forward the impossible terms, hoping that Germans would reject them.[87] However, on 9 March Ribbentrop replied that Yugoslavia would get all the guarantees regarding its territorial integrity and neither a passage of troops would be asked for, nor Yugoslavia's military assistance in the Greek conflict, as Greece was already in war. Furthermore, a secret note would be signed, promising that Yugoslavia's free access to the Aegean Sea at Thessaloniki would be taken into account. However, Yugoslavia could not be exempt from Article 3 of the Pact, which implied military support in case of attack by a power not presently involved in war.[88]

As already stressed, the moment the Italians attacked Greece, Thessaloniki became an object of frequent conversations and worries for the Yugoslav government.[89] The Yugoslavs told both the British and Americans that German occupation of Thessaloniki would not be considered *casus belli*, as it was expected the Germans would respect the existing arrangements, according to which Yugoslavia had certain rights in the free zone of Thessaloniki's port.[90] However, in case Bulgaria or Italy occupied it, Yugoslavia would have to enter the war and defend its only remaining access to the open sea, since the Adriatic was already closed off by the Italians. To the leading Serbian politicians, a situation where Thessaloniki was occupied by some either openly or potentially hostile nation was equal to a noose around the neck of Yugoslavia. The uncertainty of situation demanded military preparations. From 11 January on, the Yugoslav War Ministry began to issue regular monthly orders for mobilization of the army reserve; upon arriving in their units, these mobilized civilians remained in uniforms for six weeks, until another batch of the reserve was summoned. The Greeks estimated that in March 1941 Yugoslavia had 900,000 mobilized soldiers. However, both Maček and King Peter II in their memoirs testify of slow and unorganized procedures for mobilization, the lack of equipment and weaponry, and unacceptable living conditions of mobilized soldiers.[91] This was also suggested by the Chief of the General Staff Petar Kosić to Konstantinović as early as November 1940.[92]

On 10 March, Heeren informed Cincar-Marković about the necessity of maintaining the Article 3 clause. The Yugoslav stated that it was not possible for Yugoslavia to adhere to any pact which might bring his country in war with either the Soviet Union or the United States. Heeren was immediately instructed from Berlin to reply that although most likely there would be no invitation for Yugoslavia's military aid, it was impossible to alter any of the provisions of the Tripartite Pact, as there were equal obligations of all the members.[93] On 11 March, Heeren reported to Berlin of the great excitement that rumours of the alleged German ultimatum caused in all corners. He had learned from reliable sources that Franklin Roosevelt had sent a personal message to all the important political figures in the country and that the army was against any adherence to the Tripartite Pact, as this would dishonour the Serbian soldier.[94]

Heeren's information was correct. Although pressure was occasionally deployed ever since January, upon Paul's return from Berghof the British and Americans began a full diplomatic initiative for endorsing Yugoslavia's rejection of any German offer. Their pressures were remarkably similar in context with the German and Italian and centred around the threat that Yugoslavia's destiny after the war would depend on its attitude during the war.[95] The old-new British Foreign Secretary Eden invited the Regent to meet in Crete, which Paul rejected. Then Churchill and President Roosevelt tried to intervene. Pressure was exercised from the special American representative Colonel William Donovan, Lane and the new British Minister in Yugoslavia Ronald Ian Campbell; finally, from Terence Shone, the former official of the British legation in Belgrade, who was sent to Yugoslavia especially for this occasion with a personal message from Eden. However, none of these pressures resulted in changing Prince Paul's mind.[96] All the great powers' narratives balanced between threats and promises of bright future once the war was over. One of Lane's arguments seemed very plausible and, had the atmosphere in Belgrade not been as heated, might have borne some weight on Paul's reasoning: 'Yugoslavia is in geographically [favourable] strategic position because of common frontiers with both Germany and Italy. Neither wanted other here.'[97]

While setting excessive demands to Berlin in a hope that they would not be accepted, Belgrade sent Major Milisav Perišić to Athens on 8 March to sound out the British who had begun their landing in Piraeus the moment the German troops had crossed the

Danube into Bulgaria, about the extent of British assistance if Yugoslavia decided to enter the war on the side of Greece and Britain. Perišić also emphasized the importance of Thessaloniki for securing Yugoslavia's lines of communication.[98] His mission came in the days of great uncertainty in Belgrade, but although Yugoslavia wanted to hear both sides, this should not be taken as a sign of its willingness to consider a common front with the Greeks and British. Both Paul and Cvetković were dedicated to pursuing strict neutrality; the only considered alternative to this was to sign the Tripartite Pact under different circumstances, but certainly not to take an offensive action against the Axis. In the midst of this careful treading between the Allies and the Axis, Yugoslavia attempted to transfer its gold reserves deposited with the Federal Reserve Bank in the United States to Brazil and Argentina. Had Belgrade strictly insisted on this transfer, Roosevelt would have probably decided to freeze the assets; however, on 19 March, after Fotić's repeated pleas to his government, the Yugoslav request was withdrawn.[99]

On 12 March, instructed by Ribbentrop, Heeren issued a new formulation of Article 3 for the Yugoslavs: the Germans were willing to give in writing a promise that as long as war lasted, Belgrade would never be asked for military assistance, unless the Yugoslavs decided themselves to join. This would however have to be a secret note and would not be possible to make it public.[100] Two days later, Ribbentrop explained that it was not possible for Yugoslavia to obtain publication of any such a promise as this would set up a dangerous precedent for other countries that might wish to join the pact. He stressed that Yugoslavia got the best possible conditions and it was not possible for Germany to go further than that.[101] On 20 March, Cincar-Marković informed the Crown Council of the nature of the German request. Cvetković expressed his doubts over Hitler's sincerity, reminding the council over many agreements and promises he had already broken. Maček asked the Yugoslav Foreign Minister about the consequences of rejecting the German offer. Cincar-Marković replied that there would be no immediate consequences, but next time if the Germans returned with renewed pressure, conditions for Yugoslavia would be less favourable, 'which will leave us only one choice in the end, whether to heed to their demands or to wage war against them'. Maček then asked if that eventually meant choosing between the pact and war and Cincar-Marković confirmed.[102] His answer left an impression and on the following day, the Yugoslav Foreign Minister informed Heeren that the Crown Council had accepted Yugoslavia's adherence to the Tripartite Pact, on the base of the promise that the country would not be asked for military assistance in any forthcoming conflict in Europe.[103] It is not exactly clear what Cincar-Marković based his argument – pact or war – on, when in replying to Maček even he confirmed that 'for the time being, there will be no consequences'. No German source confirms such an ultimatum. Konstantinović later testified that Cvetković once complained about the feebleness and lack of initiative of their Foreign Minister.[104] It is hard to judge whether Cincar-Marković's attitude was determined by his lack of nerve, or a long-term assessment of a seasoned diplomat. It is even more ambiguous as the Yugoslav Foreign Minister was not among those who favoured rapprochement with Germany. As late as February 1941, Cincar-Marković would rather agree to an honourable death fighting and hoping that it would 'mean something at the moment of liquidation of [the] war', than to allow Germany to take possession of Thessaloniki and 'strangle' Yugoslavia by isolating it.[105]

Although the Germans demanded urgency and suggested 23 March as the date for signature, there were complications. Three important ministers, all Serbs, Konstantinović, Budisavljević and Čubrilović, immediately resigned upon the government was informed of the decision by the Crown Council late in the evening of 20 March and Cvetković asked for time to fill in emptied places.[106] The crux of their argument against the signing related to the political context of the Tripartite Pact, which clearly established the method of leadership, as Germany, Italy and Japan were 'to establish and maintain new order of things'.[107] The pragmatic argument against the signing, that Hitler could not care less about written contracts, was equally justified: on 17 March, commenting on the worries expressed to him by Hungarian Minister in Berlin, that his country's claims on parts of Yugoslavia might be dealt a severe blow upon Yugoslavia's accession to the Tripartite Pact, Weizsäcker clarified that Yugoslavia was not offered *guarantees* for its territory, but instead *the Reich's respect* of its sovereignty and territorial integrity. The German then added that the Reich's government 'had not forgotten' Hungary's remaining revisionist claims.[108] On 23 March in Munich, Hitler told the Hungarian Foreign Minister László Bárdossy that Germany 'did not give Yugoslavia any guaranty of its borders ... Germany merely explained the Yugoslavs that it would not attack them so long as they did not take anti-German attitude'.[109] These were clear insinuations of some future Vienna Award at the expense of Yugoslavia, as it was previously done with Czechoslovakia and Romania.

In the meantime, Berlin obtained Mussolini's acceptance of all the terms agreed and Ribbentrop instructed Heeren to explain in Belgrade that 25 March is the last possible date by when Yugoslavia could sign the pact according to the terms agreed, before the visit of the Japanese Foreign Minister Yosuke Matsuoka to Berlin the following day.[110] On 22 March, Heeren reported that he had separate conversations with Prince Paul, Maček and new Slovene leader Franc Kulovec and that all three had confirmed that difficulties would be overcome and Yugoslavia would sign the pact in time set up by Berlin.[111] The treaty was signed by Cvetković and Cincar-Marković on 25 March in Vienna. It was accompanied by four notes: on Yugoslavia's abstention from present and future military operations, on respecting its national interests regarding Thessaloniki, on Yugoslavia's sovereignty and on restriction from using Yugoslavia's territory for the transport of troops and war material. The first two notes were to remain secret, and the latter two were made public.

According to subsequent Ribbentrop's account, Hitler joked that judging by the appearance of the Yugoslavs, the ceremony in Belvedere looked more like a funeral.[112] In the words of Konstantin Fotić: 'It took Hitler more time than it had in the case of any other country to bring Yugoslavia into the ranks of the Axis, but his efforts were crowned with a success which he thought would assure him of a bloodless conquest.'[113] Two days later, some Serbian officers led by aviation Generals Borivoje Mirković and Dušan Simović overthrew the Regency; the event was followed by manifestations of public support in Belgrade and other Serbian towns. Hitler's interpreter Paul Schmidt later wrote in his memoirs that Hitler and Ribbentrop were warned by the experts that Yugoslavia's government might not survive such a decision, but as so many times before, the opinion of the 'weak diplomats' was thrown into a bin.[114] Former German minister in Belgrade and ambassador in Rome Ulrich von Hassell shared Schmidt's opinion: 'This [Ribbentrop's insisting that the Tripartite Pact had to be signed latest by 25 March] represents the true methods of our present leaders: they take no cognizance whatsoever of psychological effects [on the Yugoslav government].'[115] This remark is a testimony to an unsurmountable rift in understanding the foreign policy between the old-school Weimar and the Nazi diplomats – psychological effect caused by verbal bullying was exactly what Ribbentrop and Hitler wanted to achieve. In one of his reports from Belgrade, Lane wrote about 'the government terrified by Germans'.[116] Many reports state deterioration of Paul's mental health as a result of despair; in another interview with Lane, he apparently repeated twice that he wished he was dead.[117] Eastern parts of the country were strongly pro-British and anti-German and would not tolerate any agreement with Hitler. Maček and other Croatian leaders were mainly opposed to the Third Reich and preferred Yugoslavia's neutrality and even a fight if the country was attacked, but under specific circumstances they would agree to some kind of agreement with Hitler. As early as November 1940, Maček recommended the signing of the Tripartite Pact, provided clauses of non-violation of the Yugoslav territory and rejection of active participation in war were obtained.[118] However, Serbian interest for Thessaloniki was not recognized by the Croats and Slovenes who would not fight for it. Neither Prince Paul prior to, nor Simović after the coup, accepted suggestions about the forming of a recreated Salonika front at the Greek-Yugoslav border, as such a decision would have estranged non-Serbian parts of Yugoslavia and allowed their easy occupation by any invading army. Twenty years of bickering between the Serbian and Croatian political elites had left its toll and despite the 1939 Agreement, Yugoslavia remained a politically divided nation. In Prince Paul's words to Lane, this was also a comprehension of the army: '[The] only military possibility for Yugoslavia is to attack; defensive war would be fatal.'[119] Therefore, internal discords prevented Yugoslavia's weak leaders from reaching any firm decision which could have been unpopular with some portions of the Yugoslav nation. Eventually, it was a combination of external threats and this internal instability which doomed Prince Regent and Cvetković's government. On the other hand, agreement with Hitler by itself was not a guarantee enough against subsequent German attack or dissolution of the country. The fate of Romania stood clearly before the eyes of the Yugoslavs. Also, Italy, Hungary and Bulgaria did not relinquish their claims over Yugoslavia's territory and they all listed Hitler as an ally. This led to the assumption that if Germany ended the war victoriously, parts of Yugoslavia's territory might be ceded to its neighbours despite any signed agreements. The only answer to Yugoslavia's dilemmas was to wait for Germany's defeat. But the question remained whether to wait with or without the agreement signed with the Axis.

The argument that Yugoslavia had no other choice but to sign the Tripartite Pact or face the invasion is unsupported by evidence. Hungarian Foreign Minister István Csáky privately confessed to Prince Paul on 11 December 1940 that Hitler personally told him the only two reasons which might motivate him to consider the invasion of Yugoslavia were either the Yugoslav attack on Italian forces in Albania, or the British attempt to recreate the Salonika front with Greece and Yugoslavia.[120] No German diplomatic or military correspondence before 25 March 1941 suggests that Hitler would have attacked Yugoslavia at that moment, even if Yugoslavia rejected to adhere to the pact; no such plans were in place for any of the German military formations.[121] On 22 March, in one of his final orders to the army before the beginning of Marita, in regard to Yugoslavia Hitler said: 'It is still left to be assessed if we should count with the entry of Yugoslav troops towards Thessaloniki.'[122] Hermann Neubacher later wrote in his memoirs about the utter surprise of General List upon receiving the order to turn part of his troops towards Yugoslavia after the coup in Belgrade and the organizational headaches this sudden change caused for the Twelfth Army: 'For everyone who knew anything about this [German-Yugoslav relations], there is no doubt that Hitler never thought about *any* attack on Yugoslavia before 27 March 1941 ... War against Yugoslavia was never part of German plans for conquest.'[123] In the final instruction given to Heeren over the telephone on 19 March, Ribbentrop stressed that if the Yugoslavs did not sign immediately, after all the hitherto unprecedented concessions granted to them, 'various technical difficulties will arise and later on it will be more difficult. I accepted everything and it can't be postponed, the Japanese are coming over here on 25 [March] and they'll stay for five days, then comes something else I have to deal with and the whole thing cannot be postponed ... Any delay with the signing means a loss [for Yugoslavia] of a unique opportunity.'[124] Although semantics of this sentence could be discussed, it does not seem to indicate a threat of war.

With everything said, the most probable explanation for Yugoslavia's decision to sign the pact is that its leaders misunderstood Ribbentrop's aggressive diplomatic language for actual threats and reacted out of understandable fear. As Konstantinović wrote in his diary on 6 March, Yugoslavia lost a war of nerves.[125] The decision was made in a small circle of few people forming the Crown Council at the time when situation demanded a wide national consensus. A reminder to this was an inept sentence by Lane in a heated debate with Cvetković on 22 March: 'If Parliament existed here, he [Cvetković] would find out quickly enough ... that people [in Yugoslavia] opposed to compromise with dictators.'[126] The same assumption was hinted after the war by Radoje Knežević, one of political organizers of the coup: '[After King Alexander's abolition of the Constitution in 1929] for twelve years Yugoslavia was submitted to a regime in which all power was usurped by the Court. The nation had no say in the matter. The monarch's will was sovereign. He alone decided upon the policy to be adopted as much in foreign matters as within the country itself'.[127] Although Knežević's continued allegations against Prince Paul are widely exaggerated and unfounded, both he and Lane were right to point at the autocratic style of government which significantly contributed to the fall of the Regency.

People's contempt for the direction of Yugoslavia's foreign policy and desire for more democracy at home were at first directed against Stojadinović.[128] But it was only a matter of time before it would turn against the Regent. Prince Paul was an Oxford-educated aristocrat, with profound knowledge of arts, liberal understanding of politics and close family connections with the British Royal Family.[129] However, faced with the ways politics was run in the Balkans, his political liberalism quickly faded. Greeted by many among the Serbian and Croatian opposition politicians as a person who would restore democracy in 1934, Paul turned out to be a disappointment.[130] Thus, by failing to democratize the country Paul resorted to the old style of court politics, in both internal and foreign affairs.[131] Cvetković's government was not unified on many issues and the rift between the Serbian and Croatian ministers still remained. Korošec and Antić, two influential persons of Yugoslavia's political life in those days, unfortunately both also talented for intrigues and manipulation, were widely disliked by the rest of the government.[132] On top of everything, the government was rarely informed about the events in February and March 1941; Cvetković did not summon his cabinet even to submit a report after his meeting with Hitler on 14 February.[133] If the members of the cabinet were kept in dark, it is not surprising that the signing of the Tripartite Pact astonished the Yugoslav people. The same could be told of the army. According to the memoirs of Ilija Jukić, Maček's Chief of Cabinet and the Under-Secretary of Foreign Ministry in 1939–41, Slobodan Jovanović, a distinguished Serbian intellectual and politician, later told him that 'had the putsch leaders been aware of the gravity of Yugoslavia's external position … they would have never carried out the putsch'.[134]

This is however questionable. Already on 25 October 1940, just before the Italian attack on Greece, Heeren reported of the rumours about the possible military coup. He stated that the army and leading Serbian circles were not pleased with the course of the Yugoslav internal and foreign policy and were of the opinion that the constant concessions to the Croats damaged the unity of the country. According to this report, there was a widespread opinion that the country needed a strong man to guide it through the dangerous situation created by the events with Romania and Greece, much stronger than Prince Paul or Cvetković.[135] On 26 March 1941, German legation reported of a great surprise by the stunned masses upon hearing the news from Vienna, as 'the government had hardly prepared the people … and had until recently declared to be in favour of the policy of neutrality'.[136] It is safe to say that Prince Paul and his Crown Council, estranged from the army and isolated from most of the Yugoslav people, mainly Serbs, doomed themselves. When a debate between the most relevant political, economic and intellectual factors across the country was vitally needed, the most important decisions were reached in the small circle of men whose horizons were blurred by discord, personal animosities, panic and fear. In protest to the signing of the pact, Yugoslav minister in Moscow announced his resignation and the minister in Washington the forming of a Committee for Free Yugoslavia, with a task of rallying all people willing to leave the country and fight on the side of the Allies.[137]

If to sign the Tripartite Pact was a mistake, the coup was a rushed, irresponsible and untimely reaction. According to Maček's memoirs, Prince Paul had once told him: 'Woe to the country that is ruled by officers or priests.'[138] The events unfortunately proved him right. The problem with the coup was the lack of any coherent plan of what to do afterwards, provided it was successful. The idea was to take the country out of the hands of authoritarian regime and restore the policy of strict neutrality.[139] After the coup was executed, the conspirators discussed what to do next; proposals ranged from the Romanian-style army dictatorship, over the government of national salvation, to the full restoration of democracy.[140] However, despite sound slogans about a dishonour which the pact with Hitler had brought on a Serbian soldier, the new government made no deviation from the foreign-political course of the previous one; instead, Heeren and other foreign diplomats were informed that Yugoslavia remained the member of the Tripartite Pact.[141] Although some later testimonies tried to denounce this by claiming that the new government of General Simović in reality returned to the course of neutrality and did not intend to get involved in the ongoing conflict,[142] the argument is hollow and contradicts the facts. Simović indeed told Lane already on 28 March that the Tripartite Pact would be neither denounced nor ratified.[143] However, soon came the proper political clarification from the old-new Foreign Minister Momčilo Ninčić, who explained to the American Minister that the pact 'cannot be repudiated as [legally] terms of the pact provided that it would enter into effect immediately on signature'.[144] The following day, Ninčić received Heeren and informed him 'that the new government remains in principle faithful to all concluded bilateral agreements, to which also belongs the protocol signed in Vienna on 25 March'.[145] When British General John Dill visited Belgrade incognito on 1 April, he learned from Simović that Yugoslavia would not make any move that might provoke Hitler. After the visit, Dill reported back to London about great confusion within the new Yugoslav government.[146] There is no doubt that the officers who dethroned Cvetković's government did so out of patriotic reasons, ashamed by what they considered a treasonous pact with Hitler; but without the decisive change of direction in foreign policy, the very purpose of the coup was lost.

More importantly, if the trigger cause for the coup was a pact with Hitler, it is remarkable that it never came to the mind of conspirators that Hitler might retaliate. Although Vauhnik soon sent very precise warning from Berlin that Yugoslavia would be attacked on 6 April in the morning,[147] the new government rejected it and refused to announce a general mobilization. Instead of concentrating the troops in strategically defensible positions protected by the geography of terrain, such as mountainous Bosnia and Central Serbia, the bulk of troops remained widespread along the Yugoslav borderline. On 3 April, Simović finally sent General Radivoje Janković, Deputy Chief of the Yugoslav General Staff, to meet the British-Greek military delegation on the Yugoslav-Greek border. Upon hearing the Greek plea to dislocate majority of Yugoslav forces from western parts of Yugoslavia and focus on defending the territory of pre-1914 Serbia, which was strategically more sensible and offered possibility for joint operations with the Greek army against the Germans in Bulgaria and Italians in Albania, Janković refused any such proposal with the same excuse as the Regency earlier.[148] According to King Peter's subsequent testimony, Simović was confident until the very last moment that no imminent threat to Yugoslavia was coming from Germany.[149] The last attempt by the new Yugoslav government to ease its international position was talks in Moscow over the conclusion of a non-aggression pact; however, the most the Soviets were willing to offer was the Treaty of Friendship, signed on 5 April in the evening.[150]

When Hitler was informed about the Belgrade coup, first he thought it was a joke.[151] Mad with rage, he still managed to find something positive for Germany in the coup; before the gathered generals he said that consequences for the planned German attack on the Soviet Union would have been more serious if the Belgrade events had taken place during Operation Barbarossa.[152] There were other reasons for his swift decision to turn on Yugoslavia, such as to prevent a possible united front with Greece and Britain, to facilitate the attack on Greece, to restore his prestige worldwide damaged by the coup, and also possibly Hitler's long-held antipathies for Serbia.¹⁵³ On the same day, 27 March in the evening, he signed the Directive Number 25, general directions for the attack on Yugoslavia.

Heeren showed admirable compassion for the country where he served more than seven years and did his best to save Yugoslavia. He insisted that the coup was a deed of a small fraction in the army and was not supported by the people, not even the majority of Serbs. He described demonstrations in Belgrade as merely a manifestation of people's joy over the accession of young King Peter in the place of unpopular Prince Paul. He even tried to diminish the importance of the street attacks to his and personalities of other legation members, by ascribing the incidents to the communists.¹⁵⁴ But nothing could change Hitler's mind; importantly, Operation 25 contained special instruction for the army troops to quickly seize all the deposits of raw materials.¹⁵⁵ The attack was to be carried by the Twelfth Army, already concentrated in Bulgaria and the newly formed Second army, to attack from the north. The dual campaign against Greece and Yugoslavia began on 6 April in the morning. The German forces faced stiff Greek resistance on the so-called Metaxas line, alongside the Greek-Bulgarian frontier, but the attack westward progressed better. Yugoslavia proved to be a soft belly of Greek defence when on 8 April the Second armoured division broke Yugoslav defences around Strumica and turned south, penetrating the Greek territory down the undefended Vardar valley, capturing Thessaloniki that night and cutting off the Greek forces in east Macedonia and west Thrace. At the same time, after quickly taking Skopje on 6 April, motorized units of the Fortieth army corps turned south and passing quickly by Bitolj took Edessa in northern Greece on 10 April, thus coming from the back of the Greek and British second line of defence, formed of divisions concentrated between Kajmakčalan and Mount Olimp. On 9 April, the German forces occupied Niš and continued north to Belgrade. The capital was surrounded by 11 April from three directions, mainly by various armoured divisions of both armies and was taken in the morning of 13 April without struggle.¹⁵⁶ Yugoslav resistance lasted barely a week, although the country officially surrendered on the morning of 17 April. Bizarrely, it was Aleksandar Cincar-Marković who tried to gain time for Yugoslavia by signing the Tripartite Pact, who was urged by the remnants of the Yugoslav army led by General Danilo Kalafatović to sign Yugoslavia's surrender. Simović, his government and the King had already left the country three days earlier.¹⁵⁷

# Conclusion

In the turmoil after the Great Depression, Yugoslavia's exports to the German market and the imports of advanced German technology significantly contributed to Yugoslavia's economic recovery and stabilization. They were also important factors for Yugoslavia's industrialization and the modernization of its economy. It cannot be denied that both parties benefitted from the 1934 Trade Agreement. It is true that as the German economy recovered, Berlin's bargaining power increased. But to reduce the view of Yugoslavia's economy merely to Germany's share of its foreign trade is too one-dimensional. After all, in terms of numbers (enlarged by the value of German war reparations) and dynamism, in many aspects the mutual trade was only restored to where it had been just before the Great Depression. What is more important is to stress the differences from the 1920s. Firstly, the methods of trade and Germany's economic ideology under both Schacht's New Plan and the Nazi Four-Year Plan could not be further from the mutual economic relationship of the previous decade. Secondly, in the 1930s Yugoslavia and the other countries of the region did not have the same export possibilities elsewhere. This all led them to increased dependency on the German market; the Yugoslavs did all they could to keep that dependency under control, hoping to cut it off the moment normal economic activity in the world recovered. But whenever they made purely economic progress, the political events of the second half of the 1930s would bring them back to where they had been.

In the context of the existence of various competing institutions in foreign policy decision-making in Berlin, which all pursued their own agendas, it is not easy to define one clearly defined approach in German foreign policy towards Yugoslavia. Instead, we should stress the nature of the Reich's political interests in Yugoslavia and the Balkans, namely the elimination of the influence of other Great Powers from the region and its benevolent neutrality towards Germany in the upcoming war. This was to be achieved through a combination of careful diplomacy, aggressive economic initiatives and the deployment of soft power. But above any other considerations, the Third Reich was a revisionist country, and this fact eventually excluded any possibility for a closer partnership with Yugoslavia. Throughout the 1930s, Yugoslavia was suspicious of Berlin and its ulterior motives. Even when they were seemingly on the same side, for example in the questions of the Habsburg restoration and Italian meddling in Austrian affairs, there was an unease in Belgrade about Berlin's policy in the region after the Anschluss. Berlin's urge for Yugoslavia's neutrality from the other Great Powers stood in correlation with another of the Reich's political interests, that of securing unlimited imports of food and raw materials from Yugoslavia and the region. The history of the Third Reich cannot be studied in isolation from its war economy, which was the crux of the Nazi programme. Burdened with the memory of Germany's failure to secure enough commodities to successfully end the First World War, the Nazis were determined not to repeat the same mistake again. Before 1940, Hitler never contemplated waging war in the south-east, but securing the area as a source of commodities necessary for the German war machine was high on the list of the Nazis' political desires.

Unlike the Germans, for whom the import of goods necessary for their war economy was one of major factors in their foreign policy, the Yugoslavs never allowed economic considerations to influence their foreign policy decision-making. The problem for the German-Yugoslav economic relationship therefore was not so much whether German foreign policy needed the economy as a tool, or if the economy profited from increased German political might, although the latter is a correct conclusion. The problem was in the contrary economic ideologies in Berlin and Belgrade, which from the beginning excluded any possibility of Yugoslavia's voluntary participation in the German *Grosswirtschaftsraum* on Berlin's terms. This concept was based on the denial of free economic development to Germany's trading partners. German officials of the 1930s and leading industrialists associated with the Nazis never contemplated allowing anything more than, at most, economic development and industrialization complementary only to the Reich's needs. The economies of the European south-east were to be mere colonial suppliers of food and raw materials to Germany, with no freedom for making independent decisions. The Yugoslavs sensed this early on, but the wider context of European economics and politics worked against them.

The problem for the Germans was that their plans required either Yugoslavia's voluntary submission, or a strong political pressure in Belgrade. The former was impossible; leading Yugoslav economic officials, businessmen and experts belonged to the camp of free trade and economic liberalism. The latter eventually failed; Yugoslavia belonged politically to the camp of the pro-Versailles and anti-revisionist countries. No Nazi economic or political concessions or favours could have changed that. Hitler was probably honest when he fumed on the morning of 27 March 1941 that he had given the Yugoslavs everything they wanted and they still betrayed him. For this reason, the phrase 'German informal empire' could hardly be applied to Yugoslavia any time before the summer of 1940. To be an empire, formal or informal, a power needs to be able to decisively influence the terms of other countries' political, social, cultural and economic development in peacetime. The Third Reich had never had such an influence in Yugoslavia, at least not until the fall of France.

Yugoslavia and the Third Reich were constantly moving in opposite directions, no matter that this was not obvious to contemporaries, or to many subsequent historians. Even the Germans considered some of the Yugoslav decisions, such as the introduction of import controls in April 1936, or the enforced purchase of the total production of French- and British-owned mines in October 1939, as being results of their pressure. However, to the Yugoslavs, these measures were dictated by the economic realities of the moment. Furthermore, Yugoslavia managed to build a solid foundation for its own heavy industry, which was directly opposed to the wishes of Nazi economic planners. Sooner or later, frictions would have occurred between these two countries. Even had Yugoslavia avoided the German invasion in 1941, an alternative history of the Second World War for the Land of the South Slavs would have meant either the official restructuring of mutual economic relations with Berlin in line with the agreement Germany signed with Romania in March 1939 at best, or in the worst-case scenario the occupation of the country followed by the German management of Yugoslavia's economy, as happened to Hungary in March 1944. In any scenario, Yugoslavia was destined to become German economic prey the moment the Nazis took the reins of power in Berlin in 1933, in the form of either a satellite or a colony.

# Notes

## Chapter 1

1. Jörg Brechtefeld, *Mitteleuropa and German Politics: 1848 to the Present* (London: Macmillan, 1996), 2.
2. Bo Strath, 'Mitteleuropa from List to Naumann', *European Journal of Social Theory* 11, no. 2 (2008), 172–4.
3. Ibid., 177–8.
4. Brechtefeld, *Mitteleuropa and German Politics*, 45.
5. *Griff nach Südosteuropa: Neue Dokumente über dem deutschen Imperialismus und Militarismus gegenüber Südosteuropa im zweiten Weltkrieg*, ed. Wolfgang Schumann (Berlin: VEB Deutscher Verlag der Wissenschaften, 1973), 16.
6. Andrej Mitrović, 'Die Zentralmächte, Mitteleuropa und der Balkan', in *Mitteleuropa-Konzeptionen in der Ersten Hälfte des 20. Jahrhunderts*, ed. Richard Plaschka et al. (Wien: Verlag der Österreichische Akademie der Wissenschaften, 1995), 39–62, 56–7.
7. Brechtefeld, *Mitteleuropa and German Politics*, 48.
8. Andrej Mitrović, 'Ergänzungswirtschaft: The Theory of an Integrated Economic Area of the Third Reich and the Southeast Europe (1933–1941)', in *The Third Reich and Yugoslavia, 1933–1945* (Beograd: ISI, 1977), 7.
9. Henry Cord Meyer, *Mitteleuropa in German Thought and Action, 1815–1945* (The Hague: Martinus Nijhoff, 1955), 313.
10. Bernd-Jürgen Wendt, 'England und der Deutsche "Drang nach Südosten". Kapitalbeziehungen und Warenverkehr in Südosteuropa zwischen den Weltkriegen', in *Deutschland in der Weltpolitik*, ed. Fritz Fischer et al. (Düsseldorf: Bertelsmann Universitätsverlag, 1973), 483.
11. Henry Cord Meyer, 'Mitteleuropa in German Political Geography', *Annals of the Association of American Geographers* 36, no. 3 (1946), 190.
12. Milan Ristović, *Nemački novi poredak i jugoistočna Evropa, 1940/41–1944/45* (Beograd: Službeni glasnik, 2005), 36–8, 41–3.
13. Franz Ahlgrimm, *Die Landwirtschaft des südosteuropäischen Raumes*, Lecture delivered on 21 February 1939 (Vienna, 1939), 17, 19.
14. Walter Hoffmann, *Südost-Europa: ein Querschnitt durch Politik, Kultur und Wirtschaft* (Leipzig: Wolfgang Richard Lindner Verlag, 1932), 123–45.
15. Walter Hoffmann, *Grossdeutschland im Donauraum* (Berlin: Propaganda-Verlag Paul Hochmuth, 1939), 25.
16. Thomas Bohn, 'Bulgariens Rolle im "wirtschaftlichen" Ergänzungsraum Südosteuropa', in *Besatzung und Bündnis: Deutsche Herrschaftsstrategien in Ost- und Südosteuropa*, ed. Christian Gerlach et al. (Berlin: Schwarze Risse, 1995), 112.
17. Hermann Gross, *Die Wirtschaftliche Bedeutung Südosteuropas für das Deutsche Reich* (Berlin and Stuttgart: Rohlhammer Verlag, 1938), 9–14.
18. Kurt Erbsland, *Die Umgestaltung der deutschen Handelspolitik durch den "Neuen Plan" und die Möglichkeit ihrer künftigen Ausgestaltung* (Speyer am Rhein: Pilger-Druckerei, 1937), 61–5.

19  Thomas Mayer, 'Hermann Neubacher: Karriere einer Südosteuropa-Experten', in *"Mitteleuropa" und "Südosteuropa" als Planungsraum: Wirtschafts- und kulturpolitische Expretisen im Zeitalter der Weltkriege*, ed. Carola Sachse (Göttingen: Wallstein Verlag, 2010), 248–54.
20  Hans Zeck, *Die Deutsche Wirtschaft und Südosteuropa* (Leipzig and Berlin: Teubner, 1939), 25–6.
21  Ibid., 34–5.
22  Ibid., 39–40; Ian Innerhofer, 'The Role of the "Agrarian Overpopulation" in German Spatial and Economic Planning for South East Europe before and during World War II', in *Perpetual Motion? Transformation and Transition in Central, Eastern Europe and Russia* (London: UCL School of Slavonic and East European Studies, 2010), 47.
23  Andrej Mitrović, 'Nemački privredni prostor i jugoistočna Evropa 1933', *Istorijski časopis* 21 (1974), 229; Wolfgang Schumann, 'Aspekte und Hintergründe der Handels- und Wirtschaftspolitik Hitlerdeutschland gegenüber Jugoslawien', in *The Third Reich and Yugoslavia, 1933–1945* (Beograd: ISI, 1977), 222.
24  Živko Avramovski, 'The International Isolation of Yugoslavia: An Objective of German Foreign Policy in the Period from 1933–1939', in *The Third Reich and Yugoslavia, 1933–1945* (Beograd: ISI, 1977), 262.
25  Ibid., 263–4.
26  Leposava Cvijetić, 'The Ambitions and Plans of the Third Reich with Regard to the Integration of Yugoslavia into the So-Called Grosswirtschaftsraum', in *The Third Reich and Yugoslavia, 1933–1945* (Beograd: ISI, 1977), 186.
27  *Akten zur deutschen auswärtigen Politik, 1918–1945* (henceforth ADAP), Series C, Volume III/1, Document Number 13 (Göttingen: Vandenhoeck & Ruprecht, 1971–1981), Circular by German Foreign Ministry, 18 June 1934.
28  ADAP, C, III/1, 23, German Foreign Ministry to German Italian Embassy, 21 June 1934.
29  Hans-Jürgen Schröder, 'Südosteuropa als "Informal Empire" Deutschlands 1933–39. Das Beispiel Jugoslawien', *Jahrbücher für Geschichte Osteuropas*, Neue Folge, 23, no. 1 (1975), 94; 'Deutsche Südosteuropapolitik 1929–1936: Zur Kontinuität deutscher Außenpolitik in der Weltwirtschaftskrise', *Geschichte und Gesellschaft* 2, no. 1, Außenwirtschaft und Außenpolitik im Dritten Reich (1976), 5.
30  Johann Wüscht, *Jugoslawien und das Dritte Reich: eine dokumentierte Geschichte der deutsch-jugoslawischen Beziehungen von 1933 bis 1945* (Stuttgart: Seewald, 1969), 87.
31  Ian Kershaw, 'Hitler and the Uniqueness of Nazism', *Journal of Contemporary History* 39, no. 2 (2004), 243–4. For more on this also see: Ian Kershaw, *The Nazi Dictatorship: Problems and Perspectives of Interpretation* (London: Edward Arnold, 1989); Martin Broszat, *The Hitler State: The Foundation and Development of the Internal Structure of the Third Reich* (London: Longman, 1981); Hans Mommsen, 'Hitlers Stellung im nationalsozialistischen Herrschaftssystem' and Klaus Hildebrand, 'Monokratie oder Polykratie? Hitlers Herrschaft und das Dritte Reich', both in *Der 'Führerstaat'. Mythos und Realität*, ed. G. Gerhard Hirschfeld and Lothar Kettenacker (Stuttgart: Klett-Cotta, 1981).
32  Broszat, *The Hitler State*, 194.
33  Roderick Stackelberg, *Hitler's Germany: Origins, Interpretations, Legacies* (London: Routledge, 1999), 105–7.
34  Broszat, *The Hitler State*, 198.
35  Kurt Doß, 'Germany', in *The Times Survey of Foreign Ministries of the World*, ed. Zara Steiner (London: Times Books, 1982), 241–5; Eckart Conze, *Das Amt und die*

*Vergangenheit: deutschen Diplomaten im Dritten Reich und in der Bundesrepublik* (München: Blessing, 2010), 74–5.

36  *Institut für Zeitgeschichte* (henceforth IfZG), Munich, Folder MA 1300, Role 2, US Department of State (1945).

37  *Memoirs of Ernst von Weizsäcker*, trans. John Andrews (London: Victor Gollancz, 1951), 128.

38  Manfred Messerschmidt, 'Außenpolitik und Kriegsvorbereitung', in *Das Deutsche Reich und der Zweite Weltkrieg 1, Ursachen und Voraussetzungen der deutschen Kriegspolitik*, ed. Wilhelm Deist et al. (Stuttgart: Deutsche Verlag-Anstalt, 1979), 554–8, 569–70, 590; Dirk Stegmann, '"Mitteleuropa", 1925–1934: Zum Problem der Kontinuität deutscher Außenhandelspolitik von Stresemann bis Hitler', in *Autarkie und Grossraumwirtschaft in Deutschland 1930–1939: aussenwirtschaftspolitische Konzeptionen zwischen Wirtschaftskrise und Zweitem Weltkrieg*, ed. Eckart Teichert (Munich: Oldenbourg, 1984), 219.

39  Jost Dülffer, 'Zum "Decision-Making Process" in der deutschen Außenpolitik', in *Hitler, Deutschland und die Mächte: Materialien zur Aussenpolitik des Dritten Reiches*, ed. Manfred Funke (Düsseldorf, Droste Verlag, 1976), 188–90.

40  Stegmann, '"Mitteleuropa", 1925–1934: Zum Problem der Kontinuität deutscher Außenhandelspolitik von Stresemann bis Hitler', 215–16.

41  Transcript from the Meeting of the Headquarters of German Group of the MWT, Berlin, 19 December 1933 (Bundesarchiv Berlin (henceforth BArchB), Folder R10V-274). More on this also in Stephen G. Gross, *Export Empire: German Soft Power in Southeastern Europe, 1890–1945* (Cambridge: Cambridge University Press, 2015), 181–219.

42  Stegmann, '"Mitteleuropa", 1925–1934: Zum Problem der Kontinuität deutscher Außenhandelspolitik von Stresemann bis Hitler', 220–1.

43  György Ranky, *Economy and Foreign Policy: The Struggle of the Great Powers for Hegemony in the Danube Valley* (New York: Columbia University Press, 1983), 128–9; Robert Mark Spaulding, *Osthandel und Ostpolitik: German Foreign Trade Policies in Eastern Europe from Bismarck to Adenauer* (Oxford: Berghahn Books, 1997), 251–7.

44  Quoted in Hans-Erich Volkmann, 'Die NS-Wirtschaft in Vorbereitung des Krieges', in *Das Deutsche Reich und der Zweite Weltkrieg 1, Ursachen und Voraussetzungen der deutschen Kriegspolitik*, ed. Wilhelm Diest et al. (Stuttgart: Deutsche Verlags-Anstalt, 1979), 191.

45  Adolf Hitler, *Mein Kampf*, trans. Ralph Manheim (London: Pimlico, 1992), 126.

46  ADAP, C, III/2, No. 295. Memorandum by Ritter (German Foreign Ministry), 3 November 1934.

47  Schröder, 'Südosteuropa als Informal Empire NS Deutschlands: das Beispiel Jugoslawien, 1933–1939', 258.

48  Mitrović, 'Nemački privredni prostor i jugoistočna Evropa 1933', 234; Brechtefeld, *Mitteleuropa and German Politics, 1848 to the Present*, 53.

49  Marie-Luise Recker, 'Die Außenpolitik des Auswärtigen Amts', in *Das Auswärtige Amt in der NS-Diktatur*, ed. Johannes Hürter and Michael Mayer (Oldenburg: De Gruyter, 2014), 84.

50  Brechtefeld, *Mitteleuropa and German Politics, 1848 to the Present*, 53–5.

51  William Carr, *Arms, Autarky and Aggression: A Study in German Foreign Policy, 1933–1939* (London: Edward Arnold, 1972), 50.

52  Volkmann, 'Die NS-Wirtschaft in Vorbereitung des Krieges', 259.

53  Ibid.

54  Alfred Kube, 'Außenpolitik und "Großraumwirtschaft". Die deutsche Politik zur wirtschaftlichen Integration Südosteuropas 1933 bis 1939', *Geschichte und Gesellschaft*. Sonderheft 10, Wirtschaftliche und politische Integration in Europa im 19. und 20. Jahrhundert (1984), 187–192.
55  Tim Mason, 'The Primacy of Politics – Politics and Economics in National Socialist Germany', in *Nazism and the Third Reich*, ed. Henry Ashby Turner (New York: Quadrangle Books, 1972), 175–200.
56  Kerwhaw, *The Nazi Dictatorship*, 45.
57  Hans-Erich Volkmann, 'Politik, Wirtschaft und Aufrüstung unter dem Nationalsozialismus', in *Hitler, Deutschland und die Mächte: Materialien zur Außenpolitik des Dritten Reiches* ed. Manfred Funke (Düsseldorf: Droste Verlag, 1976), 289; Volkmann, 'Die NS-Wirtschaft in Vorbereitung des Krieges', 203.
58  Alan Milward, 'The Reichsmark Bloc and the International Economy', in *Der 'Führerstaat', Mythos und Realität: Studien zur Struktur und Politik des Dritten Reiches*, ed. G. Hirschfeld and L. Kettenacker (Stuttgart: Klett-Cotta, 1981), 377–413.
59  Bernd-Jürgen Wendt, 'Südosteuropa in der nationalistischen Großraumwirtschaft: eine Antwort auf Alan S. Milward', in *Der 'Führerstaat', Mythos und Realität: Studien zur Struktur und Politik des Dritten Reiches*, ed. Gerhard Hirschfeld and Lothar Kettenacker (Stuttgart: Klett-Cotta, 1981), 414–28.
60  Mitrović, 'Nemački privredni prostor i jugoistočna Evropa 1933', 233, 238.
61  Richard Overy, *War and Economy in the Third Reich* (Oxford: Clarendon Press, 1994), 133, 137–9.
62  Kershaw, *The Nazi Dictatorship*, 51–3.
63  *Verein zur Wahrung der gemeinsamen wirtschaftlichen Interessen in Rheinland und Westfalen*, the organization for the protection of industrial interests of the Ruhr area, founded in late nineteenth century.
64  Claus-Dieter Krohn, 'Autoritärer Kapitalismus: Wirtschaftskonzeptionen im Übergang von der Weimarer Republik zum Nationalsozialismus', in *Industrielle Gesellschaft und politisches System: Beiträge zur politischen Sozialgeschichte*, ed. Dirk Stegmann, Bernd Jürgen Wendt and Peter-Christian Witt (Bonn: Verlag Neue Gesellschaft, 1978), 120.
65  Carl Freytag, *Deutschlands 'Drang nach Südosten': Der Mitteleuropäische Wirtschaftstag und der 'Ergänzungsraum Südosteuropa', 1931–1945* (Wien: Vienna University Press, 2012), 73, 84.
66  Adam Tooze, *Wages of Destruction: Making and Breaking of the Nazi Economy* (London: Penguin, 2007), 229.
67  Volkmann, 'Die NS-Wirtschaft in Vorbereitung des Krieges', 327.
68  Holm Sundhaussen, 'Südosteuropa in der Nationalsozialistischen Kriegswirtschaft am Beispiel des "Unabhängigen Staates Kroatien"', *Südost-Forschungen* 32 (1973), 237–8.
69  In the introduction of *Griff nach Südosteuropa*, 27–8.
70  Overy, *War and Economy in the Third Reich*, 106.
71  Dietrich Orlow, *The Nazis in the Balkans: A Case Study of Totalitarian Politics* (Pittsburgh: University of Pittsburgh Press, 1968), 96.
72  Volkmann, 'Die NS-Wirtschaft in Vorbereitung des Krieges', 285.
73  Peter Hayes, 'Industry under the Swastika', in *Enterprise in the Period of Fascism in Europe*, ed. Harold James and Jakob Tanner (Aldershot: Ashgate, 2002), 30.
74  Ibid., 31–2.
75  Tooze, *Wages of Destruction*, 143; Freytag, *Deutschlands 'Drang nach Südosten'*, 79.

76 Kube, 'Außenpolitik und "Großraumwirtschaft". Die deutsche Politik zur wirtschaftlichen Integration Südosteuropas 1933 bis 1939', 192.
77 Rainer Schmidt, *Die Außenpolitik des Dritten Reiches* (Stuttgart: Klett-Cotta, 2002), 211.

## Chapter 2

1 Vuk Vinaver, *Jugoslavija i Francuska izmedju dva rata* (Beograd: ISI, 1985), 295, 305.
2 Dušan Lukač, *Treći Rajh i zemlje jugoistočne Evrope* 1 (Beograd: Vojnoizdavački zavod, 1982), 219.
3 Enes Milak, *Italija i Jugoslavija 1931-1937* (Belgrade: ISI, 1987), 38-49.
4 Vuk Vinaver, '"Austrijsko pitanje" i velika preorijentacija Kralja Aleksandra prema Nemačkoj, 1927-1932', *Istorija 20. veka* 3 (1977), 8-9.
5 Ibid., 17-21.
6 Ibid., 9.
7 Vuk Vinaver, *Svetska ekonomska kriza u Podunavlju i nemački prodor, 1929-1935* (Beograd: ISI, 1987), 65.
8 Milak, *Italija i Jugoslavija*, 59.
9 For more on this see Dragan Bakić, *Britain and Interwar Danubian Europe: Foreign Policy and Security Challenges, 1919-1936* (London: Bloomsbury, 2017).
10 Ibid., 97.
11 Srdjan Mićić, 'Jugoslovenska saradnja sa Telegrafen-Unionom i nemačkim novinarima, 1927-1934', *Tokovi istorije* 2 (2018), 43.
12 Vuk Vinaver, 'Početak nemačke orijentacije stare', *Istorijski zapisi* 34, no. 3-4 (1977), 793.
13 Ibid., 797-8.
14 Yugoslav Foreign Ministry to Royal Court, 29 October 1932 (Arhiv Jugoslavije (henceforth AJ), Fund 74, Folder 190).
15 Detlev Peukert, *Weimar Republic: The Crisis of Classical Modernity* (New York: Hill and Wang, 1992), 55-6.
16 David Thomas Murphy, *The Heroic Earth: Geopolitical Thought in Weimar Germany, 1918-1933* (Kent: Kent State University Press, 1997), 221.
17 Reinhard Frommelt, *Paneuropa oder Mitteleuropa: Einigungsbestrebungen im Kalkül deutscher Wirtschaft und Politik, 1925-1933* (Stuttgart: Deutsche Verlags-Anstalt, 1977), 80-2.
18 Gross, *Export Empire*, 162-3; Stegmann, '"Mitteleuropa", 1925-1934': Zum Problem der Kontinuität deutscher Außenhandelspolitik von Stresemann bis Hitler', 216.
19 Jürgen Elvert, *Mitteleuropa! Deutsche Pläne zur europäischen Neuordnung, 1918-1945* (Stuttgart: Franz Steiner Verlag, 1999), 104.
20 Peter Krüger, *Die Aussenpolitik der Republik von Weimar* (Darmstadt: Wissenschaftliche Buchgesellschaft, 1985), 536.
21 Otto Leichter, *Zwischen Zwei Diktaturen: Österreichs Revolutionäre Sozialisten, 1934-1936* (Wien: Europa Verlag, 1968), 67.
22 Zara Steiner, *The Triumph of the Dark: European International History, 1933-1939* (Oxford: Oxford University Press, 2013), 29-36; James Burgwyn, *Italian Foreign Policy in the Interwar Period, 1918-1940* (London: Praeger, 1997), 80-5.
23 Dufour von Feronce (German Belgrade Legation) to German Foreign Ministry, 1 June 1933 (Politisches Archiv des Auswärtigen Amts (henceforth PA), Record Group RZ 206, Folder R 30303).

24  Memorandum by Busse (German Foreign Ministry), 5 January 1934 (PA, RZ 206 R 30303); ADAP, C, II/2, Rieth (German Vienna Legation) to German Foreign Ministry, 10 March 1934.
25  Memorandum by Busse (German Foreign Ministry), 5 January 1934 (PA, RZ 206, R 30303); Srdjan Mićić, *Kraljevina Jugoslavija i Anšlus Austrije* (Beograd: Službeni glasnik, 2010), 39.
26  Memorandum by Busse (German Foreign Ministry), 29 February 1934 (PA, RZ 206, R 30303).
27  Schumann, 'Aspekte und Hintergründe der Handels- und Wirtschaftspolitik Hitlerdeutschlands gegenüber Jugoslawien', 222.
28  Burgwyn, *Italian Foreign Policy in the Interwar Period*, 72.
29  Ibid., 73.
30  Dufour von Feronce (German Belgrade Legation) to German Foreign Ministry, 27 June 1933 (PA, RZ 206, R 73123).
31  Bogdan Krizman, *Vanjska politika jugoslavenske države* (Zagreb: Školska knjiga, 1975), 80–1.
32  ADAP, C, I/2, 345, Dufour von Feronce (German Belgrade legation) to Neurath, 30 June 1933; ADAP, C, I/2, 378, Hassell (German Rome Embassy) to German Foreign Ministry, 28 July 1933.
33  ADAP, C, I/1, 99, Köppke (German Foreign Ministry) to Hassell (German Rome Embassy), 16 March 1933.
34  Avramovski, 'The International Isolation of Yugoslavia: An Objective of German Foreign Policy in the Period from 1933–1939', 262.
35  Außenpolitisches Amt der NSADP
36  ADAP, C, II/1, 72, 91, 92. Correspondence between Bülow (German Foreign Ministry) and Lammers (The Reich Chancellery), November 1933.
37  Vuk Vinaver, *Jugoslavija i Madjarska, 1933–1941* (Beograd: Narodna knjiga, 1976), 47–8; Ranki, *Economy and Foreign Policy*, 135–40.
38  Krizman, *Vanjska politika jugoslavenske države*, 80; Kube, 'Außenpolitik und "Großraumwirtschaft". Die deutsche Politik zur wirtschaftlichen Integration Südosteuropas 1933 bis 1939', 190.
39  Unsigned report about the talks with the Yugoslav minister, Berlin, 5 April 1934 (PA, RZ 206, R 73123).
40  Hassell (German Rome Embassy) to German Foreign Ministry, 22 March 1934 (PA, RZ 206, R 73123).
41  Hassell (German Rome Embassy) to German Foreign Ministry, 27 April 1934 (PA, RZ 206, R 73123).
42  Hahn (German Klagenfurt Consulate) to German Foreign Ministry, 28 December 1933 (PA, RZ 206, R 73204).
43  Alfred Kube, *Pour le mérite und Hakenkreuz: Hermann Göring im Dritten Reich* (München: Oldenbourg, 1986), 85–7; Mićić, *Kraljevina Jugoslavija i Anšlus Austrije*, 40.
44  Röhm in Dubrovnik, *Jugoslavien-Dienst*, no. 8, 15 April 1934 (AJ, 65, 255).
45  Kube, 'Außenpolitik und "Großraumwirtschaft". Die deutsche Politik zur wirtschaftlichen Integration Südosteuropas 1933 bis 1939', 191.
46  Report by Köpke (German Foreign Ministry), 23 May 1934 (PA, 73123).
47  Gerhard Weinberg, *The Foreign Policy of Hitler's Germany: Diplomatic Revolution in Europe, 1933–1936* (Chicago: Chicago University Press, 1970), 100–1; Burgwyn, *Italian Foreign Policy in the Interwar Period*, 97.
48  Ibid., 104; ADAP, C, III/1, 134, Report by Bülow (German Foreign Ministry), 30 July 1934.

49 'Teške borbe u Koruškoj', *Politika*, 28 July 1934; 'Koncentracioni logor Hitlerovaca u Jugoslaviji', *Politika*, 30 July 1934; 'Dolazak nove grupe austrijskih izbeglica', *Politika*, 31 July 1934; Heeren (German Belgrade Legation) to German Foreign Ministry, 7 December 1934 (PA, RZ 206, R 73123).
50 They were transported to Germany in November that year. Maurice Williams, 'Aid, Assistance and Advice: German Nazis and the Austrian Hilfswerk', *Central European History* 14, no. 3 (1981), 234.
51 Heeren (German Belgrade Legation) to German Foreign Ministry, 18 September 1934 (PA, RZ 206, R 73123).
52 Vinaver, *Svetska ekonomska kriza u Podunavlju i nemački prodor*, 240-1; Steiner, *The Triumph of the Dark*, 71-81.
53 He travelled by boat from Romania. 'Jugoslavija je svom svojom dušom dočekala svoga prijatelja Luja Bartua', *Politika*, 25 June 1934.
54 Vinaver, *Svetska ekonomska kriza u Podunavlju i nemački prodor*, 240; Heeren (German Belgrade Legation) to German Foreign Ministry, 18 September 1934 (PA, RZ 206, R73123).
55 ADAP, C, III/1, 39, Heeren (German Belgrade Legation) to German Foreign Ministry, 27 June 1934.
56 Heeren (German Belgrade Legation) to German Foreign Ministry, 30 June 1934 (PA, RZ 206, R 73123).
57 Heeren (German Belgrade Legation) to German Foreign Ministry, 28 March 1934 (PA, RZ 206, R 73123).
58 Weinberg, *The Foreign Policy of Hitler's Germany*, 46.
59 Klaus Hildebrand, *The Foreign Policy of the Third Reich* (London: Batsford, 1973), 34; Carr, *Arms, Autarky and Aggression*, 35-6; Messerschmidt, 'Aussenpolitik und Kriegsvorbereitung', 590.
60 *Izveštaji Ministarstva inostranih poslova Kraljevine Jugoslavije*, Volume 4 (1933), Beograd: Arhiv Jugoslavije, 2005-16, Monthly reports from Germany, 15, 57-9, 207.
61 'Previranja u Nemačkoj', *Nova Evropa*, XXVI/6, 26 June 1933, 130-2.
62 Milan Koljanin, *Jevreji i antisemitizam u Kraljevini Jugoslaviji, 1918-1941* (Beograd: ISI, 2008), 234.
63 Signed under the pseudonym 'X Y Z'.
64 'Spoljašnja politika Hitlerove Nemačke', *Politika*, 9 April 1933.
65 Freundt (German Zagreb Consulate) to German Foreign Ministry, 26 May 1933 (PA, RZ 206, R 73204).
66 Freundt (German Zagreb Consulate) to German Foreign Ministry, 21 February 1934 (PA, RZ 206, R 73204).
67 Ivo Goldstein and Slavko Goldstein, *Holokaust u Zagrebu* (Zagreb: Novi Liber, 2001), 59.
68 Heeren (German Belgrade Legation) to German Foreign Ministry, 22 June 1934 (PA, RZ 206, R 73123).
69 Avramovski, 'The International Isolation of Yugoslavia: An Objective of German Foreign Policy in the Period from 1933-1939', 266.
70 ADAP, C, II/2, 381, Memorandum by Köpke (German Foreign Ministry), 5 April 1934.
71 *Izveštaji Ministarstva inostranih poslova Kraljevine Jugoslavije* 5 (1934), Monthly Report from Germany, August 311.
72 Vinaver, *Jugoslavija i Francuska izmedju dva svetska rata*, 277.

73  Carlile Aylmer Macartney, *October Fifteenth: A History of Modern Hungary, 1929-1945*, Volume 1 (Edinburgh: Edinburgh University Press, 1957), 147.
74  Royal Court to Yugoslav Foreign Ministry, 1 August 1933 (AJ, 74, 190); Yugoslav Foreign Ministry to Royal Court, 20 October 1933 (AJ, 74, 190).
75  *Nemačka obaveštajna služba u staroj Jugoslaviji* 2 (Beograd: Državni SUP FNRJ, Uprava državne bezbednosti – Treće odeljenje, 1955), 477–8.
76  Interrogation report from the hearing of Hans Heinrich Herwarth and Andor Hencke, by the State Department Interrogation Mission (IfZG, MA 1300, 2), 4.
77  Vinaver, *Jugoslavija i Madjarska*, 82–3.
78  ADAP, C, III/1, No. 264, Heeren (German Belgrade Legation) to German Foreign Ministry, 22 October 1934.
79  Kube, *Pour le mérite und Hakenkreuz: Hermann Göring im Dritten Reich*, 95; ADAP, C, III/1, No. 263, Heeren (German Belgrade Legation) to German Foreign Ministry, 22 October 1934.
80  ADAP, C, III/2, No. 319, Heeren (German Belgrade Legation) to German Foreign Ministry, 9 November 1934.
81  ADAP, C, III/1, No. 264, Heeren (German Belgrade Legation) to German Foreign Ministry, 22 October 1934.
82  Bennett Kovrig, 'Mediation by Obfuscation: The Resolution of the Marseille Crisis, October 1934 to May 1935', *The Historical Journal* 19, no. 1 (1976), 206–7; Unsigned Report, Berlin, 26 November 1934 (PA, RZ 206, R 73123).
83  Henderson (British Belgrade Legation) to Foreign Office, 29 October 1934, Minute by Gallop, 5986/5524/92 (The National Archives (henceforth TNA), London, Foreign Office Papers, Series 371, Box 18460). For more on Hungarian harbouring of Croatian nationalists see Vladimir Šadek, 'Logor Janka-puszta i razvoj ustaške organizacije u Podravini do 1934', *Podravina* 11, no. 21 (2012).
84  Memorandum by Bülow (German Foreign Ministry), 25 November 1934 (PA, RAV Belgrad, 27/2).
85  'Terrorismus und Revisionismus', *Deutsche diplomatisch-politische Korrespondenz*, Berlin, 10 December 1934 (PA, RAV Belgrad, 27/2).
86  Heeren (German Belgrade Legation) to German Foreign Ministry, 17 January 1935 (PA, R73124); Jacob Hoptner, *Yugoslavia in Crisis, 1934–1941* (New York: East Central European studies of Columbia University, 1962), 30–1.
87  Lukač, *Treći Rajh i zemlje jugoistočne Evrope* 1, 212.
88  Carr, *Arms, Autarky and Aggression*, 45–6.
89  Živko Avramovski, *Balkanske zemlje i velike sile, 1935–1937* (Beograd: Prosveta, 1968), 32–4.
90  Eliza Campus, *The Little Entente and the Balkan Alliance* (Bucharest: Bibliotheca Historica Romaniae, 1978), 98–9; Steiner, *The Triumph of the Dark*, 83–90.
91  Ibid., 100–2; Vinaver, *Jugoslavija i Madjarska*, 104; Campus, *The Little Entente and the Balkan Alliance*, 99.
92  Heeren (German Belgrade Legation) to German Foreign Ministry, 25 April 1935 (PA, RZ 206, R 73124).
93  Heeren (German Belgrade Legation) to German Foreign Ministry, 20 June 1935 (PA, RAV Belgrad, 16/4).
94  He also kept the post of Foreign Minister for himself.
95  Avramovski, *Balkanske zemlje i velike sile*, 47–8; *Documents on British Foreign Policy* (henceforth DBFP), ed. W. N. Medlicott and Douglas Dakin (London: Her

Majesty's Stationary Office, 1972–82), Series II, Volume 15, Document No. 72, Edmond (Geneva) to Hoare (Foreign Office), 12 October 1935; Balfour (British Belgrade Legation) to the Foreign Office, 17 October 1935, 6199/6199/92 (TNA, FO 371/19580).
96 *Izveštaji Ministarstva inostranih poslova Kraljevine Jugoslavije* 6 (1935), Monthly Report from Germany, August 311.
97 DBFP II, 15, 298, Hoare (Foreign Office) to Campbell (British Belgrade Legation) and Lorraine (British Angora Legation), 3 December 1935.
98 Avramovski, *Balkanske zemlje i velike sile*, 59–60.
99 Campbell (British Belgrade Legation) to Foreign Office, 25 November 1935, 7125/241/92 (TNA, FO 371/19577).
100 Perica Hadži-Jovančić, 'Losing the Periphery: The British Foreign Office and Policy towards Yugoslavia, 1935–1938', *Diplomacy & Statecraft* 31, no. 1 (2020), 71–74.
101 Heeren (German Belgrade Legation) to German Foreign Ministry, 4 March 1936 (PA, RZ 206, R 240727).
102 Steiner, *The Triumph of the Dark*, 90–1.
103 Milak, *Jugoslavija i Italija*, 120–1.
104 Köpke (German Foreign Ministry) to Heeren (German Belgrade Legation), 18 June 1935 (PA, RZ 206, R 73124); German Prague Legation to German Foreign Ministry, 14 June 1935 (PA, RZ 206, R 73124).
105 Newton (British Berlin Embassy) to Foreign Office, 27 July 1935, 4827/4827/92 (TNA, FO 371/19580).
106 ADAP, C, IV/1, 191, Heeren (German Belgrade Legation) to German Foreign Ministry, 3 July 1935.
107 Papen (German Vienna Legation) to German Foreign Ministry, 5 November 1935 (PA, RZ 206, R 73124). German Milan Consulate to German Foreign Ministry, 18 January 1936 (PA, RZ 206, R 73124).
108 ADAP, C, IV/2, 434, Renthe-Fink (German Foreign Ministry) to Heeren (German Belgrade Legation), 28 November 1935.
109 Memorandum by Busse (German Foreign Ministry), 7 October 1935 (PA, RZ 206, R 73124); Report by Busse (German Foreign Ministry), 10 March 1936 (PA, RZ 206, R 73124). For more on the Yugoslav-German Society in Belgrade see Ranka Gašić, Jugoslovensko-nemačko društvo u Beogradu, 1931–1941, *Istorija 20. veka* 16, no. 1 (1998).
110 Avramovski, *Balkanske zemlje i velike sile*, 213; ADAP, C, IV/2, 542, Circular of the State Secretary of German Foreign Ministry, 6 February 1936.
111 Papen (German Vienna Legation) to German Foreign Ministry, 11 March 1936 (PA, RZ 206, R 73124).
112 Vinaver, *Jugoslavija i Francuska izmedju dva rata*, 311.
113 Piotr Wandycz, 'The Little Entente: Sixty Years Later', *Slavonic and East European Review* 59, no. 4 (1981), 560.
114 Steiner, *The Triumph of the Dark*, 147, 152.
115 Yugoslav Foreign Ministry to Yugoslav Paris Legation, 13 March 1936 (AJ, 334, 16).
116 Ivan Becić, 'Statistika i karakter spoljne trgovine Kraljevine SHS, 1919–1929', *Istorija 20. veka* 33, no. 2 (2015), 68–72.
117 Papen (German Vienna Legation) to German Foreign Ministry, 11 March 1936 (PA, RZ 206, R 73124).
118 Hoptner, *Yugoslavia in Crisis*, 49.
119 Milak, *Jugoslavija i Italija*, 127–8.

120 Burgwyn, *Italian Foreign Policy in the Interwar Period*, 139–43.
121 Steiner, *The Triumph of the Dark*, 155–7.
122 Bakić, *Britain and Interwar Danubian Europe*, 164–8. See also Hadži-Jovančić, 'Losing the Periphery: British Foreign Office and Policy towards Yugoslavia, 1935 –1938.'

# Chapter 3

1 Avramovski, *Balkanske zemlje i velike sile*, 109–13; Cvijetić, 'The Ambitions and Plans of the Third Reich with Regard to the Integration of Yugoslavia into the So-Called Grosswirtschaftsraum', 186; Lukač, *Treći Rajh i zemlje jugoistočne Evrope, 1933–1936* 1, 207; Milak, *Italija i Jugoslavija*, 152, 155; Philip Hepburn, 'The Origins of Appeasement and Anglo-Yugoslav Relations', in *Yugoslav-British Relations* (Beograd: ISI, 1988), 230. More recently: Vesna Aleksić, 'Nazification of the Allgemeiner jugoslawischer Bankverein AG: Political Destiny of an Economic Institution', in *Deutsch-serbische Beziehungen vom Berliner Kongress bis heute*, ed. Dittmar Dahlmann and Milan Kosanović (Bonn: Michael Zikic Stiftung, 2004), 125; Branko Pavlica, 'Nemačka kao ugovorni partner Srbije i Jugoslavije, 1892–1992', *Zbornik Matice srpske za društvene nauke* 112–13 (2002), 298.
2 Wendt, 'Südosteuropa in der nationalsozialistischen Großraumwirtschaft: eine Antwort auf Alan S. Milward', 415.
3 Frank Child, *The Theory and Practice of Exchange Control in Germany: A Study of Monopolistic Exploitation in International Markets* (The Hague: Martinus Nijhoff, 1958); Albert Hirschmann, *National Power and the Structure of Foreign Trade* (Berkeley and Los Angeles: University of California Press, 1945); Schröder, 'Südosteuropa als Informal Empire NS Deutschlands: das Beispiel Jugoslawien, 1933–1939'; William Grenzebach, *Germany's Informal Empire in East-Central Europe: German Economic Policy towards Yugoslavia and Rumania, 1933–1939* (Stuttgart: Franz Steiner Verlag, 1988).
4 Albrecht Ritschl, 'Nazi Economic Imperialism and the Exploitation of the Small: Evidence from Germany's Secret Foreign Exchange Balances, 1938–1940,' *The Economic History Review*, New Series 54, no. 2 (2001), 325; Werner Abelshauser, 'Kriegswirtschaft und Wirtschaftswunder', *Vierteljahrshefte für Zeitgeschichte* 47, no. 4 (1999), 519–521.
5 For example Peter Hedberg and Elias Hakansson, 'Did Germany Exploit Its Small Trading Partners? The Nature of the German Interwar and Wartime Trade Policies Revisited from the Swedish Experience', *Scandinavian Economic History Review* 56, no. 3 (2008).
6 John Lampe, *Balkans into Southeastern Europe, 1914–2014: A Century of War and Transition* (London: Palgrave Macmillan, 2014), 134–5.
7 Mari-Žanin Čalić, *Socijalna istorija Srbije, 1815–1914* (Beograd: Clio, 2004), 394–5.
8 Stevan Kukoleča, *Industrija Jugoslavije 1918–1938* (Beograd: Balkanska štampa, 1941), 286.
9 Nikola Vučo, *Agrarna kriza u Jugoslaviji, 1930–1934* (Beograd: Prosveta, 1968), 161–2.
10 Ibid., 163.

11 For more on this, see Zdravka Zlodi, 'Ideja Frana Ilešiča o uređenju srednjo-istočne Europe iz 1930ih godina', *Časopis za suvremenu povijest* 36, no. 3 (2004).
12 Iago Gil Aguado, 'The Creditanstalt Crisis of 1931 and the Failure of the Austro-German Customs Union Project', *The Historical Journal* 44, no. 1 (2001), 207–8.
13 David Kaiser, *Economic Diplomacy and the Origins of the Second World War: Germany, Britain, France and Eastern Europe, 1930–1939* (Princeton: Princeton University Press, 1980), 30–40.
14 Elvert, *Mitteleuropa! Deutsche Pläne zür europäischen Neuordnung*, 107–8; Stegmann, '"Mitteleuropa", 1925–1934: Zum Problem der Kontinuität deutscher Außenhandelspolitik von Stresemann bis Hitler', 219.
15 Alice Teichova, *Kleinstaaten im Spannungsfeld der Grossmächte: Wirtschaft und Politik in Mittel- und Südosteuropa in der Zwischenkriegszeit* (München: Oldenbourg, 1988), 185. For more on the British plan's origin, context and implications see Fred Stambrook, 'A British Proposal for the Danubian States: The Customs Union Project of 1932', *The Slavonic and East European Review* 42, no. 98 (1963). The Danube Federation, or the Tardieu Plan, is named after the French Prime Minister Andre Tardieu.
16 Markus Wien, *Markt und Modernisierung: deutsch-bulgarische Wirtschaftsbeziehungen 1918–1944 in ihren konzeptionellen Grundlagen* (München: Oldenbourg, 2007), 64.
17 Herbert Matis, 'Wirtschaftliche Mitteleuropa-Konzeptionen in der Zwischenkriegszeit', in *Mitteleuropa-Konzeptionen in der ersten Hälfte des 20. Jahrhunderts*, ed. Richard Plaschka et al. (Vienna: Österreichischen Akademie der Wissenschaften, 1995), 234.
18 Kaiser, *Economic Diplomacy*, 51.
19 Stevan Ćirković, *Politička i privredna Mala Antanta* (Beograd: Biblioteka jugoslovenskog udruženja za međunarodno pravo, 1935), 27–9; 'Kriza Konferencije za obnovu Srednje i Istočne Evrope', *Politika*, 9 September 1932.
20 Wien, *Markt und Modenisierung*, 65; Stambrook, 'A British Proposal for the Danubian States: The Customs Union Project of 1932', 80–2.
21 Mira Kolar-Dimitrijević, 'Privredne veze izmedju Austrije i sjeverne Hrvatske od 1918. do 1925. godine', *Historijski zbornik* 65 (1992), 57–88.
22 Matis, 'Wirtschaftliche Mitteleuropa-Konzeptionen in der Zwischenkriegszeit', 230–2; Wüscht, *Jugoslawien und das Dritte Reich*, 81.
23 Gross, *Export Empire*, 161.
24 Matis, 'Wirtschaftliche Mitteleuropa-Konzeptionen in der Zwischenkriegszeit', 242–3.
25 Božidar Jurković, *Die ausländische Kapital in Jugoslavien* (Stuttgart: Kohlhammer Verlag, 1941), 133.
26 Leonard Gomes, *German Reparations 1919–1932: A Historical Survey* (London: Palgrave Macmillan, 2010), 56.
27 Ivan Becić, *Ministarstvo finansija Kraljevine Jugoslavije, 1918–1941* (Beograd: ISI, 2012), 319, 323; 'Ratni dugovi Kraljevine Srbije u svetlu politike', *Istorija 20. veka* 28, no. 3 (2010), 54–5.
28 The General Directory of State's Debts at the Yugoslav Finance Ministry to Yugoslav Royal Delegate at the Reparation Commission (Paris), 4 September 1929 (AJ, 70, 462).
29 Becić, *Ministarstvo finansija Kraljevine Jugoslavije*, 279.

30  John Wheeler-Bennett and Hugh Latimer, *Information on the Reparation Settlement: Being the Background and History of the Young Plan and the Hague Agreements, 1929-1930* (London: George Allen and Unwin, 1930), 100, 226-9.
31  John Wheeler-Bennett, *The Wreck of Reparations: Being the Political Background of the Lausanne Agreement, 1932* (London: George Allen and Unwin, 1933), 25.
32  Wheeler-Bennett and Latimer, *Information on the Reparation Settlement*, 118, 235.
33  Ibid., 192-5.
34  Yugoslav Royal Delegate at the Reparation Commission (Paris) to General Directory of State's Debts at the Yugoslav Finance Ministry, 10 October 1929 (AJ, 70, 462).
35  Gomes, *German Reparations 1919-1932*, 162.
36  Ibid., 192-7.
37  After the American President Herbert Hoover.
38  Sally Marks, 'The Myths of Reparations', Central European History 11, no. 3 (1978), 252.
39  Wheeler-Bennett, *The Wreck of Reparations*, 69.
40  *Documents on International Affairs* 1931, ed. Wheeler Bennett, W. John (Oxford: Oxford University Press, 1932), 121.
41  Wheeler-Bennett and Latimer, *The Wreck of Reparations*, 70.
42  Gomes, *German Reparations*, 208-12.
43  German-Yugoslav agreement on 23 January 1933 about the termination of the German deliveries to Yugoslavia as part of reparations, Berlin, 23 January 1933 (PA, RZ 304, R 35318).
44  Wheeler-Bennett and Latimer, *Information on the Reparation Settlement*, 94-5; Gomes, *German Reparations*, 162; Boško Đorđević, *Pregled ugovorne trgovinske politike, od osnivanja države Srba, Hrvata i Slovenaca do rata 1941. godine* (Zagreb: Jugoslovenska akademija znanosti i umjetnosti, 1960), 139.
45  'Prezaduženost nemačke poljoprivrede', *Politika*, 13 June 1932; Tooze, *The Wages of Destruction*, 52-4.
46  Grenzebach, *Germany's Informal Empire in East-Central Europe*, 16; Gross, *Export Empire*, 168-9; Kaiser, *Economic Diplomacy*, 25-6.
47  ADAP, C, III/1, 13, Circular of the German Foreign Ministry, 18 June 1934.
48  'Pobuna nemačkih agraraca u fraku', *Narodno blagostanje*, 21 January 1933.
49  Grenzebach, *Germany's Informal Empire in East-Central Europe*, 15-16; Verband der deutschen Ausfuhrbrauereien to German Agriculture Ministry, 20 December 1932 (PA, RZ 206, R 241146); Rheinisch-Westfälisches Kohlen Syndikat to German Economics Ministry, 18 March 1933 (PA, RZ 303, R 117339); Verein deutscher Maschinenbau-Anstalt to German Foreign Ministry, 24 March 1933 (PA, R41146); Verein deutscher Eisen- und Stahlindustrieller to German Economics and Foreign Ministries, 7 April 1933 (PA, R41146).
50  Memorandum by Yugoslav Trade and Industry Ministry, 18 July 1930 (AJ, 65, 254).
51  Yugoslav Berlin Legation to Yugoslav Trade and Industry Ministry, uncertain date (AJ, 65, 252).
52  'Narodna privreda u prvom tromesečju 1932. godine', *Politika*, 3 June 1932.
53  Nikolai Momtchiloff, *Ten Years of Controlled Trade in South-Eastern Europe* (Cambridge: Cambridge University Press, 1944), 16-17; Albert George Kenwood and Alan Leslie Lougheed, *The Growth of the International Economy, 1820-1960* (London: Routledge, 1992), 200; 'Liberalizam ili intervencionizam u našoj trgovinskoj politici', *Nova Evropa* XXX/11, 26 November 1937. Gross, *Export Empire*, 185-286.

54  Michael Ebi, *Export um jeden Preis, die Deutsche Exportförderung von 1932–1938* (Stuttgart: Franz Steiner Verlag, 2004), 95.
55  Kenwood and Lougheed, *The Growth of the International Economy*, 202.
56  Reichsbank-Direktorium to German Foreign Ministry, Berlin, 4 October 1932 (PA, RZ 303, R 117338).
57  Monthly report of the Yugoslav National Bank's (henceforth YNB) Board Committee, Belgrade, November 1932 (Arhiv Narodne Banke Srbije (henceforth ANB), Belgrade, Fund 1/II, Box 11).
58  'Liberalizam ili intervencionizam u našoj trgovinskoj politici', *Nova Evropa* XXX/11, 26 November 1937.
59  For example, according to the payment agreement with Greece, 65 per cent of the value of Yugoslav exports was to be paid in foreign currency, while the rest could be traded for Greek goods valued in drachmas. Undated and unsigned document, Belgrade (ANB, 1/II, 149); Monthly report of the YNB's Board Committee, October 1932 (ANB, 1/II, 11); Monthly report of the YNB's Board Committee, February 1933 (ANB, 1/II, 12).
60  Monthly report of the YNB's Board Committee, October 1932 (ANB, 1/II, 11).
61  Memorandum on the outcome of the London Economic Conference, 10 May 1933 (ANB, 1/II, 91).
62  Monthly report of the YNB's Board Committee, November 1932 (ANB, 1/II, 11).
63  'Evolution of the Yugoslav Foreign Trade in the Period 1929–1939', Belgrade, unsigned, 1940 (ANB, 1/II, 149).
64  'Novi putevi nemačke trgovinske politike', *Politika*, 25 January 1933; Undated and unsigned report, Belgrade (AJ, 65, 255).
65  Monthly report of the YNB's Board Committee, June 1933 (ANB, 1/II, 12).
66  German Belgrade Legation to German Foreign Ministry, 11 April 1933 (PA, RZ 206, R 241597); Report by *Jugoslawien-Dienst*, 15 February 1934 (AJ, 65, 255); Milak, *Italija i Jugoslavija*, 97–8.
67  ADAP, C, III/1, 13, Circular of German Foreign Ministry, 18 June 1934.
68  'Evolution of the Yugoslav Foreign Trade in the Period 1929–1939', Belgrade, unsigned, 1940 (ANB, 1/II, 149).
69  Šumenković (Yugoslav Trade and Industry Ministry) to Srškić, 17 February 1933 (AJ, 65, 254); Ritter (German Foreign Ministry) to Dufour von Feronce (German Belgrade Legation), 2 February 1933 (PA, RZ 311, R 105940).
70  Ritter (German Foreign Ministry) to German Belgrade Legation, 30 November 1932 (PA, RZ 311, R 105940).
71  Undated and unsigned report, Belgrade, probably late 1932 (AJ, 65, 255); 'Provisional Regulation of Our Trading Relations with Germany', Belgrade, undated and unsigned document (AJ, 65, 254); Memorandum by Wiehl (German Foreign Ministry), 15 March 1933 (PA, RZ 311, R 105940); Boško Djordjević and Sava Obradović, *Pregled ugovorne trgovine od osnivanja države Srba, Hrvata i Slovenaca do rata 1941. godine* (Zagreb: Jugoslavenska Akademija Znanosti i Umjetnosti, 1960), 139.
72  'Od danas u ponoć nastaje neugovorno stanje izmedju nemačkog Rajha i Kraljevine Jugoslavije', *Vreme*, 5 March 1933; Wiehl (German Foreign Ministry) to German Belgrade Legation, 4 March 1933 (PA, RZ 311, R 105940); Fodor (Regierungsrat) to Busse (German Foreign Ministry), 22 April 1933 (PA, RZ 311, R 41146).
73  For more on this, see: Gustavo Corni, 'Alfred Hugenberg as Minister of Agriculture: Interlude or Continuity?', *German History* 7, no. 2 (1989).

74  Wiehl (German Foreign Ministry) to German Belgrade Legation, March 1933 (PA, RZ 311, R 105940).
75  Dufour von Feronce (German Belgrade Legation) to German Foreign Ministry, 27 May 1933 (PA, RZ 311, R 105940); German Foreign Ministry to German Belgrade Legation, 15 June 1933 (PA, RZ 311, R 105940); German Foreign Ministry to German Belgrade Legation, 23 June 1933 (PA, RZ 311, R 105941).
76  Grenzebach, *Germany's Informal Empire in East-Central Europe,* 27.
77  Dufour von Feronce (German Belgrade Legation) to German Foreign Ministry, 29 July 1933 (PA, RZ 311, R 105941); Jevtić (Yugoslav Foreign Ministry) to Dufour von Feronce (German Belgrade Legation), 29 July 1933 (AJ, 72, 50).
78  'Nemačko-jugoslovenski trgovinski odnosi', *Vreme,* 3 August 1933.
79  'Kriza izvoza voća u Nemačku', *Narodno blagostanje,* 19 August 1933.
80  Dufour von Feronce (German Belgrade Legation) to German Foreign Ministry, 23 August 1933 (PA, RZ 311, R 105941).
81  Yugoslav Foreign Ministry to Yugoslav Trade and Industry Minister, 9 September 1933 (AJ, 65, 254).
82  Memorandum by Ulrich (German Foreign Ministry), Berlin, 14 February 1934 (PA, R105941).
83  Ritter (German Foreign Ministry) to German Rome Embassy, 12 March 1934 (PA, RZ 311, R 105941).
84  *Izveštaji Ministarstva inostranih poslova Kraljevine Jugoslavije* 5 (1934), Monthly Reports from Germany, March, July, August, 122–3, 269–70, 309–12.
85  Grenzebach, *Germany's Informal Empire in East-Central Europe,* 39; Telegram by Sarnow (German Economics Ministry), 15 April 1934 (PA, RZ 311, R 105941).
86  ADAP, C, III/1, 13, Circular by German Foreign Ministry, 18 June 1934.
87  Secret Protocol to the German Yugoslav trade agreement, 1 May 1934 (AJ, 65, 254).
88  Djordjević, *Pregled ugovorne trgovinske politike,* 145–6; Ranki, *Economy and Foreign Policy,* 141.
89  Pavlica, 'Nemačka kao ugovorni partner Srbije i Jugoslavije', 297. In payments through clearing, tourists were goods like any other, as Germany needed to pay Reichsmarks on the Yugoslav clearing account in Berlin and issue traveller checks which were then converted into dinars upon the travellers' arrival in Yugoslavia.
90  Grenzebach, *Germany's Informal Empire in East-Central Europe,* 41.
91  Vučo, *Agrarna kriza u Jugoslaviji,* 181.
92  Grenzebach, *Germany's Informal Empire in East-Central Europe,* 42.
93  Unsigned document, appendix to Ulrich's memorandum for German European Legations, 18. June 1934 (PA, RZ 311, R 105941).
94  Secret protocol for the improvement of German-Yugoslav goods exchange, 1 May 1934 (AJ, 65, 254).
95  Additional note to articles one and two of the secret protocol, 1 May 1934 (AJ, 65, 254).
96  Memorandum on German-Yugoslav commercial relations, 31 January 1936, 664/81/92 (TNA, FO371/20434).
97  'Jugoslovensko-nemački privredni odnosi', *Jugoslovenski ekonomist,* November 1938.
98  Reichsnährstand.
99  Gross, *Export Empire,* 189.
100 *Statistisches Jahrbuch für das Deutsche Reich* 1935 (Berlin: Statistische Reichsamt), 202, 210, 242; *Statistisches Jahrbuch für das Deutsche Reich* 1937, 242, 277.
101 Ulrich's secret memorandum to German European legations, 18 June 1934 (PA, RZ 311, R 105941).

102 Antonin Basch, *The Danube Basin and the German Economic Sphere* (London: Kegan Paul, 1944), 152–3.
103 Ćirković, *Politička i privredna Mala Antanta*, 30.
104 Schumann, 'Aspekte und Hintergründe der Handels- und Wirtschaftspolitik Hitlerdeutschlands gegenüber Jugoslawien', 221.
105 'U Bukureštu je objavljen sporazum o razmeni petroleuma i bakra izmedju Jugoslavije i Rumunije', *Politika*, 8 November 1936.
106 German Belgrade Legation to German Foreign Ministry, 4 March 1936 (PA, RZ 206, R 240727).
107 Basch, *The Danube Basin and the German Economic Sphere*, 157. Although still smaller than the numbers for 1931, this increase in trade with Yugoslavia was much greater than an overall increase in Czechoslovak foreign trade.
108 German Belgrade Legation to German Foreign Ministry, 4 March 1936 (PA, RZ 206, R 240727).
109 Summary of the press reports from South-Eastern Europe, *Mitteilungen des MWT*, 16 May 1936.
110 'Naša privreda i pakt Male Antante', *Nova Evropa* XXVI/3, 26 March 1933.
111 'Diskussion über die Wirtschaftsbeziehungen Jugoslawiens', *Jugoslavien-Dienst*, 15 April 1934 (AJ, 65, 255), 6.
112 Basch, *The Danube Basin and the German Economic Sphere*, 155.
113 Volkmann, 'Die NS-Wirtschaft in Vorbereitung des Krieges', 198–200.
114 Ibid., 197; *Izveštaji Ministarstva inostranih poslova Kraljevine Jugoslavije* 6 (1935), Monthly Report from Germany, February, 80.
115 Volkmann, 'Die NS-Wirtschaft in Vorbereitung des Krieges', 208–10; Carr, *Arms, Autarky and Aggression*, 21, 61–2.
116 Ibid., 36–7.
117 Volkmann, 'Die NS-Wirtschaft in Vorbereitung des Krieges', 211.
118 Hildebrand, *The Foreign Policy of the Third Reich*, 29–30.
119 Volkmann, 'Die NS-Wirtschaft in Vorbereitung des Krieges', 222.
120 *Izveštaji Ministarstva inostranih poslova Kraljevine Jugoslavije* 6 (1935), Monthly Report from Germany, February, 81.
121 Wilhelm Treue, 'Das Dritte Reich und die Westmächte auf dem Balkan', *Vierteljahrshefte für Zeitgeschichte* 1, no. 1 (1953), 47; Volkmann, 'Die NS-Wirtschaft in Vorbereitung des Krieges', 254; Tooze, *The Wages of Destruction*, 86–8; Abelshauser, 'Kriegswirtschaft und Wirtschaftswunder', 516–17.
122 Hans-Erich Volkmann, 'Aussenhandel und Aufrüstung in Deutschland, 1933–1939', in *Ökonomie und Expansion: Grundzuge der NS-Wirtschaftspolitik*, ed. Hans-Erich Volkmann and Bernhard Chiari (München: Oldenbourg, 2003), 107.
123 Report of German Foreign Ministry, 8 March 1935 (PA, RZ 206, R 241593).
124 Basch, *The Danube Basin and the German Economic Sphere*, 168.
125 Tooze, *The Wages of Destruction*, 71–9; *Izveštaji Ministarstva inostranih poslova Kraljevine Jugoslavije* 7 (1936), Monthly Report from Germany, January, 43.
126 ADAP, C, III/1, 13, Circular by German Foreign Ministry, 18 June 1934.
127 Volkmann, 'Außenhandel und Aufrüstung in Deutschland', 108–9; Carr, *Arms, Autarky and Aggression*, 53.
128 Gross, *Export Empire*, 187.
129 Yugoslav Foreign Ministry to Yugoslav Trade and Industry Ministry, 10 June 1935 (AJ, 65, 252).

130 Basch, *The Danube Basin and the German Economic Sphere*, 169; Ljubomir St Kosier, *Grossdeutschland und Jugoslawien: Aus der Südslawischen Perspektive* (Berlin: Mitteleuropäischer Verlag, 1939), 206.
131 Michael Kitson, *The Move to Autarchy: The Political Economy of Nazi Foreign Trade*, Cambridge Department of Applied Economics, Working Paper, 1992, 6.
132 Hans-Jürgen Schröder, 'Der Aufbau der deutschen Hegemonialstellung in Südosteuropa, 1933–1936', in *Hitler, Deutschland und die Mächte: Materialien yur Aussenpolitik des Dritten Reiches*, ed. Manfred Funke (Düsseldorf, Droste Verlag, 1976), 763–4.
133 Schmidt, *Die Aussenpolitik des Dritten Reiches*, 211.
134 Karl Bopp, 'Hjalmar Schacht: Central Banker', *A Quarterly of Research* 14, no. 1 (1939), 85.
135 Amos Simpson, *Hjalmar Schacht in Perspective* (The Hague: Mouton, 1969), 94–5; Gross, *Export Empire*, 187–8; *Izveštaji Ministarstva inostranih poslova Kraljevine Jugoslavije* 5 (1934), Monthly Report from Germany, September, 357–8.
136 Kitson, *The Move to Autarchy: The Political Economy of Nazi Foreign Trade*, 5; Howard Sylvester Ellis, *Exchange Control in Central Europe* (Cambridge, MA: Harvard University Press, 1941), 19; Kaiser, *Economic Diplomacy and the Origins of the Second World War*, 140–1; Carr, *Arms, Autarky and Aggression*, 39–40.
137 Momtchiloff, *Ten Years of Controlled Trade in South-Eastern Europe*, 19.
138 Basch, *The Danube Basin and the German Economic Sphere*, 167.
139 Larry Neal, 'The Economics and Finance of Bilateral Clearing Agreements', *Economic History Review* 32, no. 3 (1979), 400; Ebi, *Export um jeden Preis*, 97–8.
140 Bopp, 'Hjalmar Schacht: Central Banker', 84; Ellis, *Exchange Control in Central Europe*, 257–8.
141 German Foreign Ministry to German Legations, 10 April 1935 (PA, RZ 206, R 241593).
142 Volkmann, 'Die NS-Wirtschaft in Vorbereitung des Krieges', 262.
143 Kaiser, *Economic Diplomacy and the Origins of the Second World War*, 153.
144 Monthly report of the YNB's Board Committee, April 1935 (ANB, 1/II, 14).
145 Yugoslav National Bank to Yugoslav Finance Ministry, 23 July 1935 (ANB, 1/II, 96).
146 Schröder, 'Südosteuropa als "Informal Empire" NS-Deutschlands. Das Beispiel Jugoslawien, 1933–1939', 247–8.
147 Ellis, *Exchange Control in Central Europe*, 259, 263; *Statistisches Jahrbuch für das Deutsche Reich* 1937, 254; Monthly report of the YNB's Board Committee, January 1936 (ANB, 1/II, 15).
148 Payment of German goods by clearing, YNB, 14 September 1934 (ANB, 1/II, 96).
149 The ban of paying in Germany before the import of goods, YNB, 13 October 1934 (ANB, 1/II, 96).
150 Hess (German Belgrade Legation) to Sarnow (German Economics Ministry), 2 November 1934 (PA, RZ 311, R 105942); Sarnow (German Economics Ministry) to Hess (German Belgrade Legation), 10 November 1934 (PA, RZ 311, R 105942).
151 Hess (German Belgrade Legation) to Sarnow (German Economics Ministry), 15 November 1934 (PA, RZ 311, R 105942).
152 Sarnow (German Economics Ministry) to Hess (German Belgrade Legation), 4 December 1934 (PA, RZ 311, R 105942).
153 Hess (German Belgrade Legation) to Sarnow (German Economics Ministry), 11 January 1935 (PA, RZ 311, R 105942).
154 Ibid.

155 Records of the first meeting of Yugoslav section of the Yugoslav-German Trading Commission, Belgrade, 6 February 1935 (AJ, 65, 255).
156 Records of the second meeting of Yugoslav section of the Yugoslav-German Trading Commission, Belgrade, 8 February 1935 (AJ, 65, 255).
157 Records of the third and fourth meetings of the Yugoslav section of the Yugoslav-German Trading Commission, Belgrade, 11 and 15 February 1935 (AJ, 65, 255).
158 Record by Clodius (German Foreign Ministry) with the secret protocol attached, 6 March 1935 (PA, RZ 311, R 105942).
159 Monthly report of the YNB's Board Committee, March 1935 (ANB, 1/II, 14).
160 'Jugoslovensko-nemački privredni odnosi', *Nova Evropa* XXVIII/6, 26 June 1935.
161 Ellis, *Exchange Control in Central Europe*, 263; Neal, 'The Economics and Finance of Bilateral Clearing Agreements', 399–400.
162 Monthly report of the YNB's Board Committee, March 1935 (ANB, 1/II, 14).
163 Privileged payment of imports from Germany, YNB, 6 April 1935 (ANB, 1/II, 96).
164 The analysis of the Yugoslav foreign trade, YNB, undated (ANB, 1/II, 96); Neal, 'The Economics and Finance of Bilateral Clearing Agreements', 400.
165 Monthly report of the YNB's Board Committee, May 1935 (ANB, 1/II, 14).
166 Private clearing with Germany, YNB, 22 November 1935 (ANB, 1/II, 96); The German payment agreement, YNB, 18 September 1935 (ANB, 1/II, 96); Private clearing with Germany, unsigned circular attached to a missing report, 23 November 1935 (PA, RZ 311, R 105942).
167 *Statistisches Jahrbuch für das Deutsche Reich* 1937, 253; Djordjević, *Pregled ugovorne trgovinske politike*, 149.
168 Reinhardt (German Finance Ministry) to Hess (German Belgrade Legation), 5 September 1935 (PA, RZ 311, R 105942); Grenzebach, *Germany's Informal Empire in East Central Europe*, 58.
169 Kube, 'Außenpolitik und Großraumwirtschaft. Die deutsche Politik zur wirtschaftlichen Integration Südosteuropas 1933 bis 1939', 195.
170 The agreement between Dr Schacht and Governor Radosavljević, YNB, 28 December 1935 (ANB, 1/II, 96); Deutsche Verrechnungskasse to Yugoslav National Bank, 10 January 1936 (ANB, 1/II, 96).
171 Deutsche Verrechnungskasse to Yugoslav National Bank, 4 February 1936 (ANB, 1/II, 96).
172 'Likvidiranje klirinškog salda sa Njemačkom', *Jugoslovenski Lloyd*, 8 January 1936.
173 Yugoslav National Bank to Yugoslav Finance Ministry, 28 December 1935 (ANB, 1/II, 96).
174 Djordjević, *Pregled ugovorne trgovinske politike*, 149.
175 'Narodna banka i privreda okoline', *Slovenec*, 22 March 1935.
176 Yugoslav National Bank to Yugoslav Finance Ministry, 29 October 1936 (ANB, 1/II, 96).
177 Hess (German Belgrade Legation) to Sarnow (German Economics Ministry), 26 April 1935 (PA, RZ 311, R 105942); Hess (German Belgrade Legation) to Sarnow (German Economics Ministry), 7 May 1935 (PA, RZ 311, R 105942).
178 Hess (German Belgrade Legation) to Clodius (German Foreign Ministry), 29 August 1935 (PA, RZ 311, R 105942).
179 Yugoslav Foreign Ministry to Yugoslav Trade and Industry Ministry, 13 January 1936 (AJ, 65, 255).
180 Wandycz, 'The Little Entente: Sixty Years Later', 559–60; Piotr Wandycz, *The Twilight of French Eastern Alliances, 1926–1936* (Princeton: Princeton University Press, 1988), 424.

181  The record of the second meeting of the Yugoslav delegation at the German-Yugoslav Mixed Committee, Belgrade, 15 March 1936 (AJ, 65, 254).
182  Undated and unsigned report, Yugoslav Berlin Legation, first half of 1936 (AJ, 394, 1).
183  The secret protocol, Zagreb, 1 April 1936 (ANB, 1/II, 96).
184  Djordjević, *Pregled ugovorne trgovinske politike*, 152; Ivan Becić, 'Finansijska politika Milana Stojadinovića', *Istorija 20. veka* 29, no. 3 (2011), 139; 'Der jugoslawische Einfuhrkontrollausschuss', *Mitteilungen des MWT*, 24 April 1936.
185  Campbell (British Belgrade Legation) to Foreign Office, 30 April 1937, 3281/8/92 (TNA, FO 371/21194).
186  Evolution of the Yugoslav Foreign Trade from 1929 to 1939, YNB, undated analysis from 1940 (ANB, 1/II, 149).
187  Annual economic report on Yugoslavia for 1936, British Foreign Office, 30 April 1937, 3281/8/92 (TNA, FO 371/21194).
188  Yugoslav National Bank to Stojadinović (Yugoslav Finance Ministry), 7 May 1935 (ANB, 1/II, 96); Balfour (British Belgrade Legation) to Foreign Office, 19 August 1935, 5150/5150/92 (TNA, FO 371/19580).
189  Yugoslav National Bank to Letica (Yugoslav Finance Ministry), 4 September 1935 (ANB, 1/II, 96).
190  Yugoslav National Bank to Letica (Yugoslav Finance Ministry), 14 March 1936 (ANB, 1/II, 96).
191  Monthly report of the YNB's Board Committee, May 1936 (ANB, 1/II, 15).
192  'Die Wirtschaftspolitik Jugoslawiens', *Mitteilungen des MWT*, 5 June 1936.
193  Milak, *Italija i Jugoslavija*, 106.
194  Grenzebach, *Germany's Informal Empire in East-Central Europe*, 63.
195  Campbell (British Belgrade Legation) to Foreign Office, 19 June 1936, 3685/81/92 (TNA, FO 371/20435).
196  Heeren (German Belgrade Legation) to German Foreign Ministry, 16 June 1936 (PA, RZ 211, R 103338).
197  Hjalmar Schacht, *My First Seventy-Six Years* (London: Wingate, 1955), 331.
198  Campbell (British Belgrade Legation) to Foreign Office, 19 June 1936, 3685/81/92 (TNA, FO 371/20435).
199  Quoted in Grenzebach, *Germany's Informal Empire in East-Central Europe*, 63.
200  Hans Raupach, 'The Impact of the Great Depression on Eastern Europe', *Journal of Contemporary History* 4, no. 4, The Great Depression (1969), 83.
201  'Oko kliringa', *Narodno blagostanje*, 13 October 1934.

# Chapter 4

1  Steiner, *The Triumph of the Dark*, 317–29.
2  For more on this see Christopher Seton-Watson, 'The Anglo-Italian Gentleman's Agreement of January 1937 and Its Aftermath', in *The Fascist Challenge and the Policy of Appeasement*, ed. Wolfgang Mommsen and Lothar Kettenacker (London: George Allen and Unwin, 1983), 267–82.
3  'Na sednici glavnog odbora Jugoslavenske radikalne zajednice, Milan Stojadinović govorio je o novom šefu Jugoslovenske nacionalne stranke Petru Živkoviću', *Politika*, 8 July 1936.
4  Heeren (German Belgrade Legation) to German Foreign Ministry, 10 July 1936 (PA, RZ 211, R 103318).
5  Vinaver, *Jugoslavija i Francuska izmedju dva svetska rata*, 324.

| | |
|---|---|
| 6 | Heeren (German Belgrade Legation) to German Foreign Ministry, 6 September 1936 (PA, RZ 211, R 103318). |
| 7 | Milan Stojadinović, *Ni rat, ni pakt: Jugoslavija izmedju dva rata* (Buenos Aires: by author, 1963), 364. |
| 8 | Hoptner, *Yugoslavia in Crisis*, 53–5; Avramovski, *Balkanske zemlje i velike sile*, 216–17. |
| 9 | Ibid., 223–30. |
| 10 | Wandycz, 'Little Entente: Sixty Years Later', 560–3. |
| 11 | Avramovski, *Balkanske zemlje i velike sile*, 242–3. |
| 12 | Heeren (German Belgrade Legation) to German Foreign Ministry, 12 November 1936 (PA, RZ 211, R 103320). |
| 13 | Weinberg, *Hitler's Foreign Policy*, 262. |
| 14 | Hoptner, *Yugoslavia in Crisis*, 62–3. |
| 15 | Avramovski, *Balkanske zemlje i velike sile*, 267–85. |
| 16 | Hoptner, *Yugoslavia in Crisis*, 67. |
| 17 | Milak, *Italija i Jugoslavija*, 136–7. |
| 18 | Živko Avramovski, *Balkanska antanta* (Belgrade: ISI, 1986), 261. |
| 19 | Heeren (German Belgrade Legation) to German Foreign Ministry, 12 November 1936 (PA, RZ 211, R 103318). |
| 20 | Heeren (German Belgrade Legation) to German Foreign Ministry, 13 November 1936 (PA, RAV Belgrad, 20/2). |
| 21 | Hoptner, *Yugoslavia in Crisis*, 85; Lukač, *Treći Rajh i zemlje jugoistočne Evrope* 2, 77; Steiner, *The Triumph of the Dark*, 362. |
| 22 | Lukač, *Treći Rajh i zemlje jugoistočne Evrope* 2, 78. |
| 23 | Bismarck (German Rome Embassy) to German Foreign Ministry, 27 February and 9 March 1937 (PA, RAV Belgrad, 20/2). |
| 24 | Heeren (German Belgrade Legation) to German Foreign Ministry, 31 March 1937 (PA, RAV Belgrad, 20/2). |
| 25 | Burgwyn, *Italian Foreign Policy in the Interwar Period*, 156. |
| 26 | Hassell (German Rome Embassy) to German Foreign Ministry, 29 March 1937 (PA, RAV Belgrad, 20/2). |
| 27 | Burgwyn, *Italian Foreign Policy in the Interwar Period*, 152. |
| 28 | Weinberg, *The Foreign Policy of Hitler's Germany*, 262. |
| 29 | Lukač, *Treći Rajh i zemlje jugoistočne Evrope* 2, 89. |
| 30 | The tools were the opposition parties from both Serbia and Croatia. Todor Stojkov, 'Čehoslovačko-francuska aktivnost protiv M. Stojadinovića (1936–1938)', *Časopis za suvremenu povijest* 1 (1979), 56–62. |
| 31 | 'Yugoslavia and Hitler: Yugoslav Fascism for German Money', *Rude Pravo*, 3 February 1937; 'Hitler Counts on Yugoslavia's Neutrality', *Rude Pravo*, 7 March 1937. |
| 32 | ADAP, C, VI/2, 309, Heeren (German Belgrade Legation) to German Foreign Ministry, 9 April 1937. |
| 33 | Heeren (German Belgrade Legation) to German Foreign Ministry, 23 June 1937 (PA, RZ 211, R 103318). |
| 34 | Neurath's report about the Belgrade visit, 16 June 1937 (PA, RZ 211, R 103318). |
| 35 | ADAP, C, VI/2, 542, Pochhammer (German Bucharest Legation) to German Foreign Ministry, 1 September 1937. |
| 36 | Minute by British Foreign Office, 16 November 1937, 7626/2597/92 (TNA, FO 371/21201). |
| 37 | Macartney, *October Fifteenth*, 151, 197. |
| 38 | Vinaver, *Jugoslavija i Madjarska*, 196. |

39 Eugene Boia, *Romania's Diplomatic Relations with Yugoslavia in the Interwar Period, 1919–1941* (Boulder: East European Monographs, 1993), 223.
40 Weinberg, *The Foreign Policy of Hitler's Germany*, 221–4; Macartney, *October Fifteenth*, 196.
41 ADAP, D, V, 141, Memorandum by Press Attaché Heck (German Bern Legation), 21 September 1937.
42 ADAP, D, V, 149, Memorandum by Meissner, State Secretary of the Chancellery, 25 November 1937.
43 Macartney, *October Fifteenth*, 202–4.
44 ADAP, D, V, 162,163, Memorandums by Neurath and Heeren (German Belgrade Legation), 15 and 17 January 1938.
45 *Nemačka obaveštajna služba u staroj Jugoslaviji* 2, 115–16.
46 Campbell (British Belgrade Legation) to Foreign Office, 3 January 1938, 147/147/92 (TNA, FO 371/22475).
47 Stojadinović, *Ni rat ni pakt*, 502–3.
48 Campbell (British Belgrade Legation) to Foreign Office, 3 January 1938, 147/147/92 (TNA, FO 371/22475).
49 Clemens Diederich to German Foreign Ministry, Berlin, 24 November 1937 (PA, RZ 211, R 103318).
50 *Izveštaji Ministarstva Kraljevine Jugoslavije* 9 (1938), Monthly reports from Belgium, Great Britain, Czechoslovakia, Hungary and Poland, March, 133, 142, 153, 166–7.
51 Lukač, *Treći Rajh i zemlje jugoistočne Evrope* 2, 132.
52 Stojadinović, *Ni rat ni pakt*, 501.
53 Lukač, *Treći Rajh i zemlje jugoistočne Evrope* 2, 150; Hoptner, *Yugoslavia in Crisis*, 111.
54 Heeren (German Belgrade Legation) to German Foreign Ministry, 22 February 1938 (PA, RZ 211, R 103318); Arnold Suppan, *Jugoslawien und Österreich, 1918–1938: bilaterale Aussenpolitik im europäischen Umfeld* (Wien: Verlag für Geschichte und Politik, 1996), 1204.
55 Ibid., 1212–13.
56 Galeazzo Ciano, *Diary, 1937–1943*, ed. Muggeridge Malcolm (London: Phoenix Press, 2002), 59.
57 Vinaver, *Jugoslavija i Francuska izmedju dva rata*, 369.
58 Robert Alexander Clarke Parker, *Chamberlain and Appeasement: British Foreign Policy and the Coming of the Second World War* (London: Macmillan, 1993), 93.
59 Avramovski, *Balkanska antanta*, 272.
60 Mićić, *Kraljevina Jugoslavija i Anšlus Austrije 1938*, 78–9.
61 Ibid., 161–3, 172–4, 197–8.
62 Suppan, *Jugoslawien und Österreich*, 1216.
63 *Foreign Relations of the United States Diplomatic Papers* (henceforth FRUS), 1938, General, Volume I, Document 449 (Washington, United States Government Printing Office, 1955), US Minister in Yugoslavia to Secretary of State, 12 March 1938.
64 'Pretsednik vlade Milan Stojadinović o prisajedinjenju Austrije nemačkom Rajhu', *Politika*, 17 March 1938.
65 Heeren (German Belgrade Legation) to German Foreign Ministry, 17 March 1938 (PA, RZ 211, R 103345).
66 'Pretsednik vlade Milan Stojadinović o prisajedinjenju Austrije nemačkom Rajhu', *Politika*, 17 March 1938.
67 ADAP, D, V, 193, Weizsäcker (German Foreign Ministry) to Erdmannsdorff (German Budapest Legation), 13 April 1938.

68  *Tajni arhivi grofa Ciana 1936-1942*, trans. Ive Mihailović (Zagreb: Zora, 1952), 226-7.
69  Lukač, *Treći Rajh i zemlje jugoistočne Evrope* 2, 175.
70  ADAP, D, II, 367, Unsigned minute, German Foreign Ministry, 18 August 1938.
71  Lukač, *Treći Rajh i zemlje jugoistočne Evrope* 2, 212.
72  ADAP, D, II, 114, Memorandum by Weizsäcker (German Foreign Ministry), 1 April 1938.
73  ADAP, D, II, 284, Memorandum by Weizsäcker (German Foreign Ministry), Berlin, 7 July 1938.
74  ADAP, D, II, 198, Werkmeister (German Budapest Legation) to German Foreign Ministry, 23 May 1938.
75  ADAP, D, II, 260, Memorandum by Ribbentrop, sometime between 21 and 24 June 1938.
76  ADAP, D, II, 367, Unsigned memorandum, German Foreign Ministry, 18 August 1938.
77  Hoptner, *Yugoslavia in Crisis*, 116; Vinaver, *Jugoslavija i Madjarska*, 287-8, 440; Vinaver, *Jugoslavija i Francuska izmedju dva rata*, 384.
78  Macartney, *October Fifteenth*, 238-47; Steiner, *The Triumph of the Dark*, 588-9.
79  Lukač, *Treći Rajh i zemlje jugoistočne Evrope* 2, 212-13.
80  William Oldson, 'Romania and the Munich Crisis, August-September 1938', *East European Quarterly* 11, no. 2 (1977), 182-3.
81  Hoptner, *Yugoslavia in Crisis*, 117-18.
82  ADAP, D, II, 412, Heeren (German Belgrade Legation) to German Foreign Ministry, 31 August 1938; ADAP, D, II, 447, minute by Weizsäcker (German Foreign Ministry) for Ribbentrop, 9 September 1938.
83  Martin Alexander, *The Republic in Danger: General Maurice Gamelin and the Politics of French Defence, 1933-1940* (Cambridge: Cambridge University Press, 1992), 232.
84  Shone (British Belgrade Legation) to Foreign Office, 29 July 1938, 6734/147/92 (TNA, FO 371/22475).
85  ADAP, D, II, 463, Heeren (German Belgrade Legation) to German Foreign Ministry, 12 September 1938.
86  Campbell (British Belgrade Legation) to Foreign Office, 21 October 1938, 8552/147/92 (TNA, FO 371/22475).
87  ADAP, D, V, 229, Heeren (German Belgrade Legation) to German Foreign Ministry, 4 October 1938; ADAP, D, V, 230, Fabricius (German Bucharest Legation) to German Foreign Ministry, 6 October 1938.
88  *Izveštaji Ministarstva inostranih poslova Kraljevine Jugoslavije* 1939, Monthly reports from Great Britain, September, 398-9.
89  ADAP, D, V, 263, Memorandum by Heinburg (German Foreign Ministry), 8 December 1938.
90  Boia, *Romania's Diplomatic Relations with Yugoslavia in the Interwar Period*, 242-3.
91  Steiner, *The Triumph of the Dark*, 688-90.
92  Betty Jo Winchester, 'Hungary and the "Third Europe" in 1938', *Slavic Review* 32, no. 4 (1973), 742, 744; Dušan Biber, 'O padu Stojadinovićeve vlade', *Istorija XX veka* 8 (1966), 7.
93  *Allianz Hitler-Horthy-Mussolini: Dokumente zur ungarischen Aussenpolitik (1933-1944)*, ed. Magda Adam et al. (Budapest: Akademiai Kiado, 1966), 31-3.
94  Ciano, *Diary*, 187.

95 *Tajni arhivi grofa Ćana*, 280.
96 Ibid., 227.
97 Campbell (British Belgrade Legation) to Foreign Office, 9 May 1938, 4721/147/92 (TNA, FO 371/22475); Campbell (British Belgrade Legation) to Foreign Office, 3 June 1938, 5482/147/92 (TNA, FO 371/22475).
98 Hoptner, *Yugoslavia in Crisis,* 114–15.
99 Dejan Djokić, *Elusive Compromise: A History of Interwar Yugoslavia* (New York: Columbia University Press, 2007), 191–2.
100 Biber, 'O padu Stojadinovićeve vlade', 63.
101 *The Goebbels Diaries, 1939–1941*, trans. Fred Taylor (London: Hamish Hamilton, 1982), 9.
102 *Izveštaji Ministarstva inostranih poslova Kraljevine Jugoslavije* 10 (1939), Monthly reports from Germany, February, 90.
103 ADAP, D, V, 285, Memorandum by Schmidt (German Foreign Ministry), 7 February 1939.
104 ADAP, D, V, 291, Heeren (German Belgrade Legation) to German Foreign Ministry, 11 February 1939.
105 Heeren (German Belgrade Legation) to German Foreign Ministry, 22 February 1939 (PA, RZ 211, R 103318).
106 ADAP, D, V, 300, Weizsäcker (German Foreign Ministry) to Heeren (German Belgrade Legation), 22 February 1939.
107 ADAP, D, V, 311, Heeren (German Belgrade Legation) to Weizsäcker (German Foreign Ministry), 7 March 1939.
108 ADAP, D, VI, 41, Heeren (German Belgrade Legation) to German Foreign Ministry, 19 March 1939.
109 Ciano, *Diary*, 179.
110 Stojadinović, *Ni rat ni pakt*, 518.
111 Hoptner, *Yugoslavia in Crisis,* 125–6; Dragan Bakić, 'The Italo-Yugoslav Conflict over Albania: A View from Belgrade, 1919–1939', *Diplomacy & Statecraft* 25, no. 4 (2014), 604–6; Vinaver, *Jugoslavija i Francuska izmedju dva rata*, 399.
112 Hoptner, *Yugoslavia in Crisis*, 138–41. Djokić, *Elusive Agreement*, 198–200.
113 Dimitrije Djordjević, 'Fascism in Yugoslavia, 1918–1941', in *Native Fascism in the Successor States, 1918–1945*, ed. Peter Sugar (Santa Barbara: Clio Press, 1971), 128.
114 Ciano, *Diary*, 222; Avramovski, *Balkanska antanta,* 303.
115 Heeren (German Belgrade Legation) to the German Foreign Ministry, 13 April 1939 (PA, RZ 211, R 103318).
116 Irina Aleksandra Nikolić, 'Anglo-Yugoslav Relations, 1938–1941' (unpublished PhD diss., University of Cambridge, 2001), 84; Avramovski, *Balkanska antanta*, 301–2; Boia, *Romania's Diplomatic Relations with Yugoslavia in the Interwar Period*, 257–9.
117 ADAP, D, VI, 198, note by Schmidt (German Foreign Ministry), 14 April 1939.
118 ADAP, D, VI, 262, 271, Memorandums by Kordt and Hewel (German Foreign Ministry), 25 and 26 April 1939.
119 ADAP, D, VI, 474, Memorandum by Ribbentrop, 7 June 1939.
120 'Eventualni svetski rat i mi', *Narodno blagostanje*, 29 April 1939.
121 Heeren (German Belgrade Legation) to German Foreign Ministry, 20 June 1939 (PA, RZ 211, R 103318).
122 ADAP, D, VI, 637, Memorandum by Weizsäcker (German Foreign Ministry), 8 July 1939.
123 Avramovski, *Balkanska antanta*, 311–12.

124 ADAP, D, VI, 675, Memorandum by Wörmann (German Foreign Ministry), 15 July 1939.
125 ADAP, D, VI, 733, 745, Weizsäcker (German Foreign Ministry) to German Belgrade Legation; Feine (German Belgrade Legation) to German Foreign Ministry, 29 and 31 July 1939.
126 ADAP, D, VII, 17, Heeren (German Belgrade Legation) to German Foreign Ministry, Bled, 10 August 1939.
127 Hoptner, *Yugoslavia in Crisis*, 166.
128 ADAP, D, VI, 503, 598, Erdmannsdorff (German Budapest Legation) to German Foreign Ministry; Weizsäcker (German Foreign Ministry) to German Belgrade Legation, 10 June and 1 July 1939.
129 Avramovski, *Balkanska antanta*, 323–4.
130 ADAP, D, VI, 680, Wörmann (German Foreign Ministry) to German Belgrade Legation, 17 July 1939.
131 Nikolić, 'Anglo-Yugoslav Relations', 98–103.Vladislav Stakić, *Moji razgovori sa Musolinijem: osovinske sile i Jugoslavija* (München: by author, 1967), 58–9.
132 Feine (German Belgrade Legation) to German Foreign Ministry, 25 July 1939 (PA, RZ 211, R 103318).
133 Heeren (German Belgrade Legation) to German Foreign Ministry, 20 July 1939 (PA, RZ 211, R 103318).
134 Ciano, *Diary*, 258–67; ADAP, D, VII, 43, Memorandum by Schmidt (German Foreign Ministry), 12 August 1939; Denis Mack Smith, *Mussolini's Roman Empire* (London and New York: Longman, 1976), 193–4; Bogdan Krizman, 'Odnosi Jugoslavije s Njemačkom i Italijom, 1937–1941', *Historijski zbornik* 17 (1964), 227–33; Živko Avramovski, 'Sukob interesa V. Britanije i Nemačke na Balkanu uoči Drugog svetskog rata', *Istorija XX veka. Zbornik radova* 2 (1961), 135.
135 ADAP, D, VII, 532, Memorandum by Wörmann (German Foreign Ministry), 1 September 1939.
136 *Winston Churchill and Emery Reves: Correspondence, 1937–1938*, ed. Martin Gilbert (Austin: University of Texas Press, 1997), 230.
137 Campbell (British Belgrade Legation) to Foreign Office, 3 January 1938, 147/147/92 (TNA, FO 371/22475).

# Chapter 5

1 Mason, 'The Primacy of Politics – Politics and Economics in National Socialist Germany', 183.
2 Carr, *Arms, Autarky and Aggression*, 53.
3 Dietmar Petzina, 'Vierjahresplan und Rüstungspolitik', in *Wirtschaft und Rüstung am Vorabend des Zweiten Weltkrieges*, ed. Friedrich Forstmeier and Hans-Erich Volkmann (Düsseldorf: Droste Verlag, 1975), 68–9.
4 Grenzebach, *Germany's Informal Empire in East-Central Europe*, 96–7.
5 Carr, *Arms, Autarky and Aggression*, 54.
6 Grenzebach, *Germany's Informal Empire in East-Central Europe*, 97–8.
7 Tooze, *The Wages of Destruction*, 207–13; Petzina, 'Vierjahresplan und Rüstungspolitik', 72–3.
8 Carr, *Arms, Autarky and Aggression*, 55.

9   Volkmann, 'Die NS-Wirtschaft in Vorbereitung des Krieges', 285.
10  Carr, *Arms, Autarky and Aggression*, 51–2; Tooze, *The Wages of Destruction*, 205. On Schacht's conflict with the military and Göring over the synthetic oil production also see: Anand Toprani, *Oil and the Great Powers: Britain and Germany, 1914–1945* (Oxford: Oxford University Press, 2019), 170–6.
11  Grenzebach, *Germany's Informal Empire in East-Central Europe*, 101.
12  Monthly report of the YNB's Board Committee, June 1936 (ANB, 1/II, 15).
13  'German Economic and Financial Policies', Yugoslav Berlin Legation to Yugoslav Foreign Ministry, 30 May 1936 (AJ, 394, 1).
14  Overy, *War and Economy in the Third Reich*, 95; Tooze, *The Wages of Destruction*, 223.
15  *Izveštaji Ministarstva inostranih poslova Kraljevine Jugoslavije* 8 (1937), Monthly Report from Germany, January, 34.
16  Grenzebach, *Germany's Informal Empire in East-Central Europe*, 102–4; Tooze, *The Wages of Destruction*, 219–22.
17  Volkmann, 'Außenhandel und Aufrüstung in Deutschland', 117–18.
18  'German Foreign Trade in the First Three Months', Yugoslav Berlin Legation to Yugoslav Foreign Ministry, 21 May 1936 (AJ, 394, 1).
19  'Yugoslav-German Trade Relations', Yugoslav Berlin Legation to Yugoslav Foreign Ministry, 3 June 1936 (AJ, 394, 1); Industrial-Trading Chamber (Banja Luka) to Vrbanić (Yugoslav Finance Ministry), 11 June 1936 (AJ, 65, 253); 'Problems with the Purchase of Goods from Germany', Industrial Union of Dravska Banovina (Ljubljana) to Trade and Industry Ministry, 11 December 1936 (AJ, 65, 253).
20  'Import of Our Cattle to Germany', Yugoslav Berlin Legation to Yugoslav Foreign Ministry, 9 July 1936 (AJ, 394, 1).
21  Monthly reports of the YNB's Board Committee, September and October 1936 (ANB, 1/II, 15).
22  'Za nemačke turiste nema više deviza', *Politika*, 9 October 1936.
23  'Trade Relations between Yugoslavia and Germany', Yugoslav Foreign Ministry to Stojadinović, 9 September 1936 (AJ, 394, 1).
24  Secret Protocol, Dresden, 20 October 1936 (ANB, 1/II, 96).
25  ADAP, C, V, 592, Sarnow (German Economics Ministry) to Ritter (German Foreign Ministry), 12 October1936.
26  Monthly report of the YNB's Board Committee, June 1936 (ANB, 1/II, 15).
27  Monthly report of the YNB's Board Committee, August 1936 (ANB, 1/II, 15).
28  Grenzebach, *Germany's Informal Empire in East-Central Europe*, 66; Gross, *Export Empire*, 200.
29  Monthly report of the YNB's Board Committee, November 1936 (ANB, 1/II, 15).
30  Kaiser, *Economic Diplomacy and Origins of the Second World War*, 17.
31  Monthly report of the YNB's Board Committee, December 1936 (ANB, 1/II, 15).
32  Monthly report of the YNB's Board Committee, January 1937 (ANB, 1/II, 16).
33  Ellis, *Exchange Control in Central Europe*, 262.
34  Reichsbank to German Economics Ministry, 26 January 1937 (Bundesarchive (Henceforth BArch), Record Group R 2, Folder 10221).
35  Schacht to Göring, 20 January 1937 (BArch, R 2/14138).
36  ADAP, C, VI, 91, 104, 150, 198, 211, Communication between German Belgrade Legation and German Foreign Ministry, December 1936–February 1937.
37  ADAP, C, VI, 219, Hess (German Belgrade Legation) to German Foreign Ministry, 19 February 1937.

38  Berger (German Finance Ministry) to German Economics Ministry, 3 February 1937 (BArch, R 2/10221).
39  German Belgrade Legation to German Economics Ministry, 26 January 1937 (BArch, R 2/10221).
40  Unsigned proposal delivered to Cincar-Marković (Yugoslav Berlin Legation), 12 February 1937 (BArchB, R2/10221).
41  German Foreign Ministry to German Economics Ministry, 4 March 1937 (BArch, R 2/10221).
42  Djordjević, *Pregled ugovorne trgovinske politike*, 157.
43  Report by Yugoslav Foreign Ministry, 24 March 1937 (ANB, 1/II, 96).
44  German Foreign Ministry to Yugoslav Berlin Legation, 24 March 1937 (ANB, 1/II, 96); Undated and unsigned document, Belgrade (AJ, 65, 254); Djordjević, *Pregled ugovorne trgovinske politike*, 157; 'Klirinški saldo sa Nemačkom na visokoj temperaturi', *Narodno blagostanje*, 3 April 1937.
45  Clodius to German Economics Ministry and German Finance Ministry, 19 March 1937 (BArch, R 2/10221).
46  Monthly report of the YNB's Board Committee, May 1937 (ANB, 1/II, 16).
47  Monthly reports of the YNB's Board Committee, December 1937 and February 1938 (ANB, 1/II, 16, 17).
48  Monthly reports of the YNB's Board Committee, May, June, July and December 1937 (ANB, 1/II, 16).
49  Vladimir Cvetković, *Ekonomski odnosi Jugoslavije i Francuske, 1918–1941* (Belgrade: INIS, 2006), 192–3.
50  Monthly reports of the YNB's Board Committee, May and September 1937 (ANB, 1/II, 16).
51  Monthly reports of the YNB's Board Committee, May and November 1937 (ANB, 1/II, 16).
52  Milak, *Italija i Jugoslavija*, 151–6.
53  Heeren (German Belgrade Legation) to German Foreign Ministry, 3 April 1937 (BArch, R 2/9918).
54  *Statistički godišnjak Kraljevine Jugoslavije*, 1937 (Beograd: Državna štamparija, 1938), 190–1.
55  'Dnevni red jugoslovensko-nemačkog trgovinskog odbora', *Narodno blagostanje*, 20 May 1939.
56  Monthly reports of the YNB's Board Committee, August and September 1937 (ANB, 1/II, 16); 'Weekly Report LIV – Relations with Other Countries: Germany', Trade and Industry Ministry, 1 November 1937 (AJ, 65, 194).
57  The fourth session of the Yugoslav Coordination Board for Foreign Trade, 27 August 1937 (AJ, 65, 194).
58  Campbell (British Belgrade Legation) to Foreign Office, 25 October 1937, 7173/76/92 (TNA, FO 371/21195).
59  'Novi trgovinski i platni sporazum sa Nemačkom', *Narodno Blagostanje*, 9 October 1937.
60  'Record of the German-Yugoslav Mixed Committee Meeting in Dubrovnik', Sarnow (German Economics Ministry) to Benzler (German Foreign Ministry), Walter (German Agricultural Ministry) and Wucher (German Finance Ministry), 4 October 1937 (BArch, R 2/14138); Fourth Secret Protocol, Dubrovnik, 29 September 1937

(ANB, 1/II, 96); 'Weekly Report LIV – Relations with Other Countries: Germany', Trade and Industry Ministry, 1 November 1937 (AJ, 65, 194).
61 Monthly reports of the YNB's Board Committee, October and November 1937 (ANB, 1/II, 16).
62 The fifth session of the Yugoslav Coordination Board for Foreign Trade, 31 August 1937 (AJ, 65, 194); Monthly report of the YNB's Board Committee, February 1938 (ANB, 1/II, 17).
63 *Statistisches Jahrbuch für das Deutsche Reich* 1938, 254.
64 Volkmann, 'Die NS-Wirtschaft in Vorbereitung des Krieges', 310–12.
65 Grenzebach, *Germany's Informal Empire in East-Central Europe,* 108–9.
66 Tooze, *The Wages of Destruction,* 231–2.
67 Ibid., 238–42. *Izveštaji Ministarstva inostranih poslova Kraljevine Jugoslavije* 8 (1937), Monthly Report from Germany, July, 363.
68 Volkmann, 'Aussenhandel und Aufrüstung in Deutschland', 123–4.
69 Petzina, 'Vierjahresplan und Rüstungspolitik', 74–5.
70 Overy, *War and Economy in the Third Reich*, 186–7.
71 Richard Overy, *Goering: The Iron Man* (London: Routledge and Paul, 1984), 62–4.
72 Richard Overy, *The Nazi Economic Recovery, 1932–1938* (Cambridge: Cambridge University Press, 1996), 27.
73 ADAP, C, VI, 198, 211, Memorandum by Janson (German Belgrade Legation), 12 February 1937; Hess (German Belgrade Legation) to Clodius (German Foreign Ministry), 16 February 1937.
74 *Nemačka obaveštajna služba u staroj Jugoslaviji* 2, 35–6.
75 Grenzebach, *Germany's Informal Empire in East-Central Europe,* 133–5.
76 Vladimir Rozenberg and Jovan Kostić, *Ko finansira jugoslovensku privredu* (Beograd: Balkanska štampa, 1940), 64.
77 Avramovski, 'Sukob interesa V. Britanije i Nemačke na Balkanu', 21–2.
78 Norbert Schausberger, 'Der Anschluß', in *Österreich 1918–1938: Geschichte der Ersten Republik* 1, ed. Erika Weinzierl and Kurt Skalnik (Graz: Styria, 1983), 521–3; Volkmann, 'Die NS-Wirtschaft in Vorbereitung des Krieges', 324.
79 'Economic Perspectives of the Anschluss', Yugoslav Berlin Legation to Yugoslav Foreign Ministry, 22 March 1938 (AJ, 394, 1).
80 Monthly report of the YNB's Board Committee, April 1938 (ANB, 1/II, 17).
81 The Fifth Confidential Protocol, 4 June 1938 (ANB, 1/II, 96); Monthly report of the YNB's Board Committee, July 1938 (ANB, 1/II, 17).
82 Yugoslav National Bank to its branch offices, 26 October 1938 (ANB, 1/II, 96); 'The Maintenance of Trade and Payment Transfer between the Sudetes and Yugoslavia', Berlin, unsigned, 30 September 1938 (PA, RZ 311, R 105942).
83 'The Eight Protocol of the German-Yugoslav Mixed Committee', Cologne, 7 June 1939 (ANB, 1/II, 96).
84 Gross, *Export Empire*, 195–6.
85 Djordjević, *Pregled ugovorne trgovinske politike*, 165.
86 *Statistički godišnjak*, 1938/39, 252–3.
87 Memorandum by the British Department of Overseas Trade, 18 May 1938, 4986/347/92 (TNA, FO 371/22477).
88 Campbell (British Belgrade Legation) to Foreign Office, 3 June 1938, 5482/147/92 (TNA, FO 371/22475).
89 *Statistički godišnjak* 1938/39, 252–3.

90  Monthly report of the YNB's Board Committee, May 1938 (ANB, 1/II, 17).
91  Monthly report of the YNB's Board Committee, September 1938 (ANB, 1/II, 17).
92  Monthly reports of the YNB's Board Committee, November and December 1938 (ANB, 1/II, 17).
93  Monthly report of the YNB's Board Committee, February 1939 (ANB, 1/II, 18).
94  'Evolution of the Kingdom of Yugoslavia's Foreign Trade, 1929–1939', Belgrade, unsigned and undated report (ANB, 1/II, 149).
95  'Privredna 1938 godina bila je u Jugoslaviji bolja od 1937', *Narodno blagostanje*, 18 February 1939.
96  Monthly report of the YNB's Board Committee, August 1938 (ANB, 1/II, 17).
97  Monthly report of the YNB's Board Committee, September 1939 (ANB, 1/II, 18).
98  Ibid.
99  Yugoslav National Bank to Yugoslav Finance Ministry, 28 January 1939 (ANB, 1/II, 92).
100 'Trgovina', *Narodno blagostanje*, 22 July 1939.
101 Monthly report of the YNB's Board Committee, September 1939 (ANB, 1/II, 18).
102 Sava Terzić, *Die deutsch-jugoslawischen Handelsbeziehungen auf Grund des Handelsvertrages 1934* (Wien: Hollinek, 1940), 72.
103 *Statistički godišnjak 1939*, 252–3.
104 Heeren (German Belgrade Legation) to German Foreign Ministry, 10 December 1938 (PA, RZ 311, R 105942).
105 Campbell (British Belgrade Legation) to Foreign Office, 9 May 1938, 4721/147/92 (TNA, FO 371/22475); Campbell (British Belgrade legation) to Foreign Office, 3 June 1938, 5482/147/92 (TNA, FO 371/22475).
106 Nikolić, 'Anglo-Yugoslav Relations', 49–52.
107 Vinaver, *Jugoslavija i Francuska izmedju dva rata*, 379–80.
108 Volkmann, 'Die NS-Wirtschaft in Vorbereitung des Krieges', 327.
109 'Development of Germany's Foreign-Economic Relations with Other Countries in the First Three Months of 1939', Berlin, 31 July 1939 (PA, RAV Belgrad, 53/4).
110 'Reichsmark Kursfrage und kein Ende', *Narodno blagostanje*, 20 May 1939.
111 'Annual Economic Report "A" on Yugoslavia for 1937', Campbell (British Belgrade Legation) to Foreign Office, 9 May 1938, 4739/146/92 (TNA, FO 371/22474).
112 'Secret Protocol of the Second Meeting of the German-Yugoslav Mixed Committee', 20 April 1936 (YNB, 1/II, 96); 'Secret Protocol of the Second Meeting of the German-Yugoslav Mixed Committee', Berlin, 15 April 1936 (BArch, R 2/14138).
113 Monthly report of the YNB's Board Committee, June 1939 (ANB, 1/II, 18).
114 Kaiser, *Economic Diplomacy and the Origins of the Second World War*, 264, 270–1.
115 *Statistički godišnjak 1940*, 234–5.
116 *Aprilski rat: Zbornik dokumenata*, ed. Dušan Gvozdenović (Beograd: Vojnoistorijski institut, 1969), Volume I, Document 76, Report on the Yugoslav foreign policy, Berlin, 21 August 1939, 302.
117 Leposava Cvijetić, 'Prodaja naoružanja kao metod pritiska Nemačke na Jugoslaviju', *Istorija XX veka* 3 (1975), 174.
118 Ausfuhrgemeinschaft für Kriegsgerät.
119 Živko Avramovski, 'Ekonomski i politički ciljevi nemačkog izvoza naoružanja u balkanske zemlje uoči Drugog svetskog rata', *Vojnoistorijski glasnik* 2 (1972), 63.
120 Volkmann, 'Ausenhandel und Aufrüstung in Deutschland', 113–16.
121 Avramovski, 'Ciljevi nemačkog izvoza naoružanja u balkanske zemlje', 68; 'A Draft for the Talks with the Yugoslav Foreign Minister regarding the War Material Deliveries to Yugoslavia', German Foreign Ministry, 22 April 1939 (PA, RZ 344, R 106181).

122 'Perspectives for the Sale of German Weaponry to Yugoslavia', Rheinmettal-Borsig to Clodius (German Foreign Ministry), Berlin, 5 March 1936 (PA, RZ 206, R 241455).
123 Dalibor Denda, 'Tenkovske jedinice u vojsci Kraljevine Jugoslavije, 1930–1941' *Vojnoistorijski glasnik* 1 (2009), 150.
124 Avramovski, 'Ciljevi nemačkog izvoza naoružanja u balkanske zemlje', 73–4; Cvijetić, 'Prodaja naoružanja kao metod pritiska Nemačke na Jugoslaviju', 182–4.
125 Avramovski, 'Ciljevi nemačkog izvoza naoružanja u balkanske zemlje', 69.
126 German Economics Ministry to Krupp, 15 March 1939 (BArchB, R2301/6471).
127 ADAP, C, VI, 91, 104, 150. Communication between the German Belgrade Legation and German Foreign Ministry, winter of 1936–7.
128 Campbell (British Belgrade Legation) to Foreign Office, 22 November 1937, 7829/21/92 (TNA, FO 371/21195).
129 Campbell (British Belgrade Legation) to Foreign Office, 20 October 1937, 6995/21/92 (TNA, FO 371/21195).
130 Stojadinović to Letica (Yugoslav Finance Ministry), 14 November 1938 (AJ, 70, 284).
131 Unsigned document, Belgrade, 6 April 1939 (AJ, 70, 284).
132 'Secret Protocol', Yugoslav Finance Ministry to Yugoslav War Ministry, 26 May 1939 (AJ, 70, 284).
133 Grenzebach, *Germany's Informal Empire in East-Central Europe*, 146; Minute by Lupin (Reichsgruppe Industrie), Berlin, 14 October 1938 (BArchB, R901/106440).
134 'Manevri izvršeni potpuno u duhu postavljenog cilja', *Politika*, 26 September 1937; Avramovski, 'Ciljevi nemačkog izvoza naoružanja u balkanske zemlje', 73.
135 Yugoslav War Ministry to Yugoslav Finance Ministry, 1 May 1939 (AJ, 70, 284).
136 Memorandum by Wiehl (German Foreign Ministry), 18 February 1939 (PA, RZ 344, R 106181); Heeren (German Belgrade Legation) to Wiehl (German Foreign Ministry), 17 February 1939 (PA, RZ 344, R 106181).
137 Minute by Clodius, Berlin, April 1939 (BArch, R 901/106440).
138 These events are documented in detail in the folder R 106181, of the record group RZ 344, in the Political Archive of the Federal Foreign Office in Berlin.
139 'The Draft for the Talks with the Yugoslav Foreign Minister regarding the War Material Deliveries to Yugoslavia', German Foreign Ministry, 24 April 1939 (PA, RZ344, R 106181).
140 Memorandum by Clodius (German Foreign Ministry), 27 April 1939 (PA, RZ 344, R 106181).
141 Heeren (German Belgrade Legation) to German Foreign Ministry, 5 May 1939 (PA, RZ 344, R 106181).
142 Reports of conversations with Neuhausen, Yugoslav Finance Ministry, 4 March, 30 March and 5 April 1939 (AJ, 70, 284).
143 Yugoslav Finance Ministry to Neuhausen, 26 April 1939 (AJ, 70, 284).
144 Volkmann, 'Die NS Wirtschaft in Vorbereitung des Krieges', 344–5.
145 Yugoslav Foreign Ministry to Yugoslav Finance Ministry, 5 May 1939 (AJ, 70, 284).
146 Djuričić (Yugoslav Finance Ministry) to Cvetković, 19 May 1939 (AJ, 70, 284).
147 Krosigk (German Finance Ministry) to German Economics Ministry, Foreign Ministry and Reichsbank, 14 June 1939 (BArch, R 901/106440).
148 Schönebeck (German Belgrade Legation) to German Air Ministry, 15 June 1939 (BArch, R 901/106440).
149 Heeren (German Belgrade Legation) to German Foreign Ministry, 28 June 1939 (BArch, R 901/106440).

150 Memorandum by Wiehl (German Foreign Ministry), 27 June 1939 (BArch, R 901/106440).
151 'Secret Protocol', Yugoslav Finance Ministry, 7 July 1939 (AJ, 70, 284).
152 'Report about the Reception of the Prince Regent Paul', German Foreign Ministry, 5 June 1939 (PA, RZ 344, R 106181); Clodius (German Foreign Ministry) to German Belgrade Legation, 16 April 1939 (BArch, R 901/106440).
153 'Delivery of War Material from the Protectorate to Yugoslavia', German Foreign Ministry, 10 July 1939 (BArch, R 901/106440).
154 'Memorandum about the Deliveries of War Material', German Foreign Ministry, 22 July 1939 (BArch, R901/106440).
155 High Command of Wehrmacht to German Foreign Ministry, 22 July 1939 (BArch, R 901/106440).
156 Unsigned report, German Belgrade Legation, 22 April 1939 (PA, RZ 344, R 106181); ADAP, D, VI, 245, German Belgrade Legation to German Foreign Ministry, 22 April 1939.
157 Record by Wiehl (German Foreign Ministry), 17 July 1939 (PA, RZ 344, R 106181).
158 *Aprilski rat 1941* 1, 88, Memorandum by Wiehl (German Foreign Ministry), 11 September 1939.
159 Overy, *The Nazi Economic Recovery*, 63–4.

# Chapter 6

1 Smiljana Djurović, 'Jedan aspekt pokušaja modernizacije države i uključivanja Kraljevine SHS u industrijsku civilizaciju zapadne Evrope', *Jugoslovenski istorijski časopis* 24, no. 1 (1989), 48.
2 More on Teichova's theories will follow further in this chapter.
3 Mijo Mirković, *Ekonomska struktura Jugoslavije, 1918-1941* (Zagreb: Školska knjiga, 1952); Smiljana Djurović, *Državna intervencija u industriji Jugoslavije, 1918–1941* (Beograd: INIS, 1986); Teichova, *Kleinstaaten in Spannungsfeld der Großmächte*; Ivan Crnić, *Die jugoslawische Eisenindustrie im Rahmen der jugoslawischen Volkswirtschaft* (Köln: Orthen, 1938); Rozenberg and Kostić, *Ko finansira jugoslovensku privredu*; Terzić, *Die deutsch-jugoslawischen Handelsbeziehungen auf Grund des Handelvertrages 1934*.
4 Mitrović, 'Ergänzungswirtschaft: The Theory of an Integrated Economic Area of the Third Reich and the Southeast Europe', Ristović, *Nemački novi poredak i jugoistočna Evropa*; Stevan K. Pavlowitch, *Hitler's New Disorder: The Second World War in Yugoslavia* (Oxford: Oxford University Press, 2008).
5 Holm Sundhaussen, *Geschichte Jugoslawiens* (Stuttgart: Verlag W. Kohlhammer, 1982), 93; Cvijetić, 'The Ambitions and Plans of the Third Reich with Regard to the Integration of Yugoslavia into the So-Called *Grosswirtschaftsraum*', 188; Avramovski, 'The International Isolation of Yugoslavia: An Objective of German Foreign Policy in the Period from 1933–1939', 268–9.
6 Sundhaussen, *Geschichte Jugoslawiens*, 93; *Statistički godišnjak* 1936, 230–1.
7 Milak, *Italija i Jugoslavija*, 89–91.
8 *Statistički godišnjak* 1933, 188–90; 'Diskussion über die Wirtschaftsbeziehungen Jugoslawiens', *Jugoslavien-Dienst*, 15 April 1934 (AJ, 65, 255).
9 Milak, *Italija i Jugoslavija*, 95–6.

10  Smiljana Djurović, 'Sankcije Društva naroda prema Italiji 1935. godine i jugoslovenska privreda', in *Sa Teslom u novi vek: nove sinteze istorije* (Beograd: Zavod za udžbenike i nastavna sredstva, 1997), 253; Terzić, *Die deutsch-jugoslawischen Handelsbeziehungen auf Grund des Handelvertrages 1934*, 83.
11  'Jugoslawische Vieh- und Holzausfuhr nach Italien', *Mitteilungen des MWT*, 28 June 1935; 'Der Außenhandel in ersten Halbjahr 1935', *Mitteilungen des MWT*, 3 August 1935.
12  Milak, *Italija i Jugoslavija*, 106–7.
13  *Statistički godišnjak* 1933, 188–9.
14  Karl Trucksaess, *Nemačko-jugoslovenski industrijski i trgovački adresar* (Berlin: Gesellschaft für Aussenhandelswerbung, 1936), 13–14; German Belgrade Legation to German Foreign Ministry, 4 March 1936 (PA, RZ 206, R 240727).
15  Monthly reports of the YNB's Board Committee throughout 1935, Belgrade (ANB, 1/II, 14).
16  Milak, *Italija i Jugoslavija*, 106.
17  Monthly report of the YNB's Board Committee, September 1935 (ANB, 1/II, 14).
18  Monthly report of the YNB's Board Committee, November 1935 (ANB, 1/II, 14).
19  'Two Years of Stojadinović's Government', 1937 (AJ, 37, 1), 32; 'Sankcije i naš izvoz', *Jugoslovenski Lloyd*, 11 January 1936.
20  *Statistički godišnjak* 1936, 242; *Statistički godišnjak* 1937, 195; 'Karakteristika razvoja naše privrede u svetlu spoljne trgovine', *Narodno Blagostanje*, 10 April 1937.
21  'Germany on the Yugoslav Market', German Belgrade Legation to German Foreign Ministry, 4 March 1936 (PA, RZ 206, R 240727).
22  Campbell (British Belgrade Legation) to Foreign Office, 30 April 1937, 3281/8/92 (TNA, FO 371/21194); 'Verdoppelung der japanischen Einfuhr', *Mitteilungen des MWT*, 3 February 1936.
23  Campbell (British Belgrade Legation) to Foreign Office, 21 December 1935, 7745/5167/92 (TNA, FO 371/19580).
24  'Jugoslovensko-nemački privredni odnosi', *Jugoslovenski ekonomist*, November 1938.
25  Avramovski, *Balkanske zemlje i velike sile*, 120–1.
26  'Naši trgovinski odnosi sa Nemačkom', *Narodno blagostanje*, 11 April 1936.
27  Miha Krek to Radosavljevic (Yugoslav National Bank), Belgrade, 6 May 1936 (ANB, 1/II, 227).
28  Avramovski, *Balkanske zemlje i velike sile*, 121.
29  Campbell (British Belgrade Legation) to Foreign Office, 13 April 1936, 2163/81/92 (TNA, FO 371/20434).
30  Milak, *Italija i Jugoslavija*, 107.
31  Trucksaess, *Nemačko-jugoslovenski industrijski i trgovački adresar* 1936, 9–13.
32  Ibid., 79.
33  *Statistički godišnjak* 1940, 247–8; Karl Trucksaess, *Nemačko-jugoslovenski industrijski i trgovački adresar* (Berlin: Gesellschaft für Aussenhandelswerbung, 1941), 16.
34  'Industry and Trade', German Finance Ministry, 13 March 1933 (BArch, R 2/10221).
35  Rozenberg and Kostić, *Ko finansira jugoslovensku privredu*, 65.
36  'Industrijska politika Jugoslavije', *Industrijski pregled*, February 1936.
37  'Entwicklung und Struktur der jugoslawischen Wirtschaft', *Mitteilung des MWT*, 17 August 1935.
38  'Jugoslawische Industrieausbau', *Frankfurter Zeitung*, 4 March 1939.
39  Jurković, *Die ausländische Kapital in Jugoslavien*, 297–314.
40  The value of equity.

41    Rozenberg and Kostić, *Ko finansira jugoslovensku privredu*, 80–103.
42    Three German enterprises invested capital in Rudokop: Elwerath Gewerkschaft-Hanover, Preußische Bergwerks- und Hutten-Hanover – shorten 'Preussag' – and Deutsche Erdöl. All three had their representatives in Belgrade. Jurković, *Die ausländische Kapital in Jugoslavien*, 318–19.
43    Secret report by Wiehl (German Foreign Ministry), 26 November 1938 (PA, RAV Belgrad, 53/3); Unsigned memorandum for German Belgrade Legation's Counsellor Feine, 22 December 1938 (PA, RAV Belgrad, 53/3). Freytag, *Deutschlands 'Drang nach Südosten'*, 220–2.
44    Rozenberg and Kostić, *Ko finansira jugoslovensku privredu*, 112; 'Jugoslovenski antimon', *Industrijski pregled*, January 1939.
45    Roland Schönfeld, 'Deutsche Rohstoffsicherungspolitik in Jugoslawien 1933–1944', *Vierteljahreshefte für Zeitgeschichte* 24, no. 3 (1976), 226.
46    Ibid., 225.
47    Schönfeld, 'Deutsche Rohstoffsicherungspolitik in Jugoslawien', 223–5.
48    Ibid., 225; Ranka Gašić, 'Prodor nemačkog kapitala u beogradska rudarska akcionarska društva tridesetih godina 20. veka', *Istorija 20. Veka* 31, no.1 (2013), 16–21.
49    Živko Avramovski, *Treći Rajh i Borski rudnik* (Bor: Muzej rudarstva i metalurgije, 1975), 51–68.
50    Freytag, *Deutschlands „Drang nach Südosten"*, 182.
51    Schumann, 'Aspekte und Hintergrunde der Handels- und Wirtschaftspolitik Hitlerdeutschlands gegenüber Jugoslawien', 226.
52    Freytag, *Deutschlands „Drang nach Südosten"*, 199–215.
53    Schumann, 'Aspekte und Hintergrunde der Handels- und Wirtschaftspolitik Hitlerdeutschlands gegenüber Jugoslawien', 228.
54    Ristović, *Nemački novi poredak i jugoistočna Evropa*, 20; Avramovski, 'Sukob interesa V. Britanije i Nemačke na Balkanu', 22; Wendt, 'England und der Deutsche "Drang nach Südosten". Kapitalbeziehungen und Warenverkehr in Südosteuropa zwischen den Weltkriegen', 494–5.
55    Milan Ristović, 'Izmedju „žrtve u krvi" i najvažnijeg „savezničkog doprinosa": Treći rajh i pitanje jugoistočnoevropske nafte u Drugom svetskom ratu', *Tokovi istorije* 1 2017, 23–4.
56    Richard Overy, 'Business in the Grossraumwirtschaft: Eastern Europe, 1938–1945', in *Enterprise in the Period of Fascism in Europe*, ed. Harold James and Jakob Tanner (Aldershot: Ashgate, 2002), 164.
57    Rozenberg and Kostić, *Ko finansira jugoslovensku privredu*, 28.
58    Schönfeld, 'Deutsche Rohstoffsicherungspolitik in Jugoslawien', 228; Vesna Aleksić, 'Nazification of the Allgemeiner jugoslawischer Bankverein AG: Political Destiny of an Economic Institution' in *Deutsch-serbische Beziehungen vom Berliner Kongress bis heute*, ed. Dittmar Dahlmann and Milan Kosanović (Bonn: Michael Zikic Stiftung, 2003), 129 -33; Mira Kolar-Dimitrijević, 'Strani kapital i Banovina Hrvatska, 1939-1941', *Povijesni prilozi* no. 9 (1990), 179; Božidar Jurković, *Das ausländische Kapital in Jugoslavien* (Stuttgart: Kohlhammer Verlag, 1941), 254–255',
59    Ristović, *Nemački novi poredak i jugoistočna Evropa*, 235–8.
60    'The Control of Foreign Capital', YNB, 5 February 1941 (ANB, 1/II, 171).
61    Wendt, 'England und der deutsche "Drang nach Südosten": Kapitalbeziehungen und Warenverkehr in Südosteuropa zwischen Weltkriegen', 495.
62    'The Control of Foreign Capital', YNB, 5 February 1941 (ANB, 1/II, 171).

63 Foreign Currency Department of the Yugoslav National Bank to the Yugoslav Finance Ministry, 4 September 1940 (ANB, 1/II, 171).
64 Schönfeld, 'Deutsche Rohstoffsicherungspolitik in Jugoslawien', 226; 'Proizvodnja aluminijuma u Jugoslaviji', *Industrijski pregled,* December 1936.
65 'Two years of Stojadinović's government', Belgrade (AJ, 37, 1), 427–33.
66 Mari-Žanin Čalić, *Istorija Jugoslavije u 20. veku* (Beograd: Clio, 2013), 31.
67 For more on Stojadinović's fiscal policies and ways for providing domestic capital for the state-funded projects see Becić, 'Finansijska politika Milana Stojadinovića', 134–41.
68 Gutehoffnungshütte Aktiengesellschaft (Oberhausen) to Stojadinović, 14 August 1935 (AJ, 37, 38).
69 Secret Protocol about the Results of the Second Meeting of the German-Yugoslav Mixed Committee, 15 April 1936 (BArch, R 2/14138).
70 'Potreba daljnjeg proširenja industrije gvoždja u Zenici', *Industrijski pregled,* May 1938.
71 'Rude i metali', *Industrijski pregled,* May 1938.
72 Siemens and Halske to Yugoslav Transport Ministry, Belgrade, 11 April 1935 (AJ, 65, 255).
73 Schönfeld, 'Deutsche Rohstoffsicherungspolitik in Jugoslawien', 217; Jurković, *Die ausländische Kapital in Jugoslavien,* 314.
74 Ibid., 42–3.
75 Djurović, *Državna intervencija u industriji Jugoslavije,* 225–6.
76 'Iz industrije za preradu gvoždja i metala', *Industrijski pregled*, February 1936.
77 Sarnow (German Economics Ministry) to Hess (German Belgrade Legation), 16 January 1935 (PA, RZ 311, R 105942).
78 Hess (German Belgrade Legation) to Clodius (German Foreign Ministry), 10 September 1935 (PA, RZ 311, R 105942).
79 Yugoslav Railways to Yugoslav Finance Ministry, 13 July 1935 (ANB, 1/II, 96).
80 Heeren (German Belgrade Legation) to Stojadinović, 8 March 1938 (AJ, 37, 30).
81 Reinhardt (German Finance Ministry) to Hess (German Belgrade Legation), 5 September 1935 (PA, RZ 311, R 105942).
82 Union of the Yugoslav Industry for Metal- and Ironworks to Yugoslav National Bank, 23 November 1935 (ANB, 1/II, 96).
83 Yugoslav National Bank to Yugoslav Finance Ministry, 7 May 1935 (ANB, 1/II, 96).
84 'Zemaljska konferencija industrijalaca', *Jugoslovenski ekonomist,* March, 1937.
85 'Law about the state accounting in Yugoslavia', Heeren (German Belgrade Legation) to German Foreign Ministry, 30 July 1934 (PA, RZ 206, R 241455); 'Eisenwerk Vareš wieder in Betrieb', *Mitteilungen des MWT,* 28 June 1935.
86 Yugoslav National Bank to Letica (Yugoslav Finance Ministry), 27 October 1936 (ANB, 1/II, 96).
87 Yugoslav National Bank to Letica (Yugoslav Finance Ministry), 17 December 1938 (ANB, 1/II, 96).
88 Stojadinović to Vrbanić (Yugoslav Trade and Industry Ministry), 13 January 1936 (ANB, 1/II, 96).
89 Yugoslav National Bank to Yugoslav Trade and Industry Ministry, 18 October 1935 (ANB, 1/II, 96).
90 Sub-Annex to Annex 6 of the Secret Protocol, Zagreb, 1 April 1936 (PA, RZ 311, R 105942).
91 Wendt, 'England und der deutsche "Drang nach Südosten": Kapitalbeziehungen und Warenverkehr in Südosteuropa zwischen Weltkriegen', 493.

92  Alice Teichova, 'Besonderheit in Strukturwandel der mittelost- und südosteuropäischen Industrie in den Zwischenkriegszeit', in *Industrielle Gesellschaft und politisches System: Beiträge zur politischen Sozialgeschichte*, ed. Dirk Stegmann, Bernd Jürgen Wendt and Peter-Christian Witt (Bonn: Verlag Neue Gesselschaft, 1978), 148.
93  Zlatko Kudelić, 'Gospodarska problematika žumberačkoga kraja uoči drugoga svjetskog rata u Žumberačkim novinama', *Časopis za suvremenu povijest* 26, no. 1 (1994), 112–13.
94  'Die Hanfausfur Jugoslawiens', *Mitteilungen des MWT*, 12 December 1935.
95  'Die Hanfernte', *Mitteilungen des MWT*, 9 September 1936.
96  Cvijetić, 'The Ambitions and Plans of the Third Reich with Regard to the Integration of Yugoslavia into the So-Called Grosswirtschaftsraum', 188–9.
97  'Soja-Produktion in Jugoslawien', *Mitteilungen des MWT*, 20 February 1939.
98  Freytag, *Deutschlands „Drang nach Südosten"*, 197.
99  Terzić, *Die deutsch-jugoslawischen Handelsbeziehungen auf Grund des Handelvertrages 1934*, 47.
100 'Promene u strukturi naše poljoprivrede', *Jugoslovenski ekonomist*, February 1938.
101 Dragan Aleksić, *Privreda Srbije u Drugom svetskom ratu* (Beograd: INIS, 2002), 31.
102 'Razvoj naše teksitlne industrije od ujedinjenja do danas', *Jugoslovenski ekonomist*, October 1937; 'Jugoslawien und seine Wirtschaft', *Aussenhandel und Devisenbewirtschaftung*, 20 November 1940 (BArch, N-1208, 36).
103 Gesellschaft für Getreidehandel.
104 Yugoslav Agricultural Ministry to Yugoslav National Bank, 8 October 1935 (ANB, 1/II, 96).
105 Presidency of Deutschen Regierungsausschusses to Pilja, 7 June 1935 (AJ, 65, 255).
106 Report by Yugoslav Trade and Industry Ministry, 21 October 1937 (AJ, 65, 253). 'Ölsaaten statt Weizenbau in Jugoslawien', *Mitteilungen des MWT*, 26 June 1936.
107 'Two Years of Stojadinović's Government: Section 3, Agricultural Policy', 1937 (AJ, 37, 1), 8.
108 'Posle opijuma – uljarice', *Narodno Blagostanje*, 12 September 1936.
109 'Yugoslavia', Reichs-Kredit-Gesselschaft, March 1936 (BA Berlin, R2/16456); Rozenberg and Kostić, *Ko finansira jugoslovensku privredu*, 190.
110 Yugoslavia's textile production, weekly report – Publications of Instituts für Konjunkturforschung, 88, 2 July 1940 (BArch, N-1208, 36).
111 'Posle opijuma – uljarice', *Narodno Blagostanje*, 12 September 1936; 'Naša industrija ulja', *Industrijski pregled*, August 1936.
112 'Državni intervencionizam', *Industrijski pregled*, March 1937.
113 Zagreb University had already had this faculty founded in 1919.
114 'Obaveštajna služba', *Narodno Blagostanje*, 17 April 1937.
115 Terzić, *Die deutsch-jugoslawischen Handelsbeziehungen auf Grund des Handelvertrages 1934*, 46.
116 'Razvoj naše tekstilne industrije od ujedinjenja do danas', *Jugoslovenski ekonomist*, October 1937; 'Deutsche Textilmaschinen – Ausfuhr nach Jugoslawien', *Mitteilungen des MWT*, 25 April 1935.
117 'Motorizovanje Jugoslavije', *Industrijski pregled*, August 1938; 'Bessserung der Automobileinfuhr', *Mitteilungen des MWT*, 16 May 1935.
118 *Statistički godišnjak* 1940, 247–8.
119 Ibid., 235, 253–4.
120 'Rude i metali', *Industrijski pregled*, May 1938.

121 'Jugoslawien und seine Wirtschaft', *Aussenhandel und Devisenbewirtschaftung*, 10 December 1940 (BArch, N-1208, 36); *Statistički godišnjak* 1940, 241–3; Terzić, *Die deutsch-jugoslawischen Handelsbeziehungen auf Grund des Handelvertrages 1934*, 84–5; 'Naša spoljna trgovina u 1938. godini', *Jugoslovenski ekonomist*, May 1938; 'Fero legure u Jugoslaviji', *Industrijski pregled*, January 1940; 'Rudarstvo', *Industrijski pregled*, January 1939.
122 Trucksaess, *Njemačko-jugoslavenski vodič za industriju i trgovinu*, 1941, 16.
123 'Yugoslavia', Reichs-Kredit-Gesselschaft, Berlin, March 1936 (BArch, R 2/16456).
124 Terzić, *Die deutsch-jugoslawischen Handelsbeziehungen auf Grund des Handelvertrages 1934*, 101.
125 Unsigned document, Berlin, 20 September 1937 (BArch, R 2/10221); 'Naš boksit i fabrika aluminijuma', *Industrijski pregled*, February 1936.
126 'The statistics of those Yugoslav products that are in greatest need at the German market', unsigned report, 18 September 1937 (AJ, 65, 253).
127 *Statistisches Jahrbuch für das Deutsche Reich* 1940, 281, 283.
128 'Fero legure u Jugoslaviji', *Industrijski pregled*, January 1940.
129 Felix Hermann, *Die Antimonerzvorkommen ehem. Jugoslawiens, Bulgariens, Griechenlands und der Türkei* (Berlin: Mitteleuropäischer Wirtschaftstag, 1941), 2; Freytag, *Deutschlands 'Drang nach Südosten'*, 207–8.
130 'Naša spoljna trgovina pod dejstvom svetskog privrednog ciklusa', *Narodno blagostanje*, 8 April 1939.
131 Cvetković, *Ekonomski odnosi Jugoslavije i Francuske*, 188.
132 'Die Ausfuhr Jugoslawiens nach dem Grossdeutschen Reich' *Mitteilungen des MWT*, 1 April 1939.
133 'Subject: Visit of the Yugoslav Prince Regent', Berlin, 31 May 1939 (BArch, R 43II/1456B).
134 *Statistisches Jahrbuch für das Deutsche Reich* 1940, 282.
135 Vereinigte Stahlwerke.
136 Stegmann, '"Mitteleuropa", 1925–1934', 205–6.
137 Ibid., 208; Wien, *Markt und Modernisierung*, 60–1.
138 Stegmann, '"Mitteleuropa", 1925–1934', 209.
139 Gross, *Export Empire*, 58–62.
140 Wien, *Markt und Modernisierung*, 51.
141 Nils Müller, 'Die Wirtschaft als „Brücke der Politik"', in *Mitteleuropa und Südosteuropa als Planungsraum: Wirtschafts- und kulturpolitische Expertisen im Zeitalter der Weltkriege*, ed. Carola Sachse (Göttingen: Wallstein Verlag, 2010), 92–5.
142 Wien, *Markt und Modernisierung*, 53; Heinz Barsche, 'Der Mitteleuropäische Wirtschaftstag', *Deutsche Aussenpolitik* 11 (Berlin: Rütten und Loening, 1960), 1296.
143 Karl Drechsler, Hans Dress and Gerhart Hass, 'Europapläne des deutschen Imperialismus in zweiten Weltkrieg', *Zeitschrift für Geschichtswissenschaft* 7 (1971), 916.
144 Wien, *Markt und Modernisierung*, 57.
145 Freytag, *Deutschlands 'Drang nach Südosten'*, 60–1, 87–8.
146 Barsche, 'Der Mitteleuropäische Wirtschaftstag', 1297.
147 Deutschen Industrie- und Handelskammerstages.
148 Matis, 'Wirtschaftliche Mitteleuropa-Konzeptionen in der Zwischenkriegszeit', 235–6.
149 Peter Krüger, 'Wirtschaftliche Mitteleuropapläne in Deutschland zwischen den Weltkriegen', in *Mitteleuropa-Konzeptionen in der ersten Hälfte des 20. Jahrhunderts*, ed. Richard Plaschka et al. (Wien: Österreichischen Akademie der Wissenschaften, 1995), 283–5.

150 Wien, *Markt und Modernisierung*, 62–3; Freytag, *Deutschlands 'Drang nach Südosten'*, 89.
151 'Wiener Tagung des Mitteleuropäischen Wirtschaftstag', Vienna, 2 September 1940, Kiel: Institut für Weltwirtschaft, 8–9.
152 *Griff nach Südosteuropa*, 17.
153 Alfred Sohn-Rethel, *Economy and Class Structure of German Fascism* (London: Free Association Books, 1987), 19, 51.
154 'Was die Statistik beweist', *Mitteilungen des MWT*, 2 March 1936.
155 Freytag, *Deutschlands 'Drang nach Südosten'*, 56–7.
156 Ibid., 168–9.
157 Ibid., 222.
158 *Griff nach Südosteuropa*, 54–8; Ristović, *Nemački novi poredak i jugoistočna Evropa*, 125–8; Gross, *Export Empire*, 298.
159 Peter Hayes, *Industry and Ideology: IG Farben in the Nazi Era* (Cambridge: Cambridge University Press, 2001), 125–7.
160 Ibid., 131–3.
161 Harm Schröter, 'Siemens and Central and South-East Europe between the Two World Wars', in *International Business and Central Europe, 1918–1939*, ed. Alice Teichova and Philip Leonard Cottrell (Leicester: Leicester University Press, 1983), 186–7.
162 Hayes, *Industry and Ideology: IG Farben in the Nazi Era*, 300–2.
163 Verena Schröter, 'The IG Farben AG in Central and South-East Europe, 1926–38', in *International Business and Central Europe, 1918–1939*, ed. Alice Teichova and Philip Leonard Cottrell (Leicester: Leicester University Press, 1983), 53, 155.
164 Schröter, 'Siemens and Central and South-East Europe between the Two World Wars', 179–81.
165 'Wiener Tagung des Mitteleuropäischen Wirtschaftstag', 20–2.
166 Ibid., 29–31, 35–40.
167 Ibid., 31.
168 Stephen G. Gross, 'Das Mitteleuropa Institut in Dresden: Verknüpfung regionaler Wirtschaftsinteressen mit deutscher Auslandskulturpolitik in der Zwischenkriegzeit", in *„Mitteleuropa" und „Südosteuropa" als Planungsraum: Wirtschafts- und kulturpolitische Expertisen im Zeitalter der Weltkriege*, ed. Carola Sachse (Göttingen: Wallstein Verlag, 2010), 130–4.
169 Gross, *Export Empire*, 33–9.
170 Max Whyte, 'The Uses and Abuses of Nietzsche in the Third Reich: Alfred Baeumler's "Heroic Realism"', *The Journal of Contemporary History* 42, no. 2 (2008), 176; Werner Daitz, *Der Weg zur Volkswirtschaft, Grossraumwirtschaft und Grossraumpolitik* 2 (Dresden: Meinhold Verlagsgesellschaft, 1942), 15; Brechtefeld, *Mitteleuropa and German Politics*, 54; Ristović, *Nemački novi poredak i jugoistočna Evropa*, 38–9.
171 Crnić, *Die jugoslawische Eisenindustrie in Rahmen der jugoslawischen Volkswirtschaft*, 138–40.
172 'Erste Geschäftsbericht der Deutschland-Stiftung des Mitteleuropäischen Wirtschaftstag, für das Studienjahr 1936/1937', *MWT Deutsche Gruppe – Deutscher Akademischer Austauschdienst*, Kiel: Institut für Weltwirtschaft, 36.
173 Ibid., 56.
174 Mitrović, 'Ergänzungswirtschaft: The Theory of an Integrated Economic Area of the Third Reich and the Southeast Europe', 18–27.
175 Ibid., 36.
176 For more see Milan Ristović, 'Rat, modernizacija i industrializacija Jugoistočne Evrope: Nemački stavovi o promenama društvene i privredne strukture "dopunskog

privrednog prostora", 1940-1943', in *Srbija u modernizacijskim procesima XX veka*, ed. Latinka Perović, Marija Obradović and Dubravka Stojanović (Beograd: INIS, 1994); Ristović, *Nemački novi poredak i jugoistočna Evropa*, 347.
177 Mitrović, 'Ergänzungswirtschaft: The Theory of an Integrated Economic Area of the Third Reich and the Southeast Europe', 27-8.
178 Innerhofer, 'The Role of "Agrarian Overpopulation" in German Spatial and Economic Planning for Southeastern Europe before and during the Second World War', 44-9.
179 Ibid., 46-7.
180 'Rudolf Bićanić o problemu "velikog privrednog prostora"', *Narodno blagostanje*, 19 August 1939.
181 Milan Ristović, 'Weder Souveränität noch Industrialisierung', in *'Mitteleuropa' und 'Südosteuropa' als Planungsraum: Wirtschafts- und kulturpolitische Expertisen im Zeitalter der Weltkriege*, ed. Carola Sachse (Göttingen: Wallstein, 2010), 221-2.
182 Ibid., 223-4.
183 Mira Kolar-Dimitrijević, 'Die wirtschaftlichen Möglichkeiten und die konkrete Integration Kroatiens in die Mitteleuropäischen Wirtschaftspläne 1918-1938', in *Mitteleuropa-Konzeptionen in der ersten Hälfte des 20. Jahrhunderts*, ed. Richard Plaschka et al. (Wien: Österreichischen Akademie der Wissenschaften, 1995), 273.
184 *People's Welfare*, a weekly economic magazine, published in Belgrade between 1929 and 1941.
185 'Jedno pitanje i jedan odgovor', *Narodno Blagostanje*, 20 October 1934.
186 'Nemačka inicijativa u privredi jugoistoka', *Narodno blagostanje*, no. 24, 15 June 1940.
187 Kosier, *Grossdeutschland und Jugoslawien*, 207-13.
188 Kolar-Dimitrijević, 'Die wirtschaftlichen Möglichkeiten und die konkrete Integration Kroatiens in die Mitteleuropäischen Wirtschaftspläne', 274. For more on *Nova Evropa* and its liberal and pro-Yugoslav leaning, see Veljko Stanić, '"Unutrašnji autsajder": Milan Ćurčin, *Nova Evropa* i Drugi svetski rat', in *Intelektualci i rat, 1939-1947: Zbornik radova s medjunarodnog skupa Desničini susreti 2011*, ed. Drago Roksandić et al. (Zagreb, Plejada, 2012); Ranka Gašić, 'Koncepcija jugoslovenstva u Novoj Evropi', in *Nova Evropa, 1920-1941: Zbornik radova*, ed. Marko Nedić and Vesna Matović (Beograd: Institut za književnost i umetnost, 2010).
189 Gross, *Export Empire*, 48.
190 'Autarkija', *Jugoslovenski ekonomist*, May 1936.
191 'Država i ekonomija', *Jugoslovenski ekonomist*, October 1938.
192 'Jugoslovensko-nemački privredni odnosi', *Jugoslovenski ekonomist*, November 1938.
193 Terzić, *Die deutsch-jugoslawischen Handelsbeziehungen auf Grund des Handelsvertrages 1934*, 63.
194 'Zemaljska konferencija industrijalaca', *Jugoslovenski ekonomist*, March 1937.
195 'Problem sirovina i devizna politika Narodne banke', *Industrijski pregled*, June-July 1939; 'Uvoz-izvoz 1939. godine', *Industrijski pregled*, January 1940.
196 'Privredni planovi Nemačke na Balkanu', printed in *Industrijski pregled*, August 1936.
197 Sundhaussen, 'Südosteuropa in der Nationalsozialistischen Kriegswirtschaft am Beispiel des „Unabhängigen Staates Kroatien"', 235-7.
198 Alice Teichova, 'Eastern Europe in Transition: Economic Development during the Interwar and Postwar Period', in *Central Europe in the Twentieth Century: An Economic History Perspective*, ed. Alice Teichova (Aldershot: Ashgate, 1997), 13; Teichova, *Kleinstaaten im Spannungsfeld der Großmächte*, 196-7.

199  Theodor Zotschew, 'Die Industrialisierung Südosteuropa', *Südosteuropa – Jahrbuch*, no. 1 (1957), 148.
200  Teichova, *Kleinstaaten im Spannungsfeld der Großmächte*, 146–51.
201  Čalić, *Socijalna istorija Srbije*, 398–9.

## Chapter 7

1   Michael Burleigh and Wolfgang Wippermann, *The Racial State: Germany, 1933–1945* (Cambridge: Cambridge University Press, 1991), 37–43; Philippe Burrin, *Hitler and the Jews: The Genesis of the Holocaust* (London: Arnold, 1994), 25–32.
2   Mirna Zakić, *Ethnic Germans and National Socialism in Yugoslavia in World War II* (Cambridge: Cambridge University Press, 2017), 12.
3   Doris Bergen, 'The Nazi Concept of "Volksdeutsche" and the Exacerbation of Anti-Semitism in Eastern Europe, 1939–1945', *Journal of Contemporary History* 45, no. 4 (1994), 570–1.
4   Anthony Komjathy and Rebecca Stockwell, *German Minorities and the Third Reich: Ethnic Germans of East Central Europe between the Wars* (London: Holmes and Meier, 1980), 11–12.
5   Laslo Sekelj, 'Antisemitizam u Jugoslaviji, 1918–1945', *Revija za sociologiju*, 11, no. 3–4 (1981), 180.
6   Robert Wistrich, *Hitler and the Holocaust: How and Why the Holocaust Happened* (London: Phoenix, 2002), 26–7.
7   Koljanin, *Jevreji i antisemitizam u Kraljevini Jugoslaviji*, 44–53.
8   Sekelj, 'Antisemitizam u Jugoslaviji', 182.
9   Dj. Bobić, *Antisemitizam: židovsko pitanje* (Zagreb: Grafika, 1935), 5–6.
10  Edo Gajić, *Jugoslavija i jevrejski problem* (Beograd: Štamparija Drag. Gregorića, 1938), 15–18.
11  Mića Dimitrijević and Vojislav Stojanović, *Naši Jevreji* (Beograd: Minerva, 1940), 25, 42.
12  Ibid., 51.
13  Ibid., 43–4.
14  Ibid., 54.
15  Ibid., 45–50.
16  Bobić, *Antisemitizam: židovsko pitanje*, 36; Gajić, *Jugoslavija i jevrejski problem*, 92.
17  Milan Ristović, 'The Jews of Serbia (1804–1918): From Princely Protection to Formal Emancipation', in *The Jews and the Nation States of Southeastern Europe from the 19th Century to the Great Depression: Combining Viewpoints on a Controversial Story*, ed. Tullia Catalan (Newcastle upon Tyne: Cambridge Scholars Publishing, 2016), 28.
18  Koljanin, *Jevreji i antisemitizam u Kraljevini Jugoslaviji*, 120–36, 147–53, 240, 353; Darko Gavrilović, *Mit o neprijatelju: antisemitizam Dimitrija Ljotića* (Beograd: Službeni glasnik, 2018), 45–51; Marija Vulesica, 'Antisemitismus im ersten Jugoslawien 1918 bis 1941', *Jahrbuch für Antisemitismusforschung* 17 (2008), 137–8; Pino Adriano and Giorgio Cingolani, *Nationalism and Terror: Ante Pavelić and Ustashe Terrorism from Fascism to the Cold War* (Budapest: Central European University Press, 2018), 13.
19  Koljanin, *Jevreji i antisemitizam u Kraljevini Jugoslaviji*, 127, 173–4, 286–7.
20  Ibid., 198–9.

21 Ibid., 188–90, 199–200; Vulesica, 'Antisemitismus im ersten Jugoslawien', 141–4.
22 Ibid., 146.
23 Koljanin, *Jevreji i antisemitizam u Kraljevini Jugoslaviji*, 258.
24 Sekelj, 'Antisemitizam u Jugoslaviji', p. 184.
25 Vulesica, 'Antisemitismus im ersten Jugoslawien', p. 148.
26 Nenad Petrović, *Ideologija varvarstva: fašističke i nacionalsocijalističke ideje kod intelektualaca u Beogradu, 1929–1941* (Beograd: Mostart, 2015), 50–1.
27 Koljanin, *Jevreji i antisemitizam u Kraljevini Jugoslaviji*, 246.
28 Goldstein, *Holokaust u Zagrebu*, 45.
29 By mainstream political parties, we imply liberal, democratic or conservative parties.
30 German Zagreb Consulate to German Foreign Ministry, 20 July 1935 (PA, RZ 206, R 241508).
31 John Pollard, *Papacy in the Age of Totalitarianism, 1914–1958* (Oxford: Oxford University Press, 2014), 279–80, 472–5.
32 Goldstein, *Holokaust u Zagrebu*, 49–50.
33 Ibid., 55.
34 Ibid., 58, 62.
35 Gavrilović, *Mit o neprijatelju*, 52.
36 Milan Ristović, 'Jews in Serbia during World War Two: Between the "Final Solution of the Jewish Question" and "the Righteous among Nations"', in *Righteous among the Nations – Serbia*, ed. Milan Fogel, Milan Ristović and Milan Koljanin (Beograd: JOZ, 2010), 261–2.
37 Sekelj, 'Antisemitizam u Jugoslaviji', 186.
38 Freundt (German Zagreb Consulate), to German Foreign Ministry, 18 April 1933 (PA, RZ 206, R 241508).
39 More on this in: Moshe Gottlieb, 'The Anti-Nazi Boycott Movement in the United States: An Ideological and Sociological Appreciation', *Jewish Social Studies* 35, no. 3–4 (1973).
40 These documents are kept in the Political Archive of the Federal Foreign Office, folder number: R 241508.
41 Daruvarska pivovara (Daruvar) to Bayerische Berg-, Hütten- und Salzwerke (Munich), 9 June 1934 (PA, RZ 206, R 241508).
42 Ivan Avakumović, 'Yugoslavia's Fascist Movements', in *Native Fascism in the Successor States, 1918–1941*, ed. Peter Sugar (Santa Barbara: Clio Press, 1971), 135–6.
43 Gavrilović, *Mit o neprijatelju*, 166.
44 Olivera Milosavljević, *Savremenici fašizma 1: Percepcija fašizma u beogradskoj javnosti, 1933–1941* (Beograd: Helsinški odbor za ljudska prava u Srbiji, 2010), 20–1.
45 Organisation of Yugoslav Nationalists.
46 Nikola Žutić, 'Niko Bartulović i slovenački Jugoslaveni', *Istorija 20. veka* 1/2014, 67–73.
47 Avakumović, 'Yugoslavia's Fascist Movements', 136–7.
48 Djordjević, Dimitrije, 'Fascism in Yugoslavia, 1918–1941' (Santa Barbara: Clio Press, 1971), 130–1.
49 Petrović, *Ideologija varvarstva*, 19, 39.
50 Godstein, *Holokaust u Zagrebu*, 33.
51 Aleksa Djilas, *The Contested Country: Yugoslav Unity and Communist Revolution, 1919–1953* (Cambridge, MA: Harvard University Press, 1996), 114.
52 Djordjević, 'Fascism in Yugoslavia', 130.
53 Petrović, *Ideologija varvarstva*, 64–71.

54 Milan Ristović, 'Rural Anti-Utopia in the Ideology of Serbian Collaborationists in the Second World War', *European Review of History* 15, no. 2 (2008), 183.
55 Godstein, *Holokaust u Zagrebu*, 62.
56 Gavrilović, *Mit o neprijatelju*, 83–4.
57 The acronym means rally, or gathering in Serbo-Croatian; analogy with 'Fasci Italiani di Combattimento' is obvious.
58 Jovan Byford, *Denial and Repression of Antisemitism: Post-Communist Remembrance of the Serbian Bishop Nikolaj Velimirović* (Budapest: Central European University Press, 2008), 47–52.
59 Ibid., 117–18.
60 Avakumović, 'Yugoslavia's Fascist Movements', 141.
61 Mark Biondich, 'Radical Catholicism and Fascism in Croatia, 1918–1945', in *Clerical Fascism in Interwar Europe*, ed. Matthew Feldman et. al. (London: Routledge, 2008), 176–7.
62 Adriano and Cingolani, *Nationalism and Terror*, 32.
63 Djilas, *The Contested Country*, 106–7.
64 IvoBanac, *The National Question in Yugoslavia: Origins, History, Politics* (New York: Cornell University Press, 1984), 262–3.
65 Ibid., 264–6.
66 Adriano and Cingolani, *Nationalism and Terror*, 33.
67 Ibid., 70–2.
68 For more on Sufflay's murder see: Bosiljka Janjatović and Petar Strčić, 'O ubojstvu Dr Milana Šufflaya', *Historijski Zbornik* 46, no. 1 (1993).
69 Fikreta Jelić-Butić, *Ustaše i Nezavisna Država Hrvatska* (Zagreb: Školska knjiga, 1978), 45–7.
70 Djilas, *The Contested Country*, 109; Avakumović, 'Yugoslavia's Fascist Movements', 141.
71 Jelić-Butić, *Ustaše i Nezavisna Država Hrvatska*, 50–2; Koljanin, *Jevreji i antisemitizam u Kraljevini Jugoslaviji*, 379.
72 Ibid., 293–4.
73 Unsigned minute, German Foreign Ministry, Berlin, 14 October 1935 (PA, RZ 211, R 103345).
74 Minute by Busse, German Foreign Ministry, 2 July 1936 (PA, RZ 211, R 103345).
75 Minute by Busse, Foreign Ministry, Berlin, 23 November 1936 (PA, RZ 211, R 103345).
76 Minute by Busse, Foreign Ministry, Berlin, 22 December 1936 (PA, RZ 211, R 103345).
77 Jelić-Butić, *Ustaše i Nezavisna Država Hrvatska*, 33; *Nemačka obaveštajna služba u staroj Jugoslaviji* 2, 116.
78 ADAP, C, VI, 234, Heeren (German Belgrade legation) to German Foreign Ministry, 26 February 1937.
79 Avakumović, 'Yugoslavia's Fascist Movements', 138; *Nemačka obaveštajna služba u staroj Jugoslaviji* 2, 46–51; *Politika* covered the whole affair with a series of articles in late January and early February of 1937.
80 Koljanin, *Jevreji i antisemitizam u Kraljevini Jugoslaviji*, 236–8.
81 ADAP, C, VI, 244, Heeren (German Belgrade legation) to German Foreign Ministry, 3 March 1937.
82 Dragan Tešić, 'Vojska Kraljevine Jugoslavije i nacionalne manjine u godinama uoči Aprilskog rata', *Istorija 20. veka* 14, no. 2 (1996), 84–5.

83 Koljanin, *Jevreji i antisemitizam u Kraljevini Jugoslaviji*, 397–408, 413–14.
84 Željko Lazić, *Uvod u smrt: Numerus clausus 1940. godine i ograničavanja prava Jevreja u Kraljevini Jugoslaviji* (Beograd: Službeni glasnik, 2016), 201.
85 Mihailo Konstantinović, *Politika Sporazuma: Dnevničke beleške 1939–1941, Londonske beleške 1944–1945* (Novi Sad: Agencija, 1998), 176; Mladenka Ivanković and Aleksandar Stojanović, 'Anti-Semitic Propaganda and Legislation in Serbia 1939–1942: Content, Scale, Aims and Role of the German Factor', *Istorija 20. veka* 37, no. 2 (2019), 88.
86 Ibid., 204–8.
87 Koljanin, *Jevreji i antisemitizam u Kraljevini Jugoslaviji*, 420–4, 428–36.
88 Milosavljević, *Savremenici fašizma*, 249.
89 Vane Ivanović, *LX: Memoirs of a Yugoslav* (London: Weidenfeld & Nicolson, 1977), 191–2.
90 Ibid., 195–7.
91 Ibid., 447.
92 Heeren (German Belgrade Legation) to German Foreign Ministry, 27 July 1940 (PA, RZ 211, R 103321).
93 Koljanin, *Jevreji i antisemitizam u Kraljevini Jugoslaviji*, 456–8.
94 Ibid., 233.
95 *Nemačka obaveštajna služba u staroj Jugoslaviji*, 70–5. For more on this see Carl Bethke, 'Da li je bilo jugoslovenskih Nemaca: Regionalne specifičnosti i procesi nacionalne integracije nemačke manjine na teritoriji jugoslovenske države, 1918–1948', in *O „nestanku" nemačkih nacionalnih manjina: jedno teško poglavlje u istoriji Jugoslavije, 1941–1955*, ed. Christian Glass (Ulm: Donauschwäbisches Zentralmuseum, 2016), 33–47.
96 Zoran Janjetović, *Nemci u Vojvodini* (Beograd: INIS, 2009), 213.
97 Johann Böhm, *Die Deutsche Volksgruppe in Jugoslawien, 1918–1945* (Frankfurt: Peter Lang, 2009), 67; Janjetović, *Nemci u Vojvodini*, 239, 261.
98 Vladimir Geiger, 'Njemačka manjina u Kraljevini Srba, Hrvata i Slovenaca/Jugoslaviji (1918–1941)', in *Dijalog povjesničara – istoričara*, ed. Hans-Georg Fleck and Igor Graovac (Zagreb: Zaklada Friedrich Naumann, 2000), 440; Zakić, *Ethnic Germans and National Socialism in Yugoslavia*, 27–30, 33, 37.
99 Ibid., 35.
100 Janjetović, *Nemci u Vojvodini*, 213–15.
101 Dušan Biber, *Nacizem in Nemci v Jugoslaviji, 1933–1941* (Ljubljana: Cankarjeva Založba, 1966), 38–9.
102 Janjetović, *Nemci u Vojvodini*, 247–9.
103 Böhm, *Die Deutsche Volksgruppe in Jugoslawien*, 77–82, 87–8.
104 Schwäbisch-Deutscher-Kulturbund.
105 *Nemačka obaveštajna služba u staroj Jugoslaviji*, 81–2.
106 Janjetović, *Nemci u Vojvodini*, 123–4; Geiger, 'Njemačka manjina u Kraljevini Srba, Hrvata i Slovenaca/Jugoslaviji', 434–5.
107 Bethke, 'Da li je bilo jugoslovenskih Nemaca', 37–8; Janjetović, *Nemci u Vojvodini*, 167.
108 For more on VoMi see Valdis Lumans, *Himmler's Auxiliaries: The Volksdeutsche Mittelstelle and the German National Minorities of Europe, 1933–1945* (Chapel Hill: University of North Carolina Press, 1993).

109 Nathaniel Reul, 'Resurrection and Revolution. Austro-Catholicism, German Nationalism and National Socialism in Slovenia, 1933-1941', *Österreichische Zeitschrift für Geschichtswissenschaften* 28, no. 1 (2017), 234-5.
110 Janjetović, *Nemci u Vojvodini*, 241.
111 Geiger, 'Njemačka manjina u Kraljevini Srba, Hrvata i Slovenaca/Jugoslaviji', 436-7; *Nemačka obaveštajna služba u staroj Jugoslaviji*, 92.
112 Goldstein, *Holokaust u Zagrebu*, 60-1.
113 Janjetović, *Nemci u Vojvodini*, 121.
114 Böhm, *Die Deutsche Volksgruppe in Jugoslawien*, 275-6; Janjetović, *Nemci u Vojvodini*, 173-5.
115 Böhm, *Die Deutsche Volksgruppe in Jugoslawien*, 266-7.
116 Lumans, *Himmler's Auxiliaries*, 119; Janjetović, *Nemci u Vojvodini*, 228-33.
117 Geiger, 'Njemačka manjina u Kraljevini Srba, Hrvata i Slovenaca/Jugoslaviji', 443.
118 Zakić, *Ethnic Germans and National Socialism in Yugoslavia*, 43-6.
119 Vladimir Barović and Dejan Pralica, 'Širenje nacionalsocijalističke propagande na teritoriji Dunavske banovine tokom 1940. godine', *Vojno delo* 63 (2011), 462.
120 Ibid., 461.
121 Zakić, *Ethnic Germans and National Socialism in Yugoslavia*, 50-1.
122 Tešić, 'Vojska Kraljevine Jugoslavije i nacionalne manjine u godinama uoči Aprilskog rata', 79-80.
123 Numerous reports on these activities are kept in the Military Archive in Belgrade, in boxes belonging to the Register 17.
124 Barović and Pralica, 'Širenje nacionalsocijalističke propagande na teritoriji Dunavske banovine tokom 1940. godine', 460-3.
125 Police Headquarters (Belgrade) to the Yugoslav Army and Navy Ministry, 12 January 1941 (Military Archive Belgrade (henceforth VA), Register 17, Box 1, Folder 4, Document 31).
126 Zakić, *Ethnic Germans and National Socialism in Yugoslavia*, 47.
127 Ibid., 51-3.
128 Lumans, *Himmler's Auxiliaries*, 120.
129 Vladimir Barović, 'Puč od 27. marta 1941 i medijsko-propagandno delovanje nemačke narodne grupe u Dunavskoj banovini', *Kultura polisa* 14, no. 33 (2017), 264-6.

# Chapter 8

1 Tooze, *Wages of Destruction*, 326-33.
2 Vladimir Vauhnik, *Nevidljivi front: Borba za očuvanje Jugoslavije* (München: Iskra, 1984), 106. For more on Vauhnik see Aleksandar Životić, 'Slovenci u vojnoj diplomatiji Kraljevine Jugoslavije', *Zgodovinski časopis* 73, no.1-2 (2019), 149-51.
3 Elisabeth Barker, *British Policy in South East Europe in the Second World War* (London: Macmillan, 1976), 29.
4 Subotić (Yugoslav London Legation) to Yugoslav Foreign Ministry, 1 August 1939 (AJ, 70, 284).
5 Subotić (Yugoslav London Legation) to Yugoslav Foreign Ministry, 11 January 1940 (AJ, 70, 284); Cincar-Marković to Šutej (Yugoslav Finance Ministry), 23 January 1940 (AJ, 70, 284).

6   Cincar-Marković to Šutej (Yugoslav Finance Ministry), 19 March 1940 and 16 April 1940 (AJ, 70, 284).
7   Avramovski, 'Ekonomski i politički ciljevi nemačkog izvoza naoružanja u balkanske zemlje uoči Drugog svetskog rata', 80.
8   Phillips Payson O'Brien, *How the War Was Won: Air-Sea Power and Allied Victory in World War II* (Cambridge: Cambridge University Press, 2015), 20.
9   Minute by Clodius (German Foreign Ministry), 7 September 1939 (PA, RZ 311, R 105943).
10  Wiehl (German Foreign Ministry) to Heeren (German Belgrade Legation), 11 September 1939 (PA, RZ 311, R 105943).
11  ADAP, D, VIII, 53, Memorandum by Wiehl (German Foreign Ministry), 11 September 1939.
12  Heeren (German Belgrade Legation) to German Foreign Ministry, 14 September 1939 (PA, RZ 311, R 105943).
13  ADAP, D, VIII, 117, Memorandum by Wiehl (German Foreign Ministry), 21 September 1941.
14  Named after the leader of the German negotiating team Friedrich Landfried of the German Economics Ministry.
15  German-Yugoslav secret protocol on 5 October 1939, Berlin (PA, RZ 311, R 105945).
16  Cvijetić, 'Prodaja naoružanja kao metod pritiska Nemačke na Jugoslaviju', 227–8.
17  Minute by Wörmann (German Foreign Ministry), 17 October 1939 (PA, RZ 211, R 103321); Cvijetić, 'Prodaja naoružanja kao metod pritiska Nemačke na Jugoslaviju', 229.
18  ADAP, D, VIII, 117, Memorandum by Wiehl (German Foreign Ministry), 21 September 1941, footnote no. 4.
19  Heeren (German Belgrade Legation) to German Foreign Ministry, 30 October 1939 (PA, RZ 311, R 105943).
20  Heeren (German Belgrade Legation) to German Foreign Ministry, 8 November 1939 (PA, RZ 311, R 105943).
21  Vauhnik, *Nevidljivi front*, 104.
22  Cvijetić, 'Prodaja naoružanja kao metod pritiska Nemačke na Jugoslaviju', 233.
23  *Aprilski rat* 1, 123, Report by Toussaint (German Belgrade Legation), 18 October 1939; *Aprilski rat* 1, 125, Report by Reichsbank, 20 October 1939.
24  Minute by Wiehl (German Foreign Ministry), 29 October 1939 and report by Heeren (German Belgrade Legation), 30 October 1939 (PA, RZ 311, R 105943).
25  Dalibor Denda, 'Jugoslovenska vojska i Treći Rajh, 1933–1941' (unpublished PhD theses, University of Belgrade, 2016), 531–2.
26  Heeren (German Belgrade Legation) to German Foreign Ministry, 26 April 1940 (PA, RZ 311, R 105943).
27  Cvijetić, 'Prodaja naoružanja kao metod pritiska Nemačke na Jugoslaviju', 241–2.
28  ADAP, D, XI/2, 370, 471, Two Memorandums by Wiehl (German Foreign Ministry), 20 November and 7 December 1940.
29  Cvijetić, 'Prodaja naoružanja kao metod pritiska Nemačke na Jugoslaviju', 248–9.
30  Monthly report of the YNB's Board Committee, December 1939 (ANB, 1/II, 18).
31  *Aprilski rat* 1, 130, Report by Toussaint (German Belgrade Legation), 3 November 1939.
32  *Aprilski rat* 1, 138, Report by Toussaint (German Belgrade Legation), 25 November 1939.
33  Monthly report of the YNB's Board Committee, December 1939 (ANB, 1/II, 18); Vinaver, *Jugoslavija i Francuska izmedju dva svetska rata*, 427.

34 Monthly report of the YNB's Board Committee, February 1940 (ANB, 1/II, 19).
35 'Jugoslawischer Aussenhandel 1939', *Mitteilungen des MWT*, 10 April 1940; 'Uvoz-Izvoz 1939', *Industrijski pregled*, January 1940.
36 Ibid.
37 Monthly report of the YNB's Board Committee, November 1939 (ANB, 1/II, 18).
38 Monthly report of the YNB's Board Committee, May 1940 (ANB, 1/II, 19).
39 'Yugoslavia's Economic Life', YNB, unsigned and undated memorandum (ANB, 1/II, 149).
40 *Aprilski rat* 1, 131, Report by Toussaint (German Belgrade Legation),10 November 1939.
41 ADAP, D, VIII, 99, Wiehl (German Foreign Ministry) to the German Belgrade Legation, Berlin, 19 September 1939.
42 Nikolić, 'Anglo-Yugoslav Relations', 166.
43 Minute by Wiehl (German Foreign Ministry) 28 November 1939 (PA, RZ 311, R 105943).
44 Šutej (Yugoslav Finance Ministry) to Nedić (Yugoslav War Ministry), 9 November 1939 (AJ, 70, 284); Subotić (Yugoslav London Legation) to Yugoslav Foreign Ministry, 11 January 1940 (AJ, 70, 284).
45 'Handelsvertragsverhandlungen mit England und Frankreich', *Mitteilungen des MWT*, 9 December 1939.
46 Report from the 104th Meeting of the Foreign Trade Coordination Committee, Belgrade, 27 October 1939 (AJ, 65, 194).
47 'Geflügel- und Eierausfuhr nach England', *Mitteilungen des MWT*, 9 December 1939; Minute by Hikel (German Foreign Ministry), 5 December 1939 (PA, R103318); Report by Freundt (German Zagreb Cosulate), 2 February 1940 (PA, RZ 311, R 105943).
48 Barker, *British Policy in South East Europe in the Second World War*, 37.
49 Minute by Wiehl (German Foreign Ministry), 10 April 1940 (PA, RZ 311, R 105943); Heeren (German Belgrade Legation) to German Foreign Ministry, 14 April 1940 (PA, RZ 311, R 105943); Barker, *British Policy in South East Europe in the Second World War*, 30–2; Ristović, 'Izmedju „žrtve u krvi" i najvažnijeg „savezničkog doprinosa"', 27.
50 'Velike količine sirovina koje kupuje u Rusiji, prevoziće Nemačka prvenstveno Dunavom', *Politika*, 19 November 1939.
51 Milan Ristović, 'Delovanje nemačke organizacije za zaštitu privrednih objekata (Werkschutz) u Jugoslaviji 1940', *Vojnoistorijski glasnik* 1 (1986), 185.
52 Ibid., 192.
53 *Nemačka obaveštajna služba u staroj Jugoslaviji*, 182–95.
54 Nikolić, 'Anglo-Yugoslav Relations', 174.
55 The Ninth Secret Protocol, YNB, 16 October 1939 (ANB, 1/II, 96).
56 The report on application of the secret protocol signed with Germany on 5 October 1939, YNB, 8 February 1941 (ANB, 1/II, 96).
57 Heeren (German Belgrade Legation) to German Foreign Ministry, 21 February 1940 (PA, RZ 311, R 105943).
58 Reich's Representative for Metals to General Consul Neuhausen, 5 December 1939 (ANB, 1/II, 140).
59 Yugoslav Trade and Industry Ministry to Yugoslav War Ministry, 30 November 1939 (AJ, 65, 253).
60 Schönfeld, 'Deutsche Rohstoffsicherungspolitik in Jugoslawien', 222.
61 Clodius (German Foreign Ministry) to Heeren (German Belgrade Legation), 29 December 1939 (PA, RZ 311, R 105943).

62 'Krupne izmene stavova u uvoznoj i izvoznoj carinskoj tarifi', *Pollitika*, 2 April 1940.
63 Cvijetić, 'Prodaja naoružanja kao metod pritiska Nemačke na Jugoslaviju', 233–4.
64 Memorandum by Gemünd (German Travel Bureau), Belgrade, 12 January 1940 (ANB, 1/II, 140).
65 Heeren (German Belgrade Legation) to German Foreign Ministry, 2 January 1940 (PA, RZ 211, R 103321).
66 Heeren (German Belgrade Legation) to German Foreign Ministry, 14 April 1940 (PA, RZ 311, R 105943).
67 *Aprilski rat* 1, 204, Italian Belgrade Legation to Ciano, 2 May 1940.
68 *Aprilski rat* 1, 205, Report by Clodius, Sofia, 3 May 1940.
69 *Aprilski rat* 1, 206, 207, Italian Sofia Legation to Ciano, 4 May and 6 May 1940.
70 German-Yugoslav Agreement, YNB, 31 May 1940 (ANB, 1/II, 96); 'Posle zasedanja nemačko-jugoslovenskog privrednog odbora', *Narodno blagostanje*, 8 June 1940.
71 Monthly report of the YNB's Board Committee, August 1940 (ANB, 1/II, 19).
72 *Aprilski rat* 1, 241, Wiehl (German Foreign Ministry) to Heeren (German Belgrade Legation), 15 June 1940.
73 Yugoslav Berlin Legation to Yugoslav Foreign Ministry, 17 June 1938 (AJ, 394, 1).
74 Unsigned and Undated Memorandum, YNB (ANB, 1/II, 96).
75 Ibid.
76 Minute by Yugoslav Foreign Ministry, 22 October 1935 (AJ, 65, 255).
77 Cincar-Marković to Djuričić (Yugoslav Finance Ministry), 12 June 1939 (AJ, 70, 300).
78 Ibid.
79 Djuričić (Yugoslav Finance Ministry) to Cincar-Marković, 12 June 1939 (AJ, 70, 300).
80 Memorandum by Šutej (Yugoslav Finance Ministry), 7 December 1939 (AJ, 70, 300).
81 http://net.lib.byu.edu/~rdh7/wwi/versa/versa9.html, last accessed on 30 October 2017.
82 Report from the first session of the Yugoslav committee, Belgrade, 20 October 1939 (AJ, 70, 300).
83 Reports from the sessions of the Mixed German-Yugoslav Committee for regulating pre-1914 German loans, on 15 November, 20 November and 21 November 1939 (AJ, 70, 300).
84 Memorandum by Šutej (Yugoslav Finance Ministry), 7 December 1939 (AJ, 70, 300).
85 Friderik Babnik to Djordjević (Department of Yugoslavia's State Loans), Maribor, 22 January 1940 (AJ, 70, 300); Martini (Counsellor of the German Government) to Djordjević (Department of Yugoslavia's State Loans), Dubrovnik, 23 August 1940 (AJ, 70, 300).
86 Berliner Handelsgesellschaft to Djordjević (Department of Yugoslavia's State Loans), Berlin, 7 October 1940 (AJ, 70, 300).
87 Memorandum by Šutej (Yugoslav Finance Ministry), 22 November 1940 (AJ, 70, 300).
88 'Südosteuropa: Vorschläge für eine neue deutsche Kapitalpolitik', Berlin, February 1940, Kiel: Institut für Weltwirtschaft, 3–8.
89 Tooze, *The Wages of Destruction*, 328–31.
90 Monthly report of the YNB's Board Committee, February 1940 (ANB, 1/II, 18).
91 Heeren (German Belgrade Legation) to German Foreign Ministry, 5 July 1940 (PA, RZ 211, R 103321).
92 Monthly report of the YNB's Board Committee, August 1940 (ANB, 1/II, 19).
93 Heeren (German Belgrade Legation) to German Foreign Ministry, 17 June 1940 (PA, RZ 311, R 105943).
94 Monthly report of the YNB's Board Committee, June 1940 (ANB, 1/II, 19).

95  ADAP, D, IX, 237, Heeren (Belgrade Legation) to German Foreign Ministry, 12 May 1940.
96  ADAP, D, X, 121, Heeren (German Belgrade Legation) to German Foreign Ministry, 5 July 1940.
97  Monthly report of the YNB's Board Committee, August 1940 (ANB, 1/II, Box 19).
98  Secret Protocol of the Eleventh Meeting of the Mixed Committee, Berlin, 31 July 1940 (ANB, 1/II, 96).
99  Djordjević, *Pregled ugovorne trgovinske politike*, 183–6.
100  Monthly report of the YNB's Board Committee, October 1940 (ANB, 1/II, 19).
101  Monthly report of the YNB's Board Committee, September 1940 (ANB, 1/II,19).
102  Monthly report of the YNB's Board Committee, October 1940 (ANB, 1/II, 19).
103  Report by Wiehl (German Foreign Ministry), 27 September 1940 (PA, RZ 311, R 105943).
104  Secret Protocol of the Twelfth Meeting of the Mixed Committee, 19 October 1940 (ANB, 1/II, 96).
105  Report on the meeting of representatives of two governmental committees, Belgrade, 24 September 1940 (ANB, 1/II, 96).
106  Yugoslavia's payment transfer with Germany during 1940, Belgrade, 31 January 1941 (ANB, 1/II, 96).
107  'Naš kliring sa Nemačkom', *Narodno blagostanje*, 7 December 1940.
108  Monthly report of the YNB's Board Committee, January 1941 (ANB, 1/II, 20).
109  Yugoslavia's payment transfer with Germany during 1940, Belgrade, 31 January 1941 (ANB, 1/II, 96).
110  Wiehl (German Foreign Ministry) to Landfried (German Economics Ministry), 27 September 1940 (PA, RZ 311, R 105943).
111  Ristović, *Nemački Novi poredak i jugoistočna Evropa*, 159–60.
112  Dimitrijević (Yugoslav Düsseldorf Consulate) to Yugoslav Foreign Ministry, 1 August 1940 (ANB, 1/II, 96); Translation of Funk's Interview, undated and unsigned (AJ, 65, 252).
113  Ivan Berend, *An Economic History of Twentieth-Century Europe* (Cambridge: Cambridge University Press, 2016), 120–1.
114  'Germany and economic reorientation of South-Eastern Europe', Yugoslav Berlin legation, 14 December 1940 (AJ, 65, 252); Stephen G. Gross, 'Gold, Debt and the Quest for Monetary Order: The Nazi Campaign to Integrate Europe in 1940', *Contemporary European History* 26, no. 2 (2017), 296.
115  Document printed in: Wuescht, *Jugoslawien und das Dritte Reich*, 286–8; Rebecca Haynes, *Romanian Policy towards Germany, 1936–40* (Basingstoke: Macmillan in association with School of Slavonic and East European Studies, University College London, 2000), 74–81; Gavriil Preda, 'German Foreign Policy towards the Romanian Oil during 1938–1940', *International Journal of Social Science and Humanity* 3, no. 3 (2013), 328.
116  Orlow, *The Nazis in the Balkans*, 101.
117  ADAP, D, VIII, 545, Clodius to German Foreign Ministry, Budapest, 17 January 1940; ADAP, D, X, 194, Erdmannsdorff (German Budapest Legation) to German Foreign Ministry, 20 July 1940; Lorant Tilkovszky, 'The Late Interwar Years and World War II', in *History of Hungary*, ed. Peter Sugar et al. (London and New York: I.B. Tauris, 1990), 342; Ivan T. Berend and György Ranki, *The Hungarian Economy in the Twentieth Century* (London: Croom Helm, 1985), 164.
118  Wien, *Markt und Modernisierung*, 304–8.
119  'Germany and Economic Reorientation of South-Eastern Europe', Yugoslav Berlin Legation, 14 December 1940 (AJ, 65, 252).

120 'Board meeting of the German Trade Chamber for Yugoslavia', Berlin, 5 December 1940 (BArch, R 43II/325).
121 The document is published in Drechsler, Dress and Hass, 'Europapläne des deutschen Imperialismus in zweiten Weltkrieg', 924–5.

## Chapter 9

1 Martin Broszat, 'Deutschland-Ungarn-Rumänien: Entwicklung und Grundfaktoren nationalsozialistischer Hegemonial- und Bündnispolitik', *Historische Zeitschrift* 206, no. 1 (1968), 70.
2 Hoptner, *Yugoslavia in Crisis,* 170.
3 Ibid., 172.
4 Stakić, *Moji razgovori sa Musolinijem*, 59.
5 'Da li će doći do rata', *Nova Evropa* XXXII/8, 26 August 1939. The similar argument was expressed in periodical press, such as *Vidici*, *Napred-list za narod* and the left-leaning *Radničke novine*, while the Belgrade-based satirical newspaper *Ošišani jež* mocked the Yugoslav government for its neutral stance towards the German attack on Poland. Being under the strict control of cenzorship, the daily press was restricted in its reporting. More on this in Rade Ristanović, 'Beogradska periodična štampa o početku Drugog svetskog rata', *Tokovi istorije* 2/2015.
6 ADAP, D, IX, 100, Heeren (German Belgrade legation) to German Foreign Ministry, 13 April 1940.
7 ADAP, D, IX, 140, Heeren (German Belgrade legation) to German Foreign Ministry, 19 April 1940.
8 ADAP, D, IX, 517, Heeren (German Belgrade legation) to German Foreign Ministry, 21 June 1940.
9 ADAP, D, X, 121, Heeren (German Belgrade Legation) to German Foreign Ministry, 5 July 1940.
10 ADAP, D, X, 215, Heeren (German Belgrade Legation) to German Foreign Ministry, 23 July 1940.
11 ADAP, D, IX, 176, Heeren (German Belgrade Legation) to German Foreign Ministry, 27 April 1940.
12 ADAP, D, IX, 258, Albrecht (German Foreign Ministry) to German Belgrade Legation, footnote 1, 17 May 1940.
13 ADAP, D, IX, 278, Heeren (German Belgrade Legation) to German Foreign Ministry, 20 May 1940.
14 Lukač, *Treći Rajh i zemlje jugoistočne Evrope* 2, 343–4.
15 ADAP, D, X, 53, 70, 173, 174, Correspondence between the German Foreign Ministry and German Sofia legation, June–July 1940.
16 ADAP, D, X, 244, 245, Two unsigned memorandums, Berlin, 27 July 1940.
17 Lukač, *Treći Rajh i zemlje jugoistočne Evrope* 2, 348–60.
18 Ibid., 372–4.
19 ADAP, D, IX, 384, Memorandum for Ribbentrop, 4 June 1940; ADAP, D, IX, 395, 403, Two memorandums by Wörmann (German Foreign Ministry), 6 June 1940 and 8 June 1940.
20 ADAP, D, X, 333, Erbach (German Athens Legation) to German Foreign Ministry, 13 August 1940; ADAP, D, X, 334, Memorandum by Weizsäcker (German Foreign Ministry), 13 August 1940.

21  ADAP, D, X, 363, 372, 377, 386, 387, 391, Correspondence between Erbach (German Athens Legation) and German Foreign Ministry, August 1940; ADAP, D, X, 394, Memorandum by Sonnleithner (German Foreign Ministry), 27 August 1940.
22  Krizman, 'Odnosi Jugoslavije s Njemačkom i Italijom', 234–5.
23  ADAP, D, X, 129, Unsigned memorandum, Berlin, 8 July 1940.
24  ADAP, D, X, 343, Foreign Intelligence Department of the High Command to the Chief of the High Command of the Wehrmacht, Berlin, 14 August 1940.
25  Ibid.
26  ADAP, D, X, 290, 348, Correspondence between Mackensen (German Rome Embassy) and Ribbentrop, 6 and 16 August 1940.
27  ADAP, D, X, 343, Foreign Intelligence Office of Wehrmacht to Chief of the High Command of Wehrmacht, 14 August 1940; ADAP, D, X, 353, Memorandum by Schmidt (Foreign Minister's Office), Berlin, 17 August 1940.
28  ADAP, D, X, 232, Heeren (German Belgrade Legation) to German Foreign Ministry, 26 July 1940.
29  ADAP, D, X, 395, Heeren (German Belgrade Legation) to German Foreign Ministry, 26 August 1940.
30  Lukač, *Treći Rajh i zemlje jugoistočne Evrope* 2, 404.
31  For more on Italian motives see: Harry Cliadakis, 'Neutrality and War in Italian Policy, 1939–1940', *Journal of Contemporary History* 9, no. 3 (1974); Krizman, 'Odnosi Jugoslavije s Njemačkom i Italijom', 235.
32  Gerhard Weinberg, *A World at Arms: A Global History of World War II* (Cambridge: Cambridge University Press, 1994), 183–4, 195–6; Detlef Vogel, 'Das Eingreifen Deutschlands auf dem Balkan', in *Das Deutsche Reich und der Zweite Weltkrieg* 3, ed. Gerhard Schreiber, Bernd Stegemann and Detlef Vogel (Stuttgart: Deutsche Verlags-Anstalt, 1984), 419.
33  Gerhard Weinberg, *Germany and the Soviet Union, 1939–1941* (Leiden: E.J. Brill, 1954), 114; Andreas Hillgruber, *Germany and the Two World Wars* (Cambridge, MA: Harvard University Press, 1981), 80–2; Richard J. Evans, *The Third Reich at War: How the Nazis Led Germany from Conquest to Disaster* (London: Penguin, 2008), 160–2.
34  Detlef Vogel, 'Das Eingreifen Deutschlands auf dem Balkan', in *Das Deutsche Reich und der Zweite Weltkrieg* 3, ed. Gerhard Schreiber, Bernd Stegemann and Detlef Vogel (Stuttgart: Deutsche Verlags-Anstalt, 1984), 427–8.
35  Ciano, *Diary,* 397.
36  Hoptner, *Yugoslavia in Crisis,* 183.
37  Weinberg, *A World at Arms,* 216.
38  Dragan Bakić, 'The Port of Salonica in Yugoslav Foreign Policy, 1919–1941', *Balcanica* 43 (2012), 206–7.
39  Danilo Gregorić, *So endete Jugoslawien* (Leipzig: Wilhelm Goldmann Verlag, 1943), 112.
40  Hoptner, *Yugoslavia in Crisis,* 186; Lukač, *Treći rajh i zemlje jugoistočne Evrope* 2, 461.
41  Hoptner, *Yugoslavia in Crisis,* 184.
42  Stakić, *Moji razgovori sa Musolinijem,* 82–3.
43  ADAP, D, XI, 324, Note by Schmidt (Foreign Minister's Office), 12 November 1940; ADAP, D, XI, 334, Heeren (German Belgrade legation) to German Foreign Ministry, 14 November 1940.
44  Gregorić, *So endete Jugoslawien,* 75–6, 96.
45  Ibid., 97.

46   Vladko Maček, *In the Struggle for Freedom* (University Park: Pennsylvania State University Press, 1957), 205.
47   Ibid., 202–5; Stakić, *Moji razgovori sa Musolinijem*, 69, 94–5.
48   For more on this see Dejan Djokić, 'National Mobilisation in the 1930s: The Emergence of the "Serb Question" in the Kingdom of Yugoslavia', in *New Perspectives on Yugoslavia: Key Issues and Controversies*, ed. Dejan Djokić and James Ker-Lindsey (Abingdon: Routledge, 2010).
49   Stevan Pavlowitch, 'Serbia and Yugoslavia – the Relationship', *Southeast European and Black Sea Studies* 4, no. 1 (2004), 101; Djokić, *Elusive Compromise*, 251.
50   Konstantinović, *Politika sporazuma*, 181, 196–200.
51   Djokić, *Elusive Compromise*, 212–22, 244–5.
52   Hoptner, *Yugoslavia in Crisis*, 191–2.
53   Vogel, 'Das Eingerifen Deutschlands aud fem Balkan', 420.
54   Ernst Presseisen, 'Prelude to "Barbarossa": Germany and the Balkans, 1940–1941', *The Journal of Modern History* 32, no. 4 (1960), 362.
55   Vogel, 'Das Eingerifen Deutschlands aud fem Balkan', 427–8.
56   Weinberg, *Germany and the Soviet Union*, 143.
57   Bogdan Krizman, 'Yugoslavia's Accession to the Tripartite Pact', in *The Third Reich and Yugoslavia, 1933–1945* (Beograd: ISI, 1977), 402.
58   Vogel, 'Das Eingerifen Deutschlands aud fem Balkan', 421.
59   Ibid., 436.
60   ADAP, D, XI/2, 397, Heeren (German Belgrade legation) to German Foreign Ministry, 25 November 1940.
61   ADAP, D, XI/2, 369, Hitler to Mussolini, Vienna, 20 November 1940.
62   ADAP, D, XI/2, 417, Memorandum by Schmidt (German Foreign Minister's Office), 29 November 1940.
63   Lukač, *Treći Rajh i zemlje jugoistočne Evrope* 2, 458–9.
64   Konstantin Fotić, *The War We Lost* (New York: The Viking Press, 1948), 38–9.
65   ADAP, D, XI/2, 465, 467, 469, Heeren (German Belgrade legation) to German Foreign Ministry, 7 December 1940.
66   ADAP, D, XI/2, 471, Memorandum by Wiehl (German Foreign Ministry), 7 December 1940.
67   ADAP, D, XI/2, 549, Ribbentrop to Heeren (German Belgrade Legation), 21 December 1940.
68   ADAP, D, XI/2, 551, Heeren (German Belgrade Legation) to German Foreign Ministry, 23 December 1940.
69   Hoptner, *Yugoslavia in Crisis*, 204.
70   Konstantinović, *Politika Sporazuma*, 259–61.
71   Hoptner, *Yugoslavia in Crisis*, 207–8.
72   Stakić, *Moji razgovori sa Musolinijem*, 98.
73   ADAP, D, XI/2, 708, Chief of the Security Police and Security Service to German Foreign Ministry, Berlin, 25 January 1941; ADAP, D, XI/2, 730, Minute by Hewel (German Foreign Minister's Office), 29 January 1941; Konstantinović, *Politika Sporazuma*, 292.
74   Ibid., 296–8.
75   Martin van Creveld, *Hitler's Strategy 1940–1941: The Balkan Clue* (Cambridge: Cambridge University Press, 1973), 97.
76   Weinberg, *Germany and the Soviet Union*, 152–3.

77  General Halder, *The Halder War Diary*, ed. Charles Burdick and Hans-Adolf Jacobsen (London: Greenhill Books, 1988), entry on 28 January 1941, 313.
78  Creveld, *Hitler's Strategy*, 126-7.
79  Ibid., 125.
80  ADAP, D, XII/1, 47, 48, Memorandums by Schmidt (German Foreign Minister's Office), 15 February 1941.
81  *The Halder War Diary*, entry on 17 February 1941, 320.
82  ADAP, D, XII/1, 130, Ribbentrop to Heeren (German Belgrade Legation), 7 March 1941.
83  *The Halder War Diary*, entry on 8 March 1941, 328.
84  Krizman, 'Yugoslavia's Accession to the Tripartite Pact', 404-5.
85  Hoptner, *Yugoslavia in Crisis*, 220; Maček, *In the Struggle for Freedom*, 209-12; Konstantinović, *Politika sporazuma*, 310. Describing this event, Terzić used Maček's version of the meeting of another session of the Crown Council, the one held on 20 March. Velimir Terzić, *Slom Kraljevine Jugoslavije: uzroci i posledice poraza* (Beograd: Narodna knjiga, 1982), 370-5.
86  *Aprilski rat* 2, 55, Heeren (German Belgrade Legation) to Ribbentrop, 7 March 1941.
87  Bogdan Krizman, 'Završni pregovori o pristupu Jugoslavije Trojnom paktu 1941. godine', *Historijski zbornik* 29-30 (1976-7), 518.
88  ADAP, D, XII/1, 144, Ribbentrop to Heeren (German Belgrade Legation), 9 March 1941.
89  For more on this see Bakić, 'The Port of Salonica in Yugoslav Foreign Policy'; Konstantinović, *Politika sporazuma*, 214, 222.
90  Ibid., 228; FRUS, 1941, II, Lane (US Belgrade Legation) to Secretary of State, 16 March 1941.
91  Peter II, King of Yugoslavia, *A King's Heritage: The Memoirs* (London: Cassell and Company, 1955), 73-4; Maček, *In the Struggle for Freedom*, 197-8.
92  Konstantinović, *Politika sporazuma*, 237.
93  ADAP, XII/1, 145, 149, Heeren (German Belgrade Legation) to German Foreign Ministry, 10 and 11 March 1941.
94  ADAP, XII/1, 151, Heeren (German Belgrade Legation) to German Foreign Ministry, 11 March 1941.
95  FRUS, 1941, II, Lane (US Belgrade Legation) to Secretary of State, 11 February 1941; Gregorić, *So endete Jugoslawien*, 95.
96  Krizman, 'Odnosi Jugoslavije s Njemačkom i Italijom', 243; Lukač, *Treći Rajh i zemlje jugoistočne Evrope* 2, 475; Vogel, 'Das Eingerifen Deutschlands aud fem Balkan', 438; Maček, *In the Struggle for Freedom*, 207; Hoptner, *Yugoslavia in Crisis*, 213-15, 222-7; *Aprilski rat* 2, 20, Heeren (German Belgrade Legation) to Ribbentrop, 5 February 1941.
97  FRUS, 1941, II, Lane (US Belgrade Legation) to Secretary of State, 21 March 1941.
98  Alexander Papagos, *The German Attack on Greece* (London: Greek Office of Information, 1946), 22-3.
99  Fotić, *The War We Lost*, 61-4.
100  ADAP, D, XII/1, 156, Heeren (German Belgrade Legation) to German Foreign Office, 12 March 1941.
101  ADAP, D, XII/1, 165, Ribbentrop to Heeren (German Belgrade Legation), 14 March 1941.
102  Maček, *In the Struggle for Freedom*, 210-11.
103  ADAP, D, XII/1, 173, Heeren (German Belgrade Legation) to German Foreign Ministry, 17 March 1941.

104 Konstantinović, *Politika sporazuma*, 350.
105 Bakić, 'The Port of Salonika in Yugoslav Foreign Policy', 211–12.
106 ADAP, D, XII/1, 187, Minute by Lohmann (Foreign Minister's Office), Berlin, 21 March 1941.
107 *Three-Power Pact between Germany, Italy and Japan*, http://avalon.law.yale.edu/wwii/triparti.asp, last accessed on 9 October 2017; Konstantinović, *Politika sporazuma*, 311–12.
108 ADAP, D, XII/1, 172, Memorandum by Weizsäcker (German Foreign Ministry), 17 March 1941.
109 ADAP, D, XII/1, 191, Memorandum by Schmidt (Foreign Minister's Office), 23 March 1941.
110 ADAP, D, XII/1, 192, Ribbentrop to Heeren (German Belgrade Legation), 22 March 1941.
111 ADAP, D, XII/1, 194, Heeren (German Belgrade Legation) to German Foreign Ministry, 22 March 1941.
112 Joachim von Ribbentrop, *Zwischen London und Moskau* (Leoni am Starnberger See, Druffel-Verlag, 1954), 224.
113 Fotić, *The War We Lost*, 72.
114 Paul Schmidt, *Statist auf diplomatischer Bühne, 1923–1945* (Bonn: Athenäum-Verlag, 1954), 529.
115 *The Von Hassell Diaries, 1938–1944: The Story of the Forces against Hitler inside Germany as Recorded by Ambassador Ulrich von Hassell, a Leader of the Movement* (London: Hamish Hamilton, 1948), 163.
116 FRUS, 1941, II, Lane (US Belgrade Legation) to Secretary of State, 11 March 1941.
117 FRUS, 1941, II, Lane (US Belgrade Legation) to Secretary of State, 18 February 1941.
118 Konstantinović, *Politika sporazuma*, 235.
119 FRUS, 1941, II, Lane (US Belgrade Legation) to Secretary of State, 21 March 1941.
120 Terzić, *Slom Kraljevine Jugoslavije 1941*, 306.
121 For example The war diary of the First Panzer Army, BArch, RH 21-1, 40.
122 High Command of the Armed Forces, 22. March 1941 (BArch, RW 4, 530).
123 Herman Nojbaher, *Specijalni zadatak Balkan*, trans. Nikola Živković (Beograd: Službeni list, 2004), 130–2.
124 *Aprilski rat* 2, 85, Ribbentrop to Heeren (German Belgrade Legation), 19 March 1941.
125 Konstantinović, *Politika sporazuma*, 312.
126 FRUS, 1941, II, Lane (US Belgrade Legation) to Secretary of State, 22 March 1941.
127 Radoje Knežević, 'Prince Paul, Hitler and Salonika', *International Affairs* 27 (1951), 39.
128 Biber, 'O padu Stojadinoviće vlade', 11.
129 For more on his private life see: Neil Balfour and Sally Mackay, *Prince Paul of Yugoslavia: Britain's Maligned Friend* (London: Hamish Hamilton, 1980).
130 Ilija Jukić, *The Fall of Yugoslavia* (New York: Harcourt Brace Jovanovich, 1974), 79–81.
131 On the attitude of Serbian opposition parties towards the idea of Yugoslavia's democratization see Mira Radojević, 'Demokratska stranka o državnom preuredjenju Kraljevine Jugoslavije, 1935–1941', *Istorija 20. Veka* 9, no. 1–2 (1991), 37–63.
132 Konstantinović's diary offers plenty of evidence. Also FRUS, 1941, II, Lane (US Belgrade Legation) to Secretary of State, 31 March 1941. Anton Korošec died on

14 December 1940. He was succeeded by Franc Kulovec as the new leader of the Slovene People's Party and Minister without Portfolio in Cvetković's government.
133 Terzić, *Slom Kraljevine Jugoslavije*, 338, 351.
134 Jukić, *The Fall of Yugoslavia*, 87.
135 ADAP, D, XI/1, 231, Heeren (German Belgrade Legation) to German Foreign Ministry, 25 October 1940.
136 ADAP, D, XII/1, 211, Feine (German Belgrade Legation) to German Foreign Ministry, 26 March 1941.
137 Fotić, *The War We Lost*, 70–1.
138 Maček, *In the Struggle for Freedom*, 198.
139 Živan Knežević, *27. Mart 1941* (New York: The Author, 1979), 252, 261.
140 Hoptner, *Yugoslavia in Crisis*, 262–6.
141 Ibid., 269–70; Peter II, *A King's Heritage*, 71.
142 Knežević, *27. Mart 1941*, 352–3.
143 FRUS, 1941, II, Lane (US Belgrade Legation) to Secretary of State, 28 March 1941.
144 FRUS, 1941, II, Lane (US Belgrade Legation) to Secretary of State, 29 March 1941.
145 ADAP, D, XII/1, 235, Heeren (German Belgrade Legation) to German Foreign Ministry, 30 March 1941.
146 Hoptner, *Yugoslavia in Crisis*, 274–5.
147 Ibid., 281–3.
148 Papagos, *The German Attack on Greece*, 26.
149 Peter II, *A King's Heritage*, 75.
150 Max Beloff, *The Foreign Policy of Soviet Russia, 1929–1941* 2 (Oxford: Oxford University Press, 1949), 36; Hoptner, *Yugoslavia in Crisis*, 276–81.
151 Presseisen, 'Prelude to "Barbarossa"', 369.
152 Weinberg, *Germany and the Soviet Union*, 158.
153 Vogel, 'Das Eingerifen Deutschlands aud fem Balkan', 443–4.
154 ADAP, D, XII/1, 259, Memorandum by Heeren, Berlin, 3 April 1941.
155 For more on preparing the plans for division, administration and economic exploitation of Yugoslavia during the period 27 March–6 April 1941, see Slavko Odić and Slavko Komarica, *Yugoslavia in the German Plans of Conquest* (Beograd: ISI, 1977), 441–57.
156 Details of this military campaign are widely described in numerous works. Here are used Creveld, *Hitler's Strategy 1940–1941*; Vogel, 'Das Eingerifen Deutschlands aud fem Balkan' and Christopher Shores, Brian Cull and Nicola Malizia, *Air War for Yugoslavia, Greece and Crete, 1940–1941* (London: Grub Street, 1987).
157 Hoptner, *Yugoslavia in Crisis*, 290–2.

# Bibliography

## Unpublished sources

Political Archive of the Federal Foreign Office (PA), Berlin:
- RAV Belgrad, Akten der deutschen Gesandtschaft in Belgrad.
- RZ 311, Handakten Clodius.
- RZ 344, Handakten Wiehl.
- RZ 304, Sonderreferat W Rep – Wirtschaft Reparationen.
- RZ 206, Länderarbeitung II, Jugoslawien.
- RZ 211, Politische Abteilung, Jugoslawien.
- RZ 303, Sonderreferat Wirtschaft.

Federal Archive (BArch), Berlin:
- R 2 Reichfinanzministerium.
- R 2301 Rechnungshof des Deutschen Reiches.
- R 10V Deutsches Kalisyndikat.
- R 901 Auswärtiges Amt.
- R 43II Reichskanzlei.

Federal Archive (BArch), Koblenz:
- N-1208, Nachlass Zimmermann.

Federal Archive – Military Archive (BArch), Freiburg:
- RH 21-1, Panzerarmeekommando 1.
- RW 4, OKW/Wehrmachtführungsstab.

Institute of Contemporary History (IfZG), Munich:
- US Department of State 1945.

Archive of Yugoslavia (AJ), Belgrade:
- 37, Milan Stojadinović.
- 65, Ministry of Trade and Industry.
- 70, Ministry of Finances.
- 72, National Parliament Papers.
- 74, Royal Court.
- 334, Ministry of Foreign Affairs.
- 394, Yugoslav Legation in Berlin.

Archive of the Serbian National Bank (ANB), Belgrade:
- 1/II, Kingdom of SHS/Yugoslavia, 1920-1941.

Military Archive (VA), Belgrade:
- Register 17, Army of the Kingdom of Yugoslavia.

The National Archives (TNA), London:
- 371, Foreign Office General Correspondence.

## Published documentary sources

*Akten zur deutschen auswärtigen Politik*, 1918-1945, Serie C, 1933-1937 (Göttingen: Vandenhoeck & Ruprecht, 1971-1981).
*Akten zur deutschen auswärtigen Politik*, 1918-1945, Serie D, 1937-1945 (Göttingen: Vandenhoeck & Ruprecht, 1971-1981).
*Allianz Hitler-Horthy-Mussolini: Dokumente zur ungarischen Außenpolitik* (1933-1944), ed. Magda Adam et al. (Budapest: Akademiai Kiado, 1966).
*Anatomie des Krieges: Neue Dokumente über die Rolle des deutschen Monopolkapitals bei der Vorbereitung und Durchführung des zweiten Weltkriegs*, ed. Dietrich Eichholtz and Wolfgang Schumann (Berlin: Berlin: VEB Deutscher Verlag der Wissenschaften, 1969).
*Aprilski rat: Zbornik dokumenata*, ed. Dušan Gvozdenović (Beograd: Vojnoistorijski institut, 1969).
*Documents of British Foreign Policy*, Second Series, 1930-1938, ed. W. N. Medlicott and Douglas Dakin (London: Her Majesty's Stationary Office, 1972-1982).
*Documents on International Affairs*, ed. John W. Wheeler Bennett (Oxford: Oxford University Press, 1932).
*Foreign Relations of the United States: Diplomatic Papers* (Washington, United States Government Printing Office).
*Griff nach Südosteuropa: Neue Dokumente über dem deutschen Imperialismus und Militarismus gegenüber Südosteuropa im zweiten Weltkrieg*, ed. Wolfgang Schumann (Berlin: VEB Deutscher Verlag der Wissenschaften, 1973).
*Izveštaji Ministarstva inostranih poslova Kraljevine Jugoslavije*, 1930-1941 (Beograd: Arhiv Jugoslavije, 2005-2016).
*Statistički godišnjak Kraljevine Jugoslavije*, since 1929 (Beograd: Državna štamparija).
*Statistisches Jahrbuch für das Deutsche Reich*, since 1880 (Berlin: Statistische Reichsamt).
*Three-Power Pact between Germany, Italy and Japan*, http://avalon.law.yale.edu/wwii/triparti.asp, last accessed on 9 October 2017.

## Contemporary literature, memoirs, autobiographies and diaries

Ahlgrimm, Franz, *Die Landwirtschaft des südosteuropäischen Raumes*, Lecture delivered on 21 February 1939, Vienna, 1939.
Basch, Antonin, *The Danube Basin and the German Economic Sphere* (London: K. Paul, Trench, Trubner, 1944).
Bobić, Dj., *Antisemitizam: židovsko pitanje* (Zagreb: Grafika, 1935).

Bopp, Karl, 'Hjalmar Schacht: Central Banker', *A Quarterly of Research* 14, no. 1 (1939), 1–91.
Ciano, Galeazzo, *Ciano's Diary, 1937–1943*, ed. Muggeridge Malcolm (London: Phoenix Press, 2002).
Ćirković, Stevan, *Politička i privredna Mala Antanta* (Beograd: Biblioteka jugoslovenskog udruženja za međunarodno pravo, 1935).
Crnić, Ivan, *Die jugoslawische Eisenindustrie im Rahmen der jugoslawischen Volkswirtschaft* (Köln: Orthen, 1938).
Daitz, Werner, *Der Weg zur Volkswirtschaft, Grossraumwirtschaft und Grossraumpolitik* 2 (Dresden: Meinhold Verlagsgeselschaft, 1942).
Dimitrijević, Mića and Stojanović, Vojislav, *Naši Jevreji* (Beograd: Minerva, 1940).
Ellis, Howard Sylvester, *Exchange Control in Central Europe* (Cambridge, MA: Harvard University Press, 1941).
Erbsland, Kurt, *Die Umgestaltung der deutschen Handelspolitik durch den "Neuen Plan" und die Möglichkeit ihrer künftigen Ausgestaltung* (Spcycr am Rhein: Pilger-Druckerei, 1937).
'Erste Geschäftsbericht der Deutschland-Stiftung des Mitteleuropäischen Wirtschaftstag, für das Studienjahr 191936/1937', in *MWT Deutsche Gruppe – Deutscher Akademischer Austauschdienst* (Kiel: Institut für Weltwirtschaft).
Fotić, Konstantin, *The War We Lost* (New York: The Viking Press, 1948).
Gajić, Edo, *Jugoslavija i jevrejski problem* (Beograd: Štamparija Drag. Gregorića, 1938).
*The Goebbels Diaries, 1939–1941*, trans. Fred Taylor (London: Hamish Hamilton, 1982).
Gregorić, Danilo, *So endete Jugoslawien* (Leipzig: Wilhelm GoldmannVerlag, 1943).
Gross, Hermann, *Die Wirtschaftliche Bedeutung Südosteuropas für das Deutsche Reich* (Berlin and Stuttgart: Rohlhammer Verlag, 1938).
*The Halder War Diary*, ed. Charles Burdick and Hans-Adolf Jacobsen (London: Greenhill Books, 1988).
Hermann, Felix, *Die Antimonerzvorkommen ehem. Jugoslawiens, Bulgariens, Griechenlands und der Türkei* (Berlin: Mitteleuropäischer Wirtschaftstag, 1941).
Hitler, Adolf, *Mein Kampf*, trans. Ralph Manheim (London: Pimlico, 1992).
Hoffmann, Walter, *Südost-Europa: ein Querschnitt durch Politik, Kultur und Wirtschaft* (Leipzig: Wolfgang Richard Lindner Verlag, 1932).
Hoffmann, Walter, *Grossdeutschland im Donauraum* (Berlin: Propaganda-Verlag Paul Hochmuth, 1939).
Ivanović, Vane, *LX: Memoirs of a Yugoslav* (London: Weidenfeld & Nicolson, 1977).
Jukić, Ilija, *The Fall of Yugoslavia* (New York: Harcourt Brace Jovanovich, 1974).
Jurković, Božidar, *Die ausländische Kapital in Jugoslavien* (Stuttgart: Kohlhammer, 1941).
Knežević, Živan, *27. Mart 1941* (New York: The Author, 1979).
Knežević, Radoje, 'Prince Paul, Hitler and Salonika', *International Affairs* 27 (1951), 38–44.
Konstantinović, Mihailo, *Politika Sporazuma: Dnevničke beleške 1939–1941, Londonske beleške 1944–1945* (Novi Sad: Agencija, 1998).
Kosier, Ljubomir St, *Grossdeutschland und Jugoslawien: aus der Südslawischen Perspektive* (Berlin: Mitteleuropäischer Verlag, 1939).
Kukoleča, Stevan, *Industrija Jugoslavije 1918–1938* (Beograd: Balkanska štampa, 1941).
Maček, Vladko, *In the Struggle for Freedom* (University Park: Pennsylvania State University Press, 1957).
*Memoirs of Ernst von Weizsäcker*, trans. John Andrews (London: Victor Gollancz, 1951).

Momtchiloff, Nikolai, *Ten Years of Controlled Trade in South-Eastern Europe* (Cambridge: Cambridge University Press, 1944).
Nojbaher, Herman, *Specijalni zadatak Balkan*, trans. Nikola Živković (Beograd: Službeni list, 2004).
Obradović, Sava, *Zwischen Clearing und Devise: Probleme der handelspolitik Jugoslawiens* (Leipzig: Felix Meiner Verlag, 1939).
Papagos, Alexander, *The German Attack on Greece* (London: Greek Office of Information, 1946).
Peter II, King of Yugoslavia, *A King's Heritage: The Memoirs* (London: Cassell and Company, 1955).
Ribbentrop, Joachim von, *Zwischen London und Moskau* (Leoni am Starnberger See: Druffel-Verlag, 1954).
Rozenberg, Vladimir and Kostić, Jovan, *Ko finansira jugoslovensku privredu* (Beograd: Balkanska štampa, 1940).
Schacht, Hjalmar, *My First Seventy-Six Years* (London: Wingate, 1955).
Schmidt, Paul, *Statist auf diplomatischer Bühne, 1923–1945* (Bonn: Athenäum-Verlag, 1954).
Sohn-Rethel, Alfred, *Economy and Class Structure of German Fascism* (London: Free Association Books, 1987).
Stakić, Vladislav, *Moji razgovori sa Musolinijem: osovinske sile i Jugoslavija* (München: by author, 1967).
Stojadinović, Milan, *Ni rat, ni pakt: Jugoslavija izmedju dva rata* (Buenos Aires: by author, 1963).
'Südosteuropa: Vorschläge für eine neue deutsche Kapitalpolitik', Berlin, February 1940, Kiel: Institut für Weltwirtschaft.
*Tajni arhivi grofa Ciana, 1936–1942*, trans. Ive Mihailović (Zagreb: Zora, 1952).
Terzić, Sava, *Die deutsch-jugoslawischen Handelsbeziehungen auf Grund des Handelsvertrages 1934* (Wien: Hollinek, 1940).
Trucksaess, Karl, *Nemačko-jugoslovenski industrijski i trgovački adresar* (Berlin: Gesellschaft für Aussenhandelswerbung, 1936).
Trucksaess, Karl, *Nemačko-jugoslovenski industrijski i trgovački adresar* (Berlin: Gesellschaft für Aussenhandelswerbung, 1941).
Vauhnik, Vladimir, *Nevidljivi front: Borba za očuvanje Jugoslavije* (München: Iskra, 1984).
*The Von Hassell Diaries, 1938–1944: The Story of the Forces against Hitler inside Germany as recorded by Ambassador Ulrich von Hassell, a Leader of the Movement* (London: Hamish Hamilton, 1948).
'Wiener Tagung des Mitteleuropäischen Wirtschaftstag', Wien, 2 September 1940, Kiel: Institut für Weltwirtschaft.
Wheeler-Bennett, John, *The Wreck of Reparations: Being the Political Background of the Lausanne Agreement, 1932* (London: George Allen and Unwin, 1933).
Wheeler-Bennett, John and Latimer, Hugh, *Information on the Reparation Settlement: Being the Background and History of the Young Plan and the Hague Agreements, 1929–1930* (London: George Allen and Unwin, 1930).
*Winston Churchill and Emery Reves: Correspondence, 1937–1938*, ed. Martin Gilbert (Austin: University of Texas Press, 1997).
Zeck, Hans, *Die Deutsche Wirtschaft und Südosteuropa* (Leipzig and Berlin: Teubner, 1939).

## Books, edited chapters and articles

Abelshauser, Werner, 'Kriegswirtschaft und Wirtschaftswunder', *Vierteljahrshefte für Zeitgeschichte* 47, no. 4 (1999), 503-38.

Adriano, Pino and Cingolani, Giorgio, *Nationalism and Terror: Ante Pavelić and Ustashe Terrorism from Fascism to the Cold War* (Budapest: Central European University Press, 2018).

Aleksić, Dragan, *Privreda Srbije u Drugom svetskom ratu* (Beograd: INIS, 2002).

Aleksić, Vesna, 'Nazification of the Allgemeiner jugoslawischer Bankverein AG: Political Destiny of an Economic Institution', in *Deutsch-serbische Beziehungen vom Berliner Kongress bis heute*, ed. Dittmar Dahlmann and Milan Kosanović (Bonn: Michael Zikic Stiftung, 2003), 115-67.

Alexander, Martin, *The Republic in Danger: General Maurice Gamelin and the Politics of French Defence, 1933-1940* (Cambridge: Cambridge University Press, 1992).

Avakumović, Ivan, 'Yugoslavia's Fascist Movements', in *Native Fascism in the Successor States, 1918-1941*, ed. Peter Sugar (Santa Barbara: Clio Press, 1971), 135-43.

Avramovski, Živko, *Balkanska antanta* (Beograd: ISI, 1986).

Avramovski, Živko, 'The International Isolation of Yugoslavia: an Objective of German Foreign Policy in the Period from 1933-1939', in *The Third Reich and Yugoslavia, 1933-1945* (Beograd: ISI, 1977), 259-77.

Avramovski, Živko, *Treći Rajh i Borski rudnik* (Bor: Muzej rudarstva i metalurgije, 1975).

Avramovski, Živko, 'Ekononski i politički ciljevi nemačkog izvoza naoružanja u balkanske zemlje uoči Drugog svetskog rata', *Vojnoistorijski glasnik* 2 (1972), 61-86.

Avramovski, Živko, *Balkanske zemlje i velike sile, 1935-1937* (Beograd: Prosveta, 1968).

Avramovski, Živko, 'Sukob interesa V. Britanije i Nemačke na Balkanu uoči Drugog svetskog rata', *Istorija XX veka. Zbornik radova* 2 (1961), 5-161.

Bakić, Dragan, *Britain and Interwar Danubian Europe: Foreign Policy and Security Challenges, 1919-1936* (London: Bloomsbury, 2017).

Bakić, Dragan, 'The Italo-Yugoslav Conflict over Albania: A View from Belgrade, 1919-1939', *Diplomacy & Statecraft* 25, no. 4 (2014), 592-612.

Bakić, Dragan, 'The Port of Salonica in Yugoslav Foreign Policy, 1919-1941', *Balcanica* 43 (2012), 191-219.

Balfour, Neil and Mackay, Sally, *Prince Paul of Yugoslavia: Britain's Maligned Friend* (London: Hamish Hamilton, 1980).

Banac, Ivo, *The National Question in Yugoslavia: Origins, History, Politics* (New York: Cornell University Press, 1984).

Barker, Elisabeth, *British Policy in South East Europe in the Second World War* (London: Macmillan, 1976).

Barović, Vladimir, 'Puč od 27. marta 1941 i medijsko-propagandno delovanje nemačke narodne grupe u Dunavskoj banovini', *Kultura polisa* 14, no. 33 (2017), 259-74.

Barović, Vladimir and Pralica, Dejan, 'Širenje nacionalsocijalističke propagande na teritoriji Dunavske banovine tokom 1940. godine', *Vojno delo* 63 (2011), 453-65.

Barsche, Heinz, 'Der Mitteleuropäische Wirtschaftstag', *Deutsche Aussenpolitik* 11 (Berlin: Rütten und Loening, 1960), 1294-302.

Becić, Ivan, 'Statistika i karakter spoljne trgovine Kraljevine SHS, 1919-1929', *Istorija 20. veka* 33, no. 2 (2015), 57-72

Becić, Ivan, *Ministarstvo finansija Kraljevine Jugoslavije, 1918-1941* (Beograd: ISI, 2012).

Becić, Ivan, 'Finansijska politika Milana Stojadinovića', *Istorija 20. veka* 29, no. 3 (2011), 125-42.

Becić, Ivan, 'Ratni dugovi Kraljevine Srbije u svetlu politike', *Istorija 20. veka* 28, no. 3 (2010), 45–56.

Beloff, Max, *The Foreign Policy of Soviet Russia, 1929–1941* 2 (Oxford: Oxford University Press, 1949).

Berend, Ivan, *An Economic History of Twentieth-Century Europe* (Cambridge: Cambridge University Press, 2016).

Berend, Ivan and Ranki, György, *The Hungarian Economy in the Twentieth Century* (London: Croom Helm, 1985).

Bergen, Doris, 'The Nazi Concept of "Volksdeutsche" and the Exacerbation of Anti-Semitism in Eastern Europe, 1939–1945', *Journal of Contemporary History* 45, no. 4 (1994), 569–82.

Bethke, Carl, 'Da li je bilo jugoslovenskih Nemaca: Regionalne specifičnosti i procesi nacionalne integracije nemačke manjine na teritoriji jugoslovenske države, 1918–1948', in *O „nestanku" nemačkih nacionalnih manjina: jedno teško poglavlje u istoriji Jugoslavije, 1941–1955*, ed. Christian Glass et al. (Ulm: Donauschwäbisches Zentralmuseum, 2016), 33–47.

Biber, Dušan, *Nacizem in Nemci v Jugoslaviji, 1933–1941* (Ljubljana: Cankarjeva Založba, 1966).

Biber, Dušan, 'O padu Stojadinovićeve vlade', *Istorija XX veka* 8 (1966), 5–71.

Biondich, Mark, 'Radical Catholicism and Fascism in Croatia, 1918–1945', in *Clerical Fascism in Interwar Europe*, ed. Matthew Feldman et al. (London: Routledge, 2008), 171–88.

Böhm, Johann, *Die Deutsche Volksgruppe in Jugoslawien, 1918–1945* (Frankfurt: Peter Lang, 2009).

Bohn, Thomas, 'Bulgariens Rolle im "wirtschaftlichen" Ergänzungsraum Südosteuropa', in *Besatzung und Bündnis: Deutsche Herrschaftsstrategien in Ost- und Südosteuropa*, ed. Christian Gerlach et al. (Berlin: Schwarze Risse, 1995), 111–38.

Boia, Eugene, *Romania's Diplomatic Relations with Yugoslavia in the Interwar Period, 1919–1941* (Boulder: East European Monographs, 1993).

Brechtefeld, Jörg, *Mitteleuropa and German Politics: 1848 to the Present* (London: Macmillan, 1996).

Broszat, Martin, *The Hitler State: The Foundation and Development of the Internal Structure of the Third Reich* (London: Longman, 1981).

Broszat, Martin, 'Deutschland-Ungarn-Rumänien: Entwicklung und Grundfaktoren nationalsozialistischer Hegemonial- und Bündnispolitik', *Historische Zeitschrift* 206, no. 1 (1968), 45–96.

Burgwyn, James, *Italian Foreign Policy in the Interwar Period, 1918–1940* (London: Praeger, 1997).

Burleigh, Michael and Wippermann, Wolfgang, *The Racial State: Germany, 1933–1945* (Cambridge: Cambridge University Press, 1991).

Burrin, Philippe, *Hitler and the Jews: The Genesis of the Holocaust* (London: Arnold, 1994).

Byford, Jovan, *Denial and Repression of Antisemitism: Post-Communist Remembrance of the Serbian Bishop Nikolaj Velimirović* (Budapest: Central European University Press, 2008).

Čalić, Mari-Žanin, *Istorija Jugoslavije u 20. veku* (Beograd: Clio, 2013).

Čalić, Mari-Žanin, *Socijalna istorija Srbije, 1815–1914* (Beograd: Clio, 2004).

Campus, Eliza, *The Little Entente and the Balkan Alliance* (Bucharest: Bibliotheca Historica Romaniae, 1978).

Carr, William, *Arms, Autarky and Aggression: A Study in German Foreign Policy, 1933–1939* (London: Edward Arnold, 1972).
Child, Frank, *The Theory and Practice of Exchange Control in Germany: A Study of Monopolistic Exploitation in International Markets* (The Hague: Martinus Nijhoff, 1958).
Cliadakis, Harry, 'Neutrality and War in Italian Policy, 1939–1940', *Journal of Contemporary History* 9, no. 3 (1974), 171–90.
Conze, Eckart, *Das Amt und die Vergangenheit: deutschen Diplomaten im Dritten Reich und in der Bundesrepublik* (München: Blessing, 2010).
Corni, Gustavo, 'Alfred Hugenberg as Minister of Agriculture: Interlude or Continuity', *German History* 7, no. 2 (1989), 204–25.
Creveld, Martin van, *Hitler's Strategy 1940–1941: The Balkan Clue* (Cambridge: Cambridge University Press, 1973).
Cvetković, Vladimir, *Ekonomski odnosi Jugoslavije i Francuske, 1918–1941* (Beograd: INIS, 2006).
Cvijetić, Leposava, 'The Ambitions and Plans of the Third Reich with regard to the Integration of Yugoslavia into the So-Called Grosswirtschaftsraum', in *The Third Reich and Yugoslavia, 1933–1945* (Beograd: ISI, 1977), 184–96.
Cvijetić, Leposava, 'Prodaja naoružanja kao metod pritiska Nemačke na Jugoslaviju', *Istorija XX veka* 3 (1975), 171–253.
Denda, Dalibor, 'Tenkovske jedinice u vojsci Kraljevine Jugoslavije, 1930–1941', *Vojnoistorijski glasnik* 1 (2009), 147–71.
Djilas, Aleksa, *The Contested Country: Yugoslav Unity and Communist Revolution, 1919–1953* (Cambridge, MA: Harvard University Press, 1991).
Djokić, Dejan, 'National Mobilisation in the 1930s: The Emergence of the "Serb Question" in the Kingdom of Yugoslavia', in *New Perspectives on Yugoslavia: Key Issues and Controversies*, ed. Dejan Djokić and James Ker-Lindsey (Abingdon: Routledge, 2010), 62–81.
Djokić, Dejan, *Elusive Compromise: A History of Interwar Yugoslavia* (New York: Columbia University Press, 2007).
Djordjević, Boško, s dopunom Save Obradovića o plurilateralnim sporazumima Jugoslavije 1934–1941 i predgovorom Mije Mirkovića, *Pregled ugovorne trgovinske politike, od osnivanja države Srba, Hrvata i Slovenaca do rata 1941. godine* (Zagreb: Jugoslovenska akademija znanosti i umjetnosti, 1960).
Djordjević, Dimitrije, 'Fascism in Yugoslavia, 1918–1941', in *Native Fascism in the Successor States, 1918–1945*, ed. Peter Sugar (Santa Barbara: Clio Press, 1971), 125–34.
Djurović, Smiljana, 'Sankcije Društva naroda prema Italiji 1935. godine i jugoslovenska privreda', in *Sa Teslom u novi vek: nove sinteze istorije* (Beograd: Zavod za udžbenike i nastavna sredstva, 1997), 239–68.
Djurović, Smiljana, 'Jedan aspekt pokušaja modernizacije države i uključivanja Kraljevine SHS u industrijsku civilizaciju zapadne Evrope', *Jugoslovenski Istorijski Časopis* 24, no. 1 (1989), 43–50.
Djurović, Smiljana, 'Značaj industrijalizacije Primorske banovine u ekonomskoj konstelaciji Jugoslavije, 1929–1941', *Istorijski Časopis* 34 (1987), 327–49.
Djurović, Smiljana, *Državna intervencija u industriji Jugoslavije, 1918–1941* (Beograd: ISI, 1986).
Doß, Kurt, 'Germany', in *The Times Survey of Foreign Ministries of the World*, ed. Zara Steiner (London: Times Books, 1982), 225–55.

Drechsler, Karl, Dress, Hans and Hass, Gerhart, 'Europapläne des deutschen Imperialismus in zweiten Weltkrieg', *Zeitschrift für Geschichtswissenschaft* 7 (1971), 916–31.
Dülffer, Jost, 'Zum "Decision-Making Process" in der deutschen Außenpolitik', in *Hitler, Deutschland und die Mächte: Materialien zur Aussenpolitik des Dritten Reiches*, ed. Manfred Funke (Düsseldorf: Droste Verlag, 1976), 186–204.
Ebi, Michael, *Export um jeden Preis, die Deutsche Exportforderung von 1932–1938* (Stuttgart: Franz Steiner Verlag, 2004).
Elvert, Jürgen, *Mitteleuropa! Deutsche Pläne zur europäischen Neuordnung, 1918–1945* (Stuttgart: Franz Steiner Verlag, 1999).
Evans, Richard J., *The Third Reich at War: How the Nazis led Germany from Conquest to Disaster* (London: Penguin, 2008).
Freytag, Carl, *Deutschlands 'Drang nach Südosten': Der Mitteleuropäische Wirtschaftstag und der 'Ergänzungsraum Südosteuropa', 1931–1945* (Wien: Vienna University Press, 2012).
Frommelt, Reinhard, *Paneuropa oder Mitteleuropa: Einigungsbestrebungen im Kalkül deutscher Wirtschaft und Politik, 1925–1933* (Stuttgart: Deutsche Verlags-Anstalt, 1977).
Gašić, Ranka, 'Prodor nemačkog kapitala u beogradska rudarska akcionarska društva tridesetih godina 20. veka', *Istorija 20. veka* 31, no. 1 (2013), 9–22.
Gašić, Ranka, 'Koncepcija jugoslovenstva u Novoj Evropi', in *Nova Evropa, 1920–1941: Zbornik radova*, ed. Marko Nedić and Vesna Matović (Beograd: Institut za književnost i umetnost, 2010), 139–49.
Gašić, Ranka, 'Jugoslovensko-nemačko društvo u Beogradu, 1931–1941', *Istorija 20. veka* 16, no. 1 (1998), 99–107.
Gavrilović, Darko, *Mit o neprijatelju: antisemitizam Dimitrija Ljotića* (Beograd: Službeni glasnik, 2018).
Geiger, Vladimir, 'Njemačka manjina u Kraljevini Srba, Hrvata i Slovenaca/Jugoslaviji (1918–1941)', in *Dijalog povjesničara – istoričara*, ed. Hans-Georg Fleck and Igor Graovac (Zagreb: Zaklada Friedrich Naumann, 2000), 429–45.
Gil Aguado, Iago, 'The Creditanstalt Crisis of 1931 and the Failure of the Austro-German Customs Union Project', *The Historical Journal* 44, no. 1 (2001), 199–221.
Gomes, Leonard, *German Reparations 1919–1932, A Historical Survey* (London: Palgrave, 2010).
Goldstein, Ivo and Goldstein, Slavko, *Holokaust u Zagrebu* (Zagreb: Novi Liber, 2001).
Gottlieb, Moshe, 'The Anti-Nazi Boycott Movement in the United States: An Ideological and Sociological Appreciation', *Jewish Social Studies* 35, no. 3–4 (1973), 198–227.
Grenzebach, William, *Germany's Informal Empire in East-Central Europe: German Economic Policy towards Yugoslavia and Rumania, 1933–1939* (Stuttgart: Franz Steiner Verlag, 1988).
Gross, Stephen G., 'Gold, Debt and the Quest for Monetary Order: The Nazi Campaign to Integrate Europe in 1940', *Contemporary European History* 26, no. 2 (2017), 287–309.
Gross, Stephen G., *Export Empire: German soft power in Southeastern Europe, 1890–1945* (Cambridge: Cambridge University Press, 2015).
Gross, Stephen G., 'Das Mitteleuropa-Institut in Dresden: Verknüpfung regionaler Wirtschaftsinteressen mit deutscher Auslandskulturpolitik in der Zwischenkriegzeit', in *„Mitteleuropa" und „Südosteuropa" als Planungsraum: Wirtschafts- und kulturpolitische*

*Expertisen im Zeitalter der Weltkriege*, ed. Carola Sachse (Göttingen: Wallstein Verlag, 2010), 115–40.

Hadži-Jovančić, Perica, 'Losing the Periphery: British Foreign Office and Policy towards Yugoslavia, 1935–1938', *Diplomacy & Statecraft* 31, no. 1 (2020), 65–90.

Hayes, Peter, 'Industry under the Swastika', in *Enterprise in the Period of Fascism in Europe*, ed. Harold James and Jakob Tanner (Aldershot: Ashgate, 2002), 26–36.

Hayes, Peter, *Industry and Ideology: IG Farben in the Nazi Era* (Cambridge: Cambridge University Press, 2001).

Haynes, Rebecca, *Romanian Policy towards Germany, 1936–40* (Basingstoke: Macmillan in association with School of Slavonic and East European Studies, University College London, 2000).

Hedberg, Peter and Hakansson, Elias, 'Did Germany Exploit Its Small Trading Partners? The Nature of the German Interwar and Wartime Trade Policies Revisited from the Swedish Experience', *Scandinavian Economic History Review* 56, no. 3 (2008), 246–70.

Hehn, Paul, *A Low Dishonest Decade: The Great Powers, Eastern Europe, and the Economic Origins of the Second World War* (London: Continuum, 2002).

Hepburn, Philip, 'The Origins of Appeasement and Anglo-Yugoslav Relations 1931–1937', in *Yugoslav-British Relations* (Beograd: ISI, 1988), 223–36.

Hildebrand, Klaus, 'Monokratie oder Polykratie? Hitlers Herrschaft und das Dritte Reich', in *Der „Führerstaat", Mythos und Realität: Studien zur Struktur und Politik des Dritten Reiches*, ed. Gerhard Hirschfeld and Lothar Kettenacker (Stuttgart: Klett-Cotta, 1981), 73–95.

Hildebrand, Klaus, *The Foreign Policy of the Third Reich* (London: Batsford, 1973).

Hillgruber, Andreas, *Germany and the Two World Wars* (Cambridge, MA: Harvard University Press, 1981).

Hirschmann, Albert, *National Power and the Structure of Foreign Trade* (Berkeley and Los Angeles: University of California Press, 1945).

Hoptner, Jacob, *Yugoslavia in Crisis, 1934–1941* (New York: East Central European studies of Columbia University, 1962).

Innerhofer, Ian, 'The Role of the "agrarian overpopulation" in German Spatial and Economic Planning for South East Europe before and during World War II', in *Perpetual Motion? Transformation and Transition in Central, Eastern Europe and Russia* (London: UCL School of Slavonic and East European Studies, 2010), 43–56.

Ivanković, Mladenka and Stojanović, Aleksandar, 'Anti-Semitic Propaganda and Legislation in Serbia 1939–1942: Content, Scale, Aims and Role of the German Factor', *Istorija 20. veka* 37, no. 2 (2019), 85–104.

Janjetović, Zoran, *Nemci u Vojvodini* (Beograd: INIS, 2009).

Janjatović, Bosiljka and Strčić, Petar, 'O ubojstvu Dr Milana Šufflaya', *Historijski Zbornik* 46, no. 1 (1993), 89–107.

Jelić-Butić, Fikreta, *Ustaše i Nezavisna Država Hrvatska* (Zagreb: Školska knjiga, 1978).

Kaiser, David, *Economic Diplomacy and the Origins of the Second World War: Germany, Britain, France and Eastern Europe, 1930–1939* (Guildford: Princeton University Press, 1980).

Kenwood, Albert George and Lougheed, Alan Leslie, *The Growth of the International Economy, 1820–1960* (London: Routledge, 1992).

Kershaw, Ian, 'Hitler and the Uniqueness of Nazism', *Journal of Contemporary History* 39, no. 2 (2004), 239–54.

Kershaw, Ian, *The Nazi Dictatorship: Problems and Perspectives of Interpretation* (London: Edward Arnold, 1989).
Kitson, Michael, *The Move to Autarchy: The Political Economy of Nazi Foreign Trade*, Cambridge Department of Applied Economics, Working Paper, 1992.
Kolar-Dimitrijević, Mira, 'Die wirtschaftlichen Möglichkeiten und die konkrete Integration Kroatiens in die Mitteleuropäischen Wirtschaftspläne 1918-1938', in *Mitteleuropa-Konzeptionen in der ersten Hälfte des 20. Jahrhunderts*, ed. Richard Plaschka et al. (Wien: Österreichischen Akademie der Wissenschaften, 1995), 263-76.
Kolar-Dimitrijević, Mira, 'Privredne veze izmedju Austrije i sjeverne Hrvatske od 1918. do 1925. godine', *Historijski zbornik* 65 (1992), 57-88.
Kolar-Dimitrijević, Mira, 'Strani kapital i Banovina Hrvatska, 1939-1941', *Povijesni prilozi* no. 9 (1990), 165-194.
Koljanin, Milan, *Jevreji i antisemitizam u Kraljevini Jugoslaviji, 1918-1941* (Beograd: ISI, 2008).
Komjathy, Anthony and Stockwell, Rebecca, *German Minorities and the Third Reich: Ethnic Germans of East Central Europe between the Wars* (London: Holmes and Meier, 1980).
Kovrig, Bennett, 'Mediation by Obfuscation: The Resolution of the Marseille Crisis, October 1934 to May 1935', *The Historical Journal* 19, no. 1 (1976), 191-221.
Krizman, Bogdan, 'Yugoslavia's Accession to the Tripartite Pact', in *The Third Reich and Yugoslavia, 1933-1945* (Beograd: ISI, 1977), 399-422.
Krizman, Bogdan, 'Završni pregovori o pristupu Jugoslavije Trojnom paktu 1941. godine', *Historijski zbornik* 29-30 (1976-1977), 517-27.
Krizman, Bogdan, *Vanjska politika jugoslavenske države* (Zagreb: Školska knjiga, 1975).
Krizman, Bogdan, 'Odnosi Jugoslavije s Njemačkom i Italijom, 1937-1941', *Historijski zbornik* 17 (1964), 227-57.
Krohn, Claus-Dieter, 'Autoritärer Kapitalismus: Wirtschaftskonzeptionen im Übergang von der Weimarer Republik zum Nationalsozialismus', in *Industrielle Gesellschaft und politisches System: Beiträge zur politischen Sozialgeschichte*, ed. Dirk Stegmann, Bernd Jürgen Wendt and Peter-Christian Witt (Bonn: Verlag Neue Gesellschaft, 1978), 113-29.
Krüger, Peter, 'Wirtschaftliche Mitteleuropapläne in Deutschland zwischen den Weltkriegen', in *Mitteleuropa-Konzeptionen in der ersten Hälfte des 20. Jahrhunderts*, ed. Richard Plaschka et al. (Wien: Österreichischen Akademie der Wissenschaften, 1995), 283-303.
Krüger, Peter, *Die Aussenpolitik der Republik von Weimar* (Darmstadt: Wissenschaftliche Buchgesellschaft, 1985).
Kube, Alfred, *Pour le mérite und Hakenkreuz: Hermann Göring im Dritten Reich* (München: Oldenbourg, 1986).
Kube, Alfred, 'Außenpolitik und "Großraumwirtschaft". Die deutsche Politik zur wirtschaftlichen Integration Südosteuropas 1933 bis 1939', *Geschichte und Gesellschaft. Sonderheft* 10, Wirtschaftliche und politische Integration in Europa im 19. und 20. Jahrhundert (1984), 185-211.
Kudelić, Zlatko, 'Gospodarska problematika žumberačkoga kraja uoči drugoga svjetskog rata u Žumberačkim novinama', *Časopis za suvremenu povijest* 26, no. 1 (1994), 109-19.
Lampe, John, *Balkans into Southeastern Europe, 1914-2014: A Century of War and Transition* (London: Palgrave Macmillan, 2014).
Lazić, Željko, *Uvod u smrt: Numerus clausus 1940. godine i ograničuvanju prava Jevreja u Kraljevini Jugoslaviji* (Beograd: Službeni glasnik, 2016).
Leichter, Otto, *Zwischen Zwei Diktaturen: Österreichs Revolutionäre Sozialisten, 1934-1936* (Wien: Europa Verlag, 1968).

Littlefield, Frank, *Germany and Yugoslavia, 1933–1941: The German Conquest of Yugoslavia* (New York: Columbia University Press, 1988).
Lukač, Dušan, *Treći Rajh i zemlje jugoistočne Evrope* (Beograd: Vojnoizdavački zavod, 1982).
Lumans, Valdis, *Himmler's Auxiliaries: The Volksdeutsche Mittelstelle and the German National Minorities of Europe, 1933–1945* (Chapel Hill: University of North Carolina Press, 1993).
Macartney, Carlile Aylmer, *October Fifteenth: A History of Modern Hungary, 1929–1945*, Part I (Edinburgh: Edinburgh University Press, 1957).
Mack Smith, Denis, *Mussolini's Roman Empire* (London and New York: Longman, 1976).
Marks, Sally, 'The Myths of Reparations', *Central European History* 11, no. 3 (1978), 231–55.
Mason, Tim, 'The Primacy of Politics – Politics and Economics in National Socialist Germany', in *Nazism and the Third Reich*, ed. Henry Ashby Turner (New York: Quadrangle Books, 1972), 175–200.
Matis, Herbert, 'Wirtschaftliche Mitteleuropa-Konzeptionen in der Zwischenkriegszeit', in *Mitteleuropa-Konzeptionen in der ersten Hälfte des 20. Jahrhunderts*, ed. Richard Plaschka et al. (Wien: Österreichischen Akademie der Wissenschaften, 1995), 229–55.
Mayer, Thomas, 'Hermann Neubacher: Karriere einer Südosteuropa-Experten', in *„Mitteleuropa" und „Südosteuropa" als Planungsraum: Wirtschafts- und kulturpolitische Expertisen im Zeitalter der Weltkriege*, ed. Carola Sachse (Göttingen: Wallstein Verlag, 2010), 241–61.
Messerschmidt, Manfred, 'Außenpolitik und Kriegsvorbereitung', in *Das Deutsche Reich und der Zweite Weltkrieg* 1, *Ursachen und Voraussetzungen der deutschen Kriegspolitik*, ed. Wilhelm Deist et al. (Stuttgart: Deutsche Verlag-Anstalt, 1979), 535–701.
Meyer, Henry Cord, *Mitteleuropa in German Thought and Action, 1815–1945* (The Hague: Martinus Nijhoff, 1955).
Meyer, Henry Cord, 'Mitteleuropa in German political Geography', *Annals of the Association of American Geographers* 36, no. 3 (1946), 178–94.
Mićić, Srdjan, 'Jugoslovenska saradnja sa Telegrafen-Unionom i nemačkim novinarima, 1927–1934. godine', *Tokovi istorije* 2 (2018), 39–65.
Mićić, Srdjan, *Kraljevina Jugoslavija i Anšlus Austrije* (Beograd: Službeni glasnik, 2010).
Milak, Enes, *Italija i Jugoslavija, 1931–1937* (Beograd: ISI, 1987).
Milosavljević, Olivera, *Savremenici fašizma 1: Percepcija fašizma u beogradskoj javnosti 1933–1941* (Beograd: Helsinški odbor za ljudska prava, 2010).
Milward, Alan, 'The Reichsmark Bloc and the International Economy', in *Der 'Führerstaat', Mythos und Realität: Studien zur Struktur und Politik des Dritten Reiches*, ed. Gerhard Hirschfeld and Lothar Kettenacker (Stuttgart: Klett-Cotta, 1981), 377–413.
Mirković, Mijo, *Ekonomska struktura Jugoslavije, 1918–1941* (Zagreb: Školska knjiga, 1952).
Mitrović, Andrej, 'Die Zentralmächte, Mitteleuropa und der Balkan', in *Mitteleuropa-Konzeptionen in der Ersten Hälfte des 20. Jahrhunderts*, ed. Richard G. Plaschka, Horst Haselsteiner and Arnold Suppan (Wien: Verlag der Österreichische Akademie der Wissenschaften, 1995), 39–62.
Mitrović, Andrej, 'Ergänzungswirtschaft: The Theory of an Integrated Economic Area of the Third Reich and the Southeast Europe (1933–1941)', in *The Third Reich and Yugoslavia, 1933–1945* (Beograd: ISI, 1977), 7–45.
Mitrović, Andrej, 'Nemački privredni prostor i jugoistočna Evropa 1933', *Istorijski časopis* 21 (1974), 225–40.
Mommsen, Hans, 'Hitlers Stellung im nationalsozialistischen Herrschaftssystem', in *Der „Führerstaat". Mythos und Realität*, ed. Gerhard Hirschfeld and Lothar Kettenacker (Stuttgart: Klett-Cotta, 1981), 43–72.

Müller, Nils, 'Die Wirtschaft als „Brücke der Politik"' in *Mitteleuropa und Südosteuropa als Planungsraum: Wirtschafts- und kulturpolitische Expertisen im Zeitalter der Weltkriege*, ed. Carola Sachse (Göttingen: Wallstein Verlag, 2010), 87–114.

Murphy, David Thomas, *The Heroic Earth: Geopolitical Thought in Weimar Germany, 1918-1933* (Kent: Kent State University Press, 1997).

Neal, Larry, 'The Economics and Finance of Bilateral Clearing Agreements', *Economic History Review* 32, no. 3 (1979), 391–404.

*Nemačka obaveštajna služba u staroj Jugoslaviji* 2 (Beograd: Državni SUP FNRJ, Uprava državne bezbednosti – Treće odeljenje, 1955).

O'Brien, Phillips, *How the War Was Won: Air-Sea Power and Allied Victory in World War II* (Cambridge: Cambridge University Press, 2015).

Odić, Slavko and Komarica, Slavko, *Yugoslavia in the German Plans of Conquest* (Beograd: ISI, 1977).

Oldson, William, 'Romania and the Munich Crisis, August–September 1938', *East European Quarterly* 11, no. 2 (1977), 177–90.

Orlow, Dietrich, *The Nazis in the Balkans: A Case Study of Totalitarian Politics* (Pittsburgh: University of Pittsburgh Press, 1968).

Overy, Richard, 'Business in the *Grossraumwirtschaft*: Eastern Europe, 1938–1945', in *Enterprise in the Period of Fascism in Europe*, ed. Harold James and Jakob Tanner (Aldershot: Ashgate, 2002), 151–77.

Overy, Richard, *The Nazi Economic Recovery, 1932–1938* (Cambridge: Cambridge University Press, 1996).

Overy, Richard, *War and Economy in the Third Reich* (Oxford: Clarendon Press, 1994).

Overy, Richard, *Goering: The Iron Man* (London: Routledge and Paul, 1984).

Parker, Robert Alexander Clarke, *Chamberlain and Appeasement: British Foreign Policy and the Coming of the Second World War* (London: Macmillan, 1993).

Pavlica, Branko, 'Nemačka kao ugovorni partner Srbije i Jugoslavije, 1892–1992', *Zbornik Matice srpske za društvene nauke* 112–13 (2002), 287–318.

Pavlowitch, Stevan K., *Hitler's New Disorder: The Second World War in Yugoslavia* (Oxford: Oxford University Press, 2008).

Pavlowitch, Stevan K., 'Serbia and Yugoslavia – the relationship', *Southeast European and Black Sea Studies* 4, no. 1 (2004), 96–106.

Petrović, Nenad, *Ideologija varvarstva: fašističke i nacionalsocijalističke ideje kod intelektualaca u Beogradu, 1929–1941* (Beograd: Mostart, 2015).

Petzina, Dietmar, 'Vierjahresplan und Rüstungspolitik', in *Wirtschaft und Rüstung am Vorabend des Zweiten Weltkrieges*, ed. Friedrich Forstmeier and Hans-Erich Volkmann (Düsseldorf: Droste Verlag, 1975), 65–80.

Peukert, Detlev, *Weimar Republic: The Crisis of Classical Modernity* (New York: Hill and Wang, 1992).

Pollard, John, *Papacy in the Age of Totalitarianism, 1914–1958* (Oxford: Oxford University Press, 2014).

Preda, Gavriil, 'German Foreign Policy towards the Romanian Oil during 1938–1940', *International Journal of Social Science and Humanity* 3, no. 3 (2013), 326–329.

Presseisen, Ernst, 'Prelude to "Barbarossa": Germany and the Balkans, 1940–1941', *The Journal of Modern History* 32, no. 4 (1960), 359–70.

Radojević, Mira, 'Demokratska stranka o državnom preuredjenju Kraljevine Jugoslavije, 1935-1941', *Istorija 20. Veka* 9 (1991), 37–63.

Ranky, György, *Economy and Foreign Policy: The Struggle of the Great Powers for Hegemony in the Danube Valley, 1919–1939* (New York: Columbia University Press, 1983).

Raupach, Hans, 'The Impact of the Great Depression on Eastern Europe', *Journal of Contemporary History* 4, no. 4, The Great Depression (1969), 75–86.
Recker, Marie-Luise, 'Die Außenpolitik des Auswärtigen Amts', in *Das Auswärtige Amt in der NS-Diktatur*, ed. Johannes Hürter and Michael Mayer (Oldenburg: De Gruyter, 2014), 79–91.
Reul, Nathaniel, 'Resurrection and Revolution. Austro-Catholicism, German Nationalism and National Socialism in Slovenia, 1933-1941', *Österreichische Zeitschrift für Geschichtswissenschaften* 28, no. 1 (2017), 229–44.
Ristanović, Rade, 'Beogradska periodična štampa o početku Drugog svetskog rata', *Tokovi istorije* 2 (2015), 57–71.
Ristović, Milan, 'Izmedju „žrtve u krvi" i najvažnijeg „savezničkog doprinosa": Treći rajh i pitanje jugoistočnoevropske nafte u Drugom svetskom ratu', *Tokovi istorije* 1 (2017), 11–46.
Ristović, Milan, 'The Jews of Serbia (1804-1918): From Princely Protection to Formal Emancipation', in *The Jews and the Nation States of Southeastern Europe from the 19th Century to the Great Depression: Combining Viewpoints on a Controversial Story*, ed. Tullia Catalan (Newcastle upon Tyne: Cambridge Scholars Publishing, 2016), 23–50.
Ristović, Milan, 'Jews in Serbia during World War Two: Between the "Final Solution of the Jewish Question" and "the Righteous among Nations"', in *Righteous among the Nations – Serbia*, ed. Milan Fogel, Milan Ristović and Milan Koljanin (Beograd: JOZ, 2010), 260–85.
Ristović, Milan, 'Weder Souveränität noch Industrialisierung', in *"Mitteleuropa" und "Südosteuropa" als Planungsraum: Wirtschafts- und kulturpolitische Expertisen im Zeitalter der Weltkriege*, ed. Carola Sachse (Göttingen: Wallstein, 2010), 219–37.
Ristović, Milan, 'Rural Anti-Utopia in the Ideology of Serbian Collaborationists in the Second World War', *European Review of History* 15, no. 2 (2008), 179–92.
Ristović, Milan, *Nemački novi poredak i jugoistočna Evropa, 1940/4–1944/45* (Beograd: Službeni glasnik, 2005).
Ristović, Milan, 'Rat, modernizacija i industrijalizacija Jugoistočne Evrope: Nemački stavovi o promenama društvene i privredne strukture "dopunskog privrednog prostora", 1940-1943', in *Srbija u modernizacijskim procesima XX veka*, ed. Latinka Perović, Marija Obradović and Dubravka Stojanović (Beograd: INIS, 1994), 261–9.
Ristović, Milan, 'Delovanje nemačke organizacije za zaštitu privrednih objekata (Werkschutz) u Jugoslaviji 1940', *Vojnoistorijski glasnik* 1 (1986), 183–203.
Ritschl, Albrecht, 'Nazi Economic Imperialism and the Exploitation of the Small: Evidence from Germany's Secret Foreign Exchange Balances, 1938-1940', *The Economic History Review*, New Series 54, no. 2 (2001), 324–45.
Schausberger, Norbert, 'Der Anschluß', in *Osterreich 1918-1938: Geschichte der Ersten Republik* 1, ed. Erika Weinzierl and Kurt Skalnik (Graz: Styria, 1983), 517–52.
Schmidt, Rainer, *Die Außenpolitik des Dritten Reiches* (Stuttgart: Klett-Cotta, 2002).
Schönfeld, Roland, 'Deutsche Rohstoffsicherungspolitik in Jugoslawien 1933-1944', *Vierteljahreshefte für Zeitgeschichte* 24, no. 3 (1976), 215–58.
Schröder, Hans-Jürgen, 'Südosteuropa als "Informal Empire" NS-Deutschlands. Das Beispiel Jugoslawien 1933-1939', in *The Third Reich and Yugoslavia, 1933-1945* (Beograd: ISI, 1977), 240–258.
Schröder, Hans-Jürgen, 'Der Aufbau der deutschen Hegemonialstellung in Südosteuropa, 1933-1936', in *Hitler, Deutschland und die Mächte: Materialien zur Aussenpolitik des Dritten Reiches*, ed. Manfred Funke (Düsseldorf: Droste Verlag, 1976a), 757–73.

Schröder, Hans-Jürgen, 'Deutsche Südosteuropapolitik 1929-1936: Zur Kontinuität deutscher Außenpolitik in der Weltwirtschaftskrise', *Geschichte und Gesellschaft* 2, no. 1, Außenwirtschaft und Außenpolitik im 'Dritten Reich' (1976b), 5-32.

Schröter, Harm, 'Siemens and Central and South-East Europe between the Two World Wars', in *International Business and Central Europe, 1918-1939*, ed. Alice Teichova and Philip Leonard Cottrell (Leicester: Leicester University Press, 1983), 173-92.

Schröter, Verena, 'The IG Farben AG in Central and South-East Europe, 1926-38', in *International Business and Central Europe, 1918-1939*, ed. Alice Teichova and Philip Leonard Cottrell (Leicester: Leicester University Press, 1983), 139-72.

Schumann, Wolfgang, 'Aspekte und Hintergründe der Handels- und Wirtschaftspolitik Hitlerdeutschlands gegenüber Jugoslawien', in *The Third Reich and Yugoslavia, 1933-1945* (Beograd: ISI, 1977), 221-39.

Sekelj, Laslo, 'Antisemitizam u Jugoslaviji, 1918-1945', *Revija za sociologiju* 11, no. 3-4 (1981), 179-89.

Seton-Watson, Christopher, 'The Anglo-Italian Gentleman's Agreement of January 1937 and Its Aftermath', in *The Fascist Challenge and the Policy of Appeasement*, ed. Wolfgang Mommsen and Lothar Kettenacker (London: George Allen and Unwin, 1983), 267-82.

Shores, Christopher, Cull, Brian and Malizia, Nicola, *Air War for Yugoslavia, Greece and Crete, 1940-1941* (London: Grub Street, 1987).

Simpson, Amos, *Hjalmar Schacht in Perspective* (The Hague: Mouton, 1969).

Spaulding, Robert Mark, *Osthandel und Ostpolitik: German Foreign Trade Policies in Eastern Europe from Bismarck to Adenauer* (Oxford: Berghahn Books, 1997).

Stackelberg, Roderick, *Hitler's Germany: Origins, Interpretations, Legacies* (London: Routledge, 1999).

Stambrook, Fred, 'A British Proposal for the Danubian States: The Customs Union Project of 1932', *The Slavonic and East European Review* 42, no. 98 (1963), 64-88.

Stanić, Veljko, '"Unutrašnji autsajder": Milan Ćurčin, Nova Evropa i Drugi svetski rat', in *Intelektualci i rat, 1939-1947: Zbornik radova s medjunarodnog skupa Desničini susreti 2011*, ed. Drago Roksandić et al. (Zagreb: Plejada, 2012), 299-308.

Stegmann, Dirk, '"Mitteleuropa", 1925-1934: Zum Problem der Kontinuität deutscher Außenhandelspolitik von Stresemann bis Hitler', in *Autarkie und Grossraumwirtschaft in Deutschland 1930-1939: aussenwirtschaftspolitische Konzeptionen zwischen Wirtschaftskrise und Zweitem Weltkrieg*, ed. Eckart Teichert (München: Oldenbourg, 1984), 203-21.

Steiner, Zara, *The Triumph of the Dark: European international history, 1933-1939* (Oxford: Oxford University Press, 2013).

Stojkov, Todor, 'Čehoslovačko-francuska aktivnost protiv M. Stojadinovića (1936-1938)', *Časopis za suvremenu povijest* 1 (1979), 41-66.

Strath, Bo, 'Mitteleuropa from List to Naumann', *European Journal of Social Theory* 11, no. 2 (2008), 171-83.

Sundhaussen, Holm, *Geschichte Jugoslawiens* (Stuttgart: Verlag W. Kohlhammer, 1982).

Sundhaussen, Holm, 'Südosteuropa in der Nationalsozialistischen Kriegswirtschaft am Beispiel des "Unabhängigen Staates Kroatien"', *Südost-Forschungen* 32 (1973), 233-266.

Suppan, Arnold, *Jugoslawien und Österreich, 1918-1938: bilaterale Aussenpolitik im europäischen Umfeld* (Wien: Verlag für Geschichte und Politik, 1996).

Šadek, Vladimir, 'Logor Janka-puszta i razvoj ustaške organizacije u Podravini do 1934', *Podravina* 11, no. 21 (2012), 47-56.

Štiblar, Franjo, 'The Rise and Fall of Yugoslavia: An Economic History View', in *Central Europe in the Twentieth Century*, ed. Alice Teichova (Aldershot: Ashgate, 1997), 61–82.
Teichova, Alice, 'Eastern Europe in Transition: Economic Development during the Interwar and Postwar Period', in *Central Europe in the Twentieth Century: An Economic History Perspective*, ed. Alice Teichova (Aldershot: Ashgate, 1997), 5–21.
Teichova, Alice, *Kleinstaaten im Spannungsfeld der Grossmächte: Wirtschaft und Politik in Mittel- und Südosteuropa in der Zwischenkriegszeit* (München: Oldenbourg, 1988).
Teichova, Alice, 'Besonderheit in Strukturwandel der mittelost- und südosteuropäischen Industrie in den Zwischenkriegszeit', in *Industrielle Gesellschaft und politisches System: Beiträge zur politischen Sozialgeschichte*, ed. Dirk Stegmann, Bernd Jürgen Wendt and Peter-Christian Witt (Bonn: Verlag Neue Gesselschaft, 1978), 131–50.
Terzić, Velimir, *Slom Kraljevine Jugoslavije 1941: uzroci i posledice poraza* (Beograd: Narodna knjiga, 1982).
Terzić, Velimir, *Jugoslavija u Aprilskom ratu 1941* (Titograd: Grafički zavod, 1963).
Tešić, Dragan, 'Vojska Kraljevine Jugoslavije i nacionalne manjine u godinama uoči Aprilskog rata', *Istorija 20. veka* 14, no. 2 (1996), 75–91.
Tilkovszky, Lorant, 'The Late Interwar Years and World War II', in *History of Hungary*, ed. Peter Sugar et al. (London and New York: I.B. Tauris, 1990), 339–55.
Tomasevich, Jozo, *Peasants, Politics and Economic Change in Yugoslavia* (Stanford: Stanford University Press, 1955).
Tooze, Adam, *The Wages of Destruction: Making and Breaking of the Nazi Economy* (London: Penguin, 2007).
Toprani, Anand, *Oil and the Great Powers: Britain and Germany, 1914–1945* (Oxford: Oxford University Press, 2019).
Treue, Wilhelm, 'Das Dritte Reich und die Westmächte auf dem Balkan', *Vierteljahrshefte für Zeitgeschichte* 1, no. 1 (1953), 45–64.
Vinaver, Vuk, *Svetska ekonomska kriza u Podunavlju i nemački prodor, 1929–1935* (Beograd: ISI, 1987).
Vinaver, Vuk, *Jugoslavija i Francuska izmedju dva svetska rata* (Beograd: ISI, 1985).
Vinaver, Vuk, '"Austrijsko pitanje" i velika preorijentacija Kralja Aleksandra prema Nemačkoj, 1927–1932', *Istorija 20. veka* 3 (1977a), 7–31.
Vinaver, Vuk, 'Početak nemačke orijentacije stare Jugoslavije', *Istorijski zapisi* 34, no. 3–4 (1977b), 785–800.
Vinaver, Vuk, *Jugoslavija i Madjarska, 1933–1941* (Beograd: Narodna knjiga, 1976).
Vogel, Detlef, 'Das Eingreifen Deutschlands auf dem Balkan', in *Das Deutsche Reich und der Zweite Weltkrieg* 3, ed. Gerhard Schreiber, Bernd Stegemann and Detlef Vogel (Stuttgart: Deutsche Verlags-Anstalt, 1984), 415–511.
Volkmann, Hans-Erich, 'Außenhandel und Aufrüstung in Deutschland, 1933–1939', in *Ökonomie und Expansion: Grundzuge der NS-Wirtschaftspolitik*, ed. Hans-Erich Volkmann and Bernhard Chiari (München: Oldenbourg, 2003), 103–44.
Volkmann, Hans-Erich, 'Die NS-Wirtschaft in Vorbereitung des Krieges', in *Das Deutsche Reich und der zweite Weltkrieg* 1, *Ursachen und Voraussetzungen der deutschen Kriegspolitik*, ed. Wilhelm Deist et al. (Stuttgart: Deutsche Verlags-Anstalt, 1979), 177–370.
Volkmann, Hans-Erich, 'Politik, Wirtschaft und Aufrüstung unter dem Nationalsozialismus', in *Hitler, Deutschland und die Mächte: Materialien zur Aussenpolitik des Dritten Reiches*, ed. Manfred Funke (Düsseldorf: Droste Verlag, 1976), 269–91.

Vučo, Nikola, *Agrarna kriza u Jugoslaviji, 1930–1934* (Beograd: Prosveta, 1968).
Vulesica, Marija, 'Antisemitismus im ersten Jugoslawien 1918 bis 1941', *Jahrbuch für Antisemitismusforschung* 17 (2008), 131–52.
Wandycz, Piotr, *The Twilight of French Eastern Alliances, 1926–1936* (Princeton: Princeton University Press, 1988).
Wandycz, Piotr, 'The Little Entente: Sixty Years Later', *Slavonic and East European Review* 59, no. 4 (1981), 548–64.
Weinberg, Gerhard, *A World at Arms: A Global History of the World War II* (Cambridge: Cambridge University Press, 1995).
Weinberg, Gerhard, *The Foreign Policy of Hitler's Germany: Diplomatic Revolution in Europe, 1933–1936* (Chicago: Chicago University Press, 1970).
Weinberg, Gerhard, *Germany and the Soviet Union, 1939–1941* (Leiden: E. J. Brill, 1954).
Wendt, Bernd Jürgen, 'Südosteuropa in der nationalistischen Großraumwirtschaft: eine Antwort auf Alan S. Milward', in *Der 'Führerstaat', Mythos und Realität: Studien zur Struktur und Politik des Dritten Reiches*, ed. Gerhard Hirschfeld and Lothar Kettenacker (Stuttgart: Klett-Cotta, 1981), 414–28.
Wendt, Bernd Jürgen, 'England und der Deutsche "Drang nach Südosten". Kapitalbeziehungen und Warenverkehr in Südosteuropa zwischen den Weltkriegen', in *Deutschland in der Weltpolitik des 19. und 20. Jahrhunderts*, ed. Fritz Fischer et al. (Düsseldorf: Bertelsmann Universitätsverlag, 1973), 483–512.
Whyte, Max, 'The Uses and Abuses of Nietzsche in the Third Reich: Alfred Baeumler's "Heroic Realism"', *The Journal of Contemporary History* 42, no. 2 (2008), 171–94.
Wien, Markus, *Markt und Modernisierung: deutsch-bulgarische Wirtschaftsbeziehungen 1918–1944 in ihren konzeptionellen Grundlagen* (München: Oldenbourg, 2007).
Williams, Maurice, 'Aid, Assistance and Advice: German Nazis and the Austrian Hilfswerk', *Central European History* 14, no. 3 (1981), 230–42.
Winchester, Betty Jo, 'Hungary and the "Third Europe" in 1938', *Slavic Review* 32, no. 4 (1973), 741–56.
Wistrich, Robert, *Hitler and the Holocaust: How and Why the Holocaust Happened* (London: Phoenix, 2002).
Wüscht, Johann, *Jugoslawien und das Dritte Reich: eine dokumentierte Geschichte der deutsch-jugoslawischen Beziehungen von 1933 bis 1945* (Stuttgart: Seewald, 1969).
Zakić, Mirna, *Ethnic Germans and National Socialism in Yugoslavia in World War II* (Cambridge: Cambridge University Press, 2017).
Zlodi, Zdravka, 'Ideja Frana Ilešiča o uređenju srednjo-istočne Europe iz 1930ih godina', *Časopis za suvremenu povijest* 36, no. 3 (2004), 981–95.
Zotschew, Theodor, 'Die Industrialisierung Südosteuropa', *Südosteuropa – Jahrbuch* 1 (1957), 141–56.
Životić, Aleksandar, 'Slovenci u vojnoj diplomatiji Kraljevine Jugoslavije', *Zgodovinski časopis* 73, no. 1–2 (2019), 138–56.
Žutić, Nikola, 'Niko Bartulović i slovenački Jugoslaveni, 1918–1935', *Istorija 20. veka* 1 (2014), 51–76.

## Unpublished PhD theses

Denda, Dalibor, 'Jugoslovenska vojska i Treći Rajh, 1933–1941' (unpublished PhD diss., University of Belgrade, 2016).
Nikolić, Irina Aleksandra, 'Anglo-Yugoslav Relations, 1938–1941' (unpublished PhD diss., University of Cambridge, 2001).

# Index

*Abwehr* 155
Abyssinian Crisis 1, 20, 29–30, 36, 54, 60–1, 97–100, 112
Aćimović, Milan 155
Adriatic 64, 66, 72, 178, 180, 182
AEG 103
Aegean Sea 69, 177, 180–1
*Agraria* 144
Albala, David 132
Albania, also Albanians 10, 20, 61, 71–2, 99, 133, 143, 171, 173, 178, 185, 188
Alexander I, King of Yugoslavia 20–1, 23–8, 32, 66, 131, 137–8, 144, 186
Alfieri, Dino 173
Altgayer, Branimir 145–6
Andres, Ivan 154
Andrić, Ivo 73–4, 95, 151
Anglo-Turkish Agreement (1939) 73
Ankara 66, 83, 172
Anschluss 12, 20–3, 25, 29, 64–8, 70, 86–7, 89–90, 96, 114, 123, 133, 145, 158, 191
Antić, Milan 175, 187
Anti-Comintern Pact 59, 70, 72, 74, 167
antisemitism 127–32, 134–6, 141, 147–8, 167
antimon 103
Antonescu, Ion 171, 173
April War (1941) 1, 168
Argentina 183
Arrow Cross Party 136
Artuković, Andrija 138
Athens 24, 57, 60, 81, 171, 182
*Auslands-organisation der NSDAP* 14
*Aussenpolitisches Amt der NSDAP*, also Foreign Policy Office 14, 24, 86, 138
Austria 2, 9, 19–26, 28–32, 36–7, 41, 43, 59, 62, 64–7, 74, 77, 84, 86–7, 89, 98–9, 101–2, 104, 116, 129, 133, 142–3, 145, 158, 172, 191
Austro-Hungary, also Habsburg Empire 6, 22, 99, 129–130, 137, 144, 158, 177

Austro-Turkish War (1716–1718) 142
Awender, Jakob 145
Axis powers, also Rome-Berlin 3, 59, 62, 69, 72–4, 92, 158, 167, 168–72, 174–6, 178–9, 183–5

Bajkić, Vladimir 122
Balkan Entente 19, 24, 27–9, 60, 62, 66, 69, 73, 81, 83, 170
Balkans 4, 9–12, 21–3, 32–3, 60, 62, 64, 70, 77, 83, 87, 89, 91, 94, 97, 104, 115, 123, 125, 127–9, 133, 140, 150, 157, 167, 169–74, 176–81, 186, 191
Baltic Sea, also Baltic states 10, 127, 142
Balugdžić, Živojin 21, 26, 39, 51
Banac, Božo 141
Banovina, Croatian province 138, 140, 146, 176
Bárdossy, László de Bárdos 184
Barthou, Louis 25, 27
Basel 39
Bauer, Antun 130
Beck, Józef 69
Belgium, also Belgium-Luxembourg Economic Union 42, 59, 83–4, 162
Belgrade 4, 6, 19–26, 28–9, 31–2, 35–6, 41, 43, 46–7, 50, 53–5, 57–8, 60–7, 69–74, 77, 79, 81–96, 98–100, 102, 106, 108, 111–12, 124–5, 127, 129, 131, 137, 140–3, 145, 150–1, 154–61, 163, 169, 171–4, 178, 180, 182–6, 189, 191–2
Belin, Ivo 80, 82–4, 88, 93, 123–4, 156–7
Benelux 105
Beneš, Edvard 60, 62–3
Berchtesgaden, also Berghof 61, 66, 74, 174, 177–80, 182
Berlin 2–3, 7, 13, 16, 19–31, 37, 39, 41–3, 46, 48–55, 58, 61–74, 79–80, 82, 85–96, 103–5, 107–8, 111, 115, 122–5, 127–8,

133, 138–40, 142, 144, 146, 150–151, 154, 156, 158, 161–4, 169–75, 177, 180, 182, 184, 188, 191–2, 193
Berlin Summer Olympics (1936) 77, 141
Bessarabia 170
Bićanić, Rudolf 121–2
Bismarck, Otto von 9
Bitolj 174, 189
Black Sea 180
Bled 20, 29, 68, 73
Blomberg, Werner von 48, 78
Bor copper mine 103, 152, 154
Boris III, King of Bulgaria 32, 60, 170, 172
Bosnia and Herzegovina 104, 106, 108, 130–1, 137, 142–2, 158–9, 181, 188
Bratislava 60
Brauchitsch, Walther von 161
Brazil 183
Breslau 115
Bristol Blenheim 91, 94, 150
Brugère, Raymond 168
Brüning, Heinrich 15, 21–2, 42
Bucharest 28, 32, 36, 46–7, 53, 60, 62–3, 69, 164, 170–1, 173
Budapest 24, 46, 57, 62–3, 67–8, 70, 72, 74, 164, 170
Budisavljević, Srdjan 141, 184
Bukovina 170
Bulgaria 10, 19, 28, 60–2, 69, 73–4, 90, 111, 129, 150, 162, 164, 170–2, 174, 177–82, 185, 188–9
Bülow, Bernhard Wilhelm von 39
Burgenland 67

Campbell, Ronald Hugh 29, 57, 64–5, 75, 85, 87, 89
Campbell, Ronald Ian 182
Carinthia 24–5
Carol II, King of Romania 170
Catholic Church 65, 130, 132, 136–8
Central Europe, also East-Central Europe 9–10, 12, 20–4, 26–7, 35–7, 41, 49–50, 54, 59, 61, 69–70, 86, 97, 115–16, 123, 128, 133
Četniks 169
Chamberlain, Neville 66
Chautemps, Camille 66
Churchill, Winston 74, 182

Ciano, Galeazzo 4, 61–2, 66–7, 69–70, 74, 170–1, 174–5
Cincar-Marković, Aleksandar 61, 70–4, 93, 157, 169, 177–8, 181, 182–4
clearing 2, 5, 35, 40–2, 44, 47, 49–58, 80–4, 86–9, 90–1, 98, 100, 105–6, 108, 122, 153–4, 161–2
Clodius, Karl 49, 82, 92, 156–7
collective security 1, 14, 29, 32, 62, 74
Cologne 87, 90, 93–4, 108, 120, 156, 158
Constantinople 172
Craiova 171
Creditanstalt, also affair, Wiener Bankverein 104, 116
Crete 182
Crnić, Ivan 120
Crnjanski, Miloš 135
Croatia, Croats 6, 20, 23–4, 27, 61–5, 70–1, 92–3, 102, 106, 121, 123, 129–32, 134–9, 140–3, 146, 148, 155, 158, 171, 175–6, 185–7
Csáky, István 185
Čubrilović, Branko 141, 184
Curtius, Julius 21
Cvetković, Dragiša 70–1, 93–4, 132, 138, 140–2, 146, 157, 174–5, 179–81, 183–8
Cvetković-Maček Agreement (1939) 138, 159, 175–6, 185
Czechoslovakia, also Bohemia 19, 28, 30, 36, 41, 46–7, 54, 56–7, 59–60, 62–5, 67–72, 75, 80, 83, 87, 91, 94, 99, 101–2, 104, 108, 116, 123, 133, 150, 153, 157, 166, 184

Dalmatia 20, 61, 131, 134, 169, 172, 178
Danube Security Pact (1935) 28–30
Darányi, Kálmán 63
Dardanelles 178
Darré, Richard Walther 45, 48, 78, 117
Daruvar brewery 133
Dawes plan (1924) 38, 115
Demajo, Samuilo 129
Denmark 84, 162
Deutsche Bank 104, 116
Dežman, Milivoj 141
Diederich, Clemens 64–5
Dienststelle Ribbentrop 14
Dill, John 188

Dimitrijević, Mića 129
Directive 25, also Operation 189
Djordjević, Vladimir 123–4
Djuričić, Vojin 93–4, 158
Dollfuss, Engelbert 23, 25–6
Donovan, William 182
Dornier 91
*Drang nach Osten, -Südosten* 23, 118, 121
Dresden 80–2, 115
Dresdner Bank 116
Dubrovnik 24, 84–5, 111, 133
Dufour von Feronce, Albert 23, 43, 52
Duisberg, Carl 116

Eastern Europe 2, 18–19, 22, 35, 37, 122, 124, 128
Eastern Locarno 25
Eden, Anthony 31, 66, 182
Edessa 189
Epirus 171
Erbsland, Kurt 11
*Ergänzungswirtschaft*, also Complementary economies 10, 18, 121, 126, 164
*Erneuerungsbewegung*, also Renewers 139, 145
*Erzgesellschaft zur Erschliessung von Nichteisenmetallen* 103

Faber du Faur, Moritz von 30
Fabritius, Fritz 145
Feder, Gottfried 47
Filov, Bogdan 170
Finland 36, 168, 173, 177
First World War, also Great War 10, 21–2, 39, 123, 130, 176, 192
Flandin, Pierre-Étienne 31
Fotić, Konstantin 4, 178, 183–4
Four-Power Pact (1933) 23
Four-Year Plan 17–18, 77, 79, 81–2, 85–6, 89, 92–3, 191
France 2, 3, 11–13, 19–21, 23, 25–33, 36–8, 40, 42–3, 59–62, 64–6, 68, 70, 72, 74–5, 83–4, 89–91, 94, 101–3, 105, 110, 114–15, 125, 133, 136, 140, 142, 146, 148–9, 152–8, 160–1, 167–8, 172–4, 192
Franco, Francisco 173
Frangeš, Oto 37
Frank, Ivica 137

Frank, Josip 137
Funk, Walther 48, 86, 92, 103, 117, 158, 163

Galli, Carlo 20
Gamelin, Maurice Gustave 74
Gavrilo, Serbian Patriarch 141
Gavrilović, Milan 168, 179
Gemünd, Karl 157
Geneva 23, 31, 38
German-Austrian customs union 22, 36, 116
German-Austrian Gentleman's Agreement (1936) 2, 31, 62–3, 65
German-British Naval Agreement (1935) 30
German Chamber of Commerce for Yugoslavia 103, 164
German-Hungarian Trade Agreement (1934) 24, 43–4
German-Polish Non-Aggression Pact (1934) 25–26
German reparations 2
German soft power 3
German-Yugoslav Mixed Committee 44–5, 51, 54–5, 80, 82, 84, 87–8, 90, 93, 100, 105, 109–11, 155, 157–8, 161–3
German-Yugoslav Society 30
German-Yugoslav Trade Agreement (1927) 40–3, 50
German-Yugoslav Trade Agreement (1934) 2, 13, 15, 25, 35, 44, 48, 50, 58, 110, 158, 163–4, 191
*Gesellschaft für Erforschung ausländische Erzvorkommen* (GEaE) 103–104
Gestapo 24, 139, 155, 175
*Gleichschaltung* 13
Goebbels, Joseph 14, 30, 70, 72
Golddiskontbank 53, 81–2
Gömbös, Gyula 23, 32
Göring, Hermann 14, 16, 18, 24–5, 27, 29, 53, 61, 64, 67–8, 78, 80–1, 85–6, 91–5, 102–4, 117, 139, 163
Gort, John 74
Gothein, Georg 116
Grassl, Georg 144
Graz 67, 159
Grdjić, Gojko 45, 124

Great Britain, also England 2, 12, 20, 28–33, 36, 55, 59–62, 69–70, 72–4, 83–4, 87–91, 99–101, 110, 114–15, 119, 141, 149–50, 152, 153–7, 160–2, 164, 167–9, 171–5, 177–83, 185–6, 188–9
Great Depression 2, 41–2, 51, 58, 97, 101, 105, 113, 116, 191
Greece 10, 19, 42, 62, 69, 71–3, 125, 129, 167, 170–1, 173–4, 176–7, 179–81, 183, 185, 187–9
Gregorić, Danilo 135, 140, 167, 174–5
Grol, Milan 141
Gross, Hermann 11
*Grosswirtschaftsraum*, also Greater economic area 10, 15–16, 119, 122–4, 126, 192

Habsburgs, also Habsburg restoration 2, 19–20, 24, 31–2, 59–60, 63, 65–6, 129, 191
Hague conference (1929) 38
Hahn, Max 116–18, 120
Halder, Franz 4, 161, 181
Halifax, Edward Wood 74, 150
Halwax, Gustav 147
Hantos, Elemér 115
Hassell, Ulrich von 13, 24, 61–2, 185
Haushofer, Karl 120, 144
Havas 21
Hawker Hurricane 92, 150
Heeren, Viktor von 25–30, 60–1, 63–6, 68, 71–4, 84, 92–5, 108, 139, 141, 150–1, 157–8, 161, 169, 173, 175, 177–8, 180–4, 186–9
Heinrichsbauer, August 117
Helfferich, Karl 120
Helm, Hans 155
Hencke, Andor 14
Henlein, Konrad 67
Hess, Rudolf 48
Hess, Walther 51, 54, 108
Heydrich, Reinhard 144
Himmler, Heinrich 14, 142, 144
Hirtenberg affair 22
Hitler, Adolf, also Führer 9, 13–20, 22–3, 25–6, 31–2, 35, 47–50, 53, 59, 61–9, 72–4, 77–9, 85, 90, 92, 94–5, 117–18, 120, 127–8, 133, 135–6, 138–9, 141, 147, 151, 161, 163, 167–81, 183–9, 192

Hodža, Milan 54
Hoffmann, Walter 10–11
Hoover memorandum (1931) 39, 41
Hugenberg, Alfred 43, 117
Hungary 2, 9–10, 13, 19–20, 22–4, 28, 30, 36–7, 40, 43–4, 46, 49, 60–70, 72, 74, 84, 98–9, 101–2, 116, 128, 131, 137, 142–3, 145, 147, 163–4, 170–2, 174, 177–8, 184–5, 193

IG Farben 17, 103, 116, 118
Ilešič, Fran 36
Ilgner, Max 118–19
Imrédy, Béla 70
import controls in Yugoslavia 1, 52, 54–6, 58, 88, 100, 109, 125, 192
Iron Guard 170
Istria 61
Italy 1, 2, 11, 13, 19–25, 27–33, 37, 42–4, 54, 56, 59–64, 66–7, 69–74, 83–4, 88, 91–2, 95, 97–100, 102, 114, 129, 134, 137–8, 151, 158, 161, 163–4, 168–82, 184–5, 187–8, 191
Ivanjica 103
Ivanović, Ivan "Vane" 141

Jäckh, Ernst 120
Jankapuszta 137
Janko, Josef "Sepp" 146–7
Janković, Djura 141
Janković, Radivoje 188
Japan 11, 174, 184, 186
Jeftić, Radovan 156
Jelić, Branimir 139
Jevtić, Bogoljub 24, 30
Jews 26, 127–33, 136, 138, 140–2, 147–8, 167
Jovanović, Dragomir "Dragi" 155
Jovanović, Slobodan 187
Jugohrom 103
Jugomontan 103
Jugopetrol 102
Jukić, Ilija 187

Kalafatović, Danilo 189
Kánya, Kálmán 63–4, 69–70
Karl I of Habsburg 137
Keks, Johann 144, 146
Keppler, Wilhelm 48

Knežević, Radoje 186
Konstantinović, Mihajlo 4, 140, 179, 182–4, 186
Koch, Erich 81, 91
Köpke, Gerhard 24
Korkut, Derviš 129
Korošec, Anton 21, 130–1, 140–2, 187
Kosić, Petar 182
Kosier, Ljubomir 123
Kraft, Stefan 144
Krakov, Stanislav 140
Kramer, Albert 41
Krauch, Carl 17
Kraus, Karl 155
Krek, Janez Evangelist 130
Krofta, Kamil 67
Krupp 92, 103, 105, 116–17
Kujundžić, Mihailo 129
Kulovec, Franc 184
Kulturbund 26, 144–7
Kumanovo 141
Kyoseivanov, Georgi 60, 74

Lamer, Mirko 122
*Landbund* 40
Landfried, Friedrich, also Landfried protocol 151, 155, 161, 163
Lane, Arthur Bliss 66, 182, 185–6, 188
Langnam-Verein 17, 116
Lausanne conference (1932) 39
Laval, Pierre 27
Lazarević, Milan 42–3, 156
League of Nations 1, 14, 21, 23, 27–9, 32, 36, 56, 60, 63, 73–4, 88, 98–9, 115, 167, 170
*Lebensraum*, also living space 14–16, 119–20, 127, 168
Leipzig 11, 108, 115
Leskovac 107
Letica, Dušan 56, 91
Levi, Juda 129
Lichtenberger, Jakob 145
Lika Uprising (1932) 138
Lisanski rudnici 103
List, Friedrich 9
List, Wilhelm 180, 186
Little Entente 13, 19–20, 23–4, 27–31, 43–4, 46–7, 59–65, 67–8, 81, 117
Ljotić, Dimitrije 135–6, 141
Locarno Treaty (1925) 21, 115

London 4, 29, 32, 37, 39, 65–6, 69, 73–4, 89, 150, 154–5, 168, 176, 178, 188
Lörch, Walter 119–20
Lorenz, Werner 144
Lorković, Mladen 139
Lovčević, Jovan 83, 124
Loznica 103
Lozovac, aluminium plant 106, 114, 155
Luftwaffe 173

Macedonia 141, 169, 174, 180
Maček, Vladko 4, 65, 71–2, 132, 138, 140, 146, 175–6, 182–5, 187
*Machtergreifung*, the Nazi seizure of power (1933) 12, 19, 48, 58, 117, 131, 133, 144
Maleš Branimir 135
Maribor 67, 73
Marić, Ljubomir 91
Marita 177, 180, 186
Marković, Edo 123
Marseilles assassination 27–8, 137–9
Masonry 140, 142, 167, 175
Matsuoka, Yosuke 184
Maurras, Charles 136
Mediterranean 10, 29, 31, 59, 61–2, 73, 171, 173
*Mein Kampf* 15
Meinl, Julius 115
Messerschmitt 95, 150–1
Metaxas, Ioannis 171, 179
Mihailović, Jovan 123
Milan 59
Military coup of 27 March 1941 3, 27, 187–8
Mirković, Borivoje 184
*Mitteleuropa* 9–10, 15, 21–2, 37, 120
Mojić, Milorad 132
Molotov, Vyacheslav Mikhailovich 170, 177, 180
Montania 103
Montenegro 6, 24
Moscow 30, 63, 168, 170, 172–3, 178–80, 188
Munich, also Munich conference 3, 47–8, 52, 54, 69–70, 88–91, 109–11, 133, 147, 184
Mussolini, Benito, also Duce 23, 25, 30–1, 60–3, 69, 74, 138, 171, 180–1, 184
*Mitteleuropäischer Wirtschaftstag* (MWT) 102–104, 115–20, 160, 173, 177–179

Naumann, Friedrich 9–10
Nazis, also National Socialism, NSDAP 1, 3, 5, 9, 12, 14–17, 19, 24–26, 28, 47–48, 63, 65, 97, 117–118, 127–129, 131, 133–134, 136, 138–139, 143, 145–148, 166, 173, 175, 185, 191–193
Nedić, Milan 95, 135, 140, 151, 174
Netherlands 58, 84, 161–162
Neubacher, Hermann 11, 104, 186
Neuhausen, Franz 86, 92–93, 103, 150, 155–156
Neumann, Erich 93, 165
Neurath, Konstantin von 12, 14–15, 26, 46, 48, 63
neutrality 2–3, 19, 74, 141, 151, 153, 168–169, 181, 183, 185, 187–188
New Plan 49–50, 77–79, 118, 191
New York Stock Exchange Crash 36
Nietzsche, Friedrich 120
Ninčić, Momčilo 21, 188
Niš 133, 189
Norway 162
Novi Sad 108, 143–144
*numerus clausus* 140
Nuremberg 145

Obradović, Sava 93, 156
Operation Barbarossa 188
Orjuna 134
Ottawa Conference (1932) 119, 126

Pact of Steel (1939) 72
Palestine 130, 133
Papen, Franz von 40, 43
Paris 27, 30–32, 37, 62–66, 69, 74–75, 89, 168
*Partei der Deutschen*, Party of the Germans in Yugoslavia 144
Pašić, Radomir 102–103
Pavelić, Ante 137–139
Peace treaties (Trianon, Saint Germain, Neuilly) 23, 28, 36
Perišić, Milisav 182–183
Pešić, Petar 74, 175, 181
Pétain, Philippe 103, 173
Peter II, King of Yugoslavia 175, 182, 188–189
Petrescu-Comnen, Nicolae 67–69
Phips, Eric 26
Pietzsch, Albert 48

Pilja, Milivoje 42, 51, 54, 80–81, 84–85, 111, 151, 156–157
Plotnikov, Viktor 169
Poland 26, 66, 69–70, 72, 74, 83, 128, 131, 142, 147, 161
Posse, Hans Ernst 15
Prague 27, 30, 46–47, 56, 60, 62–63, 68–69, 75, 81, 87, 91
Pribićević, Adam 141
Prince Paul of Yugoslavia, also Prince Regent 27, 30, 63, 65, 70–5, 92, 114, 132, 141, 157, 169, 173–176, 179–187, 189
Prizad 44, 123
Protectorate of Bohemia and Moravia 87, 90, 101, 114, 142, 153, 157
Prussia 14
Purić, Božidar 23, 25, 28–29, 31

Radić, Stjepan 130, 137
Radosavljević, Milan 52–53, 56, 156
RAF 176
Ratzel, Friedrich 120
Red Army 179
Reichsbank 7, 15, 41–42, 48–49, 81–82
Reichstag 13–14
Reichsverband der Deutschen Industrie (RDI) 17, 116
Reichswerke "Hermann Göring" 17, 85, 103
Reinhardt, Fritz 108
Revisionism 2, 19–23, 25, 28–29, 33, 46, 62, 64, 68–69, 184, 191–192
Rheinmetall 91
Rhineland 1, 29, 31, 33, 59
Ribbentrop, Joachim von 14, 27, 30, 69, 72–73, 92, 147, 170–4, 177–178, 180–1, 183–186
Riccardi, Raffaello 163
Rintelen, Enno Emil von 172
Ritter, Karl 43–44
Roatta, Mario 172
Röhm, Ernst 24
Romania 5, 10, 13, 19, 36, 40, 46–47, 60–5, 67–69, 72–74, 80, 89, 91, 93, 111, 116, 125, 128, 133, 143–145, 147, 154, 156, 160, 163–164, 166–167, 170–4, 176–177, 179–180, 184–185, 187, 193

Rome 20, 22–26, 28, 30, 43, 46, 60–3, 65, 69, 71–73, 98, 100, 138, 163, 170, 172–173, 175, 177–178, 181, 184
Rome Accords (1935) 28
Rome Protocols (1934) 13, 24, 43, 62, 70, 98, 117
Roosevelt, Franklin Delano 182–3
Rosenberg, Alfred 14, 24, 86, 138–9
Rotterdam 173
Rudokop 102
Ruhr 116
Ruthenia 69–70

Šabac 133
Sachs, Vladimir 137
Salonika front 185
Salonika treaty 69
Salzburg 170
sanctions on Italy 1, 29, 31, 56, 98–100
Sarajevo 129, 132, 141
Sarnow, Otto 44, 51, 80, 107–8
Savoia-Marchetti, bomber aircraft 151–2
Schacht, Hjalmar 4, 15–17, 36, 48–51, 53, 57, 77–9, 81, 85–6, 117–18, 125, 191
Schleicher, Kurt von 40, 43
Schlenker, Max 116–17
Schmidt, Paul-Otto, Hitler's interpreter 184
Schmidt, Paul, Press Department of the German Foreign Ministry 175
Schnitzler, Georg von 117
Schönebeck, Carl-August von 92, 94
Schuschnigg, Kurt 30–1, 66
Schwerin von Krosigk, Johann Ludwig 79, 94
Second World War 1, 3, 5, 14, 102, 104, 126, 136, 168, 193
Serbia, Serbs 2, 6, 10, 20–2, 35, 38, 62, 64–5, 72, 99, 103–4, 106, 123, 129–38, 141, 143, 146–8, 158–60, 168–9, 172, 176–7, 182, 184, 186–9
Serbian Cultural Club 123–4, 175–6
Serbian Orthodox Church 130, 135–6, 141, 176
Shone, Terence 68, 182
*Sicherheitsdienst* 155
Šibenik 106
Siemens 103, 106, 116, 118
Šik, Lavoslav 129
Simonović, Živojin 142

Simović, Dušan 92, 184–5, 188–9
Šimrak, Janko 132
Sinaia 63, 67
Skerl, Vladimir 107
Škoda 91–2, 94–5, 151
Skopje 103, 189
Slavonia 133, 142–3, 145
Slovakia 69–70, 147, 174
Slovenia, Slovenes 21, 24, 26, 29, 65–6, 73, 130, 132, 134–6, 142–3, 145–6, 148, 184–5
Social Darwinism 22, 120, 135
Sofia 53, 57, 60, 69, 170, 177, 180
Sohn-Rethel, Alfred 117
South Dobruja 69, 170–171
South-Eastern Europe 3, 10–13, 15–16, 18–24, 27, 32–3, 35–7, 41, 49–50, 53, 59–60, 62, 64, 69, 72, 77, 79, 83, 85–7, 89–90, 97, 103–5, 111, 114–21, 124–5, 128, 136, 138, 146, 149, 163, 165, 167, 173–4, 178–9
Soviet Union, also Soviets, Russia, Soviet Russia 11, 25, 28–30, 36, 60, 69–70, 72, 79, 131, 136, 146, 154, 157, 160, 168–70, 172–4, 177–80, 182, 188
Soviet-Finnish war (1940) 168
Spa conference (1920) 38
Spaho, Mehmed 130
Spain 59, 99, 152, 173
Spitfire 91
Srebrenica 104
Stakić, Vladislav 175, 179, 181
Stalin, Joseph Vissarionovich 176, 179–80
Standard Oil 102
Starčević, Ante 130, 137
Stefanović, Svetislav 135
Stepinac, Alojzije 130, 138
Stettin 139
Stojadinović, Milan 4, 12, 19, 29–31, 55, 57, 60–71, 74–5, 87, 89, 91–2, 102, 105, 108–10, 112, 131–2, 139, 145, 155, 169, 186
Stojanović, Vojislav 129
Straits 179–80
Stresa, also Stresa conferences (1932 and 1935) 28, 30, 37
Stresemann, Gustav 21, 144
Struma 179

Subotica 133
Subotić, Ivan 150
Sudetenland 67, 87, 89
*Südosteuropa Gesellschaft* (SOEG) 117
Šufflay, Milan 137
Šutej, Juraj 159
Sweden 40, 58, 101
Switzerland 40–1, 83, 101–2, 158

Tardieu plan, also Danube federation 36–7, 54
Technical Union 82, 91, 139
Telegraphen-Union 21
Terzić, Sava 124
Teschen 70
Thessaloniki 71, 162, 168, 174–5, 177–8, 181–6, 189
Thomas, Georg 149, 161
Titulescu, Nicolae 32, 60
Tomić, Jaša 130
Topalović, Živko 141
Toussaint, Rudolf 151, 153, 155
Transylvania 171
Trepča lead and zinc mine 152, 154
Trieste 29
Tripartite Pact 3, 147, 166, 168, 174, 177–85, 187–7, 189
Turkey, also Turks 10, 19, 62, 143, 162, 174, 176–7, 181
Turkish-Bulgarian Non-Aggression Pact (1941) 181

Ukraine 146
Ulmanski, Sava 122
United Kingdom Commercial Corporation Limited 154
United States of America 12, 84, 88, 102, 139, 149, 152, 178–9, 181–3
Ustaše 27, 135, 137–9, 171

Vardar 179, 189
Vardarska province 129
Vareš 108
Varnava, Serbian Patriarch 135, 141
Vatican 132
Vauhnik, Vladimir 149, 151, 161, 174–5, 188
Velimirović, Nikolaj 135–6
Velmar-Janković, Vladimir 135

Venice 25, 67, 70
Versailles, place, conference, treaty, order 14, 28, 32, 37–8, 57, 59, 63, 131, 159, 172, 192
Vienna, also Vienna Awards 12, 19, 24–5, 65–6, 69–70, 87, 104, 115–18, 122–4, 142, 163, 167, 170, 174, 178, 184, 187–8
Vinaver, Stanislav 26
Vítkovice 108
Vojvodina 130–1, 133, 142–3, 145–6, 158
*Volk* 15, 127, 146
*Volksbund für das Deutschtum im Ausland* (VDA) 144
*Volksdeutsche*, also Yugoslav ethnic Germans 22, 72–73, 127–8, 139, 142–8
*Volksdeutsche Mittelstelle* (VoMi) 14, 144–7
Vrbanić, Milan 89, 109, 124
Vukovar 141

Wagener, Otto 48
Wall Street 39
War economy of the Nazi Germany 16, 48–9, 86, 96, 161, 166, 192
Warsaw 36, 70
Washington 39, 178
Wehrmacht 96, 149, 172, 177, 180
Weimar, Republic, Germany, period 12, 15–17, 21, 24, 26, 32, 120, 144, 185
Weizsäcker, Ernst von 14, 67–8, 73, 184
Weltpolitik 120
Wiehl, Emil 43, 92, 150, 158, 163
Wilhelmine Germany, period 15, 24, 32
Wilmowsky, Tilo von 104, 116–17, 160–1, 163
Wilson, Charles 57
Wohlthat, Helmuth, also Wohlthat Treaty (1939) 93, 103, 163–165
Wörmann, Ernst 73

Young Plan (1929) 38–39
Yugoslav Action 132, 134
Yugoslav Central Press Bureau 26
Yugoslav Lloyd 141
Yugoslav National Bank 7, 39, 41, 50–57, 80–3, 85, 87–90, 99, 101, 108–9, 111, 152–3, 156–8, 162

Yugoslav-Bulgarian Treaty of Eternal
   Friendship (1937) 60
Yugoslav-German Society 30
Yugoslav-Hungarian Treaty of Eternal
   Friendship (1940) 178
Yugoslav-Italian Agreement (1937) 61, 71,
   175, 178, 181
Yugoslav-Italian Trade Agreement (1936)
   61, 100
Yugoslav-Soviet Treaty of Friendship
   (1941) 188

Zadar 138
Zagreb 26, 36–7, 54, 56, 80, 90, 99–100,
   105, 109, 129–33, 138
Zaječar 104
Zbor 82, 132, 135–6, 139–41, 145, 148,
   175
Zeck, Hans 12
Zemun 146
Zenica 106–8, 117
Zionism 130
Zurich 155

www.ingramcontent.com/pod-product-compliance
Lightning Source LLC
Chambersburg PA
CBHW072129290426
44111CB00012B/1842